THE COMPLETE
King Arthur

"The Matthews have done it again! Here is a compact assembly of Arthurian sources from ancient Rome through the classics, including many obscure bits. A wonderful and entertaining read."

GREG STAFFORD, DESIGNER OF THE
KING ARTHUR PENDRAGON GAME

"Beautifully written and extensively researched, *The Complete King Arthur* provides a thorough overview of past and present examples of the tradition and the possible sources from which they sprang. Accessible to scholars and general readers alike, this study is a necessary addition to the library of anyone who loves King Arthur."

LINDA A. MALCOR, COAUTHOR OF
FROM SCYTHIA TO CAMELOT

"What a treasure this book is, a gift of great magnitude from the Matthews to all the rest of us. I so wish I had had it when I was immersing myself in Arthur in college many decades ago. The Mathews are the rarest of writers: scholars who are poets, poets who are scholars, singers of myth and history. They understand that facts are the basis of story, but equally, story is the basis of facts. Over the years of their phenomenal body of work, they have never set aside one for the other but have fed them together, in great measure."

RACHEL POLLACK, AUTHOR OF
UNQUENCHABLE FIRE, WINNER OF THE
ARTHUR C. CLARKE AWARD

THE COMPLETE
King Arthur

Many Faces, One Hero

JOHN AND CAITLÍN MATTHEWS

Inner Traditions
Rochester, Vermont • Toronto, Canada

Inner Traditions
One Park Street
Rochester, Vermont 05767
www.InnerTraditions.com

Text stock is SFI certified

Library of Congress Cataloging-in-Publication Data

Names: Matthews, John, 1948– author. | Matthews, Caitlin, 1952– author.
Title: The complete King Arthur : many faces, one hero / John Matthews and
    Caitlin Matthews.
Description: Rochester, Vermont : Inner Traditions, 2017. | Includes
    bibliographical references and index.
Identifiers: LCCN 2016037586 (print) | LCCN 2016047993 (e-book) |
    ISBN 9781620555996 (paperback) | ISBN 9781620556009 (e-book)
Subjects: LCSH: Arthur, King. | Britons—Kings and rulers—Historiography. |
    Great Britain—Antiquities, Celtic. | Arthurian romances—Sources. |
    Arthur, King—Legends. | BISAC: BODY, MIND & SPIRIT / Mythical
    Civilizations. | SOCIAL SCIENCE / Folklore & Mythology. | BODY, MIND
    & SPIRIT / Spirituality / Celtic.
Classification: LCC DA152.5.A7 M373 2017 (print) | LCC DA152.5.A7 (e-book) |
    DDC 942.01/4—dc23
LC record available at https://lccn.loc.gov/2016037586

Printed and bound in the United States by Lake Book Manufacturing, Inc.
The text stock is SFI certified. The Sustainable Forestry Initiative® program
promotes sustainable forest management.

10 9 8 7 6 5 4 3 2 1

Text design and layout by Debbie Glogover
This book was typeset in Garamond Premier Pro with Gill Sans MT Pro, and
Iowan Old Style as display fonts

Cover image courtesy of iStock

To send correspondence to the authors of this book, mail a first-class letter to the
author c/o Inner Traditions • Bear & Company, One Park Street, Rochester, VT
05767, and we will forward the communication, or contact the authors directly at
www.hallowquest.org.uk or Caitlín Matthews at **caitlin-matthews.blogspot.com**.

To the memory of the poet
John Heath-Stubbs (1918–2006):
a poet who sang in the dark and restored the light.

Contents

Acknowledgments

We would like to thank Linda Malcor for readily sharing her work on Lucius Artorius Castus; Kristen McDermott for her expert advice on Ben Jonson; Ari Berk for continuing author outreach support; the interloan staff of Temple Cowley Library, Oxford, for their speed in acquiring obscure articles from the four corners of the land; and the staff of the Bodleian Library, Oxford, for their tireless efforts.

Dates, Names, and Time Line of Significant Events

DATES AND NAMES

Two factors weigh heavily upon anyone attempting to explore the world of Arthur. The first concerns dating, which is at best vague and at worst impossible to interpret due to the vagaries of early writers who, before the conventions of BC and AD were widely accepted, adopted different forms of dating. For example, reckoning from the birth of Jesus or the assumed date of the Crucifixion makes a difference of twenty-eight years. For this reason dates within the Arthurian period can vary, and it is difficult to be either exact or definitive. We have traced our way through as many of these inconsistencies as possible to produce the time line that follows here. All dates, unless otherwise stated, should be understood as AD.

The second factor relates to the names of people and places. Personal names can vary greatly in both form and spelling from text to text—often within the *same* text. Wherever possible we have standardized these for the sake of clarity, and throughout the book we have referred to the ancient regions of Britain by their modern names when referring to their location but have used their ancient names when referring to specific kingdoms and their rulers. The maps on pages 9, 46, 105, and 110 show the complex changing face of Britain during the second, fifth, and sixth centuries in more detail. We have used the term *the Islands* when referring to the landmasses of Britain and Ireland and their associated coastal islands. We have used the term "British" and "Briton(s)" throughout, interchangeably. The former is more familiar from modern usage, while "Britons" is more often used of earlier people. We should also make the distinction between Britons (people of Britain) and Bretons (people of Brittany). This small area, now part of France, was known as "Little Britain," due to the number of Britons who migrated to the area following the Roman invasion.

TIME LINE OF SIGNIFICANT EVENTS

55–54 BC	Julius invades Britain, taking hostages and setting a tribute
43 AD	Roman conquest of Britain begins in earnest under Claudius
61	Druids massacred on Anglesey by Suetonius
64	Boudican revolt
83	Battle of Mons Graupius between Caledonians and Agricola
122–127	Building of Hadrian's Wall between Solway Firth and Tyne
circa 140	Birth of Lucius Artorius Castus
148	Antonine Wall built between Forth and Clyde
175	Sarmatian cavalry of 5,500 garrisoned at Ribchester and Chesters
circa 184	Central Caledonian tribes overrun Antonine Wall in reign of Commodus
circa 198	Severus repairs Hadrian's Wall, which was overrun by Maeatae tribe
circa 199	Death of Lucius Artorius Castus
circa 286/7	Carausius enters Britain and declares himself emperor, creating an independent empire

293 Diocletian appoints Constantius Chlorus as Caesar of Gaul; thereafter he took over the rule of Britain, rebuilding York, the headquarters of the Dux Britanniarum, and dividing Britain into four provinces: Britannia Prima, Britannia Secunda, Maxima Caesariensis, and Flavia Caesariensis

306 Constantine the Great made emperor at York

360 Picts and Scots break their peace treaty with Roman Britain; Theodosius is sent to subdue lawlessness and incursion, rebuilds milecastles on Hadrian's Wall

367 The Barbarian Conspiracy where Picts, Scots, and Saxons strike together

383 A significant number of legions leave Britain with coemperor Magnus Maximus

385 Saint Patrick born at Bannavem Taberniae (Banwen) on the Cumbrian coast

390 Theodosius I bans pagan worship in the Roman Empire

circa 400–430 Cunedda moves from Manau Gododdin to Gwynedd to eject Irish in Wales with his militia; Stilicho is made first consul and sets out on a punitive mission against the Picts

410 Sack of Rome by Visigoth Alaric; Honorius declares Britons must defend themselves; major Roman withdrawal of troops

circa 425 Notitia Dignitatum relates Britain as "still held by the empire"

425 Vortigern in power

429 Saint Germanus visits Britain to deter Pelagianism

circa 440 Vortigern invites mercenary Jutes led by Hengist and Horsa to protect Britain from Pictish incursion

446 Britons petition Consul Aëtius to help them

447 Second visit of Saint Germanus to Britain

455 Britons synchronize their dating of Easter with European Christians according to the edict of Pope Leo in 453

469 "Riothamus" crosses into Gaul as part of an alliance

circa 470–480 Ambrosius Aurelianus defends Britain against Saxons; Wansdyke is built

circa 490–515 Eleven of Arthur's battles are fought

circa 516	Battle of Badon led by Arthur; Gildas born
circa 537/9	Battle of Camlann where Arthur and Medrawd fall
537	Death of Maelgwn Gwynedd; the yellow plague decimates Britain; King Ida establishes Anglian kingdom of Bernicia
circa 540	Gildas writes *De Excidio Britonum*
circa 550	Battle of Catraeth (Catterick), major loss of the northern British
circa 573	Battle of Arderydd; here Merlin ran mad
577	Battle of Deorham (Dyrham); Welsh lose contact with the Britons of Devon and Cornwall; Urien Rheged, Taliesin's patron, dies on Ynys Medgawdd (Lindisfarne)
circa 613	Battle of Chester; Welsh finally lose contact with Y Gogledd (Old North)
632	British Cadwallawn of Gwynedd allies with Saxon Penda of Mercia and defeats Edwin of Northumbria
635	Saint Aidan made bishop of Lindisfarne
circa 638	Territory of Gododdin overcome by Angles
663	Synod of Whitby: Roman style Christianity dominates Celtic church
664	Cadwaladr, the last high king of Britain, dies
circa 731	Bede completes *The Ecclesiastical History of the English People*
829–30	*Historia Brittonum* compiled by Nennius
circa 930–950	*Annales Cambriae* transcribed
1066	Norman invasion of Britain
circa 1120	Modena Archivolt completed
circa 1136–1148	Geoffrey of Monmouth writes *Historia Regum Britanniae*
circa 1155	Wace completes his *Roman de Brut*
1170–1190	Chrétien de Troyes writes five Arthurian romances
1191	Discovery of "Arthur's bones" at Glastonbury
circa 1205	Lawman's *Brut* completed
1215–1235	French Vulgate Cycle written
1278	"Arthur's body" magnificently reburied at Glastonbury

1485   Malory's *Le Morte d'Arthur* published

1590–1596   Spenser's *The Faerie Queene* written

1859–1891   Alfred Tennyson writes *The Idylls of the King*

1938   *The Sword in the Stone* by T. H. White published

1963   *Sword at Sunset* by Rosemary Sutcliff published

1966–1970   Cadbury Camp, possible site of Camelot, excavated

1981   *The Mists of Avalon* by Marion Zimmer Bradley published

1981   John Boorman's *Excalibur* released

2004   Jerry Bruckheimer's *King Arthur* released

2014   John James's *The Fourth Gwenevere* published

The Once
and Future King

*You will get nowhere with this material unless you
approach it obliquely. It is only by patient infiltrations that
you will begin to understand the many and varied aspects
of the geology of Arthur, [its] sedimented strata laid down
on earlier strata [its] intrusive rocks thrust up from fires
long since dead.*

DAVID JONES,
FOREWORD TO *ARTHUR OF ALBION*
BY RICHARD BARBER (1961)

It was Sir Thomas Malory, in his fifteenth-century book *Le Morte
d'Arthur,* who called the hero "The Once and Future King." This
title, redolent of prophecy and ancestral heritage, conveys the enduring essence of a hero who is known throughout the world. Yet who,
exactly, was King Arthur? This question is asked with increasing regu-
larity, both in the media and in an outpouring of books, articles, and
academic studies on the subject published every year. Yet it seems that

1

few, if any, of those who ask the question can agree upon the answer. Even those who believe that there might have been a real Arthur cannot be certain when, or where, he lived and offer a dozen or more men with his name who *could* be the one and only hero.

The first thing to state is that he was probably never a king—certainly not in the sense that we would use the word today. It is possible to say that he was a fifth- or sixth-century soldier, who may have operated in areas as far apart as Cornwall, Wales, Scotland, or Brittany. It is also possible that he was a second-century Roman officer, active in the area around Hadrian's Wall in Cumbria. Equally it can be claimed that he is entirely mythical, a fiction dreamed up by a conquered people to bring them hope in a dark period of history. For most people today, he remains a brilliant medieval monarch reigning over a fairy-tale kingdom accompanied by his brave Knights of the Round Table and their beautiful ladies.

It is clear from this that any attempt to identify a real King Arthur is fraught with danger for the unwary researcher. The simple truth is that there is *no conclusive evidence dating from the period in which Arthur is presumed to have lived.* Nowhere are there textual or archaeological remains that point definitively to a leader named Arthur who achieved specific things at a specific time.

Some researchers have declared simply that there *has* to be an Arthur because we need him to fill a gap otherwise left in the historical record. Indeed, a recent writer commented that if you remove Arthur from his assumed place in history, you leave an Arthur-shaped hole behind! Such an argument is reasonable and can be embroidered almost endlessly, as it has over the past few decades, producing a number of plausible portraits of Arthur.

It could be said that in a certain sense *all* of these images are valid; adding that the Arthur we know best from the medieval stories derives from several figures, none of whom were necessarily called Arthur, and may date from several different times. Arthur's actual life remains as hotly contentious today as it was almost from the moment he vanished from the world, though for different reasons. His existence or nonexistence currently ranges from a popular trend, which uncritically conflates sources from many eras and accepts everything on faith, to an academic viewpoint that is quick to distance itself from mythic interpretations.

The division of Arthurian scholarship into "history" and "myth" is not a new phenomenon. The earliest surviving chronicle of Arthur, the ninth-century *Historia Brittonum,* shows us that his legend was already fragmented. Within this slender account, Arthur is presented not only as a real person, a seasoned battle leader, but also as a semi-mythic character whose deeds are stamped on the landscape. In a variety of other sources, dating from within a hundred years of his lifetime, he is described as a battle leader, a "red ravager," an active and courtly king, a freedom fighter, and as the figurehead of orderly government who attempted to restore the Roman Empire in Britain. All of these Arthurs represent successive turns of a kaleidoscope and offer portraits in which we may discern the features of a man we know so well and yet hardly know at all.

The object of this book is not to insist on the validity of any one claimant or theory but to give a straightforward overview of the long history of Arthur, from its beginnings in Roman or pre-Roman Britain, via the glories of medieval romance and the romantic dreams of subsequent eras, to the latest theories of our own time. We present here the many faces of Arthur in their context, attempting to show how each is a product of the times and peoples who carried the legends forward in different ways. Finally, we bring the story up to date as we examine the twenty-first-century Arthur, watching him transform through a new range of images, reflecting our understanding of the distant past through contemporary images in film, art, music, and fiction.

At this point we might ask: Who *is* King Arthur rather than who he was—a very different question from the one we asked above. Its answer speaks more about our time than about his reality. Arthur's image can be continually fractured by a single change in our contemporary viewpoint; he can be claimed by historians, politicians, artists, and mythographers to be used for their own ends.

But stories as powerful as these are best not looked at from a single perspective; all of the various approaches discussed here alter our perception of the once and future king (see previous note). In this book we have chosen, like archaeologists, to piece together the many fragments that constitute the image of Arthur. Some are more broken than others, while some have to be placed in context before they reveal their quality. In the end, it is not one face of Arthur that emerges, but several. Each has something to offer and reminds us of the enduring power of the hero-myth, which far outreaches the existence of any historical figure and which has earned Arthur the title he first received in the fifteenth century.

1

Arthur of Rome
Commander of Legions

I can prove that Arthur existed with as certain, as clear, as true, not to mention as many, arguments as [others] can prove Caesar to have existed.

JOHN LEYLAND, *CODUS SIVE LAUS ET DEFENSIO GALLOFRIDI ARTURI* (CA. 1536)

THE SOLDIER

What is the oldest historical face of Arthur? If we exclude for the moment the ancient and misty shadows of myth, tendrils of which constantly reach out to overwhelm any traces of the real man, we find ourselves not in the Dark Ages, but earlier, when the light of Rome still shone out across much of the world and brought new ways to the so-called barbarous northern lands. Once we begin to look at the figure of Arthur, we quickly discover that he is deeply linked with Rome, and in particular the Roman presence in Britain from the first century BC to the fifth century AD. Among those who, at one time or another, have been identified as the historical Arthur, one is a full-blooded citizen of the empire, and two others are of possible Romano-British descent.

The earliest documents that record the deeds of Arthur show that he was not perceived as a king but as a soldier, bearing the much-prized Latin title *dux* (duke): a charismatic leader who fought "alongside the leaders of the British." The oldest recorded reference to anyone bearing the name Arthur (or any variant of that name) in Britain is just such a man—a career officer of the legions named Lucius Artorius Castus, who lived and fought in Britain in the second century AD— almost three hundred years earlier than the more usually accepted dates for Arthur.

Arthur is the generally accepted form today, but in reality this name has a far longer history and a variety of spellings. It can be proven with reasonable certainty that Artorius derives from either the British name Arthur or is the Latin original of that name. Not only is Artorius Castus the only documented person with such a name to serve in the legions during the Roman occupation of Britain, he is *the only known person* in Britain who bears the name Arthur between the second and fourth centuries AD. This in itself is a striking fact, but once we look closely into the life of Artorius Castus, we quickly discover there are some startling parallels between his career and that of the great British hero.

The redoubtable Arthurian scholar Heinrich Zimmer proposed Artorius as a correct version of the hero's name as long ago as 1890.[1] The American J. D. Bruce agreed with this, stating that "a strong confirmation of his historical character seems offered by the fact that his name is, in its origin, not Celtic, but Roman, being derived from the name Artorius, which occurs in Tacitus and Juvenal and which is, indeed, the name of a Roman Gens. (Family)."[2]

Investigating these claims in 1925, the American scholar Kemp Malone wrote an article titled simply "Artorius."[3] Having shown that the name Arthur can indeed be derived etymologically from a Roman source, Malone then went on to ask a simple question: Were there any instances of the name Artorius recorded in Britain? The answer was Lucius Artorius Castus, who is known to have been stationed in Britain in the second century AD. While acknowledging that this was a long time before the more usual dating for Arthur, Malone was intrigued and set out to discover more. He found two inscriptions relating to the life of Artorius Castus. The first was discovered at Podstrana, in the region of ancient Epetium (modern Stobrez) near Spalato in Dalmatia (modern Croatia); the other near a chapel dedicated to Saint Martin of Podstrana, on the road from Spalato to Almissa.

The first inscription gives us a detailed summary of Lucius Artorius Castus's career.

> To the spirits of the departed: L. Artorius Castus, Centurion of the III Legion Gallica; also centurion of the VI Legion Ferrata, also centurion of the II Legion II Adiutrix; also centurion of the V legion Macedonica; also primus pilus of the same legion; praepositus of the classis Misenatium; Praefectus of the VI Legion Victrix; dux of the cohorts of cavalry from Britain against the Armoricans; procurator Centenarius of the province of Liburnia with the power to issue sentences of death. In his lifetime, for himself and his family, he made this.[4]

The inscription is slightly damaged and at times difficult to read, but is quite clear in its essentials. It appears to end with the words *H[ic] s[itu] est,* "lies buried here," suggesting that the inscription was originally part of a stele intended to be attached to a mausoleum. As was the custom of the time among wealthy Roman families, Castus himself probably had this constructed. Ruins of a villa in the immediate vicinity, perhaps occupied by Artorius when he was procurator of the area, suggest that the inscription was intended as a memorial stele attached to the outer walls of the villa, rather than as part of an actual tomb. It was, to all intents and purposes, an address label stating the name of the villa's occupant and outlining his history. For the moment we should notice in passing the reference to the post of *dux* on the inscription, and to Artorius's leadership of a cavalry unit from Britain.

The second inscription adds little to the first. It is probably a memorial plaque and reads simply:

Artorius Castus,

primus pilus, V legion Macedonica;

praefectus, VI Legion Victrix.[5]

These inscriptions clearly record the lifetime achievements of a career soldier who served in at least five legions, in each of which he received further promotion, and that he ended up with the rank of procurator of a province. If we knew nothing more than this, we could be forgiven for supposing that this was a man of courage and note, whose career stretched over some forty to fifty years. From their design, the dating of the two inscriptions can be made to the second century, certainly no later than AD 200, by which time we may assume Artorius was dead.

This is all we possess by way of actual recorded evidence for the life and deeds of Lucius Artorius Castus. Yet it is both more and less than we have for other Arthurs: more in that it definitely establishes that a person named Artorius actually lived, less in that it gives us almost nothing by way of dates or settings for this remarkable military career.

However, it is possible to infer a great deal from the inscriptions. By consulting historical records relating to the movements and dispositions of the various legions listed in what is effectively Artorius's service record, we can arrive at a surprisingly detailed account of his life—though all dates are currently speculative—augmented by the contemporary accounts of two Roman historians: Dio Cassius and Herodian. When these details are placed side by side, a portrait of an extraordinary soldier begins to appear.

Kemp Malone himself, after prolonged study of the inscriptions, arrived at a brief biography for Artorius. From this he was able to suggest that since Arthur and Artorius were the only people with this name in the historical record, at least up until the time shortly after the supposed existence of the sixth-century hero, when the name became suddenly popular, that it was worth exploring parallels between the two. He concentrated on the expedition led by Artorius to Armorica (Brittany), referred to in the longer inscription, which bore a marked

Map 1. The Dioceses of Britain.
(courtesy of Wil Kinghan)

resemblance to an expedition ascribed to Arthur in several later texts. Malone's conclusion was that "the only historical character with whom Arthur can with any plausibility be connected is the second century Lucius Artorius Castus."

Malone's article did not provoke any immediate or significant response. Perhaps it was too shocking to those already convinced of the existence of a fifth- and sixth-century Arthur. However, the theory did not die. Helmut Nickel, the curator of the Arms and Armor Department at the New York Metropolitan Museum of Art, took up the idea and advanced it significantly. In a series of articles published between 1973 and 1975,[6] he drew attention to the fact that Artorius Castus, during his service in Britain, had commanded squadrons of cavalry made up of warriors from a group of Indo-European tribes. These Steppeland warriors, the Sarmatians, suffered defeat at the hands of the emperor Marcus Aurelius in 175, and were subsequently drafted into the legions and posted as far from their homeland as possible. In this instance 5,500 Sarmatian warriors were sent to Britain and stationed at the Roman fort of Bremetennacum (modern Ribchester, Lancashire). Nickel suggested that traditions held by these people bore striking resemblances to later Arthurian legends.

Around the same time C. Scott Littleton and Ann C. Thomas published an article titled "The Sarmatian Connection: New Light on the Arthurian and Holy Grail Legends." They pointed out more parallels between the later Arthurian mythos and the history and traditions of the Sarmatian, Iazyge, and Ossete tribes, who came from an area between the Black Sea in the west and the Caspian Sea in the east. A few years later a book by Littleton and Malcor[7] brought forward a huge range of materials that helped establish a number of connections between Sarmatian and Arthurian legends.

ARTORIUS OF ROME

Who then, exactly, was L. Artorius Castus? Since Kemp Malone wrote his seminal article in 1925, a great deal of new evidence has been discovered (and is still turning up). We are now able to put forward a far more detailed biography of the man whose career provides enough material for any number of legendary tales.*

As Malone noted, the Artorii, to whose *gens* or family Artorius belonged, were part of the high-ranking equestrian class, the second tier of Roman nobility, who were either landholders or worked for the state. The history of this particular branch of the family can be traced back to at least as early as 80 BC. They appear to have come originally from somewhere in Greece, from where they were forced to flee by one of several Celtic incursions. They settled in the area of Italy known as Campania, apparently bringing with them a religious devotion to the goddess Flora, worship of whom appears suddenly in this area at the same time.[8]

We can date Artorius Castus's probable birth by counting back from his attainment of the rank of *dux* listed on the inscription, apparently as a result of his actions in an offensive against the Armoricans (Bretons), which seems to have taken place in AD 185–186. If Artorius had indeed served five or six tours of duty by this time, as listed on the inscription, each lasting approximately five to six years, this takes us back to approximately 158, during the reign of the emperor Antoninus Pius (186–161). Since it was usual for men to enlist at the age of eighteen, this gives us a birth date for Artorius of approximately 140.

As a member of the equestrian class, Artorius would have been destined either for a career in the army, with the rank of centurion, or in the civil service. Since an equestrian was required to maintain an income of 400,000 sesterces, it is possible that Artorius was a younger son, with a smaller income, and that his inability to raise the necessary funds forced him into the army, which offered a means of attaining a higher military rank than his social status allowed. The applicant first joined the equestrian *cursus,* a designated path upward through

---

*We currently await the publication of the monumental study of the life of Artorius Castus by Linda Malcor.

the ranks to the position of *primus pilus*. On attaining this rank, the officer's former social status was restored, and if he had saved enough money, he could maintain this permanently. However, to enter the legion as a centurion, specifically *decimus hastus posterior*, meant surrendering an already existing social position, and this is what Artorius would have been forced to do.

A long road lay before him. To reach the position of *primus pilus*, he would have to survive a minimum of four tours of duty and rise through fifty-eight ranks or grades—no small task for a boy entering the legion at eighteen years of age!

Artorius's first tour, lasting from circa 158 to circa 162, would have taken him to Syria, where the III Legion Galicia was stationed at this time. The duty of the military there was to maintain peace and keep a watchful eye on the activities of Jews and Christians within the province. He must have experienced at firsthand the delicate matter of keeping peace in an always combustible area.

In 162 the Parthians invaded the Roman province of Armenia, and the III Gallica, along with IV Scythia and the XV Flavia Firma, were sent to combat this. However, Artorius did not go with them. Having completed his first tour of duty, he transferred to the IV Ferrata in Judea around 162, with a probable promotion. Once again his duties seem to have been primarily concerned with peacekeeping in the villages of Judea, with occasional guard duties in Jerusalem. He seems to have spent the next four years in the Middle East, at the end of which time he once again transferred—this time to the II Adiutrix Legion, then stationed on the Danube.

This was to be an important move for Artorius. The II Adiutrix was one of two new legions led by the emperor Marcus Aurelius himself. This extraordinary man, more philosopher than soldier, had come to power in 161 at the age of forty. His first challenge was the war with the Parthians over possession of Armenia, which acted as a buffer zone between the empire and the Steppelands. But in 169 he was called to defend the northern frontier of the empire when the Marcomanni and Quasi tribes cut their way deep into Italy.

Artorius Castus was now approximately twenty-two years of age. Already a veteran of numerous skirmishes and encounters with the natives of the Middle East, he now entered a whole new arena of war, facing savage German tribes in a period of intense strife. It was at this time that he seems to have come in contact with a people who were to play an important part in his life. These were the Sarmatians, a group of Indo-European tribes whose home lay between the Black Sea in the west and the Caspian Sea in the east, extending as far as the Urals in the northeast. They belonged to an Iranian-speaking (Ossetic) community and were called Sauromatae by Herodotus, and Sarmatii by most other classical writers. The former name has been interpreted as meaning "Lizard People" and may equally derive from a Greek misunderstanding of the name, from their use of scalelike body armor, or from their use in battle of a wind-sock-style standard in the shape of a dragon—a device that holds great significance to their connection with the later figure of Arthur, as we shall see.

Classical sources list over a hundred distinct tribes in the Sarmatian group, including the Roxolani, Iazyges, Alani, Saboci, and Nasci. They were also closely related to the Scythians, whose lands were adjacent to theirs in the second century AD and who shared a number of their beliefs and traditions. The poet Ovid, in a collection of poems written in exile, painted a less than enamored picture of the Sarmatians in the first century:

> One sees them scamper about,
> bareback, quivers and bows at their backs, their arrows
>   dipped
> in venom, their faces covered over with hair,
> and the hair on their heads so shaggy they look rather
>   like human bushes.
> They all carry knives at their belts
> and you never know whether they're going to greet you
>   or stab you.
> Cut out your liver, and eat it.[9]

Despite their unprepossessing appearance (at least to Roman sensibilities), their fighting skills were legendary and left a deep impression on their enemies. They were skilled horsemen, able to shoot with deadly accuracy with short recurved bows, using arrowheads dipped in venom, as well as fighting with long lances. They had developed scaled body armor, made of overlapping plates of bone, as early as the first century AD, which made them formidable opponents, and it is here that we may see the alternative origin of their name as "the covered people"—those who wear armor.

A third interpretation, proposed by Dr. Ilya Yakubovich,[10] suggests that Syawa-arma-tya, or black arms, is a possible reference to the heavy tattooing common among the related Pazyrk people, perhaps similar to the Picti, or Painted People, of Northern Britain. Curiously, the Saxon historian Bede, writing some five hundred years later, described the Picts as originating in Scythia. If this were true—though there is no real evidence to support it—it would have made the two forces confronting each other neighbors from adjacent parts of the empire.

The Roman historian Strabo, who writes extensively about both communities, suggests the existence of a strong Celtic presence among these people, even referring to one group as Keltoskythai, Celtic Scythians. If this linguistic or cultural link really existed (and it remains unclear), then it would certainly explain the overlap between Sarmatian and Celtic traditions in Britain during and after the lifetime of Artorius.[11]

Artorius Castus's new legion, the II Adiutrix, was stationed at the time in Lower Pannonia, at Aquincum (modern Budapest). They were on a constant state of alert against attacks by the Sarmatians and Iazyges, as well as the Quasi and Marcomanni—all of whom Marcus Aurelius declared his intention of eliminating.

After a prolonged period of fighting, diplomatic emissaries from these tribes approached Marcus Aurelius with a view to arriving at a peaceful settlement. It is likely that Artorius Castus first encountered the Sarmatians at this time—a contact that was to bear fruit several years later. At the time, diplomacy failed, and in either 173–174 or

174–175, war broke out again. It was then that a battle took place in which Artorius Castus apparently took a leading part and which was to bring him to the notice of his superiors.*

Around 170 Artorius's third tour of duty was up, but though he had achieved some promotion, he was still some way off from reaching the rank of *primus pilus* and thus restoring his equestrian status. He therefore transferred to yet another legion, the V Macedonian, stationed at this time in Potanisa, Dacia (modern Turda in Transylvania). Here, around 172–173, Artorius finally achieved the long-desired rank of *primus pilus,* and his life changed once and for all.

In 175 the V Macedonian were engaged in a series of battles with the Iazyges, whom they pursued as far as the River Ister, which happened to be frozen at the time. The Iazyges led their pursuers to this spot in expectation of easily overcoming them on the slippery ice. However, they reckoned without the foresight of a particular Roman officer, who had prepared his men for just such an encounter. According to Dio Cassius:

> The Iazyges, perceiving that they were being pursued, awaited their opponents' onset, expecting to overcome them easily, as the others were not accustomed to the ice. Accordingly, some of the barbarians dashed straight at them, while others rode round to attack their flanks, as their horses had been trained to run safely even over a surface of this kind. The Romans upon observing this were not alarmed, but formed into a compact body, facing all their foes at once, and most of them laid down their shields and rested one foot upon them, so that they might not slip so much; and thus they received the enemy's charge. Some seized the bridles, others the shields and spearshafts of their assailants, and drew the men toward them; and thus becoming involved in close conflict, they knocked

---

*There is also a suggestion, made by Linda Malcor (personal communication), that the Artorii had long-term dealings with the Sarmatians and were in fact "specialists" who had fought against this particular ethnic group before.

down both men and horses, since the barbarians by reason of their momentum could no longer keep from slipping. The Romans, to be sure, also slipped; but in case one of them fell on his back, he would drag his adversary down on top of him and then with his feet would hurl him backward, as in a wrestling match, and so would get on top of him. . . . The barbarians, being unused to combat of this sort, and having lighter equipment, were unable to resist, so that few escaped.[12]

These were far from normal military tactics and sound, instead, like the inspired reaction of a quick-thinking legionary commander. Malcor[13] believes the man responsible for leading his troops to victory here was Artorius Castus, suggesting that the reason why Dio does not mention him by name is because there was some kind of rivalry between Artorius and Dio's father, who were both stationed in Liburnia at the same time and may have known each other. Such rivalry was not unusual in a situation where several officers were jostling for promotion. Since it was at this time that Artorius finally obtained the rank of *primus pilus,* it is therefore not unreasonable to surmise that his actions at the battle on the River Ister ensured this promotion. Malcor also points out that the Romans were using a technique familiar to the tribes of the Steppelands to capture horses—suggesting that the unnamed officer was familiar with Sarmatian horse wrangling and therefore with the Sarmatians themselves.[14]

As *primus pilus* Artorius could have left active service and opted for a quiet life in the civil service, but apparently he preferred the life of the soldier because he now opted to follow the remainder of the equestrian *curcus,* a route that required him to serve four years each as a *praefectus,* either a *tribune militum* or *legionis* and finally as a *praefectus alae.* He seems at this point to have reenlisted in the V Macedonica. Since most of the men joining the Legion at this point had little or no military experience, Artorius's splendid service record would have made him an unusually valuable officer who would very likely be singled out for special duties.

Around 178/9, the year of his death, Marcus Aurelius beat the Sarmatian tribes into submission until a rebellion in Syria forced him to make hasty terms with them. These included a promise to keep clear of the Roman frontier and to supply 8,000 horsemen to form cavalry wings for the legions. Of these warriors, 5,500 were sent to Britain. The task of transporting this huge force, along with at least two horses for each soldier, all their equipment, wagons, weapons, armor, and (we may assume) families, was no small task. It appears that it fell to Artorius.

If we are correct in our assumption that Artorius reenlisted around 175, he would either have held the rank of *praefectus* of either *auxilia* (allied non-Roman troops without citizenship) or *numeri* (foreign conscripts without citizenship). At this time the only known movement of a large group of conscripted warriors was that of the Sarmatians, more than half of whom went to Britannia and the rest into another part of the empire. Given that Artorius was later to become their commander; it is more than likely he who led them across the empire to the far distant shores of Britain.

Once they arrived in the country and were assigned to the VI Victrix, then under the command of Julius Verus, they would have required time to settle in, to be trained and taught sufficient Latin to enable them to follow commands. Artorius may have been appointed this task also and could have remained with them for over a year. However, he was not at this juncture their official commander, nor was he to remain in Britain for long. According to the inscription, in 176–177 he returned to Rome and took up the much sought-after post of *praepositus,* overseeing the disposition of the Roman fleet stationed at Naples.

This was a hugely important post, considered something of a sinecure since it involved no active service in the front line. Rather, it involved the overseeing of supplies to the emperor on his long and wearisome campaigns in the north and east. It was a position only likely to be granted to someone who had distinguished himself in some way. The assumption is that Artorius was given the job because he had successfully carried out a task for the emperor—the escorting of the Sarmatians to Britain—and that this was his reward. Since the post was also close to Campania, where several members of the Artorii family lived, it must have been a moment of supreme personal satisfaction.

Fighting between Rome and the tribes along the German borders of the empire continued sporadically into 178. On the death of Marcus Aurelius, his son, Commodus, became emperor and required that the treaty agreed between his father and the Iazyges be implemented. Artorius, meanwhile, remained in his comfortable post in Naples for almost four years until 181, when he was posted back to Britain to join the VI Victrix with the rank of *praefectus*. Now aged around forty or forty-one, Artorius found himself commander of the fort at Bremetennacum, which happened to be the permanent home of the Sarmatian troops he had conveyed there five or six years previously.

The likelihood for this rests on a number of suppositions; however, when Artorius took up the post of *praefectus* in the VI Victrix, it seems more than reasonable to believe that he would have been given command of the unit of *numeri* with whom he was already familiar. And since the principal base for the Sarmatia *alae* was at Bremetennacum, it makes sense that Artorius would not only be their commander but also commander of the fort. In the light of subsequent events, this seems the most viable scenario.

THE FORTRESS OF VETERANS

Bremetennacum (modern Ribchester, Lancashire) was one of the most important strategic centers in Northern Britain. Here, one Roman road crossed the River Ribble from south to north, while a second went east to the great legionary fortress at York (Eboracum) and a third northwest to the area known as the Fylde, a flat plain ideally suited to cavalry maneuvers.

Archaeological evidence shows that throughout the period of the Roman occupation, cavalry regularly used Bremetennacum—at least from the beginning of the second century. A third-century inscription found in the ruins of the fort names the unit *numerus equitum Sarmatarum Bremetennacensium*, while another, dating from the fourth century, calls it the *cuneus* (wedge) *Samatarum*. This testifies to the longevity of Sarmatian presence at Bremetennacum and suggests that this fort became a permanent base for the conscripted horsemen. The fort itself could only hold around five hundred men at a time, so that others of the original fifty-five thousand would have been posted elsewhere. Fragments of horse armor found at Chesters fort on the River Tyne and at several sites along Hadrian's Wall tell us where they went. The presence of Sarmatian cavalry on the Wall will be shown to play an important part in the association of Artorius Castus with the later Arthur.

The *Ravenna Cosmography*, which lists Roman forts in Britain in the second century, gives a further definition to Bremetennacum, calling it Bremetennacum Veteranorum (Fort of the Veterans). This means there was a settlement of some kind, probably formed from legionary veterans and the Sarmatian cavalry stationed at the fort. Archaeological evidence in the form of horse armor and weapons, cloak pins, and pieces of jewelry makes it clear that the Sarmatian presence was a strong and well-established one.

In addition, there is more concrete evidence in the form of personal inscriptions and dedications found in the area. It was common for both auxiliaries and numeri who had served out their time to become Roman citizens (legionaries were already citizens). At retirement they usually took the name of the emperor responsible for subduing them, along with an additional name of their own choosing. The area around Richborough provides several inscriptions, mostly dating from the beginning of the third century, several of which portray warriors in the garb of the Steppelands or bear the cognomen Marcus Aurelius. Interestingly, there are a number who bear the name Lucius—further attesting to the probability that Artorius was the fort commander at this time—and that the auxiliaries chose their names in his honor.

The Sarmatian auxiliaries must have been an outlandish sight to the native people in the area. Stockily built, with Asiatic features and colorful clothing, they would have seemed utterly strange and even barbaric to the Britons. Yet there would have been no avoiding their presence or their astonishing skills with the bow and lance, as well as their ability to guide their horses and to attack with lighting speed before withdrawing just as swiftly. Aside from any other aspects of their lives, this would not easily be forgotten.

It seems clear that the Sarmatians created a distinct cultural enclave around Bremetennacum and may well have made use of the flat grazing lands of the Fylde to breed and train their horses—thus keeping up the supply of mounts for their military service. What is beyond question is that they continued to live in the area and seem to have retained a far more distinct sense of cultural identity, as well as religious independence, than other racial groups in the legions.

This makes it even more probable that the beliefs, traditions, and stories of the Sarmatians were preserved in Britain and that they would in all probability have been heard by the native bards and storytellers who regularly traveled the country. If, as we will show, some of the stories closely resemble those later applied to the life and deeds of Arthur, it may well be that these were the origin (in part at least) of these later tales. That their own revered commander happened to bear the Latin form of the name Arthur makes this even more telling.

The veteran settlement probably began around 200, about the time when the normal period of service for men conscripted in 175 would have ended. If, as has been suggested, the Sarmatians were *dedicatii* (men selected to serve for as long as possible), they would have been discouraged from returning home. The likelihood is that they founded a settlement outside the walls of the fort and that this became their home for several generations afterward. Here, their lives and traditions would have continued, amalgamated perhaps with native British ones, introduced by intermarriage between the two cultural groups, and including, in all likelihood, stories about their most distinguished commander—Artorius Castus.

The area around Bremetennacum appears to have been granted the title of *regio* (region), a rare designation that suggests that there may even have been a specific recognition of the Sarmatian enclave as an independent area within the Roman compartmentalization of Britain. Again, this implies that the Sarmatians were able to maintain a degree of independence within the civic structure of Roman Britain.

I. A. Richmond, in an important essay,[15] notes that the Sarmatians (however independent) would have been subject to Romanization and that among the influences to which they would also have been subjected were British (Celtic) traditions and, of course, the multiracial stew of the legions, which, from the time of the emperor Severus, were allowed greater independence of belief and cultural identity.

THE CALEDONIAN REVOLT

When Lucius Artorius Castus arrived back in Britain in 181, he would have found himself in the middle of a crisis. Caledonian tribes had breached Hadrian's Wall and were ravaging much of the eastern side of Britain as far as York (Eboracum). Dio Cassius, writing of this, gives us a very Roman view of the wild tribespeople from the north.

> There are two principal races of the [northern] Britons, the Caledonians and the Maeatae. . . . The Maeatae live next to the cross-wall which cuts the island in half, and the Caledonians are beyond them. . . . They dwell in tents, naked and unshod, possess their women in common, and in common rear all the offspring. Their form of rule is democratic for the most part, and they are very fond of plundering; consequently they choose their boldest men as rulers. They go into battle in chariots, and have small, swift horses; there are also foot-soldiers, very swift in running and very firm in standing their ground. For arms they have a shield and a short spear, with a bronze apple attached to the end of the spear-shaft, so that when it is shaken it may clash and terrify the enemy; and they also have daggers.[16]

It was to protect the south from these fearsome tribes that the emperor Hadrian initially commanded the building of the Wall that bears his name to this day. Begun in 122, it took ten thousand men a total of eight years to complete and underwent many rebuildings, repairs, and extensions during the Roman occupation until it finally extended for 120 kilometers, running east–west from Maia (Bowness) on the Solway Firth (with a later spur running down to Maryport in Cumbria) to Segedunum (Wallsend) on the River Tyne. At the time of its completion it measured ten feet in diameter and varied in height between fifteen and thirty feet. There were twenty-eight forts along its length with a dozen or more fortified watchtowers set between them.

Though the purpose of the Wall was primarily defensive, it also had gates leading from south to north, indicating that it also acted as a border checkpoint and customs station for civilian and mercantile movements. Effectively it marked the border of the empire in the west, and the strong military presence based there never declined until the legions began to withdraw. The strategic roads leading to it and garrison forts that supplied it were to be of later assistance to the defenders of Britain in the fifth and sixth centuries, and there are still "Arthurian" associations with several of the forts upon the Wall, which may well stem from the presence of Artorius Castus and the Sarmatians stationed there.

In 181 the Wall failed to keep the Caledonii out. Now, as they moved south, they encountered at least one large force and, according to Dio, slew their commander, a legate of the VI Victrix—indicating that it was part of this legion they met in battle. They then progressed to York, where they killed the acting governor of the province (probably Marcus Antius Crescens Clapurnianus). The Victrix were so shocked by this, and perhaps by the battle with the Caledonii, that they began to fall apart. According to Dio, they attempted to raise up one of their own, a prefect named Priscus, to the status of emperor (one of several such revolts that took place at this time across the empire). However Priscus declined, declaring: "I am no more an emperor than you are soldiers!"

When the emperor Commodus received word of the unrest in Britain, he dispatched Marcellus Ulpius, a stern and unpopular general, to restore order. But during the period between the start of the uprising and the arrival of Ulpius (almost two years from the start of the attacks), something happened that turned the tide in favor of Rome. The one stable area during this time was around Bremetennacum—the fort and region almost certainly commanded by Artorius. *Someone* organized a campaign against the Caledonians before the arrival of the new commander, so that by the time Ulpius reached Britain, fighting had moved back beyond Hadrian's Wall to the area below the Antonine Wall (more or less abandoned at this time).

Two lines of research suggest that this someone was Artorius. First, that it is possible to match several possible battle locations in which he fought with a list of later Arthurian battle sites, and second that within a short space of time Artorius was given the rank of *dux* with the task of putting down a far more serious revolt in Armorica (Brittany). Recent suggestions have been put forward that the fragmentary word on the Podstrana stele is actually *Armenians* rather than *Amoricans*. However, a careful examination of the inscription shows that this would almost certainly not have fitted the space.

One of the few surviving pieces of documentary evidence for the existence of a later Dark Age Arthur, and the first place where he is referred to by the title *dux,* also contains a list of battles. This book, the *Historia Brittonum* (History of Britain), is attributed to a ninth-century monk named Nennius, who tells us that in the face of a Saxon invasion in the late fifth century, Arthur, the British *dux bellorum* (duke of battle), fought twelve encounters with the enemy. The first of these battles takes place "at the mouth of the River Glein"; the second to fifth are "on the river Dubglass in the region of Linnus"; the sixth is "on the river called Bassas"; the seventh is "in the forest of Calydon, or Cat Coit Celidon"; the eighth is "at the fort of Guinnion"; the ninth is "at the City of Legions"; the tenth is "on the banks of the river Tribuit"; the eleventh is "on a mountain called Agned or Cat Breguion"; and the twelfth is "at the Mount (or Hill) of Badon."

We shall examine the historical evidence for these battles, as fought by an Arthur who lived in the fifth and sixth centuries in chapter 3; for the moment, we want to explore another possibility—that Nennius's list may have derived, in part or wholly, from a lost account of Lucius Artorius Castus's campaign against the Caledonians.

In fact we have no means of knowing whether any of these battles actually took place at all, either in the sequence given by Nennius, or with someone called Arthur as a protagonist. They all may not have been full-scale battles but rather skirmishes. Nor can we say with any degree of certainty where they took place, despite numerous attempts to place them at specific points on the map of post-Roman Britain, since place names have mutated so much over the centuries. We shall present our own suggested sequence for this later, locating many of them in the north. If this suggestion is correct, and a later Arthur did indeed fight a campaign in the northern half of Britain, and if we then take the timing of these battles back three hundred years to the second rather than the fifth century, a pattern does emerge—suggesting that it could have been Artorius's exploits that furnished the original battle list, rather than the later Arthur. By applying the battle list from the *Historia Brittonum* to the situation in Britain around 181, we arrive at a scenario that seems to echo uncannily the campaign of Artorius Castus.[17]

One of the most important battles in Nennius's list—the eleventh—takes place at the Hill or Rock of Agned, also called Breguion. The latter could derive from an earlier version of the name Bremetennacum, which was initially a native British name (Bremetanna or possibly Bremetenraco—the Stronghold of the Breme), rather than Roman. An alternative site would be the fort at Bremenium (High Rochester, Northumberland), which would still be close to the path of the advancing Caledonians and within the area controlled by Bremetennacum. If, once they had sacked Eboracum, the tribes pushed farther west, following the Roman roads across the Pennines, it is likely that they met Artorius and his Sarmatian cavalry for the first time and fought a battle, which they lost.

At this point the assumption is that if Artorius was the victor of this first encounter, he drove the Caledonii west along the River Ribble toward the tidal estuary where two more rivers, the Douglas and the Dow, add their flow to the waters. This area, which would have made a good "killing field," may have possibly borne the name Tribuit in Nennius's time, and here he places another of Arthur's battles. Local tradition makes Cei or Kai the leader of this encounter, and it is possible that Artorius might have had an officer named Caius on his staff in Britain who could have led a separate cohort of Sarmatian cavalry against the Caledonii at this site. This is, of course, only speculation.[18]

Nennius describes the next four of Arthur's battles happening along the Dubglass, which has been identified with the River Douglas in Lancashire.[19] Assuming that the Caledonii fled south, away from the high escarpments of the Pennines in an attempt to shake the fast-moving Sarmatian cavalry off their tails, they could have followed the course of the River Douglas. If they indeed fought four more battles here, all would have taken place within the region of Bremetennacum.

These battles seem to have halted the headlong rush of the Caledonii, after which they turned back across the high ground toward York—which was also known as the City of the Legions—the site of Arthur's ninth battle in Nennius's list. This would have taken them back into the area controlled by the VI Victrix, to which legion some, at least, of the Sarmatian cavalry were attached, and this may have encouraged Artorius to follow up his initial success. Since that legion was still in a state of disarray, the commander of Bremetennacum seems to have decided to continue chasing the Caledonii—now definitely in flight—back above Hadrian's Wall.

Their inevitable direction would have been along Dere Street toward the fort at Vinovium (Binchester, Durham). Here, it seems, the Roman force caught up with them and were once again victorious in another skirmish. Nennius names Arthur's eighth battle as having been fought at Castle Guinnion—a name that can be shown to derive from Vinovium.[20] From here, the beaten Caledonii had only one place to go—through Hadrian's Wall, across the no-man's-land between there and the abandoned Antonine Wall—back to their own lands. Along the way, they passed the River Glen, not far from the site of the fifteenth-century Battle of Flodden, northwest of Wooler in Northumberland.

Nennius sites another of Arthur's battles on the River Glen, again etymologically shown to derive from Glein.[21]

From here, the tribesmen fled farther north, but if we are correct in our reading of the landscape and the places, Artorius continued his pursuit, possibly now under orders from the newly arrived Ulpius Marcellus to exterminate the invaders completely. The next battle seemed to have taken place at Cat Coit Celidon, the Caledonian Forest, located in the Scottish Lowlands and again close to the Roman road of Dere Street, where the now demoralized Caledonii were beaten yet again.

Nennius lists this encounter as the seventh of Arthur's battles; but we must remember that he may well have jumbled the original order— possibly because he was working from a source that rhymed—so that an earlier poet may have reorganized or even reinvented battles to make his poem sing.

On the final leg of their flight to their homelands, the Caledonii seem to have turned at bay again. If so, as it is the only unidentified site from Nennius's list, this battle probably took place at the river he calls Bassus.

The twelfth and final encounter took place at the Mount, Hill, or Rock of Badon, which some researchers have identified as Dumbarton Rock in Strathclyde, or possibly Buxton in Derbyshire, where a Roman road known as Bathamgate passes through the hills of the Peak District.[22] Curiously the twelfth-century *Historia Regum Britanniae* (History of the Kings of Britain) of Geoffrey of Monmouth, describes Dumbarton as a place where Arthur fought against the Scots (the Irish) and Picts (the descendants of the Caledonii) and killed them in enormous numbers, treating them with unparalleled severity and sparing none that fell into his hands. This adds fuel to the suggestion that the campaign was a success, as does the fact that in 184, just after these events, the emperor Commodus assumed the title of *britannicus*—a usual indication of a victory against a specific enemy of the empire.[23]

If we follow this line of reasoning, which fits the known facts, we can see that all twelve battles, as listed by Nennius and applied to those of the later Arthur, also parallel those of Artorius Castus's campaign some three hundred years earlier. If Artorius did indeed lead the campaign against the Caledonii, then the story of his deeds would have lasted; they would have been the stuff of bardic song throughout Britain and would have passed down through generations of storytellers. In addition to the named battles against the Caledonii, there would have been others—skirmishes along the Wall itself—where archaeological record places units of the Sarmatian cavalry. Perhaps they were the inspiration for a poem attributed to the sixth-century bard Taliesin, writing during the lifetime of another Arthur. The poem is called "Kadeir Teyrnon" (The Sovereign's Seat, p. 355. The full text will be found in an appendix at the end of the book.)

> *Declare the clear* awdl *[an epic poem]*
> *In* awen's *own metre. [inspiration]*
> *A man sprung of two authors,*
> *Of the steel cavalry wing,*
> *With his clear wisdom,*
> *With his royal rule,*
> *With his kingly lordship,*
> *With his honour of scripture,*
> *With his red lorica,*
> *With his assault over the Wall,*
> *With his poet-praised seat,*
> *Amongst the defenders of the Wall.*
> *He led from the enclosed Wall*
> *Pale saddled horses.*
>
> *The venerable lord,*
> *The nurturing cup-bearer,*
> *One of three wise ones*
> *To bless Arthur.*
> *Arthur the blessed,*
> *In harmonious song,*
> *In the forefront of battle,*

Trampling down nine.
Fleets shall come [. . .]
Strange accents flow,
Eloquent assaults,
Of sea-farers.

The implication here is clear. Arthur is a man "sprung of two authors," or nations, and from the steel of the cavalry wing. He fights on the disputed territory of the Wall against the "seafarers" (almost certainly the Saxons, who have replaced the Caledoni here), and makes enough of an impression to be considered a hero of no small stature. There is nothing in the story to indicate whom the phrase *Arthur the blessed* refers to. Other poems written at this time, but partly based on much earlier songs, use Arthur as a benchmark for bravery; thus in a battle fought at Catraeth (Catterick), not too far from the Wall, a warrior is praised for his ability even though "he was not Arthur."

THE ARMORICAN CAMPAIGN

The next event in Artorius Castus's life also echoes that of the later Arthur. In Geoffrey of Monmouth's *Historia Regum Britanniae,* an important Arthurian text that we shall explore in chapter 5, we are told that after a campaign in which he defeated the Scots, Arthur returned to York and almost immediately set sail for the Continent to attack Rome itself. Artorius Castus, having completed his battles against the Caledonians, also returned to York (Eboracum) and almost immediately was posted to the Continent (Armorica, Brittany), commanding a troop of Sarmatian cavalry, to put down a rebellion led by disaffected Roman soldiers.

When those responsible for the attempt to make Priscus emperor were executed or banished, one officer of the VI Victrix, rather than receive punishment, was given an important task, commanding two legions: probably drawn from the still-shattered VI and the XX Valerio Victrix. The inscription from Artorius's tomb at this point describes him as "*dux* of the cohorts of cavalry from Britain against the

Armoricans," and it was with this title (possibly a temporary one) that he undertook the repression of an uprising among legions based there in 185–186.

Both Dio Cassius and another Roman historian, Herodian (born 178), describe how trouble flared up in Armorica. Under the leadership of a disaffected ex-legionary named Maternus, a group of deserters formed themselves into a formidable force and began ravaging through Gaul and into Spain, attacking cities and setting free any prisoners they discovered until their numbers grew to dangerous proportions. When news of this reached Commodus, he sent letters to the governors of the threatened regions, which included Pescennius Niger in Aquitania, Clodius Albinus in Belgica, and Septimus Severus in Lugdunensis, accusing them of failing to keep control of their provinces.

Exactly what happened next is difficult to say. Dio and Herodian give conflicting accounts, and other sources are scanty. We know from Artorius Castus's inscription that it was at this point that he led "the cavalry from Britain against the Armoricans." We may assume that either one of the accused governors or the emperor himself ordered the crack unit of Sarmatian cavalry from Britain to put down the rebellion. Both accounts tell us that Maternus's ambitions had grown to the point that he considered taking the empire and assassinating Commodus. However a warning reached the emperor—according to Dio—via fifteen hundred "javelin men" who came from Britain into Italy to warn Commodus. This term is unusually specific since, as Malcor points out, it would have been more normal to call them simply legionaries or soldiers. Javelin man, *iaculator* in Latin, refers to the light lance or *iaculor* used by most Roman cavalry. This ties in precisely with the Artorius inscription. It is possible that the newly appointed *dux,* as the leader or coordinator of the military response to Maternus, learned of the plot against Commodus and sent a force to Rome to warn the emperor and help in his defense.[24]

An alternative scenario, based on Dio's *Roman History* (book 73), describes the plot against Commodus as led by Perennius, the commander of the Praetorian Guard, who grew tired of running the empire while Commodus enjoyed himself with chariot racing and orgies. Dio says that "the lieutenants of Britain" sent fifteen hundred men to Italy to warn Commodus that Perennius was plotting against him, showing him coins struck by the would-be emperor with his own name (or that of his son) inscribed upon them. Perennius was duly captured and executed, together with the rest of his family.

The two accounts seem to have become muddled. A more likely reconstruction of events would be that Dux Artorius led some of the fifteen hundred Sarmatian cavalry from Britain against Maternus and defeated him somewhere in Gaul or Armorica, receiving as a reward the governorship of Liburnia. It seems unlikely that he would have known about the plot conceived by Perennius, which seems to be a separate incident unconnected to the Armorican uprising.

In any case, we hear no more of the fifteen hundred javelin men, but given that Artorius's next post was as *procurator centenarius* of the province of Liburnia (in Dalmatia), we may assume that this high office was granted as a reward by the grateful emperor. This post was certainly an important one, carrying with it a salary of 100,000 sesterces a year—enough for Artorius to maintain his equestrian standing and to purchase a villa and build the mausoleum for himself and his family from which the inscription comes. That he also had "the power to issue death sentences" suggests that he was a magistrate.

A LAST ADVENTURE

When most men might have been expected to retire after a stint of twenty-five to twenty-six years in the army, Artorius still had one final adventure ahead of him. He seems to have lived comfortably in Liburnia for nearly a decade, and inscriptions found in the area suggest that other members of his family had settled there.[25] Possibly his own children had homes in the area or shared the villa at Podstrana.

Commodus was assassinated in 193, and Pertinax, whom Artorius may have known from the period when they served together in Pannonia and Britain, became emperor. His reign lasted only eighty-seven days, however, and Didius Julianus replaced him for an even briefer period of sixty-six days. At this point, the powerful and wily Septimus Severus succeeded to the imperial throne. Dio Cassius records that he held a state funeral for his old comrade Pertinax, which important members of the equestrian order were commanded to attend. Artorius would almost certainly have been present and may have renewed his earlier acquaintance with the new emperor.

Then, around 196, when Artorius would have been in his fifty-fourth year, the prefect Albinus, who had also played a part in the Armorican uprising and who was now governor of Britain, was declared emperor by his legions and invaded Gaul. Severus led a counterattack, marching north through Pannonia, Noricum, Raetia, and through Upper Germania into the threatened province. Though we have no means of knowing this for certain, he may well have called upon Artorius to aid him in the campaign. Certainly, he passed through the area of Liburnia, where the now-aging commander still lived, and he would almost certainly have remembered the leader of the Sarmatian cavalry from a decade earlier when he (Severus) was still governor of Lugdunensis and had become involved in the Armorican revolt. In addition, Artorius would have been familiar with some of the forces commanded by Albinus, which may have included Sarmatian cavalry from Bremetennacum.[26]

Two battles were fought against Albinus. The first was at Tinurtium (modern Tournus) in circa 197 and another at Lugudunum (Lyons) later in the same year. Dio, who gives the best account of this, mentions heavy losses to the *British* cavalry unit and is also clear in stating that Severus himself was not present at the first battle. The implication is that whoever was leading the Roman forces had sufficient knowledge of the Sarmatian cavalry to enable them to be beaten. This could have been Artorius, or if not, he may have advised the actual commander. If so, he would have been fighting against his own old unit.

Albinus withdrew south with Severus in pursuit. The second battle at Lugdunun was a bloody affair, and once again it was the cavalry—this time Severus's men, led by one Laetus—who turned the tide. Albinus fled the field and, having been surrounded at a nearby villa, took his own life. Dio describes the battlefield as "covered with the bodies of men and horses." It is possible that Artorius also took part in this battle and that he fell here, since there is no further mention of him in the historical record. If so, his body would have been taken back to Liburnia and buried in the mausoleum he had already prepared. The second plaque found in the area, which honored his deeds, may have been erected at this time or soon after.

Thus ended the astonishing career of Lucius Artorius Castus, whose exploits would have been remembered long after his passing and may, with the traditions handed down in Britain by the Sarmatian warriors he had commanded, have influenced the growing number of tales of a British cavalry leader who bore the title of *dux* and fought over the same area of Britain against a similar enemy to the later Saxon invaders of the fifth and sixth centuries. Curiously, the sixteenth-century antiquarian John Leyland mentioned an ancient wax seal preserved at Westminster that listed the later Arthur's conquests as: Patricus Arturus Brittaniae Galliae Germaniae Daciae Imperator (Noble Arthur, Emperor of Britain, Gaul, Germany, and Dacia). All the places listed are areas where Artorius Castus fought.[27]

ECHOES FROM THE STEPPE

The parallels between the life of Artorius and that of the later Arthur are distinctive enough to give us pause. The picture jumps into focus even more sharply when we examine other details from the lives and beliefs of the Sarmatians.

An image that is constant in the later historical accounts of Arthur is his use of armored cavalry. In each instance his men fight from horseback wearing armor and carrying long lances as well as swords and shields. The Sarmatians also were noted for their use of scale armor; they, too, fought from horseback, carried shields, and defended themselves with long lances. Like the medieval Knights of the Round Table, whose favorite weapon was also the lance, they believed themselves all to be of equal status.

The story of Arthur's success against the Saxons, three hundred years after the events described above, lies exactly in the mobility and shock tactics of his mounted troops and accounts for the wide area over which he is said to have fought his battles. By the early fifth century, even the Roman legions were discovering that they needed mounted divisions to counter the barbarian hordes that had begun to threaten Rome. They learned the use of the stirrup, which gave stability to the mounted warrior and enabled him to stand in the saddle to thrust with sword and spear against infantry, from the very people they were fighting. The Sarmatians were well versed in this form of warfare and may well have passed it on to their Roman masters.

But there is a still more significant detail connecting the Sarmatians to the later Arthurian knights. In battle they fought under a bronze dragonhead with a wind-sock-style banner attached. This may have originated as a directional aid for archers in battle, but by the second century, it was an important symbol of Sarmatian strength. This standard, known as a *draco,* which was said to roar as the wind blew through it when the warriors rode into battle, may account for the later cognomen *pendragon* (head or chief dragon) applied to Arthur and his father Uther. A fourteenth-century image from the *L'Histoire de Merlin* of Robert de Boron shows Arthur riding into battle under just such a banner. Although the Roman legions had their own standards (notably the eagle), they adopted the *draco* after the arrival of the Sarmatian auxiliaries. It became a permanent feature during the Dacian Wars of circa 101–106, during the rule of the emperor Trajan. At this time the equipment carried by the legions was generally revised to enable them to withstand the attacks of barbarian horsemen, and it was at this time that the heavily armed cavalry wings (*alae cataphractori*) became an important part of the army. The office of *draconius* (standard barer) also appears at this time, almost certainly as a direct result of the incorporation of Steppe units into the legions.[28]

The *draco* standard would certainly have been seen along Hadrian's Wall, where one or more contingents of the Sarmatian cavalry (attached to Artorius's old legion, the VI Victrix, who built several of the forts along this stretch of the Wall) were stationed at various times. Arthurian associations with this same area are well attested. Discussion still continues over the identification of the fort known as Camboglanna. Some authorities maintain that it should be identified with modern Birdoswald, others with the adjacent fort at Castlesteads. Both have possible Arthurian connections and have been cited as the place where Arthur fought his final battle at Camlann.

Archaeological evidence confirms that the fort at Birdoswald was reoccupied and a large timber hall built there during the period of the Dark Age Arthur, probably at the behest of an important local chieftain or military commander who could have been Arthur himself. Memories of the presence of Artorius and the Sarmatian cavalry at this site may have influenced local traditions that claim this as a center of Arthur's military activities in Cumbria and in the ancient Caledonian forest. A mere twenty miles farther down the Wall from the fort at Camboglanna, a name that has been put forward as a possible site of the Battle of Camlann, a second fort, named Aballava (Burgh-by-Sands), once stood. Though nothing of this now remains, it was pointed out some years ago that this is almost exactly the distance that the body of a wounded man could have been carried from the field of battle—to be buried in Avalon![29]

THE ROSE ON THE SHIELD

In the *Historia Brittonum* Nennius tells us that Arthur carried the image of the Virgin on his shoulder when he fought the Saxons at the Battle of Badon. This has long been of interest to those debating whether or not Arthur was a Christian. The suggestion most usually accepted is that this arose from confusion between the British words for shield (*scuit*) and shoulder (*scuid*), meaning that Arthur bore an image of the Virgin painted on his *shield*.[30] However, there is another possible explanation; one that takes us back once more to the Artorius's inscription, which is notably surrounded by carvings of rosettes. This may simply be a reference to the fact that the symbol for the *dux* was a golden rose-shaped brooch, worn on the shoulder to fasten the military cloak, but it can also be seen as a sign of devotion to the goddess Flora.[31]

The worship of this goddess began in Artorius's homeland of Campania around 238 BC and, as noted above, may have risen from an older Greek cult, brought to Campania by the Artorii themselves. Flora may seem a strange choice of devotion for a military family, until one remembers that in Roman mythology Flora impregnates Juno by giving her a rose so that she gives birth to Mars—the god of war. Roses were also seen as symbols of death and rebirth and continued to be important in the religious symbology of the legions. "Flora" seems to have been used as a coded reference to Rome itself in private messages between high-ranking generals and the emperor himself.

Among second-century Christians, Flora, along with Isis and several other goddesses, was often conflated with Mary the Mother of Jesus—to the extent that some church fathers disapproved of the worship of the Blessed Virgin because she could be seen as Flora in disguise. In addition the symbol of the rose was taken over in Marian worship (the rosary beads are to this day an expression of this).

Could this be the origin of Arthur's Marian devotion? In Artorius's day the image of the golden rose would have been seen as a representation of Flora; but to a fifth-century Christian author like Nennius, it would have been seen as a sign of Mary. Another possibility is that Artorius converted to Christianity toward the end of his life and that the roses on his tomb signified a devotion to Mary. This would be in line with the idea of Arthur as a Christian king as he appears in medieval literature.[32]

SARMATIAN ECHOES

It is when we look at the traditions of the Sarmatians who served under Artorius Castus that we find remarkable echoes of the legends of Arthur and his knights. One particular tribe, called the Narts, numbered among their possessions an extraordinary object known as the Nartamonga. This was a type of cauldron that would only feed heroes of significant stature, and in one tale, centering on the hero Batradz, we can see more than one echo of later Arthurian legends. The story can be summarized as follows:

> The Narts were quarrelling among themselves over who should keep the Nartamonga, the sacred cup that would only serve the most perfect hero, and for which they had sought for a long time. First Urzymag said that without him they would not have succeeded in their quest for the cup, so he should have it. Then Soslan and Sozyryko, who were also famous warriors, claimed to be the greatest hero. In each case Batradz, who was the leader of the Narts, refuted their claims, instancing times when they had failed to live up to the highest standards of heroism where he had not. Finally Batradz challenged any man there to find one time when he personally had failed them. No one could do so and he therefore kept the Nartamonga.[33]

This is interesting for a number of reasons. The nature of the Nartamonga, its ability to enhance heroic abilities and bring inspiration to the one who owns it, suggests similarities with a number of Celtic cauldrons of inspiration and life, which possess similar qualities and which are also associated with Arthur, as we shall see in chapter 4. This leaves little room for doubt that the Nart sagas represent an important link in the chain of chronology that leads in time to the Grail quest of later Arthurian legend.[34]

Batradz himself has a number of parallels with Arthur—one of the most startling being the story of his death. As he lies wounded on the field of battle, he asks his lieutenant to throw his magical sword into a nearby lake. The lieutenant tries to do this three times, finally carrying out his master's wishes after two failed attempts. This is so remarkably like the later stories in which Bedivere, Arthur's lieutenant, is asked by the wounded king to do exactly the same thing with Excalibur, that one has to consider these stories as either following each other or both drawing upon the same or similar sources. In addition it should be noted that the battle that ends in Batradz's death is also an internecine one, as was Arthur's battle against his son/nephew Mordred, and that at the time of his birth, Batradz is described as "tempered like steel in a forge," which makes him invulnerable. Arthur in the poem quoted above, on pages 27–28, is described as born of the cavalry's steel wing. Later, as long as he carries the magical Excalibur and the sheath in which it is held, he also cannot be hurt.[35]

These parallels are striking and suggest a long-standing connection between the two cultures. Nor is it necessary to believe that the Sarmatians posted to Britain in the second century were the only means by which these stories could have cross-fertilized each other and thus influenced the later Arthurian saga. T. Sulimirsky, the great expert on Sarmatian history, points out that there were a number of opportunities for contact between the Sarmatians and the Celts during the sixth to first centuries BC. During this period the Celts migrated across Europe and Asia Minor into the area of the Danube and across the plains of central Europe, to what is still today Southern Russia. Sulimirsky adds that by the first century AD, the Iazyges occupied the plains of Northern Hungary and had "partly displaced, but mostly subdued, the Celto-Dacian occupants" of this area.[36] Even earlier evidence for a Celtic influence on the Sarmatians is evidenced by the discovery of Celtic-style helmets and weapons found at Sarmatian sites in the Ukraine and Crimea. There was, in effect, sufficient contact between the two cultures for a particular type of Sarmatian brooch to have evolved from a Celtic original, making it more than likely that a transmission of stories and traditions could also have flowed between the two peoples at this early date. The Sarmatians who found themselves in Britain in the second century may well have recognized elements of story and myth among the natives with whom they were suddenly associated. Later contact was also possible, as we shall see shortly.

Given that another tradition among the Sarmatians was the worship of a sword stuck point down in the earth, we may be forgiven for suggesting that this practice, carried by the Sarmatians to Britain, influenced the later Arthurian legends. In these Arthur draws a sword from a stone to prove his right to the kingship of Britain. The fourth-century writer Ammianus Marcellinus says of the Alans (a subtribe of the Sarmatians) that their only idea of religion was "to plunge a naked sword into the earth with barbaric ceremonies, and they worship that with great respect, as Mars, the presiding deity of the regions over which they wander."[37] Elsewhere, the fifth-century Greek historian Herodotus gives a lengthy description of Scythian practices in which a kind of wooden pyramid was constructed, flat on top, into which an ancient iron sword was stuck to represent the war god Ares. Sacrifices, both animal and human, were made to this god. The Scythians were cousins to the Alans, Iazyges, and other Sarmatian tribes, and it is more than likely that they shared such ceremonies.[38]

Even the name of Arthur's magical weapon, most often given as Excalibur, may derive from a Sarmatian source. An older name for the sword is Caliburnus (White-Steel) from *chalybus* (steel) and *eburnus* (white). A tribe of Sarmatian smiths from the area of the Caucasus were known as the Kalybes—suggesting that the very name of Arthur's sword may have originated with the warriors from across the sea.[39]

This may seem a long way in time and space from the more usual setting for the Arthurian period in the late fifth to early sixth centuries. However, oral memory can extend over much greater lengths of time and old stories have a way of resurfacing, as well as affecting those that come after. As we have noted above there was a good deal of contact between the Celts and the Sarmatians. Later, as we shall see in chapter 5, the crusaders added elements to the Arthurian legends from contact with Eastern traditions. It is by no means impossible that Sarmatian/Ossetic stories could have been circulating in the crusader kingdoms at this time (the thirteenth century onward) and that, for example, the tale of Batradz's magical sword and its return to the water could have been brought back to the West, where it reappeared in the French text *La Mort du Roi Artu* (ca. 1230–1240).[40]

Other writers have speculated that the Sarmatian contingent of the legion settled in Britain (this much is clear from archaeological evidence alone) and that actual descendants of Artorius Castus (easily possible if Artorius had a liaison with a British woman) or descendants of the original warriors may still have been around in the fifth or sixth centuries.

Certainly, a Cuneus Sarmatarum is still listed in the *Notitia Dignitatum,* a list of legions complied at the end of the fourth century—barely a hundred years before the time when Arthur is believed to have flourished. Another theory suggests that, as expert horse breeders, the Steppe warriors may have continued to supply mounts to a native militia gathered together under the dragon standard some three hundred years after the time of Artorius.[41] Archaeological evidence of an important equestrian center producing horse leather and decorative harness at Trimontium (between the Antonine and Hadrianic Walls) suggests the continuing importance of horse training in Britain. It is more than likely that the Sarmatians could have established a strong presence as horse breeders and that their increasing interaction with local tribespeople and the Romano-British enclave would have made them familiar and socially acceptable figures. This would have enabled the sharing of memories as well as stories and traditions among the native British. The story of Lucius Artorius Castus may well have lived on, embroidered and altered and finally merging with older British mythic heroes and perhaps with a new rising star—Arthur, duke of battles.

THE FIRST ARTHUR

To sum up, we have accounts of the career of a second-century Roman officer who distinguished himself in a number of daring actions and who was a charismatic and memorable leader. We find him in Britain as the leader of a group of warriors, fighting from horseback with long spears, wearing heavy armor. We find these men fighting under a dragon banner described in exactly the same terms as that used by Arthur in later stories. We find him associated with a people who worshipped a sword stuck point down in the earth or on a wooden platform—a theme that would also reoccur in Arthurian legend as the sword in the stone.

In addition, we find among the traditions of the Sarmatians stories of a hero who possessed a magical vessel and a sword that went back into a lake. We find the same Roman officer—Lucius Artorius

Castus, the only man recorded with this name in Britain at this time—commanding the same warriors on Hadrian's Wall, stationed at a fort the name of which can be shown to have connections to the site of Arthur's last Battle of Camlann. Nearby is a fort with a name that recalls Avalon, Arthur's legendary last resting place.

We also have Nennius's account of twelve battles fought by the fifth- and sixth-century Arthur—battles that can be shown to parallel the campaign of the second-century Artorius. Finally, we have a poem, "Kadeir Teyrnon," that describes the warrior Arthur leading his men in defense of the Wall—surely Hadrian's Wall—where Artorius Castus and his Sarmatian cavalry are known to have fought.

If the theory of Artorius as the first Arthur is correct, it need not cause us to reject other contenders. Lucius Artorius Castus flourished in the second century AD; he is not the Arthur who fought the Saxons in the fifth or sixth centuries and helped to preserve Roman civilization in Britain. However, his battles against the Caledonii in that earlier time left a legacy that could, either consciously or not, have been taken up by the storytellers who turned the life of a great British (or Roman) leader into the stuff of myth and legend.

2

Arthur of the Shadows
A Hero in the Making

If his forehead is radiant like the smooth hill in
the lateral light, it is corrugated like the
defence of the hill, because of his care for the
land and for the men of the land.

DAVID JONES, *THE ROMAN QUARRY* (1981)

THE MISSING HERO

When archaeologists excavated the great East Anglian ship burial of
Sutton Hoo in the 1930s, they found no actual human remains. Because
of the acidic sand in which the dead king or nobleman and his atten-
dants had been interred, there were merely a series of faint impressions
where bodies had been, and the placement of swords, helmets, and belt
clasps, to show where the bodies had been laid.[1]

The evidence for Arthur in the historical record of the Dark Ages is
much the same: the impress of his presence is almost all that survives to
suggest he once existed. This does not, however, mean that he did not
exist, just that we need to scrutinize the evidence more closely.

When we look at the end of the fifth century, at a time when

Britain was in turmoil, abandoned by Rome, rent by internecine strife, and struggling against invaders on many shores, we see a shadowy figure who steps out of the darkness to bind together the warring regions into a brief unity and bring a measure of peace. Arthur emerges on the scene abruptly and without warning, and we do not even know from whence he came or what subsequently became of him.

This Arthur is not yet the king of legend, but a military commander whose exploits echo down the ages. His name flashes briefly like a comet in the darkness of the age, while his exploits, so briefly recorded, send a disproportionate shadow across the folk memory and literary traditions of Britain.

When we consider the volume of writing that the figure of Arthur has generated, it seems impossible that he did not exist at all. But to find the man behind the legends, we have to strip away the accretions with which our imagination has invested him. Beyond the medieval trappings of kingship and the glorious deeds of knighthood was an age that was still part of the late classical world, and as the mighty Roman Empire was steadily being assaulted by peoples beyond its domains, so too the same scenario was working out within Britain.

We have explored some of the evidence for a second-century Arthur: now we pass to a time when Rome was no longer a force in Britain. It is necessary to chart the events that led up to Arthur's appearance in the fifth century so that we can appreciate the unique context of his times. Then we can examine the written sources that offer the primary evidence for the man in the shadows.

A PEOPLE ALONE

The incredible flash point where Rome retreats from Britain, and where Saxon, Pict, and Scot pour into its undefended shores, is the place we would expect to find at least one freedom fighter—a leader who could galvanize resistance and have the authority to command armies.

The British chronicler Gildas, writing at the remove of a hundred and fifty years from this difficult time, speaks of the successive withdrawal of the legions in 383 and of emergency rescue campaigns to Britain by generals (possibly Carausius and Stilicho) until the final withdrawal. The Romans advised that "the British should stand alone, get used to arms, fight bravely and defend" themselves with all their power.[2] Gildas ingenuously adds that they also "left them manuals on weapons training."[3] He continues that despite the breakdown of normal life during this period, "kings, public and private persons, priests and churchmen, kept to their own stations," perhaps maintaining the barest skeleton of infrastructure together.[4]

For centuries Britain had sufficient cohorts and legions to defend its coasts. The ultimate decline of the Roman presence in Britain was due to factors that were to change the face of Europe in the fourth to fifth centuries. These included a concerted attack upon the empire by what Rome called "barbarian peoples," an increasing reliance on people of the same races to provide both soldiers and commanders for the Roman army, the subdivision of the Roman Empire into western and eastern halves, and the increasing thirst for reinforcements from outlying provinces to help prosecute campaigns of defense or to support imperial usurpations or to quell uprisings outside Britain—all these factors played their parts in Rome's abandonment of Britain.

In 383 Magnus Maximus, a Spaniard who held high military office, was proclaimed emperor in Britain by his troops; he later went on to murder the true Western emperor Gratian, before being slain himself by Emperor Theodosius I. Magnus Maximus's departure with his troops severely depleted the defensive strength left in Britain. It was remembered for a long time: bards referred to this departure as one of three military hemorrhages that bled Britain of its troops in time of need. The figure of 21,000 men is remembered, though time and grievance may have exaggerated the number.[5] The troop strength in Britain at that time numbered only 50,000.

During the somewhat nominal rule of the Western emperor Honorius (384–423), son of Theodosius I, the Vandal Flavius Stilicho wielded power as his military chief minister. He drew increasingly upon barbarian federates to bolster the strength of his armies. He gained victories in 398–399 over the Saxons, Picts, and Scots and seems to have been part of the last wave of Roman rescue missions sent to bail the British province out of trouble. A series of disastrous usurpations ensued. First Marcus, then Gratian, and last Constantine III were elected emperor by the British army. The system of tetrarchy, with its pairs of Eastern and Western emperors, and the immense demands made upon the army during this period of barbarian expansion in Europe had begun to destabilize the empire and to put Britain out on a limb. Many soldiers from the remaining Roman units left in Britain chose to throw in their lot with the usurper Constantine III to support his invasion of Gaul in 407. Honorius recognized him as co-emperor, needing his help to deal with the Visigothic attack on Rome by Alaric in 410, but a year later he had Constantine assassinated in Arles in 411.

The Byzantine historian Zosimus writes that the Britons drove out the men who had moved over to Constantine's party and began to govern themselves. In 409–410 an authoritative document, which has not survived but which is referred to elsewhere as the "rescript of Honorius," addressed itself to the *civitates* or the lower ranks of the bureaucratic structure in Britain formalizing the Roman position: the message was that, from here onward, the British must now take what measures they could to govern themselves.

In circa 425 the *Notitia Dignitatum,* which recorded the military strength in Britain, relates that the land was "still held by the empire," a good fifteen years after the main withdrawal of troops. This piece of wishful thinking is not justified by events and reads more like a stubborn man's mind-set, unable to envisage any future beyond Roman order. While a single Roman standard still flew and while one soldier still carried arms, Britain was, indeed, still "held by the empire"; but the glory days were over, and the sunset of empire already sent its last rays across the land.

We do not know the size of the standing army left behind at the Roman withdrawal, nor how long it held out, nor how many native-born sons followed in their fathers' military career of protecting the farthest northerly boundary of the empire. The *Notitia Dignitatum* was maintained up until circa 428. Then we hear no more. But it is clear from the actions of Vortigern, the first emergent British leader, that there were insufficient trained warriors to defend the land because he invited Jutish federates to perform this task. Gildas would have us believe that the remaining troops were too lazy to fight and that the barbed spears of Picts brought them to a swift end. Rather than the finality of Roman withdrawal, these remarks seem better to fit the "barbarian conspiracy" of AD 367, when the long-held northern frontier of Britain collapsed and Picts, Scots, and Saxons made common cause, swarming south, killing two Roman generals and pillaging the land.[6]

In Europe, the Huns of the Steppe had been undergoing their own expansion and had been migrating farther west, putting pressure on all lands in their path. Many displaced peoples accordingly moved south and west to avoid them, a migration that may have affected the Saxons. Germany became an important buffer zone between the empire and the new wave of barbarians at its borders. This mass migration was one of the factors that brought Britain nearer to the abyss as Rome attempted to defend itself along an immensly long front. In the face of the complex barbarian conflicts that beset the boundaries of the empire, not only strength in arms but also religion was seen as a unifying factor reinforcing those within its bounds, with Christianity defining the civilized from the pagan barbarian.

Writing in the ninth century, Nennius says of these times that Britain "went in fear for forty years" after the withdrawal. What manner of government emerged after the Romans left? The urban model of government in Roman Britain before this time had been based on councils made up of about thirty councillors of the rich elite, per town, or about 720 individuals in the country, plus their families.[7] It may have been from councils of such notables that Vortigern, the first British leader, emerges. Britain was sick of trusting in usurpers who lined their own pockets and then withdrew troops to prosecute their claims overseas. This steady ebbing away of men had robbed the long coastline of Britain of its defenses.

Given the examples of previous usurpers and military coups, of which

Map 2. *The North of Lucius Artorius Castus.*
(courtesy of Wil Kinghan)

the church father Saint Jerome writes that Britain was "particularly fertile," it is clear that urban councils would have needed military support. The power vacuum left by Rome's withdrawal was immense. Not only did the country no longer have a coherent structure—although magistrates and other officials may still have struggled on—but there was no one left to police civil society, never mind maintain order in the face of invasion and banditry. Trade with the Continent was almost certainly halted, and the safety of markets and the internal movement of goods would have been compromised. In the face of shortages and the breakdown of order, Gildas writes that "the pitiable citizens . . . resorted to looting each other." This was the result of famine following the failure of agriculture and the breakdown of food distribution following the disruption of Saxon raids and incursions.[8]

An independent, go-it-alone attitude may have briefly surfaced in the breasts of emergent native rulers and their peoples as they regarded themselves free of their overlords, but no one took the wider view of the whole country. Pax Romanitas and its laws were no longer supported from Rome. The four regions of the ex-diocese of Britain reverted to smaller units, probably predicated on original tribal regions and their elite rulers. In the face of the dismaying assaults by Scots, Picts, and Saxons, these smaller regions further fragmented the unity of Britain, which in many places reverted to tribal disputes and civil wars, as the squabble for power ensued.

With the possible exception of Saint Germanus's visit to Britain in circa 429, we simply have no firsthand information about the state of Britain in the period between 410 and 450, and the dates, which follow here, must be understood to be approximate.

There had been only regional and nominal kingship in parts of occupied Britain since before Julius Caesar's first appearance 450 years ago, but now a leader was needed to weld the country together. We assume that the urban councils and notables of the different regions made their own arrangements to govern Britain during the fifteen years after Roman withdrawal because no one emerges as a national leader until circa 425, when Vortigern came to power.

THE HIGH LORD

"Vortigern" means high lord, and is a title, not a personal name. It may have been awarded to him or he may have taken it upon himself. His personal name may have been Vitalinus, though this is often disputed: it could have been his father's name. We immediately note that Vitalinus is a Roman name while Vortigern is a British one: between 410 and 425, British names began to make a comeback. In Welsh he is called Gwrtheyrn Gwrthenau or Vortigern the Thin. His territory may have been around Gloucester, the home of Gloyw his ancestor and the eponymous founder of that city, although his descendants seem to have settled later in Radnorshire.

On the Pillar of Eliseg, a stone erected by a king of Powys in about 800, the inscription mentions Vortigern and his family lineage: it still stands near Valle Crucis Abbey, a few miles from Llangollen in Clywd. It reads:

> Maximus of Britain, [Conce]nn, Pascen[t], Mau[n], An[n]an [+] Britu, moreover, [was] the son of Guorthi[girn], whom Germanus blessed and whom Severa bore to him, the daughter of Maximus the king, who slew the king of the Romans.

If we look at the Welsh Genealogies, a sometimes unreliable collection of dynastic records transcribed during the early Middle Ages but containing earlier records, we find that they confirm this inscription. It states that Vortigern's wife, Severa, is the daughter of Magnus Maximus. If this is true, Vortigern certainly came from a wealthy and well-connected family, possibly with royal pretensions like those of his father-in-law.

However he came to power, Vortigern is said by Gildas to be part of a council that is called to discuss the defensive options of Britain. The muster of the standing army left by Rome must have fallen below sustainable continuance, for the troops along Hadrian's Wall could not adequately defend the north. The Picts of Northern Britain and the

THE FAMILY OF VORTIGERN

The characters in square brackets are interpolated from the Welsh
Genealogies; the rest are from Nennius and the Pillar of Eliseg.

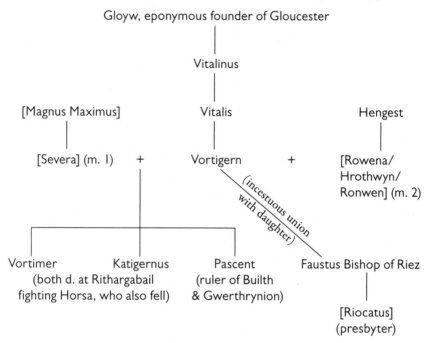

Scots from Ireland were taking advantage of the weakened military
presence to raid farther south. Around 428 Vortigern made the decision
to invite Jutish federates into Britain to act as professional defenders.

Existing records call the Jutish leaders Hengest and Horsa. They
and their men were settled on the Isle of Thanet. We do not know
how Vortigern came to appoint them: they may have been kin to
retired German veterans of the Roman army settled in Britain. *The
Kentish Chronicle,* a lost source that was used by Nennius, tells us that
Vortigern, who had married Hengist's daughter, accepted his father-
in-law's advice to send his son Octha and his cousin Ebissa north to
Dumfriesshire to fight against the Irish when they had done with the
Picts. Dumfries "the place of the Friesians" retains memory of these
troops, as do the place-names like Pennersax, Glensaxon, and Glensax
in that region.[9]

Much blame has been placed on Vortigern for inviting these

federates into Britain, but his major mistake may have been in allowing them to have their own, rather than British, leaders. Had he done so, the situation may not have escalated so quickly. The use of federate troops from barbarian nations had become a more frequent option within the Late Roman Empire. Even before the Roman withdrawal, it is clear that in Britain there had been levies of Saxons, Germans, southern Irish (Attacotti), and others to help defend the island. However, no Pictish or Scottish (northern Irish) federates were ever asked to serve in this capacity! The dilemma for Vortigern and the rulers of Britain in the early fifth century was that there were no experienced British military commanders available and too many fronts to oversee. Payment of mercenaries was their most expedient option. But even under the late Roman occupation, federates and irregular auxiliaries of British origin had been employed, especially in Demetia (Dyfed), which had already had its share of trouble with the Irish who had settled there.

The Expulsion of the Déissi, an Irish migratory epic first transcribed in the eighth century, relates the transit of the Ui Bairrche clan, expelled by King Cremthan of Leinster from southern Ireland, and their settlement in southwest Wales during the fourth century. It was to deal with this Irish settlement that the Northern British leader Cunedda and his eight sons were said to have come from Manau Gododdin (the area around Edinburgh), finally settling in Gwynedd in the 430s. This may be the first account that we have of a British mobilization of its native forces in their own defense. The Votadini, as the Gododdin people were originally called, had maintained skill in arms and probably fought as legionary irregulars along the borders of their own territory with the Picts. But whatever their skill, they were clearly insufficient to police the whole country.

It is also clear that Hengest was shrewd enough to size up the island's military weakness and Vortigern's dependency upon him; he suggested sending home for more men. The first federates had come as soldiers, but the following waves came to put down deeper roots, lured by reports of Britain's fertile acres. These were settled by treaty in Kent, which was the bride-price asked when Vortigern made a second marriage to Hengest's daughter, whom Geoffrey of Monmouth later calls Rowena and the Welsh sources, Ronnwen. But in order to settle the Saxons in Kent, Vortigern displaced its ruler, Gwyrangon. This set a dangerous precedent, causing Vortigern to become deeply unpopular. It was one thing to have Saxon federates billeted upon the people and quite another to have British lands annexed for their occupation.

Soon, Vortigern not only had Irish, Picts, and Saxons to contend with, but in addition he had to deal with civil strife caused by rebellious Britons. In circa 437, he (or the person known as Guitolin or Vitalinus) fought the Battle of Guoloph (Wallop in Hampshire, about eighteen miles northwest of Salisbury). It was fought between the supporters of Vortigern and those of the opposing party who resisted the imposition of Saxon federates. These troops were probably led by a man called Ambrosius, whom, Nennius tells us, Vortigern "greatly feared." There is some dispute as to whether this man was the Ambrosius Aurelianus whose defense of Britain is understood to have preceded Arthur, or his father, since the time scales involved (ca. 430–480) are very long for even the most active campaigner. Whichever is the case, someone headed the opposition to Vortigern's policies. This division among the British may have led to the building of a massive defensive earthwork known as Wansdyke, which, despite its later Saxon name that remembers Woden, was probably built by the British at about this time. It later served as a border dividing Saxon and British territory.

Wansdyke stretches in a west–east line from Maes Knoll, near Norton Malreward, below Bristol, to Savernake Forest, just below Marlborough: it may have been constructed to keep peace between the British tribe of the Durotriges on its south side and the Dobunni on its northern side. Ken Dark writes, "Wansdyke cannot be the southern border of a political unit to its North, because its ditch is to the North and the hill-forts it encompasses are to the South. So it faces North and defines the northern boundary of a southern (probably Durotrigan) territory in which other hill-forts were refurbished at this date."[10] This would make sense if Vortigern's home territory was indeed on the

Dobunni side. The place-name Amesbury, which lies on the southern side of Wansdyke, associated by several scholars with Ambrosius, may be taken as evidence of the struggle between Vortigern and his Saxon federates and the pro-British forces.

As if this civil insurrection were not enough, there was worse to come. Controlling federate troops was always a chancy proposition unless good discipline and firm control were exercised. There were also the problems of pay and supplies: as Nennius tells us, "the barbarians increased in number and the British were unable to feed them."[11] It would appear that the semi-independent British were not just unable but perhaps unwilling to go on supporting foreign troops on their soil.

It has been recently argued that there is insufficient evidence for a heavy settlement of Saxons in Britain in the fifth century and that they were merely plunderers who came and went. However the archaeological evidence of burials and patterns of material goods speaks of an increasingly dense pattern of settlement along the eastern side of Britain, east of the Fosse Way, with concentrations in Kent and East Anglia (see Map 2, page 46). While the first federates may have only been men, subsequent levies of Angles, Saxons, and Jutes brought their families with them. From recent DNA research, it is clear that many Saxons took wives in Britain.[12] In between Saxon settlements, there were still areas of British occupation, and there may well have been areas where Britons and Saxons lived intermixed in relatively peaceful ways. Ken Dark has suggested "the unthinkable"—that substantial regions of the southeast might have remained under British control, since there are few or no Saxon-style burials in certain regions of the south Essex coast, through to north Hampshire.

Either these British enclaves defended themselves well, as they certainly did at Silchester, or the two communities kept to their distinct regions, or perhaps they fraternized. Such a view is considered untenable by those who take Gildas's anti-Saxon vituperations at face value. That some degree of trust existed between peoples can be seen in the fact that the federate Saxons had been known as Gewissae, which

Dark and others have interpreted as meaning "the entrusted ones."[13] Native Britons might have experienced their presence with less sense of trust. Even a small, armed foreign force billeted upon a region can be intimidating and create terror among the local populace. But when such a force changes its allegiance, the result is unimaginable; yet this is what ensued.

The contemporary continental *Gallic Chronicles* say that in circa 441 "the Britons . . . yielded to the power of the Saxons," which may have been the impression of Britons who fled to Gaul, never to return to the site of past terrors.[14] Having had time to assess the potential of Britain, Hengist and his followers threw off federate status and loyalties and swept across the land, looting, raping, killing, wasting unprotected settlements, and setting the island "aflame from shore to shore." In the words of Gildas, "bodies went unburied," and people fled to woodland, hill, and cave.[15]

We sense the gathering gloom and increasing panic in an appeal sent in circa 446 to Flavius Aëtius, the Roman consul and *magister militum,* the supreme military commander of the west, based in Gaul. Gildas knew of this appeal or had seen a copy of the letter. "To Aëtius, thrice consul: the groans of the British," is how the letter begins, but he does not quote it in full, merely giving his own account of it: "The barbarians push us back to the sea, the sea pushes us back to the barbarians; between these two kinds of death, we are either drowned or slaughtered."[16] Aëtius's response is not recorded, but he was in any case too busy fighting against Attila and the Huns in Gaul and was subsequently killed in 454.

Britain was not however without its defenders. Vortimer, son of Vortigern, fought several actions against the Saxons, expelling them from the Isle of Thanet, after besieging them there. Vortimer seems to have been an active commander, fighting against not just the Saxons, but against his own father, whose second marriage to a Jutish woman and anti-British actions must have caused his family great disquiet, as more and more of their patrimony shifted sideways into the possession of the Saxons.

The twelfth-century historian, William of Malmesbury, possibly working from a lost source, writes of Vortimer: "That he saw himself and his Britons circumvented by the craft of the Angles, turned his thoughts to their expulsion, and stimulated his father to make the attempt. At his suggestion the truce was broken seven years after their [the Saxons] arrival."[17]

Despite Vortimer's spirited defense of his country, the *Kentish Chronicle* tells us that the Saxons merely sent home for reinforcements. Vortimer was killed after winning four battles against the Saxons, one at a place the Saxons called Episford and the British Rithergabail (Aylesford in Kent), where Horsa also fell, along with Vortimer's brother Catigern ("Battle-Lord"). These events possibly took place over the period of 441 to 450, and both British and Saxon sources reliably cross-refer to these battles. During this period, London, as well as most other fortified cities, seems to have been successfully held by the British, and the Saxons were eventually brought to a temporary halt. But both sides were weary, and the Saxons sent to Vortigern to sue for peace and a permanent treaty.

Nennius relates the story of how the British council of elders met with the Saxons under the chairmanship of Vortigern. In the memory of Britons, this fateful conference was forever afterward called the Treachery of the Long Knives, after the *saex* or long knife carried by the Saxons. The standard protocol of "no weapons at peace negotiations" was not observed by the Saxons who, at a signal from Hengest, took knives from their boots, each killing the Briton sitting beside him. Nennius speaks of three hundred British elders dead. Vortigern, presumably because of his marriage to Hengist's daughter, was spared but was forced to cede even more territories to Saxon control, namely Middlesex, Essex, and Sussex.

AMBROSIUS AND ARTHUR

Vortigern's remaining credibility, along with his shaky power base, fell at one stroke. Between 455 and 460, a British power vacuum saw the

Saxons reach ever farther into the rich heartland of the country, and many Britons fled to Armorica or Gaul. The leader who arises from these catastrophic years to defend his country is Ambrosius Aurelianus. That he took over from Vortigern is clear for, as we saw, Vortigern's two eldest sons, Vortimer and Catigern, died fighting the enemy. Ambrosius took no retaliatory action again Vortigern's family but gave permission to Vortigern's younger son, Pascent, to settle in the region of Builth, called Gwerthrynion, after his father's death. Ambrosius seems to have been the most able leader to galvanize resistance after the death of Vortimer, who would probably have been his elder by a few years. During the period 460 to 480, it may have been Ambrosius who was responsible for refortifying the Iron Age hill forts in the southwest and raising troops for the defense of Britain. John Morris suggests that Ambrosius raised units and garrisoned them in places along the edge of the war zone from the Severn to East Anglia; these places, now discernible by their place-names like Ambrosden, Amesbury, and Amberly, may recall the "Ambrosiaci" once stationed there.[18]

Britain's failure to mount an effective self-defense reveals its past dependency upon Rome, its internal fragmentation, and its inability to combine forces. Military service may have become associated in many minds with a task suitable for foreign troops to undertake. To understand the British reluctance to engage in arms, we might look back to the conscription and forced exile of native troops during the Roman occupation: apart from a few British irregulars, scouts, and commissary suppliers, only one British legion, the First Cohort Cornovoriorum, raised from the West Midlands and serving on the Wall, seems to have served within its own country in the Late Roman Empire.

The death of Hengest, sometime between 460 and 470, gave Ambrosius a temporary breathing place, but the Saxons were not slow to find new leaders. In Kent, Aesc, the son of Hengest's first lieutenant, succeeded to the kingship, while Aelle came to Britain in the 460s, landing near Chichester and taking over the Weald near Andrerida or Pevensey. More intriguing is the later appearance of a British name among the Saxon leaders: Cerdic. This suggests that, if this was not just a British mother's name for a son fathered by a Saxon, then this was a Briton who had joined the foe. There is some evidence to suggest that Cerdic and other disaffected Britons joined forces with the Saxons and intermarried with them. Cerdic's area of operation was around Winchester and Southampton. He later gained control of the Isle of Wight, and his campaigns would have brought him face-to-face with the troops of both Ambrosius and later, Arthur.

It was a period of mixed fortunes at home and abroad. Ambrosius's spirited defense of the island may have created a brief state of order, for in 469 a Briton named Riothamus, with a substantial number of men at his back, took over a part of southwest Armorica, in return for being active in the defense of Gaul. But in the same year, Aelle besieged the fort at Anderida (Pevensey), burning all the British inhabitants within it. It was not the only loss.

Around the Solent, there are reports of more Saxon incursions: Port, Bieda, and Maegla landed at Portsmouth and killed "a very noble (unnamed) Briton," according to Bede. These men may have been Cerdic's backup force, and we note again that one of them, Maegla, has a British name. Morris has suggested that the nobleman whom they slew may have been the ruler of Devon, Geraint, or Gerontius, son of Erbin, who is remembered in a ninth-century Welsh elegy that speaks of his death at the Battle of Llongborth.[19] Some have identified the site of this engagement as Langport, which means "long market," on the River Parret in Somerset. However, although more navigable in earlier times, it is an unlikely place for an attack from the sea. Llongborth in English literally means "ship port" and is perhaps more justifiably applicable to the area around Porchester and Portsmouth with its huge natural harbor, rather than the inland Langport in Somerset. Another possible site has been suggested, Llamporth on the south of Cardigan Bay where a Beddgeraint (Geraint's Grave) is in evidence. Saxon sources date this battle in the 480s, while British sources suggest a later date, but sometime before the decisive Battle of Badon, in which Arthur fought. An anonymous British poet takes an eyewitness view of Llongborth/Longport:

In Llongborth, I saw Arthur's,
Heroes who hewed with steel.
The Emperor, leader of the toil.

At Llongborth, Geraint was slain.
Brave men from the land of Devon;
*But before they were slain, they slew.**

This poem does not necessarily imply that Arthur was present, only that Geraint's men were of his party, or that others emulated him. The battle may well have been part of a defense of the Solent by a rising commander among Ambrosius's troops. The reference to Arthur as *amherauder* or emperor is necessarily a later interpolation, for the medieval Welsh accorded him this title. But the term *llwydiaudir llawur,* or leader of toil, is more in keeping with what we know of Arthur's career, as we shall see from his military campaigns. Geraint ap Erbin himself reappears in later Arthurian romances as one of the foremost Knights of the Round Table.

We now enter debatable territory as we approach the end of the fifth century and Arthur briefly emerges from the shadows. From the key sources below, we shall see that these mentions are not extensive. Something halted the Saxon expansion in the years following the 480s, which would have marked the declining years or perhaps death of Ambrosius. A different form of warfare seems to have emerged, with the British increasingly using cavalry against the Saxons. Nennius's list of Arthur's twelve battles, given below, shows that Arthur was vigorous in his campaigns, for they seem to cover a wide area of the country: as far north as above Hadrian's Wall and as far east as Lincolnshire, to the Anglian settlements. The twelfth battle, said to have been fought at Badon, brought a victory so substantial that it has echoed down the ages very clearly in both the historical records and the legendary accounts. Fought somewhere between 495 and 516, Badon is a battle

---

*Our translation.

that seeks a location, but seems to have been fought somewhere in the southern heartland along or just above the line of the Saxon war zone. We will explore a possible location for this and Arthur's other battles in chapter 3.

The crashing success of Badon seems to have brought Britain a brief era of peace. Certainly, Gildas looks back to a peaceful era, stating that he was born in the year of that battle. Peace may have been achieved by a partition treaty, during which time the settled Saxons of the south and east were contained within fixed limits, making certain areas of the country into no-go zones. Gildas laments the loss of pilgrimage access to the tombs of martyrs in Saint Albans and elsewhere, caused by "the lamentable partition with the barbarians."[20] There may have been other sanctions levied upon the Saxons, such as an exchange of hostages to maintain good behavior. In the later legendary material we find that Arthur has Saxons at his court, including an Osla Gyllellfawr, or Big Knife, whom we can identify as Octha, the son of Hengist, as Nennius calls him, although Bede calls him the son of Oisc or Aesc.

Twenty-one years after Badon, at a date between 516 and 537, Arthur fights another battle, at Camlann, also unlocated. In this battle the sources tell us that Arthur fell—a statement that the British found subsequently hard to believe, for they accorded him undying fame and immortal return, as we shall see. The *Anglo-Saxon Chronicle* does not mention Badon or Camlann but gives the death year of Cerdic as 534, about three years before Camlann.

Between them, Ambrosius and Arthur kept the Saxons at bay, but they had not succeeded in driving them from British shores. They were too well established, although there were Saxon migrations to Europe between 530 and 550, which is suggestive of increasing numbers, an internal dispute, or a military overthrow. The eleventh-century chronicler Adam of Bremen, in an entry for 531, writes that the Saxons left the Angles of Britain and sailed to Hatheloe on the German coast in order to find new homes and to fight on behalf of Theodoric of the Franks (511–534). In 545 there was an outbreak of plague that weakened the country as a whole. By 552 the Saxons who had been contained by Arthur and Ambrosius resumed their advances.

In the succeeding years of the sixth century, the battle lines split into different fronts with a steadily increasing Saxon menace westward beyond the Fosse Way, pushing ever deeper into the country, and with a series of battles fought against the British. Sometimes the British managed to combine their forces, as at the Battle of Dyrham in 577 when three kings of Bath, Gloucester, and Cirencester—Coinmail, Condidan, and Farinmail, respectively—died. Nennius also speaks of a British leader called Outigirn who died sometime later, having "fought bravely against the English nation," in the generation after Arthur's time.

The development of the Saxon kingdoms is beyond the scope of this book, but suffice it to say that the British continued their struggle against the incomers. Cities, strongholds, and British territories were increasingly colonized farther west and north. Around 613 the Battle of Chester saw a disastrous overthrow of the British, who finally lost contact with the kingdoms of Y Gogledd (the Old North), as it was known. Around 638 the territory of Manau Gododdin around Edinburgh was overcome by Angles, while in 664 Cadwaladr, the last High King of Britain, died. England had begun to emerge from the ruin of Britain.

The tenth-century chronicle *Annales Cambriae* (Welsh Annals) tells us that even the vastness of Snowdonia was attacked by the English—as the Angles, Saxons, and Jutes must now be called—in 816, and the hill fort of Deganwy was taken. But the raids, conflicts, and colonizations the English had inflicted upon the British were soon to be visited upon themselves as, by the late eighth century onward, the English themselves came under attack from the pagan Danes. There followed a two-century period in which the story of spirited defense followed by concession and a takeover of the rulership of Britain ensued, a tale already familiar to Britain from the fifth to sixth centuries, until a compromised Anglo-Saxon kingdom, split by civil strife as well as by Danish attack, fell in turn to the Normans in the eleventh century.

❖

It took the Saxons one hundred and fifty years to subdue Britain, a considerable period if we compare it with the swift thirty-year campaign of Clovis the Frank to subdue Gaul between 486 and 511. Arthur's campaign is almost exactly contemporaneous with those of Clovis. The long-fought British defense against the Saxons is a testament to the power of men like Ambrosius and Arthur and those who succeeded them. For three to five generations, the Britons had held out as a people alone and were pushed ever westward into Wales, but in that period was kindled the gleads of a story whose flame would never die.

THE WISEST OF THE BRITONS

Despite the fame of the historical Arthur's exploits in later ages, none of the written sources contemporary with his presumed existence between circa 470 and 537 mention him by name. We would be entirely dependent upon much later sources such as the ninth-century writings of Nennius and the tenth-century *Annales Cambriae* if it were not for the cleric Gildas, who claimed to have been born circa 516—the year of the Battle of Badon—and whose life may have overlapped that of Arthur. In addition there are references in Welsh poetry, which may or may not be of historical value. Foreign sources do not help us either. The Britons "revolted against the Roman Empire, no longer submitted to Roman laws and reverted to their native customs," writes the sixth-century Byzantine historian Zosimus, at some remove from the main action.[21] The Saxon sources tell us predominantly about Saxons; unsurprisingly, they fail to record or remember the names of British heroes, however valiant. The English monk and historian Bede, writing in circa 731, records Brocmail, who was a British leader at the Battle of Chester in 613, and Cadwaladr, who ravaged Northumbria in 633. Cerdic and Cynic are said to have killed a Welsh king called Natanleod and his four thousand followers in 508. Both the *Anglo-Saxon Chronicle* and Bede fail to mention Arthur.

The writer living in closest proximity in time and place is Gildas. He wrote his letter *De Excidio Britonum* (The Ruin of Britain) in Latin, during his forty-fourth year, around 560 in the generation following Arthur's demise. Called "the wisest of the Britons," Gildas died, according to *Annales Cambriae,* in 570. His work looks back down the previous century without, as he himself attests, access to all the sources:

> Using not so much literary remains from this country (which, such as they were, are not now available, having been burnt by enemies or removed by our countrymen when they went into exile) as foreign tradition: and that has frequent gaps to blur it.[22]

However, Gildas lives near enough to events at the turn of the sixth century to be able to draw upon the living memory of the previous generations.

Irritatingly from the viewpoint of Arthurian studies, Gildas had a pastoral rather than military brief for his account. Writing in a vein similar to the late Israelite prophets of the Babylonian captivity, he castigates the laxity of British leaders and draws parallels between ungodly vice and the deserved punishment of invasion as an instrument of divine correction. He is a Christian commentator writing a pastoral letter to a people massively displaced and shocked by the traumatic events of the last hundred years, but his primary concern is with corrupt leaders, lax priests, and faint-hearted Christians, not with the creation of a historical record of events. He gives us an abbreviated account of what has befallen since the Roman conquest, before turning his admonitions upon his mid-sixth-century contemporaries, the five kings who govern what is left of Britain in his vicinity. These leaders seem to hail from Wales and the southwest: Maglocunus of Gwynedd, Aurelius Caninus (possibly of Gwent), Constantine of Dumnonia, Vortiporus of Demetia, and Cuneglassus, who is not located.[23] Gildas writes nothing about the north, but inhabits an insular isolation, made considerably worse by his extreme erudition. With no access to historical sources or to fellow churchmen in either Gaul

or Ireland, he may have believed himself to be the last recorder of a
vanishing world and his letter to be the last possible chance to morally
exhort his fellow Britons to turn things around.

Looking back into the past to where the rot starts, Gildas pours
his contempt upon "the proud tyrant," who, though he doesn't mention
him by name, is clearly Vortigern. Gildas uses the term *superbus tyran-
nus,* which is a plausible translation of the title high high king or overlord. Vortigern's invitation to the Saxons to police the Picts has Gildas's
full contempt: "nothing more destructive, nothing more bitter has ever
befallen the land," he declares.[24] This is the British voice of Gildas
speaking, not the colonized tones of a Romanized Christian Gildas,
who speaks elsewhere of the Roman conquest with astounding compla-
cence as a just punishment for a pagan, cowardly, and naturally servile
people: "It became a mocking proverb far and wide that the British are
cowardly in war and faithless in peace."[25]

He describes the devastation following Saxon raids, with the
country burning from end to end, the demolishing of towns and
churches, the martyrdom of Christians, and the heaps of unburied
bodies. This leads into the one battle that Gildas names as a victory
for the British: the siege of Badon Hill. He is the only person to call
this action a siege rather than a battle and says that this marked "the
last defeat" of the Saxons, perhaps meaning it was the last known
defeat since his birth. He remarks that, in his own time, although the
cities are ruined and depopulated, external wars have ceased but not
the civil wars. He also says that the tremendous storm of those times
has been forgotten in the calm of the present time, "leaving no trace,
not even a memory," because so many people have died. However, one
name shines out of that era. The demoralized British were rallied by
Ambrosius Aurelianus:

*a moderate (or gentle) man who, perhaps alone of the Romans, had sur-
vived the impact of this storm; his parents had certainly worn the purple and been slain in it. In our times his descendants have fallen away
from their grandfather's excellence. Under him, our people regained*

their strength and challenged the victors to battle, in which the Lord granted the victory to us. From that time onward victory now went to our citizens and then to the enemy, just as the Lord makes trial of his latter-day Israel to see whether it loves him or not. This continued until the year of the siege of Badon Hill, almost the last defeat of the gallows-fodder, and certainly not the least.[26] (our translation)

As the only person of whom Gildas speaks with any approval, Ambrosius Aurelianus stands out from the letter as very different from the British kings castigated by Gildas's glancing "rock-words." Ambrosius is described as neither a man of named rank nor specifically as a war leader, although he seems to have been well born. Many have seen in Gildas's allusion to Ambrosius's parents a connection to the Roman usurpers of two generations back. Indeed, there is a well-attested mythic thread connecting him to Constantine III, a legend that is further developed by Geoffrey of Monmouth when he gives Arthur a family in his twelfth-century *Historia Regum Britanniae,* but there is no documentary evidence that Constantine left behind any family. Indeed there is no evidence to suggest that the purple into which Ambrosius's parents were born was the imperial purple at all, but rather the same purple blood that Gildas continually mentions as being spilt by martyrs in this book-length letter to the British. He may state that Ambrosius's parents had been "slain in the purple," but Gildas is a stylist schooled in the declamatory Hisperic or western Latin mode that recalls the poetry of Virgil. He makes use of extended metaphors and allusions like these, writing as an educated man to clerics of equal knowledge. For this reason alone, we must be careful not to impute a bald meaning to some of his constructions.

We may see Ambrosius's leadership of the British as approved by Gildas because he comes from both Christian and well-to-do Roman stock, a suitable person to bring order to chaos. Gildas does not approve of kings who are elected by the people rather than by God, holding with the prophet Hosea that it is an immoral election: "They have made kings for themselves and not through me."[27] But he approves of Ambrosius, who is unequivocally named as the one who led and inspired the British and encouraged them to be the victors of the siege of Badon. Gildas does not explicitly state that Ambrosius led the offensive personally. British victories and defeats continued until this decisive siege, for Gildas states that after Badon there followed a period of peace in which he himself is living and that, although the defense against the Saxons seems to have abated, the specter of civil war still rumbles on.

One question echoes back down the ages. Why does Gildas not mention Arthur? Part of this is answered by Gildas himself, as the primary reason for his letter: "I had decided to speak of the dangers run not by brave soldiers in the stress of war but by the lazy."[28] He comes not to speak of heroes and their military deeds but, like Christ, to turn his apostolate to the sinful rather than the saved, to stir up impotent, self-promoting leaders to virtue and action. For Gildas, "soldiers" means not only warriors but "Soldiers for Christ."

However, the two main objects of his diatribe nicely frame what little history we are given around the period of Arthur's life: Magnus Maximus of the late fourth century and Gildas's own sixth-century contemporary, the ruler Maglocunus, identified as Maelgwn Gwynedd (died ca. 547–549), one of the five tyrants singled out for castigation. Gildas attacks Magnus Maximus for removing needful defenders of the realm, for usurping imperial status, and for treachery to Rome. He attaches a much longer list of vices to Maglocunus, including parricide, adultery, breaking monastic vows, and murder. Both Magnus and Maglocunus later became important links for Welsh genealogists of subsequent periods; both men may have already been enjoying their own celebrity legends at the time, an infamy that Gildas sought to decry.[29]

Gildas may not mention Arthur because there is nothing to blame him for, or perhaps because everyone living had knowledge of the exploits of Ambrosius's generals at that action. Another reason that is often given for Gildas's silence about Arthur is based upon a much later source, the twelfth-century *Life of Gildas* by Caradoc of Llancarfan, who tells us that "the most holy Gildas was the contemporary of Arthur, the king of the whole realm of Britain, whom he attentively loved and sought always to obey. But his twenty-three brothers continually resisted the war-like king."*

Caradoc continues to relate how Gildas's brother Hueil was a notable raider who swept down from Scotland to loot and pillage until Arthur killed him. Gildas showed great Christian restraint in forgiving his brother's murder for which Arthur did penance. But after moving to Glastonbury, Gildas found himself besieged by the tyrannical Arthur who was attempting to retrieve his kidnapped wife, Gwenhwyfar, from Melwas, the king of the Summer Country (a title that stood for both the area of land known today as Somerset and for the otherworld). This incident is one of several in which Arthur ends by killing Hueil, but this late hagiological source is open to dispute. According to the twelfth-century writer Gerald of Wales, Gildas wrote as he did because "he was infuriated by the fact that King Arthur had killed his own brother. . . . When he heard (this) . . . he threw into the sea a number of outstanding books which he had written . . . about Arthur's achievements."[30]

Hagiography and blood feuds aside, how trustworthy is Gildas as a source? Past generations looked back upon Gildas as a revered monk: he is nearly always called Gildas the Wise. The nature of his stylish Latin demonstrates that he is the product of a rich education, and his familiarity with biblical events is appositely applied to the British situation. He likens himself to a latter-day Jeremiah, a prophet lamenting the ruin of his country. This high-flown polemic may blind us to Gildas's insular and clerical isolation: his native sources are scant and are reliant upon "foreign tradition." These sources may include the fourth-century Christian apologist Orosius, the Roman Dio Cassius, and other late classical writers, as well as the testimony taken to Gaul, Brittany, or Northern Italy by exiles whose accounts may have become part of the record.

In one important respect, Gildas differs from the English chronicler Bede, who wrote in the eighth century and used *De Excidio Britonum* as a primary source. Gildas tells us that Vortigern invited in the Saxons,

---

*Our translation.

while Bede adds that "the nation of the Angles, or Saxons, being invited by the aforesaid king, arrived in Britain with three long ships."[31] Nennius, working from Kentish sources, tells us that these people were Jutes who were "driven into exile from Germany."[32] Both Gildas and Nennius were Britons who used the term *Saxon* generically to cover all Germanic invaders. But Bede was himself an Anglian.

In the grip of renewed pagan assaults, Gildas asks, "What will our unlucky commanders do now?"[33] Let us see how the first major source for Arthur handles the story.

NENNIUS AND THE CHRONICLES

The *Historia Brittonum* (ca. 829–830) is a complex chronicle from a much later date than the Arthurian period. It was attributed to a monk named Nennius who, in his own words, made "a heap of all he could find," drawing on at least two verifiable sources, including the late fifth-century *Life of Saint Germanus* and the lost *Kentish Chronicle,* as well as another unknown source, which gives an unlikely childhood to Ambrosius, laying down a story that will, in time, with the aid of Geoffrey of Monmouth, develop into the nascence myth of Merlin. Nennius sewed together these sources, gathering disparate materials into one place from as far afield as the Irish origins legends and some unnamed Latin sources, which he refers to as the "Annals of the Romans and from the Chronicles of the Holy Fathers." Uniquely, he draws together the Saxon Kentish material and British sources in one place.

Nennius introduces himself at the head of what is known as the Nennian recension of this manuscript as "the pupil of holy Elfoddw," an archbishop of Gwynedd who died in 809. The author is familiar with the area around the Severn Valley, and we may speculate that his interest in Vortigern may arise from patronage by a local British king in the Builth area, possibly Farinmail, who is said to descend from Vortigern.

Nennius gives us the six ages of the world from creation down to the battle of the pagan king Penda of Mercia against Christian Oswald of the Bernicians in 644. On the way he deals with much the same territory as Gildas, but in a much less censorious and much more mythically persuasive way. He relates how the British originate from Troy, how the Picts came to the north, how the Irish arrived in successive waves, and how the Dalriadan Gaels of Northern Ireland came to live in western Scotland. He dates the coming of the Saxons back 429 years from the fourth year of King Merfyn of Gwynedd's reign. This helps us date the writing of Nennius's chronicle, for King Merfyn is known to have reigned from 825 to 844, which would date the Saxons' arrival to 400, rather too early for this event.

In Nennius's relation of the history of Britain, he tells us that "after the death of Maximus [in 397] and the end of the Roman Empire in Britain, the British went in fear for forty years." This is followed by the line, "Vortigern ruled in Britain." Nennius goes on to tell how he was under pressure from fear of attacks by the Picts and Irish, of a Roman invasion, and, not least, of Ambrosius.[34]

Drawing on the lost *Kentish Chronicle,* Nennius speaks of the coming of Horsa and Hengest and how Vortigern welcomed them, giving them the Isle of Thanet, called Ruoihm by the Saxons. After this point, the narrative is broken up between parts of *Life of Saint Germanus,* the *Kentish Chronicle,* and the astounding story that is attached to Ambrosius. We hear how the Saxons and Hengest in particular saw the military weakness of the British and, in a dispute over supplies, offered to send home for more of his countrymen to reenforce Vortigern. At a Saxon feast, Vortigern got drunk and found himself in love with Hengest's daughter. Displacing Gwyrangon, king of Kent, Vortigern gave the county to the Saxons and the lands north of the Wall to Octha, Hengist's son, and his cousin Ebissa with forty shiploads of warriors. Vortigern then slept with his own daughter who had a child called Faustus whom Saint Germanus blessed and adopted as his protégé. Saint Germanus of Auxterre did indeed come to Britain in 429 to suppress the spread and influence of Pelagianism, a particularly British form of Christian heresy, and would have doubtless been up to censuring any unchristian behavior in Vortigern, but this connection between the saint and the king is reported only in Nennius.

Nennius next tells us why Vortigern is so frightened of Ambrosius: in his flight from the condemnation of Saint Germanus, Vortigern decides to build a fortress in Snowdonia, only it keeps tumbling down. His "magicians" say that only the blood of a fatherless boy will keep the fortress standing. Reverting to a foundation-sacrifice solution, Vortigern's magicians eventually find a boy in Maes Elledi in the region of Glywysing (Glamorgan). His mother attests to her ignorance of his conception and swears to her virginity. As the boy is about to be sacrificed, he challenges Vortigern's magicians, saying he knows what is causing the problem. In the face of their ignorance, the boy tells them about a lake beneath the hill.

The foundations are dug up, revealing two vessels in the lake, nesting one inside the other. When separated, they are found to contain a cloth in which are two worms—one red, the other white—striving for mastery. The red worm fights off the white worm, which flees across the lake. The boy then explains that the cloth represents the kingdom and the two worms, two dragons. The white represents the English and the red the British, who will ultimately be successful in expelling the English. The astounded Vortigern asks the boy, who knows so much, who he is, and he replies, "I am Ambrosius," revealing himself to be none other than Emrys Guledic or Ambrosius the Mighty. When asked about his family, Ambrosius answers (for all that he was supposed to be fatherless), "My father is one of the consuls of the Romans." Vortigern then gives the fort to him as well as the western part of Britain, and he himself goes north to build Caer Gwrtheyrn in the region of the Gwynessi.[35]

This fable is interesting, for it graphically unfolds the struggle between the betrayer of Britain, Vortigern, in conflict with virtuous Ambrosius. The two worms or dragons are like the standards of their armies, which, as we saw in chapter 1, date back to a much earlier time. The western part of Britain is ceded to Ambrosius along with North Wales, while Vortigern retires to his own exile.

The story now immediately doubles back on itself, and we hear about Vortigern's son, Vortimer, who dies after another battle, possibly near the Medway, telling his followers to bury his body at the port from whence the fleeing Saxons departed, whose shore he will defend even in death. But his command is disobeyed, and the Saxons return in force. After the famous episode of the Treachery of the Long Knives, p. 54, Vortigern is imprisoned and cedes the counties of Essex, Sussex, and Middlesex to his father-in-law. Then we hear how Vortigern is pursued by a righteous Saint Germanus who, by prayer and fasting, causes Vortigern's stronghold to be consumed by fire. Thus Nennius, working from his many sources, gives us three possible ends for Vortigern: ignominious British exile, Saxon imprisonment, or Christian combustion.

Nennius tells us that Vortigern's rule in Britain was in circa 425, the year of the consulship of Theodosius and Valentinian, and that there are twelve years between the beginning of Vortigern's rule to the quarrel between Vitalinus and Ambrosius at the Battle of Cat Guoloph (Wallop, Hants). This gives us some notion that Ambrosius was still disputing with other British leaders well into the fifth century. If these dates are correct, then Ambrosius lives an astounding span of years to be old enough to fight in 437 and still be able enough to be the victor of Badon in 516, as described in *Annales Cambriae*. Clearly, there must have been someone in the generation after Ambrosius. This is where many scholars, notably Morris, have speculated about the Battle of Wallop being fought by Ambrosius's father, with the later actions, including Badon, being those of his son. Alternately, as later sources suggest, Badon was Arthur's great victory, achieved after the death or retirement of Ambrosius.

The *Historia Brittonum* shows us two very different Arthurs. In a section concerning "the Wonders of Britain," Nennius reveals a more mythological figure, one whose name and deeds have already become stamped upon the landscape.[36] Arthur is remembered in two places in the Builth region of Wales: telling of Arthur's hunting of a great boar and his slaying of his son Amr or Anir. Of the latter event, we have no further information, but of the boar hunt, we have a whole Welsh story, *Culhwch and Olwen*, which we will examine in chapter 4. These mythic fragments stand alongside Nennius's historical descriptions of

Arthur's campaign, which we give in full as the first chronicle reference to Arthur:

> In that time, the number of the Saxons increased and grew strong in Britain. On the death of Hengist, his son Octha came from the northern part of Britain to the kingdom of Kent and from this man arose the kings of Kent. Then Arthur fought against them in those days with the kings of the British, but he was their battle-leader. The first battle was in the mouth of the river called Glein. The second, third, fourth and fifth battles were near another river called Dubglas, in the region of Linnuis. The sixth battle was on the river that is called Bassus. The seventh battle was in the Caledonian Forest that is Cat Coit Celidon. The eighth was the battle in the fortress of Guinnion, in which Arthur carried an image of the holy Mary, ever virgin, upon his shoulders, and the pagans were turned in flight on that day, and a great slaughter was done upon them by the power of the Our Jesus Christ and by the power of Holy Mary, his virgin mother. The ninth battle was fought in the City of the Legions. The tenth battle was fought on the banks of the river which is called Tribuit. The eleventh battle was made on the hill called Agned. The twelfth battle was on Badon Hill, in which fell in one day, nine hundred and sixty men in one attack of Arthur's; and no one brought them low save he alone, and in every battle he was the victor.
>
> When they were laid low in all the battles, they [the Saxons] sought for help from Germany, and greatly reinforced themselves without cessation, and they brought kings from Germany to reign over them in Britain up to the time when Ida reigned, who was the son of Eobba. That one [Ida] was the first king in Beornica, that is to say Berneich [Bernicia].[37] (our translation)

This time we read that *Arthur,* not Ambrosius, is the battle leader of the British kings: he is not a king himself but fights "with the kings of the British," making him a *dux belli* or commander of forces, a suggestion that we will examine further in the ensuing chapter. Arthur appears only as a battle leader, for Nennius tells us nothing more about the man, nor about his parentage, deeds, or death.

Following the battle list, which as we saw in chapter 1 may refer back to the exploits of Lucius Artorius Castus in the second century, Nennius goes on to give brief genealogies of the English kings, though he mentions one further British leader: "Then in that time, Outigirn fought strongly against the English nation. Then Talhaern Tataguen [Tad Awen or Father of Inspiration] was poetically acclaimed; and Neirin and Taliesin and Bluchbard and Cian, who is called Gueinth Guaut, were all celebrated in British poetry."[38] (Our translation.)

This passage seems to relate to the generations following Arthur's last battle. We have no further information about Outigirn, but Neirin, or Aneirin, as he is better known, is the composer of the oldest British poetic epic, *Y Gododdin,* which describes a battle fought in the mid-sixth century (see pp. 74–77). The poet Taliesin, a contemporary of Urien Rheged (d. ca. 572–580) and possibly of Maelgwn Gwynedd (d. ca. 547–549), later becomes retrospectively sewn into the Arthurian record as the royal bard.

How trustworthy is Nennius? Like Gildas, he is ignorant of the finer details of Roman government, confusing consuls and emperors. But his manner of dating is based closely upon "consular dating," whereby events are pigeonholed as occurring during the annual term of individuals who shared mostly honorary consular appointments in the Late Roman Empire. The *Historia Brittonum* seems to have been composed in Latin and is not merely a translation of an earlier British source. All the battle names are given in Latin, with only two being glossed by British names: Trwyfuit or Tribuit and *silva Celidon* or Cat Coit Celidon. Another recension of the list also gives the Welsh name Bregion or Bregouin as the eleventh battle. While Nennius is obviously writing long after these events, we can already see how the stories relating to the fifth and sixth centuries have grown in the telling. Nennius is uncritical of myth and fable, mixing it with what we would term history. Like anyone living at a remove of some centuries from original events, he dips into a deep bucket of available sources, not able to discern clearly what belongs where, or what motivations may pertain to the times and persons he is writing about. The copies of the *Historia Brittonum* that have survived suggest that more than one person found this story fascinating. We will see later how Nennius, or whoever actually compiled this chronicle, lays the basis for Geoffrey of Monmouth, who in the twelfth century gave us a far more detailed portrait of the shadowy hero.

The next most important source for Arthurian dating is the *Annales Cambriae*, written in the mid-tenth century. This chronicle consists of a list of notable events, annotated by year of occurrence. The brevity of the entries is terse in the extreme, and some events are without dates whatsoever. Despite the fact that both this manuscript and the *Historia Brittonum* are bound together within one manuscript, Harleian 3859, they have no other correlation, and neither author knew the other. While there are thirty-six later editions of *Historia Brittonum,* there are only three recensions of *Annales Cambriae.* The first entry that refers to Arthur:

516: The Battle of Badon in which Arthur carried the cross of our Lord Jesus Christ for three days and nights upon his shoulders, and the Britons were victorious.[39]

Nennius and the *Annales Cambriae* agree on one point: Arthur is the victor of Badon. We will discuss his "carrying the cross" further in chapter 3. The other Arthurian entry:

537: The Strife of Camlann, in which Arthur and Medrawd fell; and there was death in Britain and in Ireland.[40]

Medrawd is known to us from later literary texts as Modred or Mordred, where he is the son or nephew of Arthur who became his implacable enemy. The "death" that is mentioned here may have been an early visitation of the yellow plague that swept the country again only eight years later. We also note that, in this early version of the *Annales*

Cambriae, Arthur and Medrawd are given no specific rank. But their inclusion in this chronicle is notable since *they are the only secular men not called kings to receive any mention whatever in its pages,* outside the death and birth of saints, bishops, popes, notations of extreme weather, celestial phenomena, and plagues.

In a later recension of the *Annales Cambriae,* the last entry reads somewhat differently:

> **537:** The Battle of Camlann in which the famous Arthur, King of the Britons, and Mordred, his betrayer, fell by each other's wounding.[41]

This gives us more information, in that Arthur and Medrawd are responsible for each other's death. We note that he is not called Arthur's son but rather "his betrayer." This is also the first of the references to call Arthur a king, and king of the Britons at that, suggesting that the later recension has received additional attention from the scribe, who knows from circulating stories that Arthur is now known as a king. The key phrase that betrays how very much later this recension is, occurs at "in which the *famous* Arthur": Arthur's celebrity is evidently already well established, suggesting that his legend had already begun to develop by the time the gloss was written.

REMEMBERING THE WARRIORS OF THE NORTH

There is nothing more forgetful than popular memory. When knowledge is so ubiquitous that everyone fails to write it down, it may soon become lost. However, in considering the memorials of Arthur, or our lack of them, we must remember the primacy of the oral tradition within Britain, an art that preceded Roman records and Christian chronicles. The bardic tradition of praise song and elegy ran alongside these written sources. The Celtic peoples of the Islands depended upon the memories and performance skills of their poets who, from before the Roman occupation, maintained a primary function in society as the public memory of the tribe. From the evidences of Ireland, which Rome never conquered, we know that the bardic memory was well honed, and the relation of genealogy, history, tribal epic, and a great deal more was committed to the memories of poets. Before Christianity and the clerical transcription of such early traditional lore, memory was supreme and kept alive the names and deeds of those long gone.

Within the time frame of our consideration, the craft of memory was upheld by poets such as Aneirin and Taliesin, who still retain a talismanic position in the annals of Welsh poetry as the earliest bards of our remembrance. In Aneirin's epic poem *Y Gododdin,* we find what may well be a nearer contemporary reference to Arthur, earlier than Nennius: the poem derives from a bardic and nonclerical source written not long after Gildas. Since the people of Manau Gododdin will figure largely in the deeds of Arthur, let us explore this poem and its context.

Y Gododdin is a northern British epic poem that relates an action that took place between the Britons of Manau Gododdin, whose capital was Din Eidyn or Edinburgh, and the pagan Angles of Deira (modern Humberside). Although this poem is often called "the earliest Scottish poem," this is an inexact description because, although the territory Manau Gododdin may have covered the Lothian area that is now part of Scotland, back in the sixth century the inhabitants were northern Britons of Y Gogledd, the homeland of the Old North, as the medieval north Welsh nostalgically remembered it. Manau Gododdin is believed to have stretched from the area around Stirling to the region of the Tyne, and its peoples, whom the Romans called Votadini, were known by this time as the Gododdin.

As Christopher Gidlow remarks, "The Votadini/Gododdin were only occasionally part of the Roman Empire," suggesting that they were too rebellious and undisciplined to be contained by Rome.[42] It was from this region that the famous Cunedda and his sons came in circa 430 to clear the Attacotti (Irish) from Demetia (Dyfed) and to settle in Gwynedd. This same Cunedda was the great-grandfather of Maelgwn Gwynedd, the Maglocunus whom Gildas so hotly castigated.

This northern people left a heroic record of their battle against the invaders. The battle of the Gododdin was fought in the mid-sixth century at Catraeth (modern Catterick), once the Roman fort of Cataractonium or Cataracta, named for the local falls on the River Swale. This site maintains its military connotations right up to the present age, being the location of the largest British army garrison. The date of the battle is disputed. It has been argued that if the Gododdin army marched down from Dun Eidyn to Catraeth, they would have to have crossed the land of Bernicia (Northumbria), which was established by the Anglian king Ida between 547 and 559 and which would surely have been heavily defended. No such engagement is mentioned, which presupposes that the poem has an earlier date. The reason for the engagement is unknown, although it may have been a rescue mission to release a Votadinian captive or a punitive assault.[43]

The manuscript of *Y Gododdin* exists only in a late thirteenth- or early fourteenth-century copy, although the Welsh one is of much greater antiquity. The greatest exponent of this poem, John Koch, believes that some of the archaic material of the poem was "handed down from the ancestor of Welsh, a 'Common Archaic Neo-Brittonic,' which had been spoken along the 800-mile span between the Rivers Forth and Loire in the period during which the poems are set."[44] This was the language that Arthur would have spoken. The poem is a memorial, listing the battle leaders and individual men who fell at Catraeth. Their British ruler appears to have been Mynyddog Mwynfawr (Mynyddog the Wealthy), who royally fêted the troops for a year in his own fortress of Edinburgh before they set out, though he did not go with them. Many notable men from other regions joined the assault, including men from Strathclyde and Venedotia (Gwynedd). The men of Gododdin were practiced in fighting against the Picts whose kingdoms bordered their own. They had no mercy upon the Saxon, whom they regarded as like a swarm of insects. They acted forthrightly as many Britons of those disordered times aspired to do, revenging themselves on the enemy for houses burnt and family slain or enslaved:

What Bradwen would do, you would do,
You would kill, you would burn . . .[45]

These poetic portraits of named but largely unknown heroes are moving in their archetypal depiction: they could worthily stand for any unknown band of combatants lost in any war, in any time or region, for they sing across the centuries. They give us some sense of emotional engagement with the sixth century that no amount of chronicles could evoke. The irresistible sequence of the attack turns relentlessly, in the course of one dreadful week, from confidence to slaughter:

On Tuesday, they dressed in their finery
On Wednesday, their common desire was bitter,
On Thursday, envoys were chosen,
On Friday, bodies were counted,
On Saturday, action was forthright,
On Sunday, bloody blades were redistributed,
On Monday, they were thigh-deep in blood.[46]
(our translation)

But there is one particular entry that catches the eye, the two stanzas that remember Gwaurdur, pronounced Gorthur:

Of the best, more than three hundred were killed.
At the centre and on either flank he struck.
Most generous of men, splendid before the host,
Horses from the herd would he give out in winter.

Gwaurdur picked off black crows before the wall
Of the fort—though he was no Arthur—
Mighty his deeds among men.
Before the alder palisade was Gwaurdur.[47]
(our translation)

It has become academically fashionable to slight this important reference by explaining it away as a late interpolation, but in one of the most recent and authoritative translations, Koch writes that the style is in no way later or different from the rest of the text and that the poets of the era must have either invented some previously unknown warrior called Arthur or that the timings of the battle list in *Historia Brittonum,* as well as those Arthurian entries in *Annales Cambriae,* must "reflect a radical and untraditional chronology for Arthur devised between circa 638 and 829."[48] By which statement, Koch disagrees with the current trend of investing in the nonexistence of Arthur, since any invention of Arthur must clearly come *after* the composition of *Y Gododdin,* which recounts a battle fought in the middle of the sixth century. Moreover, to secure the authenticity of this source, we should note that the Arthurian reference in this stanza appears in the most archaic of the three extant versions. The internal rhyme schemes make it unlikely that the lines referring to Arthur are interpolated from another source.

As we see above, mighty though Gwaurdur's deeds were, he was not Arthur. The points of comparison between the two men may turn on many things: that his body count was less than Arthur's, that he is besieging a fort in the same manner, that his way of assaulting the enemy lines was like Arthur's, that he was as generous in distributing horses to remount men, or all of these things. Another possibility is that Arthur's name may have been a useful rhyme for Gwaurdur's. Whichever of these aspects may be true, it still remains a reference to Arthur from only one generation after his time and so becomes a potent witness. *Y Gododdin* gives us the very earliest mention of Arthur in one small colloquial comparison that is beyond price.

The written sources that we have explored here reveal the scant historical evidence for Arthur, but we shall track his military rise and campaigns in chapter 3 and his career further through the legends, stories, and folk traditions—especially in the Welsh material—in chapter 4. That the name of Arthur already shone in the sixth century is perhaps no surprise to us, but what of his name itself? We must consider where it comes from, for it is not a name hitherto used among the British.

THE NAME OF ARTHUR

The shadowy figure of these early sources has a cache of heroic deeds but just a single name—Arthur—devoid of title. In his study of British names, Toby Griffen asks two important questions: "Why was there no Arthur before Arthur?" and "Why were there many Arthurs after Arthur?"[49] With the exception of Lucius Artorius Castus, there are no mentions of any man simply called Arthur living before the fifth century. Indeed, as Peter Bartrum, the renowned expert on Welsh Genealogies, points out, Arthur is a surprisingly rare name among Welshmen: "I have found no example of its occurrence from the time of Arthur ap Pedr of Dyfed (late sixth century) up to the end of the sixteenth century."[50]

In British, as in modern Welsh, Arthur seems to derive very simply from *arth,* meaning "bear." The Latin form Artorius may be borrowing from a British name or possibly derive from a Roman source. But the way the name Arthur first appears in *Y Gododdin,* with its *ur* ending, it is clearly not of Latin but of British derivation. Nennius retains this British form Arturus even within his Latin chronicle.

Considering Arthur's later royal status, he disappointingly appears in the early record without any patronymic or implied status. This is suspicious, for notable people are always mentioned in context with their precedents and ancestors as, for example, Owain son of Urien or Cenau ap Llywerch. It is only in nonnoble persons that we see a name stand by itself or in the case of a person distinguished by an epithet like Rhydderch Hael, *hael* meaning "generous." Our Arthur of the shadows has no epithet or byname to distinguish him. Does this imply that he is neither royal nor notable but perhaps a bastard? But when paternity is unknown or disputed, men are still distinguished by a matronymic like Mabon son of Modron or Constans Fawr fab Elen. Can this omission mean that Arthur is from the rank and file of men?

In the Sawley glosses (two anonymous commentaries written into a copy of the *Historia Brittonum* sometime in the late twelfth or early thirteenth centuries), there is a note that a possible patronymic for

Arthur is Mab Uter (son of Uther), which means "son of terror," since from his youth he was cruel. Arthur in Latin translation means "horrible bear" or else "iron hammer by which the jaws of lions were broken."*

The commentator knows his Welsh, for *uthr* is indeed Welsh for terror. Arthur's name might indeed be assembled from the Welsh for bear *arth,* but how the glossator arrives at iron hammer as a Latin meaning for Arthur is puzzling, unless we consider the Welsh word for hammer is *gordd.* This gloss doesn't necessarily stand as proof of Arthur's parentage, for "son of terror" may be an epithet of his savagery in war rather than standing for a patronymic. That Arthur is said to "break the jaws of lions" immediately puts us in mind of the deeds of Heracles or Samson. The defense of Britain is certainly a job for a strong man, but we should bear in mind that this gloss certainly postdates Geoffrey of Monmouth's twelfth-century story of Arthur's parentage in which Uther is invariably named as his father.

The medieval Welsh Genealogies retrospectively give Arthur an impressive roster of forefathers, including Coel (or Old King Cole as we know him), Gwrtheyrn (Vortigern), Emrys (Ambrosius), and Uthr, but these ascriptions cannot be accurately dated. Moreover, they are highly suspect because of the Welsh genealogists' desire to reflect glory upon their patrons by fabricating connections with notable ancestors, especially ones that hail from the Roman or early British heroic period. Today, we recognize Uther Pendragon as the father of Arthur, but he is not so called until the twelfth-century *Historia Regum Britanniae.* There is one early Welsh poem of uncertain date that makes a link between the two men: "Marwnat Uthyr Pendragon" (The Death-Song of Uther Pendragon) states that Uther shares "a ninth part of Arthur's courage" and that "the world would not exist if it were not for my offspring."[51] But it does not explicitly make Uther Arthur's father.

In regard to his lack of a patronymic and other antecedents, are we to think the unthinkable, that Arthur was not British after all but a foreigner? If this were so, surely he would still come with a

---

*Our translation.

parental name or at least a locality attached to him, like Llenleawg the Irishman?

As we have said, among the Brythonic speakers of Celtic Britain, the word *arth* means "bear," but Latin-speaking Britons might have drawn a phononymic similarity between Arthur and *arator*, which means "ploughman." Many have noted that Arturus, a Latin form of Arthur's name, shares a similarity with the star Arcturus, which is the brightest in the constellation of Boötes; this constellation is called the Bear-ward or Guardian of the Bear. The play upon "the bear" in Arthur's name may well have been intentional on Gildas's part, for he would assuredly have been familiar with the Latin poet Claudian's allegory on the constellations.[52]

Even today, Ursa Major is known throughout Europe as the Wagon, originating from the Roman title Plaustrum Magnum (Great Cart), while in the folklore of Britain, the Great Bear is sometimes known as Arthur's Wain, the handle of which points downward to Arcturus. This is intriguing because in Gildas we hear about his castigation of the tyrant Cuneglassus, whom he calls "you bear, rider among many and driver of the chariot of the Bear's Stronghold."[53] *Auriga,* the term for "charioteer," is another constellation, which is in close proximity to Ursa Major and can be located in the sky by connecting stars Alpha and Delta of the Great Bear. The Romans called the seven stars of Ursa Major the Septentriones (Seven Plough Oxen), which pulled a cosmic plough. This allusive combination of bears, oxen, and ploughmen with stars may have well been in the minds of Arthur's contemporaries when they considered his name. In fact, several later documents alternate spellings between Arthur and Arcturus. Much later, a collection of Saxon riddles, compiled in the eighth century by the monk Ældhelm of Malmesbury, includes one headed "De Arturo."

With starry troops I am environed, in the pole of the world;
I bear a war chariot with a famous surname of the vulgar,
Rolling in a circle, continually, I do not decline downward,
As the other luminaries of the heavens hasten to the sea,
I am enrich'd with this gift, forasmuch as I am next to the pole,

He who wanders in the Ryphaean mountains of Scythia,
Equaling, in numbers, the Seven Stars, in the top of the
    poles;
Whose lower part, in the stygian and lethean marsh,
Is reported to fall down in the black bottom of hell.

The reference to "starry troops" is intriguing, but of course this may have been added as a result of post-Arthurian writings.

Might Arthur's name then be merely an epithet? Just as Vortigern is not a personal name but a title for high king, it may be possible to see Arthur's name in this light, if we consider the British word *aruthr,* pronounced "a-rith'ir," which means both "terrible" and "wonderful." Such a title applied to a military leader would make him sound indomitable, as in "the Awesome." We have already seen how the name Uther is an epithet of terror: terrible to Saxons, wonderful to Britons. The medieval Welsh Triads call Arthur one of three "red ravagers," attesting to his ferocious deeds of arms and possibly to his raiding.

Another curious fact is that the name Arthur appears not in British usage, with one single exception, but springs up in immediate *Gaelic usage* within only a generation or so of his life. Oliver Padel asks, "If Arthur was primarily a figure of folklore, regarded as superhuman and with exceptional awe, then the lack of examples of the use of his name in Britain is explicable."[54] He excepts Brittany in which the name Arthur is used through the ninth century onward, but suggests that the Gaelic settlers in the west of Britain "need not have felt such reverence or reluctance," as was experienced by Arthur's fellow countrymen. We can see a similar restraint at work today in the choice of the name Jesus as a suitable name for a child. In the northern latitudes of Europe, it is rarely used as a personal name, although in the Catholic countries of southern Europe, especially in Spain, it is frequently employed.

Whether Arthur's name originates in Ireland, as Richard Barber has proposed, or whether it is a name that resurfaces in Britain from some unrecorded descendant of the Roman Artorius *gens* via Lucius Artorius

Castus cannot be finally known, but the candidates for the post begin to accumulate around the time of Arthur's late career.[55]

DARK AGE PRETENDERS

Many Arthurian explorers in recent times have seized upon a particular similarly named historical individual and tried to pin the deeds of Arthur upon him. Before we look at some of these, we should bear in mind that the identity of Arthur is something we may never fully know. The possibility is more likely that the myths and legends give us a composite Arthur, made up of many strata of history, hope, and dream. In the British struggle against the English and then the Normans, the name of Arthur became a banner of hope and his deeds an inspiration. These and many other factors shaped him just as much as the bare historical records.

There are several Britons who bear the *arth* part of Arthur's name: Arthwys ap Mar who lived in Elmet, the area around Leeds in the fifth century; Arthfael ap Einudd (ca. 480–550) who is mentioned in the *Life of Saint Cadog* as a king of Neath in Glamorgan. Then there is Arthfoddw ap Boddw (ca. 540–610) of Ceredigion whose son was named Arthlwys. Last there is Arthrwys ap Meurig who was the ruler of Gwent and Glywsying in the seventh century.[56] However, none of these British individuals bears the exact same name, nor are their deeds and dates comparable with the campaigns and time frame of Arthur.

Possible claimants to the name of Arthur have been discerned in the probable or near-contemporary lives of the following men, each of whom has his own promoter among Arthurian enthusiasts: Arthur ap Pedr (ca. 550–620) and Artuir mac Aedan (late sixth century). But as we see from their dates, these men are born too late to be encompassed by the *Annales Cambriae*'s datings of Badon and Camlann in the first third of the sixth century.

For those who look to the north for a possible Arthur, then Arthur mac Aedan seems to be well situated in time and place. His father, Aedan mac Gabran (574–608), was king of Dalriada on the Argyll coast, and his kingly inauguration was overseen by Saint Columba of

Iona himself. Dalriada on the western coastlands of Argyll and Kintyre was founded in about 500 by Gaels from Ireland. They are the people who brought the name Scot to Scotland, derived from an eponymous ancestress called Scotia. Dalriadan Gaels displaced native Pictish inhabitants north of the Antonine Wall and made alliances with their southern neighbors, the British rulers of Strathclyde. Aedan fought against his overlord Baetan mac Cairill in Ultonian Dalriada, as well as a campaign in Orkney, before conquering the Isle of Man. His last battle against the Angles in 603 was a crashing defeat for him. That he chose to name his son Arthur rather than a more Gaelic name is perhaps unsurprising: Aedan's mother and one of his wives were British. Arthur mac Aedan seems to have died at the Battle of Circhind (possible Coupar Angus) in the 590s, fighting against the Pictish tribe of the Miathi. Aedan was then succeeded by another son, Eochaid Buide, in whose reign we hear about another Arthur.

That Arthur's name inspired or appealed to British Gaels but not to Brythonic Britons is itself intriguing. The linkage between the British and Gaelic Arthurs becomes more difficult to untangle in subsequent centuries as folk story and legend erode their historic derivations. The deeds of any of these men may have flowed like tributaries into the river of recollections about the older, fifth-century Arthur. Such identifications are examples that show how fragments of history insinuated themselves into the ever more complex mosaic of the Arthurian era. All these men appear to be reflections of an earlier, warlike leader, but they are not the man we are looking for.

Clearly there is no Arthur before Arthur, although there are certainly many of them after his passing, some of whom may have been named in his honor or used to amplify Arthur's virtues by his namesakes. May we regard as evidential to Arthur's existence the fact that his name suddenly becomes popular immediately after the time of his supposed lifetime? The popularity of names given to children in any society is always reflected by the esteem or loyalty felt by people at the time, whether they live through the era of a notable monarch or the campaign of an inspiring leader.

RIOTHAMUS THE GREAT

One further claimant for the deeds of Arthur has been suggested, one who is squarely situated and active within the 460s: a man called simply Riothamus. Several of the later medieval writers who deal with Arthur, including the redoubtable Geoffrey of Monmouth in the twelfth century, mention how Arthur led an army out of Britain to fight against a Roman leader (afterward described as emperor) named Lucius Hibericus (of Ireland). This story becomes firmly lodged in the Arthurian corpus, and by the fifteenth century, when Sir Thomas Malory wrote his great book *Le Morte d'Arthur,* it had become a central episode in the saga of Arthur, with the British king matched against the might of Rome.

As already mentioned, this incident may have grown out of a garbled memory of Lucius Artorius Castus's expedition to Armorica, the fact that the enemy is named Lucius being perhaps no more than a coincidence. Riothamus has found a number of supporters, each of whom has advanced the theory that a man bearing this name led an army from Britain in AD 468 and fought against a Visigothic king named Euric in Gaul.[57] The fact that this personage is nowhere named as Arthur is generally set aside by regarding *rio-thamus* (great king) as a title rather than a name.

The sources for the story are certainly intriguing, though admittedly sparse. There are three mentions of Riothamus in the historical record: in the writings of a sixth-century author named Jordanes (who interestingly describes himself as an Alan, one of the tribes belonging to the Sarmatian group!), a couple of letters from a fifth-century Roman bishop named Sidonius, and a brief but remarkable passage in the life of an obscure Breton saint.

The story can be summarized as follows: by the middle of the fifth century, Gaul, like Britain, was under attack from Germanic tribes, and from 466, it also feared the threat of attack by Euric, who became leader of the Visigoths in that year. Jordanes supplies the following account from his book *De Rebus Gothicis* (The Story of the Goths):

Euric, king of the Visigoths, perceiving the frequent change of Roman Emperors, strove to hold Gaul by his own right. The Emperor Anthemius hearing of this, asked the Brittones [sic] for aid. Their king Riotimus [sic] came with twelve thousand men into the state of the Bituriges (Bourges, in central Gaul) by way of the Ocean, and was received as he disembarked from his ships. Euric, king of the Visigoths, came against him with an innumerable army and after a protracted fight, routed Riotimus, King of the Brittones, before the Romans could join him. He, having lost the greater part of his army, fled with all the men he could to the lands of the Burgundians, a neighbouring tribe then allied to Rome. But Euric seized the Gallic city of Arverna, for the Emperor Anthemius was now dead.[58]

The first thing we notice about this is the fact that Riothamus is called "King of the Brittones," which, assuming Riothamus is Arthur, would make it the earliest reference to the British leader as a monarch. The dating for the episode must be between 466, when Euric came to power after murdering his brother Theoderic, and 472, when Anthemius was killed. That Riothamus brought an army of twelve thousand men into Gaul suggests that Britain was in a more settled state at this time (perhaps as a result of Ambrosius's victories against the Saxons) so that he felt it was safe to lead so large a force onto foreign soil. He may also have been seeking something in return for his aid— perhaps the restoration of a lifeline to Rome—or lands in Armorica on which Britons wishing to leave the island could settle. Since he is described as coming "by way of ocean," we must assume that he originated in Britain and not, as some have suggested because of the unusual spelling "Brittones," from Brittany (Armorica).

The second piece of evidence comes from a letter addressed "to his friend Riothamus" from Sidonius, a former prefect of Rome recently appointed as bishop of the Arverni at Clermont. It is dated to circa 468 and refers to the complaint of a landowner whose slaves were being lured away—presumably to join Riothamus's army or to help maintain, supply, or serve it, perhaps in return for their freedom.[59]

What happens next offers a glimpse into the dark times in which these events took place. It appears that Riothamus was expecting to be joined by a much larger force of Roman troops, but if so, this never happened, as we are told that Euric fell on the British force and routed them. Though he fails to mention Riothamus, the sixth-century historian Gregory of Tours describes how: "The Britons were driven from Bourges by the Goths, and many were slain at the village of Deols. Count Paul with the Romans and the Franks made war on the Goths and took booty."[60]

Deols is near modern Chateauroux and seems to have been the site of a disastrous defeat for Riothamus and the Britons who, betrayed by the very people they had come to aid, were vastly outnumbered. Geoffrey Ashe suggests that the expected Roman forces were led by Syagrius, the Roman governor of an area in Northern Gaul. Presumably, Count Paul may have been a local commander who swiftly dealt with the Goths or else the force that failed to show up in time. We do not know if Riothamus survived the battle, but no further mention is made of him in the historical record. He may have returned to Britain and become the leader of the defense against the Saxons following the death of Ambrosius, though he would have been somewhat old to fight at Badon.

The reason for the nonappearance of the Roman army was brought about by the treachery of the imperial prefect of Gaul, a man named Arvandus, who wrote a letter to Euric advising him not to make peace with the Greek emperor Anthemius and urging him instead to crush the Britons posted north of the Loire (Ligeris). This British force must be those led by Riothamus, as we know of no other Britons in the area at this time.

Though it was of no help to Riothamus, a copy of Arvandus's letter to Euric was intercepted, and the prefect was arrested shortly after. The same Sidonius, who had addressed Riothamus, wrote (ca. 469) "to his friend Vincentius":

> I am distressed by the fall of Arvandus the Imperial prefect of Gaul. . . . He was arrested and brought in bonds to Rome. . . . Amongst other pleas . . . the provincials . . . were bringing against him an inter-

cepted letter which Arvandus' secretary (who had been arrested) admitted to have written at his master's dictation. It appeared to be a message addressed to the king of the Visigoths, dissuading him from peace with the "Greek Emperor" Anthemius, insisting that the Britons stationed beyond the Loire should be attacked, and declaring that Gaul ought according to the law of nations to be divided up with the Burgundians, and a great deal more mad stuff in the same vein, fit to rouse a war-like king to fury and a peaceful one to shame. The opinion of the lawyers was that this letter was red-hot treason.[61]

Perhaps if this was the only evidence we had for a "King of the Brittones," called Riothamus, leading an expedition to Gaul at this time, we might be forgiven for relegating it to a footnote. However, there is one more piece in this puzzle to be considered. Admittedly, it is a comparatively late one and possibly none too reliable, but if nothing else, it demonstrates how a story could continue to be told over a long period of time and how easy it is to forget that sources can be lost just as easily as they are found.

More than a hundred years before Geoffrey of Monmouth wrote his *Historia Regum Britanniae,* in which he described Arthur's expedition to fight the emperor Lucius, a scribe named William wrote a Latin *Life of St. Goeznovius* (ca. 1019). Just as Geoffrey himself was to do, William claimed to have had access to an ancient book called *Ystoria Britannica* (History of Britain) from which he took the following account:

The usurper Vortigern, who held the land of Britain without right, summoned warriors from the land of Saxony to strength the defences of Britain. Since they were pagans and possessed by Satan, they brought great evils on Britain, lusting for innocent blood.

Not long after this their pride was limited for a time by the great Arthur, king of the Britons. They were for the most part dispelled from the island and brought to submission. However, when this same Arthur, *after many glorious victories in Britain and Gaul,* was summoned at last from human activity, the way was open for the Saxons to re-enter the island and in that time there was great destruction of churches, persecution of saints and a general oppression of the Britons. (our translation and our italics)

The words *not long after this* have suggested to some that Arthur came to power immediately after Vortigern, which fits both with Gildas's account of the coming of the Saxons and of the subsequent troubles wrought by rebellion and partition, as well as with the generally accepted period of Arthurian Britain. In fact, this brief account is actually one of the soundest historical references we have for Arthur. It fits the pattern of known events, makes no extravagant claims for Arthur's immanent return, and describes the state of events in sixth-century Britain much as we believe them to have been, even though it does ignore the part played by Ambrosius.

The fact that the *Ystoria Britannica* has never been located or identified, as we will see later of Geoffrey of Monmouth's supposed source—"an ancient book in the British tongue"—does not mean it did not exist. There were almost certainly documents relating to the Arthurian period that failed to survive. What is interesting here, and bears an important relationship to the Riothamus material, is the mention of Arthur's "many glorious victories in Britain and *Gaul*" (our italics). This stands with the Riothamus sources to suggest that a British leader was fighting in Gaul. As in the passage from Jordanes, this leader is described not as *dux* but *rex* (king).

The main problem with the Riothamus material is the dating. If the British leader really was Arthur, it brings his dates back some years from the later accounts to around the middle of the fifth century and would make him rather old to have fought the Battle of Badon in the 490–510s. There are two possible alternatives. One is that Riothamus actually refers to Ambrosius. This would fit the dating better and has a certain logic in that Ambrosius would be more likely to have led such an expedition rather than sending a deputy to fight in Gaul. The second possibility is that the deeds of an independent commander called Riothamus fed into the story of Arthur, adding to his role of honor and preparing the way for Geoffrey on Monmouth and others to describe a continental expedition against, rather than for, Rome. What does emerge from this tangle of facts is that Britain still maintained contact with Rome and that British leaders still saw themselves as, in some way, part of the crumbling empire.

In this list of possible claimants for Arthur's name and deeds, we have seen how easy it is to attach these to any convenient individual. What gives us pause is the extent of Arthur's campaigns over a great part of Britain. This battle leader is clearly no mere regional commander.

The medieval Welsh Triads name Arthur as the chief prince of Britain who holds three thrones: those of Mynyw or Saint David's in Dyfed, of Celliwig in Cornwall (possible candidates for this are Callington in South East Cornwall, or Calliwith near Bodmin, or even Kelly, a hill fort in Egloshayle), as well as that of Pen Rhionydd in Northern Britain (an unidentified place that might be Loch Rion in Galloway).[62] This triad speaks not of a historical person but perhaps of a *composite Arthur,* made up of many overlays: a man who might be claimed by the Cornish, as well as by the Welsh or the Gaelic Dalriadans. The constituent parts of this composite Arthur are sometimes discernible, but in later legend they become so mixed that it is hard to separate them. It is impossible to claim a prior or exclusive Arthur who is "the Arthur," unless we accept the possibility that Lucius Artorius Castus was the original or *first* Arthur as suggested in chapter 1. But the regions cited in the triad are notably all located along the far western coast of Britain, which itself echoes a historical fact: there were no Britons holding any kind of rule beyond the eastern regions of Cornwall or Wales from the early seventh century onward, and a bare few holding on in Y Gogledd or the Old North.

We have examined the sources for Arthur in the earliest written records, revealed some of the possible candidates for his name, and set the scene. The man in the shadows has many namesakes, but it is time for him to come into the daylight and be seen in the context of his times as the leader of the British, allowing us to assess his military deeds in these turbulent times.

3

Arthur of the Battles
Defender of the Land

From the slaughter of the chieftain,
From the radiant ranks,
From loricated Lleon,
Will arise a gwledig
For the fierce border.

"KADEIR TEYRNON,"
BOOK OF TALIESIN
(SIXTH CENTURY)

A WAR LEADER'S RISE TO POWER

In the written sources, as we have seen, Arthur appears as a *dux bellorum* or "leader of battles," not yet a king. In describing *de mirabilibus Britanniae* (wonders of Britain), Nennius calls Arthur simply a *miles*, or soldier.[1] In the Vatican recension of *Historia Brittonum*, we hear that "although many were more noble than he, Arthur was the leader and victor in twelve battles."[2] How did a man so obscure rise from the ranks to gain twelve famous victories? How he came to this position, what military methods he used, and who his allies and enemies were will be

examined here as we seek the motivations for Arthur's battles beyond
the bare accounts of the chronicles.

Gildas's insistence that Ambrosius was the victor at Badon is not
necessarily at odds with Nennius's account of Arthur's victory. If
Ambrosius had been Arthur's commander in chief, both men could
have taken part in the battle and could therefore both be said to be
victorious. In the common parlance of war, a battle is normally attributed to its commander in chief, not to any subordinate general, however valiant, although special campaigns might single out an individual
as particularly successful. Thus, during the Second World War, while
the Allied armies of Britain might be said to have been the victors, the
North African offensive against Rommel is rightfully assigned to the
individual general, Montgomery of Alamein.

Was Arthur known to *his* contemporaries as Arthur of Badon?
The historian William of Malmesbury, writing in the first quarter of
the twelfth century, gives us a brief glimpse of Arthur at the side of
Ambrosius:

> When [Vortigern] died, the British strength decayed; their hopes
> becoming diminished, fled; and they would have soon perished alto-
> gether, had not Ambrosius, the sole survivor of the Romans, who
> became monarch after Vortigern, quelled the presumptuous barbar-
> ians by the powerful aid of warlike Arthur. This is that Arthur of
> whom the Britons fondly fable, even to the present day: a man wor-
> thy to be celebrated, not by idle fictions, but in authentic history.
> He, indeed, for a long time upheld the sinking state, and roused
> the broken spirit of his countrymen to war. Finally, at the siege
> of Mount Badon, relying on an image of the Virgin which he had
> affixed to his armour, he engaged nine hundred of the enemy single-
> handed, and dispersed them with incredible slaughter.[3]

The jibe at "idle fictions" is clearly directed at the writings of Geoffrey
of Monmouth, William's contemporary, considered by several of his peers
to have been a fabulist, but here we notice that Arthur aids Ambrosius

in prosecuting the British defense. The passage is largely attributable to Nennius's *Historia Brittonum,* and the variations may be of William's own creation, but even here we have "a warlike Arthur," not a king.

We do not know the nature of Ambrosius's relationship to Arthur. Had Arthur been a relative this would surely have been remembered in the genealogical record. In terms of the military emergency in which Britain found itself, it is possible that Ambrosius, acculturated in the Roman way, adopted Arthur. Adoption of a successor was a Roman custom among both its emperors as well as its citizens, recognized within Roman law so that childless men could appoint responsible inheritors. There are two obstacles to this, for Ambrosius had descendants, according to Gildas, and if Arthur had been formally adopted, we would expect to have some account of him as "Arthur, son of Ambrosius."

We have already seen how Vortigern continued to rule as king while his son Vortimer acted as the active general of his forces, only a generation before Arthur's time, and it is more likely that Arthur was Ambrosius's military successor rather than his adopted son. Ambrosius Aurelianus is a resoundingly Roman name with no British equivalent until Nennius calls him Emrys Guledic, or Ambrosius the Sovereign. In the mid-fifth century, British men still bore Latinate names, but successive generations favored British ones. What if Ambrosius had a British military nickname like Uter Pendragon or the Terrible Draco-Leader. Such a nickname would explain why Ambrosius is associated with the story of Vortigern's tower and the dragons, as well as providing a battle cry to rally behind. Nennius's story about a cloth with two worms upon it could well represent the two standards of the British and Saxons. As we have seen in chapter 1, a *draco* standard, so much a part of the legionary insignia of Lucius Artorius Castus, was the rallying point both for the British and the Sarmatians he led.

If such a nom de guerre had been applied to Ambrosius, it might well have led to the later association between Uther and Arthur as father and son, for while it is clear that Arthur is no one's son in the early record, both he and his predecessor bear the name Pendragon in later legend. The *draco* standard of the legions gradually mutated into the red dragon emblem of Gwynedd, still in use today as the national standard of Wales.

So where did Arthur of the Battles originate? There is a poem in the *Book of Taliesin* (*Llyfr Taliesin*) that gives us a clue to his antecedents and makes powerful sense. Already mentioned in chapter 1, where it has been seen as complementary evidence for the Roman origins of Arthur, "Kadeir Teyrnon" may also support the antecedents of a fifth-century northern Arthur. The poem discusses the ruler of Britain as a man born and bred on the Wall, as well as one militarily qualified to its supervision.

> *A man sprung of two authors,*
> *Of the steel cavalry wing,*
> *With his clear wisdom,*
> *With his royal rule,*
> *With his kingly lordship,*
> *With his honour of scripture,*
> *With his red lorica,*
> *With his assault over the Wall,*
> *With his poet-praised seat,*
> *Amongst the defenders of the Wall.*
> *From the slaughter of the chieftain,*
> *From the radiant ranks,*
> *From loricated Lleon,*
> *Will arise a gwledig*
> *For the fierce border.*[4]

The "fierce border" is none other than Hadrian's Wall. This poem suggests a man who was born either of native stock and of Roman lineage, or perhaps one who is half-native and half-foreigner: we might take our pick from the men of Rheged, the Gododdin, or of Pictish or Dalriadan origin, which might help explain whence the name Arthur was first introduced. But is the *Guledic* or Ruler of this poem actually Arthur? In the same poem he is addressed as:

Arthur the blessed,
In harmonious song,
In the forefront of battle,[5]

Arthur gains his position after "a slaughter of chieftains," possibly a reference to the Treachery of the Long Knives, in which the next or most qualified leader had to step forward. Arthur's heritage is from the breast-plated legion that served along the Wall: even a hundred and fifty years later in *Y Gododdin,* warriors are still called *cinthrenn* or centurions.[6] Could Arthur's father have been a descendant of one of those who was stationed there, or even a descendant of Lucius Artorius Castus? We know that many forts along the Wall were refortified in the fifth century and that there was significant military continuation, perhaps by soldiers who as "caretakers and military police . . . merged into a Celtic social world defined not by empire but by warband and clan."[7] The peoples who lived in the environs of the Wall would have been most concerned to keep the peace in that region. These were the men of Rheged south of the Wall and above it the kingdoms of Strathclyde to the northwest and Manau Gododdin in the northeast.

We are merely told that the man in this poem is sprung from this region and is of "two authors," meaning that he has parents of different stock, and that he has the cavalry wing's steel in his blood. The message is clear: this is a soldier whose upbringing and natural dispositions led him to rise to the position of *gwledig.* That he comes from obscure northern parentage doesn't seem to matter; that he can bring the hereditary skills of a mounted warrior to defend the shores of Britain means everything.

When we look more closely at the location of Arthur's battles, we will find that many of them are fought around the northern territories. It is possible that a well-decorated military campaigner of the north came south with his men to deal with the defense of Britain and stayed on after the death of Ambrosius to govern. We will return to this poem in the course of the chapter to reveal a man who rose to be battle leader not only of the disputed territory of the Wall but of Britain itself.

KINGS AND OVERLORDS:
BRITAIN'S DEFENDERS

Arthur's role in the protection of Britain must be set against the administration that was evolving in the wake of the Roman withdrawal. Who
was left to defend the island after the death of Ambrosius? Gildas tells
us that "Britain has her governors, she has her watchmen . . . but they
are bowed under the weight of their heavy burdens, scarcely having time
to draw breath."[8] In speaking of governors, he uses the term given by
the Romans to their own official governor: *rector*.

The Roman military infrastructure had been headed by the *magister
militum* (military commander) in Gaul, to him reported the senior officer, *comes Britanniarum* (count of Britain,) who had the mobile reserves
at his disposal. Under him was the *comes litoria Saxonici* or count of the
Saxon shore who attended to the coastal defenses of the southeast and
south. In the north, in the area of Britannia Secunda, which covered
the Humber up to the Wall, was the *dux Britanniarum*. The earliest
titles bestowed upon Arthur, in the Harleian recension of the *Historia
Brittonum,* are soldier and *dux belli*—war leader. All seem to be variations upon the Roman military titles of *dux* or *comes*.

In the late fourth century, the Roman military title of *dux* signified
a commander of a stationary force, usually in a garrison or other fort.
In the same century the title *comes Britanniarum* had been created in
response to the worsening severity of enemy attack. It was accorded to
a mobile commander who led forces that could be speedily transported
to troublesome regions. However, Arthur is never referred to as *comes
Britanniarum,* although many modern commentators have suggested
that this title would have explained his ability to move rapidly about
the land.

We must judge from the evidence below whether Arthur was acting as the supreme commander of British forces. Whether it would
have been possible for him to have authority over the whole of the land
rests upon where he stood in the British hierarchy, about which we
know very little in this period. He could not have acted without direct

support from one or more of the kings and administrators who arose in the period following the Roman withdrawal and who, by the time of his birth, circa 460–470, would have been established for at least two generations.

The variety of names given by early sources for governing titles from this time may reflect the difficulty that faced post–Roman British leaders in finding designations for themselves that struck a nice balance between Roman authority and native authenticity. Some chose to remain with Roman style titles like *decurion* or magistrate at a local level, while older British titles and newer ones were given or assumed by high-status men of power. We see this evidenced in an Ogham inscription upon a memorial stone in Castell Dwyran in Carmarthenshire, commemorating Voteporigas, one of the tyrants whom Gildas castigates. Carved in Latin on the same stone is the following:

MEMORIA/VOTEPORIGIS/PROTICTORIS

"The memorial of Vortiporix the Protector." A protector, in Roman terms, was a bodyguard of a provincial governor. This inscription, dated to 540–550, is evidently the bearer of a title that he has inherited from his family. Vortiporus's family was used to the hereditary task of defending the island, for they had been bred to it. The names of Vortiporus's forebears, Tryphun and Aircol, are derived from the Latin words *tribune* and *agricola* (farmer), suggesting a long link with the Roman defense of Britain.

Regional rulers had long played their part under the Roman administration as lawgivers who listened to cases in the vernacular: by this method Roman justice could be done through the mediation of rural courts overseen by British rulers. This is clear from the number of men who bear the title judge. From the descendants of such local lords and lawgivers, kings may well have arisen, some still bearing the titles of Roman appointments, which had become hereditary, as in the case of Saint Patrick's father, who was a *decurion,* a late imperial title denoting official status in the local administration, law court, or army. From among men like this, a king's council would have been drawn. This perhaps shows us how Ambrosius himself may have arisen from the remnants of the Roman administrative system to emerge as a leader.

The title of high lord, or *vor-tigern*, had no negative connotation in British parlance and must be seen, not in terms of a classical tyrant or dictator, but rather as a ruler who simply has the capacity to wield power.[9] We must remember that it was the custom of Celtic peoples to acclaim kings by a congress of peers rather than by primogeniture, a custom that did not fully obtain until the Norman invasion.[10] A British or Irish leader would have been chosen from among the suitably qualified or ancestrally related adult men of a clan: in this way, infants and weaklings were never exposed to certain overthrow. In addition, a legally recognized successor or *tanaiste,* as he was known in Gaelic-speaking regions, would have been appointed, so that disputed successions were avoided. It is possible that Ambrosius Aurelianus as *Emrys Guledic,* appointed Arthur as the most able man to succeed him, putting aside even his own family to do so.

One specific title arises during the early British independence: it is *guledic* (modern Welsh *gwledig*): "it was originally applied to the leader of a local, native militia," later used to denote an overking or supreme leader who is also victorious in battle.[11] *Gwledig* has its roots in the word *gwlad,* Welsh for land. It is a supreme title of honor, awarded to not just any notable or royal leader but to one whose deeds excel the commonplace. In the *Historia Brittonum,* Ambrosius is called "King among all the kings of the British nation" and is only the second person to receive the title *emrys guledic,* after the usurping Roman emperor Magnus Maximus, who entered British legend as an important ancestor of the Welsh. We can parallel the distinction between just any ruler and a *guledic* from *Y Gododdin* where the poet Aneirin refers to the ruler Ureuei as Ut Eidin, or judge of Edinburgh, but tells us that he "was no Guledic."[12] As we have seen, the "Kadeir Teyrnon" poem recognizes Arthur as a *guledic.*

Nora Chadwick points out that the title of *guledic* only appears in the language "at a time when the Saxon kingdoms were in process of formation."[13] Intriguingly, the Saxons had their own supreme title that seems to reflect that of *guledic: bretwalda* or *brytenwalda,* meaning "ruler of Britain." Bede lists six kings between the fifth and seventh centuries who assume the title *bretwalda,* the holders of this title all coming from widely differing regions. Some scholars have seen the use of *bretwalda* originating as "a defiance of British chiefs rather than an assertion of a claim to over-lordship over them."[14] Arthur's Saxon enemy Aelle was the first to assume the title.

We have no means of knowing how consistently any of these titles were recognized across the country. What emerges is that in the fifth century most independent British regions acknowledged the protection of a strong overlord, except in those places of dense settlement by Saxons or Scots, although there is some evidence to show that in the northeast, accommodations between British natives and Anglian settlers led to more cordial relations. It is possible that local rulers had representatives, sons, and supporters whom they sent to back the overrulership of the *guledic,* who may have operated more as a military governor than as a king himself, perhaps even at the behest of a national council composed of local rulers and their representatives, as we see from the council of Vortigern.

Kingship was only conferred upon Arthur posthumously by legend. But where does he fit in this picture? Nennius says clearly that Arthur fought the Saxons "with the Kings of the Britons." This could imply that Arthur himself was not British but perhaps a Breton, a Gael, or even a Pict. How plausible is it that a foreigner, whether a skillful mercenary or not, would be employed in a British army? There was the obvious example of Hengist and the Saxon mercenaries from the time of the hated Vortigern. But the later Roman Empire was used to the appointment of what would once have been considered "barbarians" as generals—such as the late fourth-century Vandal Stilicho—to whom fell the task of loyally defending the empire. On his deathbed Emperor Theodosius had entrusted his sons Arcadius and Honorius to rule respectively in Constantinople and Milan, with Stilicho as guardian of the nine-year-old Honorius, thus making Stilicho virtual ruler of the

West. If such a man might rise from the ranks of barbarians to lead Rome, then Arthur could have done the same.

Within these early sources, we may discern a professional soldier who rises through the depleted ranks of capable captains and generals to assume supreme command. The ability to not only strategize, maintain authority, and be mobile in parts of Britain that spoke and believed in many diverse ways suggests a man who had not just a common touch but a persuasive way of welding together disparate rulers or receiving a regular levy of troops and supplies. Such a man would have to embody an equal share of military ability and confidence to persuade regional lords to trust in his skill.

In military terms and considering the desperate nature of the national security in the fifth- to sixth-century Britain, it is not difficult to imagine how a successful battle leader could receive adulatory acclaim and gratitude, as well as a rapid advancement, that might have led to his being "raised to the purple." Roman troops and auxiliaries already had a recent history of acclaiming their generals as emperors of the West, as we can see from the usurpations of Magnus Maximus and Constantine III in the late fourth century. Even if we temper Gildas's poor opinion and experience of the kings and tyrants of Britain with justice, it may be seen that most of them were men whose reigns were upheld by strong military support. As Gildas states, "As far as possible, they exalt their military companions to the stars."[15] As the commander of Emrys Guledic's troops, Arthur was well placed to succeed him as battle leader of Britain, although it is only his growing posthumous reputation that has "raised him to the stars" and to the overkingship of Britain.

THE PEOPLES OF BRITAIN: FRIEND OR FOE?

Arthur had inherited the Roman task of fighting on many fronts around the coast of Britain. The challenge of uniting its people under a single banner was no mean task for any military commander. Some sense of the division of Britain may be appreciated from the writings of Saint Patrick, Constantius of Lyon, and the authors of the *Gallic Chronicles,* who all refer to Britain as "the Britains," perhaps referring to the fivefold Roman diocesan divisions of the island.[16] Britain in the Dark Ages is not yet the Great Britain of King James I's seventeenth-century vision, but rather a fragmented set of kingdoms, still divided in ways that are hard for us to imagine today.

What people call themselves and how they refer to others demonstrates both their state of being and attitude to strangers. The Roman view of the Britons had been limited by prejudice. The correspondence discovered at Vindolanda on Hadrian's Wall speaks of *Britunculi* or "the wretched little Brits," while a humorous epigram by the fifth-century Gallic poet Ausonius suggests that there was no such thing as "a good Briton."[17] Even the British Gildas assumed a Roman style of exasperation when considering his fellow countrymen, betraying the depth of the national inferiority complex left by colonization.

The British called themselves *Cambrogi,* or fellow countrymen— a name that still exists in Cymru, the Welsh name for Wales, and in the word *Cumbrian*—while Britons collectively called *all* the invading peoples from northwest Europe Saxons, after the short sword or *saex* carried by their warriors, regardless of whether they were Saxons, Jutes, or Angles. In their turn, the English, as they would collectively call themselves a century or so later, called the Britons *wealh* or *wylisc,* meaning "foreigners." This ancient enmity still remains barbed upon the Welsh tongue today, for the English are still regarded as Saeson or Saxons by the Welsh and Saesnaeg/Sasenach by the Gaels of Scotland and Ireland. The sense of the Welsh as "foreigners," because they speak another language, is still to be found today among the English, who have forgotten that the Welsh are the descendants of the British people whom Arthur defended. The same prejudice was originally tendered to the Gaelic invaders of Caledonia, who were called Scot—a Gaelic word for raider— a connotation only recalled by the expression "getting away Scot-free."

The mutual suspicions of border peoples were categorized by fear and hatred to such an extent that the *Synod of the Grove of Victory,* a confessional manual written in Wales around 567, prescribes a penance of thirteen years to be given to those "who afford guidance to the barbarians!"[18] This perhaps explains why, when Saint Augustine came to convert the Kentish Saxons in 597, the British Christians were seen as lacking in missionary zeal toward their pagan neighbors: it is clear that few could bring themselves to deal with those who had overrun their country.

Ancient prejudices show through not only in the common assumptions of the present peoples of Britain about each other, but are often revealed by those who study the ancient past. We must be careful of such assumptions, for some of the four peoples of Britain living during Arthur's time had allegiances beyond the merely territorial: both Britons and Gaels shared Christian affiliation while Saxons and Picts maintained their own ancestral pagan beliefs, creating a commonality beyond nationality. Nor must we forget that there were admixtures of one people with another along every border.

The question of identity was very much bound up with language. Bede tells us that there were five languages and four nations on the island of Britain: English, British, Irish, Pictish, and Latin.[19] The English language evolved from the languages spoken by the Saxons, Angles, Jutes, and Friesians, whose individual traces remain in the regional accents of English today. The British language of Arthur's time is an earlier form of the Welsh still spoken today. What Bede calls Irish is Gaelic, of which three forms survive today in Ireland, Scotland, and the Manx people of the Isle of Man. Latin became the unifying language of the church rather than of the empire throughout Europe. Of the Pictish language, we have no record, since they left no books, only a form of Ogham, which they adopted from the Irish, to use solely as an inscriptive alphabet upon the edges of memorial stones. It is clear that anyone traveling about Britain would have needed interpreters, as indeed we see happening when Vortigern meets Hengist; the Saxon host lays on a feast for the British king and his interpreter, who is called Ceretic or Cerdic, before he makes them drunk. Vortigern aparently did not speak Jutish, or Hengist British.[20]

The lack of a common idiom or shared cultural values makes

strangers even stranger. Britain had to find new ways to comprehend the intentions of those who now lived on their island. We already know that there had been considerable levies of Germanic soldiers serving within Britain even before the Roman withdrawal and that this may have explained how Ceretic spoke Saxon.[21] Such bilingual people were immensely useful as interpreters and spies, and a basic ability to understand and speak two languages was probably common among those who lived along borderlands. Hostage taking or the servitude of slavery must also have enabled many Britons to be able to speak Saxon.

In order to move about the country, to gain the trust of allies and parley clearly with enemies, Arthur would have needed good interpreters among his staff, as well as officers who could command regional troops in their own language. It is necessary to consider who were the most prominent enemies and allies of Arthur if we are to understand how and why he fought his battles.

Arthur's enemies were not just the Saxons. His battles in the north speak of another enemy: the Picts. Pict is the name given by the Romans to the peoples of Caledonia after the end of the second century. They seem to have been a reinforcement of southeastern and northeastern Caledonian tribes who emerged as a confederacy, possibly combining the Maeatae and the Caldonii of the northeast. Pictish origins are given a mythical and romantic treatment by Bede, who, along with many historians since, regarded them with intrigued bafflement. He relates an origin myth about the Picts coming from Scythia, before seeking a homeland of their own. They settled the farthest north of Britain, but having come with no women, they took wives from the Scots (Irish Gaels) on condition that the Picts choose their own kings from the offspring of the female royal line.[22] If the Scythian connection were proven, it might make the Picts cousins to the Sarmatians led by Lucius Artorius Castus in the second century. However, no one has been subsequently able to pinpoint Pictish origins with any certainty.

Not Christianized until the early sixth century, the Picts remained the rulers of the far north until the eighth century when they were assimilated into the dominant Gaelic kingship of Kenneth mac Alpine.

Part of this assimilation may have been to do with the Picts' complex matrilinear kingship patterns, by which male rulers gained their status via their descent from royal women, who did not rule in their own right. In such a kinship group, the important offspring is the sister's son or nephew, a strong factor within the Arthurian legend, where Arthur's nephews provide the core leadership of his military force as well as creating some of its worst family feuds.

The Picts were mighty fighters, "the flower of warriors" as Tacitus has their first-century AD leader Calgacus say. They were "hidden in the far and secret places away from the stain of tyranny."[23] Their continuous and concerted attacks by land and by sea kept the Romans busy for the duration of the occupation. It is not without reason that both the Antonine and Hadrianic Walls stretch from shore to shore to guard against Pictish and Scottish pirates. We have seen how Lucius Artorius Castus spent many years fighting against the Caledonians. The virtually constant war of attrition was sometimes halted by means of currency payoffs, such as those given by Septimus Severus as protection money to the Maeatae and Caledonii in the third century, some of which was discovered recently in a silver denari hoard found near the Moray Firth. It is possible that the hoard of late Roman silverware discovered at Traprain Law may have been a sweetener to Pictish chieftains. Not until the payment of Danegeld to fend off the Vikings in the ninth centuries was so much wealth expended to keep a foe from the door.

The long habit of cross-border raiding continued right up until the eighteenth century. Keeping the Picts at bay required energetic determination and constant vigilance. Gildas writes that the Picts and Scots are "readier to cover their villainous faces with hair than their private parts and neighboring regions with clothes."[24] This seems to reference the nakedness of Pictish warriors or at least to their wearing the barbarian kilt rather than the more civilized trews, or close-fitting tartan trousers, of the Romano-British.

The other outlandish combat wear that typified Britons to the classical eye was the use of woad. Derived from the dye plant *Isatis tinctoria,* its pigment oxidizes to a brilliant or dark blue, which was used both as body paint and in tattooing. Antiseptic woad may have been applied to the body before battle to help minimize infection; applied with an agent like fat, it would have also insulated warriors against the cold.[25] Woad was also used as naval camouflage. In his *Epitoma Rei Militaris* (A Summary of Military Defense), the fourth-century Roman military strategist Vegetius wrote of the scouting vessels, which "the Britons call Pictati,"[26] which intercept enemy shipping: "their sails and rigging are dyed sea-green, and even the tar that caulks them and the clothing of the mariners is of the same shade." In dim light and overcast weather, these Pictish vessels would have been able to bypass the eyes of lookouts and steal ashore. Of all the peoples of Britain at this era, and despite the brief Roman foray into their territory, the Picts maintained their original integrity and identity longer than any others, giving them a single-minded determination to defend it.

The poem "Kadeir Teyrnon" reminds us that Arthur lived at a time when

> *Strange accents flow,*
> *Eloquent assaults,*
> *Of sea-farers.*
> *From the children of Saraphin . . .* *

"The children of Saraphin" is a poetic gloss for the Saxons, which appears also in *Y Gododdin,* where they are called *sarph sarim,* or armored serpents, possibly a descriptive reference to the mail shirts of their warriors or a distant memory of the scaled armor worn by the Sarmatian *federati* in the second century.[27]

The people whom the British called Saxons originated from the northwest coastlands of what today are called the Netherlands (Friesians), northwest Germany from Hanover and Hamburg, westward (Saxons), southern Denmark (Angles), and northern Denmark (Jutes.) These peoples lived beyond the northern limits of Rome and were not subject to the Roman Empire. They settled in Kent and along the south

---

*Our translation.

Map 3. Peoples and kingdoms of Britain circa 500.
(courtesy of Wil Kinghan)

coast, as well as in East Anglia, and spread northeastward. The Picts had a tendency to make alliances with the Saxon incomers from early on, all the better to squeeze the British kingdoms of Manau Gododdin and Bryneich (Northumberland), which lay between Pictland and Anglian Deira (South Humberside.)

Sidonius Apollinaris, a fifth-century Gaulish bishop with British connections, writes of the Saxons as raiders whose oared sailing ships with curving prows and hide keels made surprise attacks along the coast of Gaul as well as upon Britain; he knows that they have blue eyes and that they shave the front of their foreheads, leaving their hair long at the back to add to their fearsome appearance.[28] He says they practice human sacrifice, cast lots (a method of divination involving the casting of stones or bones onto the ground), and are pagans, though his descriptions may reflect the terror of a first encounter rather than of reasoned assessment. Sidonius was personally acquainted with exiles from Saxon depredations. There is a long history of expedient migrations between the Islands and the Continent, from the first-century BC Gaulish exiles who fled to Britain in the wake of Caesar's bloody suppression of Gaul, to the fifth-century British exiles who fled from Saxon incursion to Armorica in such numbers that their presence caused it to be called Little Britain or Brittany. The many locations with the place-name Bretteville (literally Brit-Town) make a telling line along the Breton and Normandy coasts.

Along the south coast of Britain itself a number of Saxon rulers settled: Hengist and his successor Aesc in Kent, Aelle in Sussex, and the British-sounding Cerdic and his son Cynric who ruled in Hampshire. These founded the West Saxon kingdom that would later become Wessex and that came to dominate England by the ninth century. The Wessex line may indeed have arisen from an alliance between an elite British family and the Saxon incomers.

Aelle of the south Saxons is the earliest named *bretwalda,* a title that he may have earned as the result of making a treaty with the British after that battle. Evidence of partition treaties may be perceived in the Saxon name for a battle fought in circa 485 at Mearcredesburna (possibly the River Cuckmere on the Hampshire-Sussex border), a name meaning "stream of the agreed frontier."[29] The far south and east of Britain was largely in Saxon hands, and these long-term settlements provided supply lines for the inevitable push westward into the heartland of the southern British territories now known as Somerset and Gloucestershire where the cities of Bath, Cirencester, and Gloucester maintained stubborn resistance until 577, when the Battle of Dyrham saw the overthrow of three British kings.

The Roman title count of the Saxon Shore, an appointment about which we have little information, may bear more than one interpretation: Does the Saxon Shore mean "the shore . . . *attacked by* Saxons or *settled by* Saxons"[30] (our italics)? In which case, this military post may have been created for a Roman commander to lead troops of Saxon federates against the further incursions of their own people, just as Vortigern himself later appointed the Jutes to defend his eastern and northern shores. It is an intriguing thought that would help explain how the Saxons managed to establish a southern settlement so early on. Excavation of the central Saxon Shore depots like that at Porchester Castle show no sign of attack, unlike the utter destruction wrought at Pevensey by Aelle, which may suggest a continuity of Saxon settlement from before the Roman withdrawal.

A state of Anglian expansion had existed from before Arthur's birth. The eastern and northeastern coastlands saw a steady spread of settlers, first in East Anglia and slowly up into Lincolnshire, which is where it had reached by Arthur's time. Shiploads swollen with fresh Anglian incomers began to spread northward, founding the kingdom of Deira (Humberside), though it has been suggested that the Anglian settlers in Deira may have been federates "originally in the pay of the Roman commander at York."[31] The timescales involved in the establishment of the northeast Anglian kingdom of Bernicia (Northumbria) are disputed, though as we shall see from the disposition of Arthur's battles, he seems to have been engaged in this region as well as limiting Anglian expansion in Lincolnshire.

Anglian expansion was so successful that there are two continental reports about their emigration from Britain: Adam of Bremen speaks of them seeking service with Theodoric of the Franks in 531, while, in Byzantium, the historian Procopius reports that multitudes of Anglians migrate every year in vast numbers with their wives and children. The excuse given for this migration is that Britain was overpopulated with Britons, Friesians, and Angles, but it is equally possible that such migrations may have their origin in a succession of Arthurian campaigns.[32] Descendants of these Anglian migrants later caught the attention of Pope Gregory, who commented on some fair-haired slaves in the Roman market: *Non Angli, sed angeli* (Not Angles, but angels). This encounter prompted Saint Augustine's mission to convert the English.

Many scholars have recently questioned the actual quantity of Germanic incomers and their possible displacement of Britons. Instead of a massive genocide, genetic research reveals that the Saxon contribution to the British gene pool is barely 5.5 percent, rising to about 15 percent in the eastern counties.[33] This reveals that the British were not massacred wholesale, but rather lived on and intermarried. Given this evidence, the final ascendancy of the English language over the British tongue remains a puzzle.

Arthur's foes on the northwest frontier were the latest incomers into Britain: the Gaelic Dalriadans had established themselves in Argyll sometime in the second half of the fifth century, crossing from Ulster and overrunning the south of Argyll. We have already considered the Dalriadan leader, Aedan mac Gabrain's son Arthúir, as a possible contributor to Arthur's reputation. By 500 the boundaries of British Dalriada stretched as far east as Drumalban in the Grampians, where the Pictish runs began, and as far north as Loch Linnhe. The only point where they were not bordered by Picts or by the sea was at Altclud, modern Dumbarton, which was the British fortress of the independent kingdom of Strathclyde until the early tenth century. There is still a stone named Clach nam Bretann on the western side of Glenfalloch at the head of Loch Lomond, which may be a boundary marker between the Britons of Strathclyde and the Dalriadan Scots.[34]

Arthur had to keep an eye not only on the Saxons of the south and eastern coasts and the Picts and Scots Dalriadans of the north, but also on the southern Irish who raided the western coastline of what is now Wales. The Romans had placed three great fortresses in Wales: Segontium (Caernarvon), Maridunum (Carmarthan), and Isca (Caerleon) to subdue the western British peoples, but southwestern Wales had settlements of Irish from the fourth century onward, following the withdrawal of troops by Maximus in 383. There is some evidence to suggest that some of these Irish were not opportunistic raiders but in fact mercenaries appointed by the Romano-British government or more likely the magistrates and depleted local military to defend Dyfed and western Wales from Irish raiders.

The name given to these Irish raiders by the Romans is Attacotti, a name that seems to derive from the Gaelic *aithechtuatha,* the term for subject peoples who had been reduced to rent-paying status on their own land. There were many such tribes in Ireland who had become vassals of more powerful families. Philip Rance posits that mercenary Irish in Roman pay called themselves *aithechtuatha,* as a generic title for a federate group.[35] That such men from Ireland rose to positions of trust in Dyfed is borne out by the records.

An examination of the eighth-century text *The Expulsion of the Déssi* reveals that the Irish tribe of the Déssi, expelled from County Meath, settled in Britain sometime in the mid-fourth century, led by Eochaid Allmuir (Over-Sea). A comparison of these accounts with the Welsh Genealogies makes it clear that the rulers of Dyfed in the time of Arthur of the Battles are descended from *Irish forebears.* They clearly received official recognition as defenders of Britain, becoming, in the aftermath of Roman withdrawal, more British than the British.[36]

It would appear that many of those we have regarded as the enemies of the British are in actual fact foreigners who have become naturalized Britons, or mercenaries, possibly even allies to Arthur. It seems likely that if Arthur fought his battles over so much of the country, then some part of his troop strength was made up of mercenaries or naturalized

Battle sites, some with O.S. references,
others not identified.

1 River Glein (NT 9030)

2 5 Campaign area only
   - not identified.

6 Bassus (NS 6459)

7 Celidon - (Caledonian Forest)
   - not identified.

8 N. Guinnion (Stow) (NT 4644)
   S. Guinnion (Binchester)

9 York and Lincoln

10 Tribuit (Edinburgh area) (NT3073)

11 Agned (Penango - ancient name)
   (approx. NT 4605)

12 Badon (Liddington) (SU 2079)

6 Bassus

Camelon

Tribuit 10 Guinnion
                 8

Celidon
   7

           1 Glein

11 Agned

Camelon

Guinnion
   8

Dubglas

2 3
4 5

? 9
City of Legions

Pen Rhionydd

9 ?
City of Legions

NORTH
SEA

Camelon

Afon Gamlan

Mynyw

Thanet

Badon 12

Glastonbury

Guloph

Cadbury

Longborth

Tintagel

Camelford

Pevensey

Kelliwig

✗ Battles   ⊗ Arthur's battles
▲ The courts of Arthur (according to Triad 1)
Camelon 'Cam' places, possible sites of Camlan

Map 4. The defense of Britain in the fifth and sixth centuries.
(courtesy of Wil Kinghan)

foreigners who already had experience in defending British territories: men who would have provided him with well-drilled troops as well as a wide palette of languages.

In the last analysis, Britain was ultimately overthrown not solely by its Saxon enemies, but by a variety of factors in which its own civil wars and fragmented disputes must also be counted. About these we have little evidence. Gildas states that the British kings continually fought each other, and we have already seen how the building of Wansdyke between the Durotriges and the Dobunni regions is an indication of ongoing civil war between them. Some of those regarded as Arthur's enemies included some allies, while some of those thought of as his allies proved to be his enemies. There can be no 100 percent heroes or 100 percent enemies in this context; the four peoples of Britain were each striving for their own native or naturalized territories in the context of uncertain times during the rulership of jumped-up or self-proclaimed kings. In an island with navigable seaways and vulnerable coastlines, deeply penetrated by river estuaries, there were many fronts to defend. Let us look among these to find Arthur's allies, companions, and, possibly, his kindred.

ARTHUR'S BRITISH ALLIES

It is clear that no one commander could have simultaneously kept watch over all the coastlines and foreign settlements of Britain; other leaders and their troops must have contributed to their defense. Who ruled these kingdoms and what relationship they have to Arthur's cause helps us set the battles in context. Arthur's allies may have been drawn from among the fathers of the five tyrants castigated by Gildas's "word-rocks." These rulers all seemed to have lived within what would once have been Britannia Prima (see map 1, p. 9). Gidlow has suggested that Arthur might well have been one of the provincial governors of Britannia Prima, which would explain why he is said to fight *with the kings of the Britons*.[37] Unfortunately, as among many recently colonized people whose resentments and deprivations have created in them a disproportionate need for restitution, civil power struggles were all too common. In an earlier generation, Ambrosius and Vortimer had ranged themselves against the ill-judged policies of Vortigern: it is possible that internal relations between British leaders had not improved in succeeding generations. It is in such a context that we must consider Gildas's accusations against the five tyrants and ascertain whether they might have been Arthur's allies. Gildas's list includes some of the most powerful leaders of southwestern Britain: Vortiporus, Constantine, Aurelius, Cuneglassus, and Maglocunus—names that reveal both Roman and British antecedents.[38]

Vortiporus of the Demetae (Dyfed) is castigated by Gildas for the usual list of murders and adulteries, but he is called the aging son of a good king. He joins Gildas's list of men who rape their own daughters after putting aside their wives. Vortiporus's "good father," Aircol Llawhir, might have fought shoulder to shoulder with Ambrosius, just as Vortiporus himself is surely old enough to have known and fought with Arthur.

Constantine of Dumnonia (roughly Devon, Cornwall, and part of Somerset) is described by Gildas as having sworn on the sacrament not to deceive his people, and yet disguised "in the habit of a holy abbot," he slew two royal youths "in the bosom of two mothers he should have respected"—namely the church and the youths' actual mother. Gildas speaks as if Constantine were alive and possibly as if the youths were dynastic rivals. This is borne out in Geoffrey of Monmouth's medieval version of this incident, where Constantine succeeds Arthur as ruler and assassinates the two sons of Mordred who had sought sanctuary in the church, suggesting that some kind of power struggle in the far southwest played out after Arthur's downfall. In Welsh legend Gereint the son of Erbin is the prince of Dumnonia who dies fighting for Arthur at Llongborth. His successor is Cador or Cadwy, Constantine's father.

Aurelius Caninus may have ruled the Dobunni territories of the lower Severn Valley, Bath, Gloucester, and Cirencester.[39] He stands accused like Constantine of similar crimes of patricide and adultery, but he is specifically singled out for his "unjust thirst for civil war and plunder." We are not told with whom he is conflicted, but it is more than possible that he continued the long tribal enmity between Dobunni and Durotriges (Dumnonian) tribes. Aurelius may be the grandson of Ambrosius Aurelianus, whose lineage Gildas says has degenerated since his grandfather's time. Evidence of the Aurelii family was found in 1992, when a hoard of silverware and coins was discovered at Hoxne, near Norwich. Originally deposited around 450, when its British owners would have needed to flee from the Saxons, the hoard contained items with the Christian Chi-Ro design upon them. "The name most frequently found on the treasure—on no less than ten spoons—was that of *Aurelius Ursicinus,* 'the bear like,' probably the head of the family, whose name seems to be the same as that of Geoffrey's *Aurelius Ambrosius* and of Gildas's *Aurelius Caninus.*"[40]

Cuneglassus is called by Gildas "a bear, a rider of many and driver of the chariot of the Bear's Stronghold" (Receptaculum Ursi). Gidlow notes that *receptaculum* is often translated by Dark Age writers as *din* and that there is the possibility that this place-name may refer to Din Eirth or Din Arth, which are in the eastern region of North Wales and Dyfed, respectively.[41] We have already noted that Arthur's name derives from the British word *arth* or bear, but Cuneglassus may have deeper connections with Arthur. He is accused of fighting against his own countrymen and of putting away his wife in favor of her widowed sister. This latter accusation has its Arthurian resonance in the Triads, as we see below.

Cuneglassus's Arthurian connections may be simply due to his inheritance of what had once been Arthur's fortress. This would put an Arthurian stronghold in either Dyfed—famously a region where foreign federates were settled as well as unseated by the Gwyr y Gogledd, or Men of the North—or else in Powys.[42] A. O. Anderson believed that *multorum sessor,* usually translated as "rider among many," might actually indicate "occupier of many seats," which might imply that Cuneglassus unseated others in order to enjoy their territories or that he was known as one who changed sides to his advantage.[43]

Maglocunus (Great Hound) or Maelgwn Gwynedd, whose seat was

a hill fort, Deganwy in North Wales, is said by Gildas to have "removed many of these tyrants from their country and even their life." He is described as "the dragon of the island," suggesting a possible provenance for the later Arthurian title pendragon, which might have been a title for supreme battle leader of the kingdom of Gwynedd. Ifor Williams posits the term *dreic*—a standard description for a warrior—was applied to leaders before whom the *draco* wind-sock-style standard was carried.[44] But if Maglocunus had deposed some of the tyrants listed by Gildas, then he sounds formidable or well supported by troops.

Gildas doesn't mention outlying kingdoms beyond the southwest, but if we look at the other British rulers during the period of Arthur's lifetime, we find an interesting and perhaps familiar collection. March, the son of Meirchion the Thin of Rheged (Cumbria and parts of Yorkshire), was the ruler of Cornwall and later the King Mark of the Tristan cycle. In Manau Gododdin there was Lot Lwyddog (of the Host) and Gwalchmai Gwalltafwyn—both names that reappear in the Arthurian legend in the guise of Lot and Gawain. In Gwent (southeast Wales), there is Caradog Freichfras (Strong Arm) and Gereint of Dumnonia who died at Llongborth, both of whom found their places in Arthurian legend. It is only Strathclyde that fails to give us an Arthurian retainer, at least until the late sixth century when Myrddin Wyllt or Merlin was subsumed into the legend.

There are many historical kings and leaders of later generations who became woven into the later legend: Urien of Rheged and his son Owain, from the late sixth century, as well as Peredur of Ebrauc (York) whom we remember as the Grail-seeking Sir Perceval; other names and titles are adopted and adapted during the legend-making process, co-opted because of their heroism or commitment to the British defense along with Arthur. The ancestors of Urien of Rheged were potential beneficiaries of Arthur's northern victories, which clawed back the northern territories into British control once more.[45] Arthur would have needed the support of such men to back up his successes.

The stubborn belief that Arthur had Pictish allies as well as enemies is strong in the folk tradition. One name continually recurs, Hueil, son of Caw, with whom Arthur has an acrimonious relationship. According to the eleventh-century Welsh story *Culhwch and Olwen,* Hueil refuses to be subject to any other king, while the medieval *Life of Gildas* relates that the people hoped that Hueil would become king. Did he have the same ambitions as Arthur? As we shall see below, the death of Caw at the hands of Arthur had reverberating consequences.

One of Arthur's legendary knights, Sir Tristan, starts out with the resoundingly Pictish name of Drustan map Talorc, nephew of Cornish King Mark. Both Drustan and Hueil feature with Cei (the original of Sir Kay) in the Welsh Triads concerning the "Three Diademed Warriors of the Isle of Britain." The diadem or *talaith,* a crested band worn about the brows possibly over a helmet, was a battle honor awarded only to the fiercest warriors, perhaps those who led the charge and were in the forefront of battle. (A *talaith* believed to belong to Arthur was taken from Llywelyn ap Gruffud, the last Prince of Wales, by Edward I and bestowed in the treasury of Westminster Abbey.)[46] That two out of three of Arthur's premier war captains are from Pictland may lead us to the conclusion that he was allied by blood or marriage to the families of the northern kingdoms.

The Men of the North play a more substantial part in the Arthurian picture than those of the Welsh kingdoms. This may have been due to their ability to deliver first-class military assistance. Already, the Votadinian Cunedda had come south from Manau Gododdin in about 430 to help clear western Britain of Irish settlers. This influx of Gwyr y Gogledd, or Men of the North, enabled the emerging rulers of Wales to protect their shores. Such men received land and monthly rations as their pay. The land they were given or which they subsequently took formed the basis of the dominant British kingdom of Gwynedd, which was originally known as Venedotia. We may speculate that the very name of the kingdom derives from the name for the mercenary or professional soldier (via the Old Welsh *guined* from Old Irish *féni,* plural *fianna*). North Wales had originally been held by the Ordovician people, but they were clearly displaced by a group of Votadinian *féni* led by Cunedda from the north. As John Koch suggests, in a "sort of uncontrolled land grab that characterized Britiain post-Roman Migration Period," the Votadinian mercenaries established themselves in North Wales, calling themselves the Venedotes or Gwynedd-folk.[47] Here in these Votadinian irregular mercenaries, we may perhaps see the very roots of Arthur's Round Table knights.

The core of Arthur's army depended upon experienced men. There were no better troops for the job than the Men of the North. In earlier times of the Roman Empire, the Votadini had served as *laeti* or irregular federate troops, especially cavalry forces.[48] One of the fourth-century Votadini leaders was known as Patern Pesrut or Paternus of the Red Cloak, whose father and son are called respectively Tegid (Tacitus) and Uetern (Aeternus), suggesting that Arthur was not the only one whose lineage drew upon the legions of Rome. Perhaps it was from here among the folk of the Gododdin that Arthur had his own birth and training. Like the roving *fianna* warriors of the Irish hero Fionn mac Cumhail, Arthur's men may have been born in the saddle, able to attend swiftly to flash points along the borders.

The internal evidence of *Y Gododdin* reveals that the British Votadini from Manau Gododdin fought as vigorously against the Picts and Irish as they did against the Anglians. In prosecuting war so far south as Catraeth, they may have been attempting to follow through Arthur's attempt to hold off the Anglian stranglehold that threatened the northeast. Saxon Bernecia had once been British Bryneich, ruled by the southern Votadini until the mid-sixth century: if Arthur had his origins among them, his defense of this region makes good sense.

One very surprising factor in the leadership of the Gododdin in the mid-sixth century is that Uruei, the Lord of Eidin (Edinburgh), had a Saxon father called Uolstan or Wolstan, who was described as "no sovereign lord."[49] This perhaps suggests that "a small Germanic military elite were peacefully infiltrating an intact Gododdin tribal society at its upper levels" or that German legionary descendants had settled in that region and intermarried.[50] We know little of Votadinian regnal and leadership customs, but if they, like their neighbors the Picts, drew their descent from the maternal line, this would have been no bar to Uruei's leadership as the tribe's judge. Uruei's father, the Saxon Wolstan, would have been of Arthur's generation, perhaps providing him a friendly Saxon ally.

How Arthur maintained alliances and continued support from allies is worth considering. Since he was evidently not a man of notable family, we can perhaps rule out the possibility of creating kinship by the marriage of his female relatives to men of power. It does seem likely, however, that Arthur himself would have been offered the relative or daughter of a notable king as wife. Of course, such dynastic considerations obtain more centrally in the life of the literary character than in that of the historic battle leader, about whose wife we can only speculate; however, there is a long tradition of Arthur having married three women called Gwenhwyfar.

The glue wrought by such dynastic marriages had brought together the Strathclyde British and Irish Dalriadans, as well as the Pictish, Votadinian, and Saxon kingdoms, creating kinship between friend and foe. But the ultimate dynastic marriage between foes took place in 640: in a union unthinkable only a hundred years previous, Urien of Rheged's great-granddaughter Rienmelth of the British married Oswy, the son of Aethelfrith, Saxon victor of the Battle of Chester, where so many Britons died. Such marriages may have brought peace, but in actuality they often reduced national conflicts to the level of civil kinship feud and dynastic overthrow.

Alliances are kept by the making of agreements, gifts of land, the granting of positions, as well as by the exchange of hostages, envoys, or ambassadors. One of the standard methods of retaining goodwill was the giving of gifts: we have seen from *Y Gododdin* that Arthur had a reputation for generosity. The model of generosity in the poem is the Lord of Eidin (Edinburgh) who summons and maintains a great army of men for a whole year in preparation for the raid upon Catraeth: this would constitute a vast outlay of resources in food and drink as well as in arms and horses, if it is not mere epic hyperbole.

Arthur's alliances would have helped maintain the mobility of his forces, giving him a distinctive military advantage over his enemies, but how did he command his men? What were his fighting methods?

ARTHUR'S FIGHTING MEN

Nennius relates, strangely, how "the British were unused to weapons" before the Romans came.[51] This remark is clearly nonsense: early British society revolved around the honor of the warrior, his feats of arms, and prowess in combat and war. Flavius Arrianus in his *Ars Tactica* of 136 describes the Celtic feat of throwing spears at a target from a galloping horse—a tactic he called *xunema,* meaning "a deed well done."[52] *Y Gododdin* supplies us with a similar feat where a warrior "sowed ash spears from the grip of his hand, from [up]on a slender chestnut battle horse."[53] This sounds like a feat that would need long practice from youth upward. We can surmise from insular Celtic accounts that the coming-of-age tradition of young men consisted of minimal arms training for all; a noble youth could have looked forward to the gift of adult arms and a horse to mark his adult status. The rapid throwing of spears or javelins from horseback is also remarked upon from military accounts of Gaulish and Breton tactics.[54] British cavalry drill may have retained this same Celtic panache that had so impressed Arrianus in the second century. Certainly, the Vindolanda tablets speak of British cavalry using throwing spears.[55] Similar feats of fighting horsemanship had also been practiced by the Sarmatians under Lucius Artorius Castus.

Arthur's recruitment of men may have involved a form of conscription, for he certainly could not have raised sufficient troops without the aid of regional kings and local rulers, upon whom the burden of supplying a standing army must fall. With no centralized government, how did Arthur deal cooperatively with so many different regions? He must have possessed persuasive methods or a diplomatic staff whose job would have been to keep regional rulers sweet while extracting the support and men that they needed. If he had a standing army or at least a central company of his own picked men, then this would have been supplemented by seasonal levies or local troops urgent to defend their own territories, with contingents of troops grouped under their own commanders, like Eliffer ruler of York, whose epithet Gosgorddfawr means "of the Great Host." One of the reasons why Arthur is remembered throughout Britain could be because so many regions sent troops to serve under him.

As the military commander of the British, perhaps initially under the authority of Ambrosius, Arthur had the status of someone like the legendary Irish hero Fionn mac Cumhail who, with his *fianna,* supported the high king of Tara. The *fianna* were a band of professional mobile troops, used to be being billeted upon the populace wherever they served. Such a band would answer best to the status of Arthur's military leadership: a core group whose regional loyalties were subsumed in the greater loyalty that they owed their battle leader. The Roman appellations such as centurion or *cinthrann* remained in use, as did the name of a company of men, *canhwr* or century.

Whether Arthur regarded his men as roving *fianna* or disciplined *canhwr,* they had to be rewarded. Throughout the fifth century, we see evidence of coin clipping—always a sign that the fresh minting of coinage has ceased. The Romans themselves used hack-silver—chains of silver that could be literally hacked off—as payment to barbarians. No British leader after the Roman withdrawal minted any coins, although some continental coinage was in circulation, so we may discount any such payments. Arthur's British troops may have been paid in kind: in land, booty, and beasts, similar to the way in which barbarian federate troops had been paid under Rome. This "pay" very often entailed the simple drawing of a monthly ration. But, like many commanders of large armies, Arthur may at times have been in arrears with his payment and forced to depend upon the goodwill of local regions, especially in the parts of his campaign where his lines of supply were overstretched.

That Arthur is called "the Red Ravager" in the Welsh Triads suggests that his negotiations may have been none too polite and that certain regions might have objected to his form of taxation, which would have included the billeting and feeding of men and horses. The title suggests someone who would take if not freely given supplies at first asking, but it may equally arise from the usual military alternative to paying the troops—the taking of booty from the enemy or from obstructive noncombatants.

Fabio Barbieri regards Arthur as "an outstanding military leader, perhaps not of very high rank, who rebelled against the successors of Ambrosius over a matter of taxes."[56] He backs this up with evidence derived from two Welsh poems, "The Dialogue of Arthur and the Eagle" and "Pa Gur," which we will consider further in chapter 4. In the first poem, Arthur's nephew castigates him for committing perjury to obtain land and reminds him that he who is "guilty of treason against his own lord, shall repent at the Day of Judgment." Was Arthur's rise to power a result of the overthrow of his overlord? The early medieval saints' lives in which Arthur figures all depict him as self-serving and corrupt, as we shall find in chapter 5. "Pa Gur" (What Man?) tells us that Arthur's man Cei had "fought against the servants of Emreis," which may refer to the staff of Ambrosius, suggesting that Arthur's rise to power may not have been with the assent of Ambrosius or his followers. This may go some way to explain why Arthur does not feature more fully in the pro-Ambrosian chronicle of Nennius. Arthur's men could have been billeted in the remaining legionary cities and garrison fortresses, though any barracks would have been nearly a hundred years old, if indeed they were still standing. Stabling for horses may have decayed, and troops would have reverted to guarded horse lines at night. Some reoccupation of forts has been discerned, as well as the continuation of many cities like Calleva Atrebatum (Silchester), which shows no sign of disturbance, surrounded as it is by a series of dikes. During the fifth to sixth centuries, many Iron Age hill forts were refortified and reoccupied, often with the addition of a new timber palisade, watchtowers, and fighting platforms like those at South Cadbury and Congresbury in Somerset. Other such hill forts were given new dry stone and timber defenses or strengthened with earthen banks and ditches.

Collingwood and Myers long since proposed that Arthur's men would have consisted largely of mounted troops.[57] The defeat by Gothic cavalry of the Byzantine armies at Adrianople in 378 has been much quoted as a precedent for this kind of overwhelming force. Barber, in a reaction to this argument, has refuted the effectiveness of such heavy cavalry, especially without horses of sufficient size and stirrups, which do not appear in Britain before the Viking era.[58] The Sarmatian troops of Lucius Artorius Castus brought their own stirrups with them, for some have been found at forts along the Wall, but any such nonregulation use is not yet borne out by evidence from later on in Britain. However, Arthur's troops need not have been heavy cavalry, but rather lightly armored, extremely mobile in both battle and maneuver. Roman cavalry was expected to charge up and down hills, as well as to swim its horses across bodies of water, so why not British cavalry?[59] Good riding has always depended on the primary ability of the rider to keep a firm, deep seat without the aid of either saddle or stirrups. The weapons used in battle included shields, swords, and spears, but a trained battle horse will fight with its hooves, as the *Book of Taliesin* asserts: "Arthur's horse boldly delivered blows."[60] Mounted troops can also act as scouts and foragers, harry retreating enemies, and recover booty and captives.

The cavalry argument will doubtlessly rage on, but the facts about possible cavalry armoring must rest upon the kind of mounts available. The average height of native British ponies is not high. From the excavation of horse bones, most British mounts of the post-Roman era would have been fourteen hands on average, which is still ridable, although this is much shorter than the sixteen- to seventeen-hand horse of today.[61] Taller mounts may also have been imported from the Continent.

The Welsh Triads describe three men so tall that no horse could be found for them: Cadawaladr, Rhun ap Maelgwn, and Rhiwallawn. They are called "the three fettered men": in order to accommodate their height, they wore a kind of knee stirrup, attached both to the crupper of the saddle as well as to a ring about their shins, thus lifting their legs and keeping them from dragging on the ground.[62] This sounds like an unlikely arrangement, but we recall that even Gildas describes the extreme lofty stature of Maelgwn Gwynedd, and these descendants of Maelgwn lived in the sixth century or beyond, by which time any Roman blood stock, brought in to give height to the native breeds, would have begun to perhaps diminish. However, there is also the possibility that the Sarmatian auxiliaries who settled in Britain in the second century may have continued to breed horses for the legions.

The makeup of an average cavalry troop may be inferred from the Welsh poetic sources: Cunedda is said to lead 900 horses, while the mounted troops in *Y Gododdin* number 300, enough for a punitive raid of 150 miles. The average Roman *ala* or auxiliary cavalry wing in Britain would not have been as great as the standard *ala quingenaria* of 512 enlisted soldiers, made up of sixteen groups, with each group commanded by a decurion leading 32 men and horses, nor anything like as large as the *ala miliara* composed of 1,008 men and horses. "Kadeir Teyrnon" states that Arthur had the cavalry wings' steel in his blood: with his hereditary skill with horses and the drilling of cavalry, he was a ready spear to be thrown in the defense of his land.

It has been argued that the Saxons did not have cavalry and that their armies were composed of infantry only: this may have been true initially on their arrival but perhaps not later on. The two horse-and-warrior burials uncovered at Lakenheath in Suffolk reveal the panoply of mounted Saxon horsemen from the mid-sixth century but do not illuminate how many such warriors would have taken part in any battle: the fact that such finds are extremely rare testifies to an army composed predominantly of infantry.[63] The effect of a cavalry attack upon infantry depends very much upon surprise and upon the nature of the terrain, as well as upon how men are mustered and defended.

The ability to call upon reserves of grain and of fresh mounts for his cavalry suggests either a landed nobleman or else a persuasive and very organized campaign leader. Certainly Arthur is said to be a generous provider of horses in both the Triads and, by inference, in *Y Gododdin*. "The Chair of the Sovereign" poem says of Arthur that:

> *He led from the enclosed Wall*
> *Pale saddled horses.*[*64]

---

*Our translation.

The ability to supply ready-broken horses for cavalry supply was essential.

It seems possible that Arthur's main horse levies came from the north, which is reasonable considering the heavy Roman presence along the Wall and the necessity for a local horse-breeding program to remount the ten mounted units once stationed there. We have already seen such a breeding ground surviving in the area of the Fylde, near to the Sarmatian fort of Bremetennacum.

While we consider methods of warfare, it is worth bearing in mind that six of Arthur's battles take place on or around rivers, while one is on a shoreline or estuary. Leslie Alcock has noted that many of the refortified hilltop settlements are located near coasts and waterways, to give warning of sea-going attacks.[65] Few, save Bernard S. Bachrach, have seriously factored into the military picture the possibility of a British fleet or of the sea-going capability of the Saxons, which must have been considerable since their ancestors sailed from Europe, so we must also bear in mind the possibility of sea-going engagements. Southern Britons may have been inexperienced in the arts of war, but one thing is certain of an island people, that those who lived around the coast or on the banks of navigable rivers were fully qualified to sail its waters.[66] Arthur would most certainly have drawn upon the local knowledge of skilled watermen and mariners and may have had his own fleet. In the "Sovereign's Chair" the *gwledig* is exhorted to draw upon the sea defenses, for:

> *Fleets will come.*
> *The wave covers the shingle,*
> *Dylan's country, the sea, is inevitable.*
> *There will be neither shelter nor refuge,*
> *Neither hill nor dale,*
> *Nor any refuge from the storm. . . .*[*67]

---

*Our translation.

THE LUCK OF THE GODS

However Arthur fought his battles, however he disposed and armed his troops, it was ultimately their morale that decided the day. Soldiers are superstitious. Before a great battle they look for signs and omens of its outcome. Celtic legend speaks of the Washer at the Ford whom warriors encounter on the eve of battle. This haglike laundress beats the shirts of those soon to be slain upon the stones, washing away their blood in the running stream, rendering souls pristine and fit for metempsychosis. To view her on the eve of combat, or to see the scavenging raven women who descend like Celtic Valkyries to bear away the souls of the slain, as well as to feast upon their flesh, is to know yourself marked for death.

Soldiers like a lucky leader, one who has the charismatic common touch combined with the last-minute swerve of the truly daring, one who comes up smelling of roses after a debacle, a lucky lad whose trophies of war will be a trivial cut at the end of the day and a heap of fallen enemies. With such a one you know you are safe, because lucky leaders have the gods at their back. When you have spiritual assistance on your side; that same luck might extend to your followers; Arthur seems to have had this quality, which inspires troops and elevates leaders to high office.

Within memory there had been the vision of the British-born emperor Constantine the Great at Milvium Bridge: the Christian sign of the Chi-Ro that appeared in the sky brought him victory in the early fourth century. Nearer to home in circa 440 had been the extraordinary "Alleluia Victory" of Saint Germanus of Auxerre, who commanded his men to shout alleluia at the same time, thus confusing their adversaries and giving the British a bloodless victory. It is perhaps not therefore surprising that Arthur has his own miraculous Christian legend. In his eighth battle at Caer Guinnion, Arthur is said to have carried the picture of the Virgin Mary upon his shoulder or upon his back. Whether this is evidence of his Christian conviction or merely an interpolation on the part of Nennius, the image of the Mother of God borne upon the armor of a British war leader needs to be examined in more detail.

Although they both inveigh against apostates and heretics, neither Gildas nor Saint Patrick speaks of the Britons and their leaders as anything but Christian. Britain had been Christian for generations, long before Christianity's adoption as the official Roman religion from 380 onward. Apart from Christ, if Arthur needed a divinity to inspire his own troops he had a great choice at his disposal, from the legionaries' god Mithras to local divinities of war like Cocidius, Camulos, and Maponos the Hunter. As a lucky leader, he might have kept a boot in either camp, if only to assure those troops who hailed from different spiritual backgrounds that he was not prejudiced. That he might choose a Christian image such as the Blessed Virgin or the cross of the Savior as a rallying symbol is not unlikely. British Christianity would have been seen as a clear differentiation point between the Britons and their pagan Saxon enemies.

We find many historical references to men marking their shields with devices; before the formulation of heraldry, this was the best way to be recognized in the tumult of a battle. Apart from the strategist Vegetius's advice to soldiers to write their names upon their shields, in an early attempt to identify the fallen, there is an ivory carving from the early fifth century depicting what is thought to be Stilicho, the Vandal commander of the Western Empire. He is attired in a Late Roman Empire tunic, topped by a cloak fastened by a fibula in the German manner, but more tellingly, he bears a shield on which is an iconic medallion, showing the heads of the coemperors Arcadius and Honorius. As such, it is a badge of his loyalty. As the general who implemented the new state religion, Stilicho was the first military commander to fall into line behind the Christian banner. This carving gives us a brief glimpse of a Late Roman Empire shield and its insignia. Might not the benighted troops of Britain have inscribed their own supernatural help upon their own shields rather than the images of earthly emperors who had washed their hands of any responsibility for Britain?

In one of the Sawley glosses to the *Historia Brittonum,* written into the margins sometime during the late twelfth or early thirteenth centuries, we find the following comment:

> Then Arthur went to Jerusalem. There he made a cross of the same measure as the health-bringing Cross. And there it was consecrated. And for three continuous days he fasted and kept vigil, praying in the presence of the Lord's Cross, so that the Lord gave victory by this sign over the pagans, so was it done. And he himself carried the image of Holy Mary, fragments of which were saved and greatly venerated at Wedale. (our translation)

The Stow of Wedale, about twenty-three miles south of Edinburgh and at this time within Gododdin territory, is remembered as the place of a great battle. The folkloric interpretation of the name Wedale is Dale of Woe, commemorating, according to local tradition, a battle fought here by King Arthur. The name Stow is thought to be from the Old English for holy place, and Wedale from the Old English *wiche* meaning "shrine" and *dahl* meaning "valley," making it the Valley of the Shrine. There was indeed a church here from about 600, dedicated to the Virgin, and its well still survives. It is believed to be one of the earliest Scottish sites with such a dedication, although no record of any relics remains.

For anyone familiar with the gospels, the account in the *Historia Brittonum* of Arthur carrying the cross of Christ upon his shoulder conveys another image, that of Simon of Cyrene who was commandeered to shoulder the cross of an exhausted Jesus to the Mount of Golgotha. It is an image that connects the Mount of Golgotha to Mount Badon and may reflect the manner in which the Welsh regarded Arthur as a national savior from the English yoke. Though we know that there may have been confusion between the British words *scuit* meaning "shield" and *scuid* meaning "shoulder," the understanding is ultimately the same. For the beleaguered British, Christianity was the badge of civilization, distinguishing Briton from pagan barbarian. Arthur carrying or bearing a holy icon upon his shield may not be a late pious anachronism but a real possibility.

ARTHUR'S TWELVE BATTLES

It is now time to look more closely at the battle list of Nennius. The consideration of historical battles is usually accompanied by maps of troop movements, real or suppositional, and by the assessment of the equality or disparity of opponents, as well as the terrain over which they fought. In the case of Arthur's campaign, we cannot give even this much. Not only are four battles unnamed, most are unlocatable by any authoritative means, which is not to say that many writers have not tried. Authorities as far distant in linguistic and strategic know-how as the nineteenth-century translator of the *Four Ancient Books of Wales,* W. F. Skene, who sets Arthur's campaigns in Scotland, and Nikolai Tolstoy, who brings a formidable knowledge to his theories, have spilt much ink over the identification of the battles. Some historians work solely from geographic (Collingwood) or philological (Jackson) grounds, while others favor strategic options in their consideration of the battles; however, all of these must be weighed in the balance.

Is the Nennius battle list all that it seems? (See page 70.) H. M. Chadwick was the first to suggest that this list might have come from a poem recalling famous battles. Thomas Jones agreed that it was probably based upon a preexisting Welsh poem in which Arthur's battles were recited and remembered down many generations before their transcription in Nennius.[68] Such a source poem is not immediately apparent from a study of the *Historia Brittonum,* which is written in Latin. However some of the battle titles have rhyming potential: Bassus and Dubglas, Guinnion and Celidon. Other famous military leaders were remembered in epic poems, including the seventh-century Cadwallawn map Cadfan of Gwynedd who is accorded a set of twelve battles. His victory against King Edwin of Northumbria at the Battle of Meicen (known to the English as Haethfelth) in 633 was a battle so famous that it acquired iconic status for the Welsh. Also, in the *Book of Taliesin,* there is a poetic list of seven battles fought by Urien of Rheged, who lived in the late sixth century.

Thomas Jones suggests that the battle list ascribed to Arthur may contain battles belonging to a number of other leaders, refuting the possibility that no one war leader could have covered so much ground on different fronts.[69] There are indeed battles in the *Historia Brittonum* list that could be ascribed to others. The seventh battle of Cat Coit Celidon, which is fought in the Caledonian Forest, might refer to the Battle of Arfderydd of 573, which was certainly within the boundaries of Calydon. Arfderydd has its own sub-Arthurian connections, for it was in this battle that Myrddin ran mad into the depths of the forest, according to early Welsh poetic sources (see chapters 4 and 5). Could Arthur's ninth battle "in the city of the Legions" be identified as the Battle of Chester in 613? This would be highly unlikely, since Chester was known as a crashing defeat for the British and hardly a matter of boasting that "Arthur was victorious in all of these battles." In a variant edition of the *Historia Brittonum,* the eleventh battle is called, not Agned, but Bregouin, which could possibly be identified as the Kat Gellawr Brewyn or Battle of the Cells of Brewyn, a victory gained by Urien Rheged in the late sixth century.

In considering the battles, a few caveats will help keep us from rushing away down suggestive paths. One of the things seldom considered is that this list may not be the original order of engagement, nor should we see the sequence as necessarily deriving from one continuous campaign. It is quite likely that these battles may have been part of a longer series of campaigns, or might have been fought by many British generals and simply attributed to Arthur. We must also continually bear in mind the movements and settlements of Arthur's enemies, including not just Saxons, but also Angles, Scots, and Picts. Nor must we rule out the possibility that some of these battles may have been part of civil strife rather than enemy actions. We must also submit that some of these location names have not survived at all, or at least not in forms wherein their British originals can be detected. Let us look at the battles in their given order.

Battle 1: Glein. "In the mouth of the river that is called Glein." This name derives from the British *glanos,* meaning "clean," not from *glen,* as some have said. There are two possible Rivers Glen in Britain, but one of them has no mouth or estuarial opening, namely the Northumberland River Glen, which runs past Yeavering Bell, the capital seat of the Angles of Bernicia and once the British hill fort of Gefrin. Tolstoy argues that *ostium,* or estuary, might also stand for *aber,* or confluence: in which case, the Northumbrian River Glen does indeed meet the River Till, about twelve miles inland from Lindisfarne. He sees a possible motivation in this battle as an assault upon an early Anglian expansion in this region.[70] The alternative River Glen is situated in Lincolnshire and does have a mouth of sorts. With the immense system of dikes that have reshaped this region, it is perhaps impossible to say where the river made its way to the sea in Arthur's time, but it is well placed for the following battles that may have been fought in Lincolnshire.

Battles 2, 3, 4, and 5: Dubglass. These four battles were "by another river called Dubglas in the region of Linnius." The fact that these four battles have no specific names suggests that we are looking at some form of intermittent engagement over difficult terrain or at least a series of smaller conflicts in one leg of a campaign. *Dubglas* means "blue-black," a good description of peaty water. However, it should be noted that *glas* is a shifting color that can include gray, green, or blue: with the dark appellation of *du,* we might be equally looking at dark gray or dark green. River names that draw upon this meaning include Douglas, Dawlish, Dulas. The area of Linnius has been located anywhere from Lennox, which has a River Douglas, to Lincolnshire, which retains no memory of a River Dubglas. Tolstoy points out the strip of land at Arrochar in Lennox, the only land bridge between British and Dalriadan territories, is only three miles north of the River Douglas, constituting a flash point of possible conflict between Strathclyde Britains and Dalriadans. Agreeing with Skene's placement for a northern location, Tolstoy further notes that Glen Douglas "is overlooked by a mountain called Ben Arthur, and the British chief is also associated with the region at Arthur's Face in

Glenkinglas and Suidhe Artair at Dumbarton."[71] However, it must be said that any remembrances of Arthur in this region could as well commemorate Dalriadan Artúir mac Aedan as much as the British Arthur.

In terms of a likely place of enemy engagement, it would seem plausible for Linnius to be Lincolnshire, since that was a point of considerable Anglian settlement. We know that there was a later expansion from this region, since the Anglian king Ida established his kingdom of Bernicia or Northumbria from later in 547, and that Britons like Urien of Rheged with other British leaders besieged King Deodric of Bernecia on Metcaud (Lindisfarne) in the later sixth century, in an attempt to reduce the powerful hold of the Anglians. If Arthur's four engagements were fought about a river in Lincolnshire, then they may have been very difficult: the visibility of opponents in flat fen country leaves little option for surprise except in fog or by water. The use of cavalry in fen lands may have been impractical over shifting or marshy terrain, and this may have been a war where lightly armored men and surprise raids by low-lying coracles, or small boats, played a greater role. Settlement usually begins near a river, so Arthur may have launched a series of attacks upon early Anglian civilian settlements, making them think twice about remaining.

What proof do we have for Arthur's success in subduing his foes? Apart from the archaeological observation that the production of Saxon material culture in this period fell off, we can point to the dikes of Cambridgeshire, certainly built by the Angles to protect their settlements from attack from the West.[72] One of these, Fleam Dyke, derives from the Old English *fleminga-dic* or "dyke of the fugitives," perhaps suggesting that those who survived Badon might have sought the protection of the East Anglians.[73] The Byzantine historian Procopius wrote in the sixth century that many Angles had to migrate from Britain to Gaul in large numbers; from which we may infer that, just as many British had been forced to flee abroad in the mid-fifth century, so now the Angles sought better prospects elsewhere, away from the swingeing retaliations of Arthur.[74]

Battle 6: Bassas. "The sixth battle was by the river that is called Bassus." The name derives from the British *bas* or shallow. Tolstoy connects this unknown location with a Pictish raid by Caw of Prydain.[75] This tale is related in the eleventh-century *Vita Sancti Cadoci* (Life of Saint Cadog) when the saint goes to dig the foundations for a monastery at Cambuslang on what is now the outskirts of Glasgow. After digging up a monstrous collarbone, the ghost of the bone's owner appears to him, identifying himself as Caw. He tells the saint:

> Beyond Mount Bannawc where I once reigned for very many years, it happened that by devilish instinct, I arrived on these shores with troops of my raiders in order to pillage and lay them waste. But the true king who reigned at that time over this kingdom, pursued us with his army, and killed me and my host, when we had joined battle together. (our translation)

Mount Bannawc has been identified as a range of hills around Bannockburn, near Stirling, where there are two further Cambus names: Cambuskenneth and Cambusbarron. *Cambus* means "the crooked shallow" and could describe the bend of a fordable river or stream. A raid led from Stirling to Glasgow is strategically possible. We must also consider what Arthur was doing in this territory. We are told by many sources that he was the killer of Caw the Pict, so it may be that Arthur was on secondment to aid the British kingdoms of Strathclyde and Manau Gododdin.

Battle 7: Celidon. "The seventh battle was in the wood of Caledonia, that is Cat Coit Celidon." This battle is explicitly identifiable as taking place in the Caledonian Forest, which covered the south of Scotland, and although the battle site cannot be pinned down with any precision, it was certainly fought north of Hadrian's Wall and in the territory of the Picts. Tolstoy argues for a restitution of the northern British territories overrun by Picts as part of the outcome of this campaign, citing the northern extremity of the borders of Rheged as proof of this.[76]

Battle 8: Guinnion. "The eighth battle was in the fort of Guinnion." The fact that this battle is at a fort could mean a Roman fortification or a hill fort, and Vinovium or Binchester in County Durham has been suggested as a possibility.[77] Nearby is the River Glen, which flows by Yeavering Bell and was the home of British kings before the Northumbrian kings established themselves there. This battle is the one where Arthur "bears the image of the Virgin on his shoulder."[78]

Tolstoy is alone in suggesting that this might be located at Caerguidn near Sancreed in Cornwall, basing his argument on late folkloric evidence and on the tenth-century chronicle of Aethelweard, which has Cerdic sailing round the southwest coast past Land's End. Though not impossible, this is not well supported. There are traditions that connect Stow in Wedale with the location of Guinnion (see page 127). Again this puts Arthur in the region of the Gododdin or Bryneich where he might have been fending off either Pictish or Anglian enemies.

Battle 9: City of the Legions. "The ninth battle was fought in the City of the Legions." This title has given historians much to fight over, since the City of the Legions could refer to Caerleon (Chester) or to Caerleon on Usk or to a variety of Roman city garrisons. However, Nennius was quite familiar with both locations, since they are mentioned in his list of the twenty-eight cities of Britain, so it may be that he himself is unsure of the location and simply gives us the Latin *in urbe legionis,* meaning "a walled city of the legions." This description fits a few places where legions were garrisoned, including York and Exeter. We should also note that this and the tenth battle are the only ones named by Nennius in Welsh, suggesting that they were traditionally remembered by the British, though not known to Nennius himself. In selecting locations, we must consider exactly whom Arthur might be fighting.

Both Chester and Caerleon are on the western side of Britain, approachable by sea through estuaries, which might suggest an Irish attack; however, the kind of opportunistic Irish raids that affected the coast were more likely against undefended coastal settlements rather than walled cities; a concerted attack on a defensible fortress is the work of a more serious foe. Chester and Caerleon are too far west for a Saxon attack in this era and too far south for a Pictish assault. Tolstoy has suggested Isca Damnoniorum or Exeter, which the British knew as Cair wisc, arguing that the Battle of Llongborth, at which the hero Geraint died, might have been fought in Exmouth and have been a suitable location for the ninth battle.[79] This is possible, but we might also consider York, another "walled city of the legions," which lay in the path of expansionist Angles, or even Lincoln itself, a legionary fort, which was once home to the sixth and second legions, as well as being a *colonia* or legionary retirement city. Lincoln is strangely not mentioned in Nennius's list of cities, suggesting that, in his sources, it had already fallen under Anglian settlement and that he cannot with certainty identify which legionary city is intended.[80]

Battle 10: Tribruit. "He fought the tenth battle on the shores of the river called Tribruit." This British location appears in the Welsh poem "Pa Gur," which is a semimythological account of a defense of Edinburgh or an adventure in that region by Arthur and his men. In it we are told:

> By the hundred they fell. . . .
> Before Bedwyr the brave.
> On the shores of Tryfrwyd.*

The Traethev Trywruid, or "the shores of Tribruit," in this poem gives us pause. Many have looked for a river of this name, but perhaps they should be looking for a beach. *Traeth* means "the sands between the high and low tide marks" and is usually applied "to the sandbanks of a tidal estuary." Kenneth Jackson tells us that *tribruit* means "very pierced or broken," suggesting a rocky inlet.[81] Skene locates this battle along the banks of the Forth, Jackson on the Solway, while Tolstoy suggests Stert and Barrow Flats on the Parret Estuary, based solely on his location of the next battle at Brent Knoll in Somerset.[82] A location on

---

*Our translation.

the Forth would suggest Arthur fighting against Picts, perhaps as support for the Gododdin folk as the "Pa Gur" poem seems to imply (see chapter 4 for a further discussion of this).

Battle 11: Mount Agned. "The eleventh battle was made upon the mount that is called 'Agned.'" Andrew Breeze has suggested that Agned is a clerical mistranscription of *n* for *u*. The original word was *agued* (modern Welsh, *agwedd*), a word meaning "death, strait, or adversity." He locates Agned as Pennango, a hill in southern Scotland, near the junction of Teviot and Allan Water, which is remembered only in a fourteenth-century document.[83]

However, the Vatican Recension of the *Historia Brittonum* exchanges the battle of Agned for one fought "on the mountain called Breguoin where [the Saxons] were put to flight, which we call Cat Bregoin, or the Battle of Bregion in Welsh." A further recension glosses the Battle of Mount Agned "that is Cat Bregomion." It is clear that this battle has two titles: a Latin and a British one. In chapter 1 we noted as an important site for the Lucius Artorius Castus claimant, the Roman fort of Bremenium or High Rochester, which is north of Otterburn in Northumbria. This location has a number of possible hills and is strategically near the tenth battle, if we take the region of the Forth as a possibility, but it cannot be a doublet for Bregion or even Bregomion. Another suggestion is Branogenium, modern Leintwardine in Herefordshire, a site well within the range of Nennius's stamping ground in Ercing, though not so explicable as a place requiring defense from Saxons, since it is so far west. Tolstoy favors Brent Knoll solely on the literary evidence of Malory and medieval traditions that cite Agned as Castellum Puellarum, the Castle of Maidens near the Severn.[84] However, it must be added that the Castle of Maidens is also a title given to Din Eidyn (Edinburgh.)

Battle 12: Badon. "The twelfth battle was on Mount Badon." Badon is the only battle called an *obsessio* or siege: we are not told whether the Britons or the Saxons were the besieged or the besiegers, although it is often assumed that the Britons were the ones being attacked. Neither the *Anglo-Saxon Chronicle* nor Bede mentions what, for the Saxons, must have been a humiliating defeat. The *Annales Cambriae* merely calls it "the Battle of Badon." It also mentions a second Battle of Badon in circa 665: a battle for which there is no other independent source.[85]

For such a strategically important and resounding victory, Badon has not been located definitively, despite the many *bad*-sounding locations in Britain. Some, like Badbury Rings in Dorset, are unlikely candidates, being too far into British territory for a concerted Saxon attack. One of the most popular sites for Badon is Bath, the British city of Caer Baddon, surrounded, like Rome, by seven hills. One of these, Little Solsbury, overlooking the Avon, has also been suggested. It is steep and protected by the river on two sides, being vulnerable only to the north where it faces the city. Excavations prove it to have been heavily fortified and reoccupied in the fifth century, but it may just have acted as a small swift-response garrison with a lookout post. As a location for Saxon attack, Bath was very far into British territory in the early sixth century. It would have been extremely foolhardy for the Saxons to have penetrated this deeply, for their retreat and supply lines would have been easily compromised.

Another suggestion for Badon is Liddington Castle near Badbury in Wiltshire; this is a huge hill fort, which stands at the junction of three major roads from Winchester and Silchester as well as being approachable along the Ridgeway, the oldest road in Britain. This is a more likely location, for it borders the British territories, with Cirencester as the concentration point for the Britons, and gives access for Saxon retreat and supply along the Ridgeway.[86] The last suggested place is Great Bedwyn, also in Wiltshire. It is the highest point in the county and is capped by a hill fort now called Chisbury. It stands in a river valley at the extreme east of Savernake Forest and overlooks all approaches. Like Liddington, it stands in the British region, which was not yet occupied by Saxon expansionists who, only hundred and fifty years later, had gained Wiltshire, North Somerset, Gloucestershire, and the Thames Valley from Berkshire to Oxfordshire.[87]

Nennius's insistence that Arthur alone brought down 960 men may denote many things, the most unlikely being that he personally slew them all. Victories are accorded to the leader of the triumphant force, and so Arthur may well have been victor, possibly leading the charge. However, there is another possibility. The *Historia Brittonum* insists upon Arthur's victory in specific terms: *et nemo prostavit eos nisi ipse solus*—"and no one brought them low *save he alone*"—this may refute some other text or story that *someone else* had been the victor, such as Gildas's account, which accords the victory to Ambrosius.[88]

The peace that followed this battle, or at least the rout of the Saxons from the central and southern regions, may be inferred from the cessation of Saxon material culture in early mid-sixth century. This so-called pottery break indicates an interruption to Saxon settlement and may have been due to Arthur's victory.[89] This suggests that Arthur's Badonic victory was decisive in keeping the Saxons within agreed borders and might well have been a peace maintained by treaty and the exchange of hostages.

From the evidence of these battles, we can infer a number of things. They are often fought at rivers, which act as natural boundaries between Saxons, Picts, and Scots with the British. The battles are fought over a vast expanse of Britain but largely in the east and north where Anglian expansionism was threatening British rule. It is clear that the long-settled Saxon areas of the south and east are excluded from Arthur's campaign: they had been part of the struggle of a generation before Arthur. Whichever British leader it was who contained the Saxon expansionism of these southern settled territories, it was someone other than Arthur, especially if he was absent in the far north. The battle locations above the Wall suggest that Arthur was subduing Picts and/or Scots, just as the Romans and northern British kingdoms had done in previous centuries. As we have seen, the containment and defeat of the Picts required a commander of some forthright courage and wily strategy. No leader would wish a repeat of the barbarian conspiracy of 367 when Picts allied with Saxons and Scots:

such an alliance would have proven deadly to the British kingdoms. Arthur's campaigns may have been motivated by the need to drive a wedge between these enemies.

In summing up, we must consider the strategic motivations of Arthur. If we allow these battles to have been fought in this order, then in what sense can we understand his movements? Strikingly, Arthur does not give battle to the settled Saxons of the south coast where they had their greatest concentration. Perhaps they had been contained by dikes, had signed treaties, or were held at bay by sufficient British troops. If so doughty a fighter as Arthur was to be sent north, surely the south must have been left in the hands of another capable defender? Perhaps here we see revealed the roles of Ambrosius and Arthur. The aging Ambrosius might not enter the field of battle himself, but he could yet draw upon the strength and support of the southern British kingdoms to help defend the south. Arthur, as a younger commander with a mobile force, could fulfill Ambrosius's orders to secure areas of fresh encroachment from invaders, before going north to contain and divide Picts and Scots. Before he ventures north of the Wall, Arthur must be assured that the eastern coast is subdued so that his supply lines are not compromised. We would expect any commander worth his salt to first gather sufficient troops to slam into this region, which is exactly what Arthur does, with no less than five engagements in the Lincoln region.

Battles 6–11 are all fought farther north, some above Hadrian's Wall. The decision to go north is backed up by the eleventh-century tradition that states Arthur kills Caw of the Picts. The tradition recorded in the Triads, where Caw is one of his battalion commanders, may recall a failed Pictish alliance with the British kingdoms of Manau Gododdin and Strathclyde. Arthur might have had orders to give aid to the northern British kingdoms and perhaps also sought alliance with their commanders who were well used to enemy incursions from Picts. It would make sense if he was a northerner himself, better able to negotiate with the northern leaders, who might have looked askance at a southerner coming to embroil himself in their affairs; as a northerner he would both understand the terrain and its specific dangers. Having given battle and subdued these shared enemies, leaving securer borders behind him, Arthur then comes south to engage a new expansionist attack by the Saxons somewhere along the central southern border between Saxon and British territory, to give them a crashing defeat at Badon. This suggests that whoever commanded the south had died and that the most militarily able man must take up the defense of Britain. This reading follows the scant textual and historical evidence available, making Arthur the successor to Ambrosius.

Nennius records how, in the wake of Arthur's campaign, "when they were laid low in all the battles, they (the Saxons) sought for help from Germany, and greatly reinforced themselves without respite, and they brought kings from Germany to reign over them in Britain up to the time when Ida reigned, who was the son of Eobba. That one (Ida) was the first king in Beornica (Bernicia)"[90] (our translation).

Arthur's battles in the northeast speak of a significant expansion that he was seeking to block. We note that the Anglian king Ida of Northumbria established himself at Yeavering (British Gefrin) in circa 547, in the immediate decade after Arthur's passing. Ida's success in settling here in the area where Arthur fought a major part of his campaign bespeaks a power vacuum or cave-in or at least a compromise on the part of local British rulers.

We should see the Battle of Catraeth, as described in *Y Gododdin*, as part of the British struggle for the northeast. We saw earlier evidence for a relationship between British Gododdin and Anglian Bernicia from the fact that Uruei, the lord of Eidin, and one of the rulers of Manau Gododdin, had an Anglian father called Wolstan. This suggests that a dynastic marriage for the purpose of securing peaceful boundaries had taken place. But by the mid-sixth century, "Catraeth would have been in English hands for two generations before the battle."[91] This would mean that Arthur, in his campaign in Linnius, could well have been fighting on the borders of Deira south of the Tees and perhaps protecting the British Northumbrian kingdom of Bryneich north of the Tees before it eventually changed hands to become the Anglian kingdom of Bernicia. If his first battle brought him from the defense of Gefrin southward, it may be that we can see him as a man of the southern Votadini.

The poem "Kadeir Teyrnon" offers us a northern provenance for Arthur. Can this be borne out? Although it cannot be finally established, if Arthur's antecedents do lie with the folk of Manau Gododdin, then he would have had kin farther south in Gwynedd to back him. The descendants of Cunedda, the mercenary who helped expel the Irish from Dyfed, had settled in Gwynedd: they founded a kingdom that would assume a dominant part in the defense of Britain after Arthur's time. It is from Gwynedd that the red dragon standard derives, symbol of the indomitable British spirit, perhaps originally the *draco* borne before the Pendragons. The fact that nonallied Dalriadan Gaels of Argyll named their children so readily after Arthur may perhaps also support his true origins as a man of the north, a local man who came to national acclaim.

Although he came from humble or unremarked parentage, Arthur had the military background and experience to rise through the ranks to become supreme commander of the British. After his victory at Badon, there were no other honors left to claim. He had achieved the leadership of the British, becoming their *gwledig*. As supreme military commander, he could only now maintain his position and hope to deter younger, ambitious men from casting him down.

THE THIRTEENTH BATTLE

The Strife of Camlann

If Arthur is accorded twelve victorious battles, then what can be said of the thirteenth battle recorded in the *Historia Brittonum* and *Annales Cambriae,* in which he is said to have met his end? Anyone with a passing knowledge of the Arthurian legend knows of the battle in which Arthur fought his nemesis Mordred. But where is Camlann? The many *cam* names of Britain have furnished possible locations for "the last battle" from the northern Camboglanna, the Roman fortress of Birdoswald on Hadrian's Wall, right down to the southern Camelford

in Cornwall. The fort of Camboglanna is known to have been refortified during the early sixth century, when a large hall was built over one
of the ruined granaries. Along with Camelon on the Antonine Wall,
Camboglanna has also been instanced as a possible origin for Camelot.
However, Arthur's legendary placement at Camelot was the attribution
of the twelfth-century French poet Chrétien de Troyes. Gidlow has
argued that "Arthur's death at a Roman fort in the north is one of the
features which he had in common with Gwauthur of the *Gododdin*,"
whom we remember also died in a fort, though "he was no Arthur."
The River Camel running by the South Cadbury hill fort in Somerset
may also have given its name to the battle, and there is also a cluster
of Camlann names in Wales, by the River Dyfi, on the main route
between Gwynedd and Powys: "Above it is a second hillside Camlann
and tributary Afon Gamlan."[92]

In order to get a sense of which of these is most likely, we need
to consider the causes of the battle. If we are looking at a civil conflict rather than an enemy action, as implied by later accounts, then
the suggested locations above make more sense because, apart from
Camboglanna where Arthur could only have been fighting against
Dalriadans, Picts, or stray Friesians, the sites are all firmly situated
within British territory.

Set some twenty-one years after Badon, Camlann is of a different order to the preceding engagements: the extant sources and Welsh
poetic records show how shocking and memorable this battle was.
Could it have been so because it was a battle fought not against the
enemy but as part of a civil strife and a British betrayal? Traditions have
indicated this likelihood for several hundreds of years. Camlann does
not appear in the *Anglo-Saxon Chronicle*, nor in Bede, which has been
taken as evidence that Arthur did not exist. However, one good reason
why it may not appear in the English record is because it was an internecine strife fought among the Britons, and therefore something best
forgotten or remote from the Saxon wars.

In *Annales Cambriae*, three names are generally given for the word
battle: gueith, cat, and *bellum. Bellum* is the Latin and *cat* the British

word for battle. But *gueith* is British for strife, carrying the connotation of "struggle or toil." The earliest entry for Camlann calls it a *gueith,* perhaps denoting a civil conflict or particularly bloody engagement. There is evidence for this, outside the medieval literary stories. As late as 1777, in a life of the historical, long-lived Dark Age poet Llywarch Hen by Richard Thomas, the nature of the Battle of Camlann was well known: "Llywarch took no part in the civil war that brought on the catastrophe at Camlann, so fatal to the cause of the Britons; for he was then in his own principality of Argoed, in Cumberland."[93] Llywarch Hen, whose extant poems testify to his outliving his twenty-four sons, was believed to have enjoyed a near-fabulous lifespan, being associated with Arthur as well as with the seventh-century prince Cadwallawn ap Cadfan. Despite the lateness of this source, it is well attested that older traditions survived, often accidentally, for long periods after the fact.

What were the causes of Camlann? Twenty-one years of peace following Badon would have seen the return of many soldiers to their homes, giving them time to sire a new generation of children. Any internecine power struggles, perhaps set aside during war, could rise to the surface again during peacetime. With so little information other than the bare chronicle entry for Camlann to go on, we must here anticipate some of the mythic material of the next chapter in order to find clues because they will give us some inkling of what might lie at the root of civil strife.

Annales Cambriae merely gives us the entry that in "537: The Strife of Camlann, in which Arthur and Medrawd fell."[94] If this had been merely an enemy engagement, we would naturally assume that these two British commanders fell together in battle. Much turns upon the nature of Arthur and Medrawd's relationship. While it is difficult to set aside the medieval Arthurian story, with Arthur's nephew/son Mordred as the betraying culprit, it is actually only a later recension of the chronicle that speaks of Medrawd's betrayal of Arthur and of their slaying each other. Medrawd/Mordred has no relation to Arthur in the early sources but is remembered as the son of Llew ap Kynfarch, who later becomes King Loth of Lothian in the literary traditions. If an early tradition of his birth

could be established, this would make Medrawd hale from the Manau
Gododdin region, but we have no certain location for his provenance.

There are three Welsh Triads that speak of Medrawd: the fact
that they are late and may be influenced by the stories of Geoffrey of
Monmouth has to be borne in mind, yet they seem to point to an earlier tradition that Geoffrey sidesteps, suggesting an independent source.
Triad 54 speaks of three wasteful raids. The first is when Medrawd
descends upon Arthur's court at Celliwig in Cornwall: he seized all the
food and drink in the court, and dragged Arthur's wife Gwenhwyfar
from her chair and struck her. The second is a similar retaliatory raid
by Arthur upon the court of Medrawd. Could this be evidence of
Medrawd's first disaffection from Arthur?[95]

In Welsh the root of Medrawd's name is *medryd,* which means "to
be able or skillful," or *medru,* meaning "to strike," which implies a clever
person or one likely to lash out. That he is remembered in the Triads for
just this quality may be seen as suspicious: Has the myth attempted to
fit the deed to his name, in the manner of the characters of Sheridan's
Mrs. Malaprop or Shakespeare's Pistol? While Medrawd is said to
strike Gwenhwyfar, there is another triad about a further blow, which
is said to cause the Battle of Camlann. Triad 53 speaks of the blow
that Gwenhwyfach struck upon Gwenhwyfar.[96] *Culhwch and Olwen*
tells us that Gwenhwyfach was the sister of Gwenhwyfar, but this story
has not been transmitted fully to our time. Gildas writes of the tyrant
Cuneglassus and the rejection of his own wife in favor of her villainous widowed sister.[97] Perhaps Arthur had similar woman trouble, putting
aside one wife to marry her sister? Arthur's early reputation for having
married multiple Gwenhwyfars stretches from the Triads into medieval
literary tradition, where it appears as the literary device in the Vulgate of
Prose Lancelot Cycle as the story of "the false Guinevere," an enchanted
look-alike who leads Arthur astray. The existence of more than one
Guinevere is supported also in the disinterment of a body claimed to
be Arthur's at Glastonbury in the twelfth century: an accompanying
inscription stated that this was the grave of Arthur with his *second wife
Guinevere* (chapter 7). However, it should be noted that a variant version

of triad 53 gives *Medrawd* as the culprit who struck Gwenhwyfar. Under ancient British law, to strike the wife of a notable person was an insult to the husband, carrying a grievous *sarhad* or honor price.

As a literary character, Medrawd became fused with Melwas, the ruler of Somerset who was the abductor of Gwenhwyfar in the *Life of Gildas* by Caradoc of Llancarfan (see chapter 5). We see that in the early medieval stories, such as Geoffrey, Wace, and Layamon, Mordred becomes Arthur's nephew, taking his uncle's wife, Guinevere, as his own and establishing his kingship in Arthur's absence, ruling by right of his wife in an almost Pictish fashion. It is not until after the introduction of the Lancelot stories by Chrétien de Troyes in the thirteenth century that Mordred becomes Arthur's son, his earlier role subsumed by the French knight. This transposition is important, for it tells us that the role of Mordred in the earlier stories may be as a lover or abductor of Gwenhwyfar/Guinevere, a role taken up by Lancelot in the later stories. Somewhere within this theme of stolen wives and usurped thrones, Medrawd has a role to play, though it is certainly not as Arthur's son, as the medieval writers made him, attempting to wrestle with his motivations. In Norman terms, primogeniture, even of a bastard, made sense of Modred's claim; without the ancient kingship models of the Picts in mind, they could make less sense of Arthur's nephew making an attempt on the throne.

Setting aside any possible amatory causes, there may be other political reasons for the battle. We stated above that there are no battle dispositions for any of Arthur's battles; however, there is one exception in the case of Camlann, from a later source. Triad 59 speaks of the three unfortunate counsels of Britain, leading to battles of great futility, of which Camlann is the chief.[98] This was caused by "the threefold division of troops by Arthur with Medraut at Camlann." Arthur's division of his forces into three companies seems to imply the standard battle arrangement of a central body of men with two mobile wings, each at the command of a different captain. Somewhere in this division of troops lay disaffection, willful misunderstanding, or veiled betrayal. The later material of the Middle Ages gives us a possible story of a misunderstood signal as Arthur and Mordred face up against each other in parley: an adder stirs in the grass, scaring a horse, while its rider draws his sword to sever the snake, the opposing side takes this as a breaking of truce and conflict ensues. But the phrasing of the triad above suggests not a meeting of opponents but the members of a single host, perhaps with an undisclosed antipathy between them. The two other incidents of bad advice in this triad each concern allowing foreigners into the land, so perhaps the threefold division of troops between Medrawd and Arthur suggests a placement of foreign mercenaries or of men of uncertain loyalty among the army.

The final breakdown of accord between Arthur and Medrawd at Camlann is explained within the early thirteenth-century Welsh story "The Dream of Rhonabwy" as being caused by Iddawc, the Churn of Britain, a herald whose careless words agitate gossip and create dissention in the ranks. Iddawc says that he was one of the messengers between Arthur and Medrawd, his nephew, at the Battle of Camlann; through his youth and desire for battle, Iddawc: "Kindled strife between them and stirred up wrath, when I was sent by Arthur the Emperor to reason with Medrawd, and to show him, that he was his foster-father and uncle, and to seek for peace, lest the sons of the Kings of the Island of Britain . . . should be slain. And whereas Arthur charged me with the fairest saying he could think of, I uttered unto Medrawd the harshest I could devise."[99]

This suggests that Iddawc's intervention brought cessation to a truce or parley. Even though the original source of the story is lost, it may recall an actual event, since the cause of Camlann was independently remembered by the Welsh.

There is another theory proposed by Nikolai Tolstoy that also gives us a valid reason for the enmity between Arthur and Medrawd, as well as the cause of the raids and insults. In Tolstoy's argument connecting the death of Caw the Pict at the hands of Arthur with the sixth battle of Bassus, he proposes that this may have started a blood feud between members of Caw's family and Arthur's.[100] That there is enmity between them is evident, for there are several instances in early British tradition where Arthur fights, maims, tricks, and eventually kills Caw's son, Hueil. But there is a further twist: in the twelfth-century Welsh *Bonedd y Saint* (Descent of the Saints), we hear of Cwyllog, daughter of Caw. Later tradition makes Cwyllog not only the sister of Gildas ap Caw *but the wife of Medrawd!* The consequences of this relationship for the state of Britain become immediately apparent: "as son-in-law of Caw, Medrawd also inherited the blood-feud, and finally avenged his father-in-law."[101] The evidence upon which this marriage rests is slender, for it comes only in *Celtic Remains,* a work by the seventeenth-century poet Henry Vaughan, who nonetheless was a Welsh speaker and may have had access to records now lost to us. If we were to follow this line, there are further dynastic consequences for the role of Medrawd in the downfall of Arthur.

The Pictish succession always ran through the female line so that the daughter of a king was the woman whose husband and sons were qualified to reign. All of Caw's twenty-four sons were killed, except Gildas, we hear in the *Vita Gildae* (Life of Gildas) by Caradoc of Llancarfan (ca. 1120–1130). *If Cwyllog was Caw's oldest remaining daughter, then Medrawd, as her husband, would have been ipso facto a king among the Picts.* This seductive theory gives us a plausible motivation for Medrawd to change sides and fight against Arthur with the help of his in-law Picts and with Saxon allies to back up his claim.

If Arthur killed Caw during one of his northern battles against the Picts, and if Medrawd, as one of his British allies, were married to Caw's daughter, then the defender of Britain might indeed have had a potentially difficult situation on his hands. Blood feuds could pass down through generations, which is why Celtic laws gave specific fine payments or "honor prices" for different categories of people who might be injured or killed, in order to avoid the perpetuation of tribal strife. If both Arthur and Medrawd were of northern lineage, there may also have been an incipient power struggle between them. If this were the spark that kindled the conflict, then it would seem that Camlann was a battle fought as a result of civil war. Internal political tensions must have also played in the background to any such personal enmity: factors that we cannot now confidently reconstruct.

Whatever its cause, Camlann's outcome left Britain in a dangerously divided condition, with not only the loss of many of its finest warriors in battle but also a visitation of yellow plague that struck Britain in the same year. If Camlann was indeed fought at Camboglanna, then Avalon was not far distant, in the presence of the fort of Aballava or Burgh by Sands in Cumbria, just a few miles west down Hadrian's Wall, which may have been where Arthur's body was taken, helping to create an ever-living legend. Or Camlann may have been fought else-where, somewhere in Wales or Cornwall. We shall never know perhaps.

It is the fate of Arthur to have no grave. As the medieval Welsh "Stanzas on the Graves" tells us, though there are graves for many heroes including,

> *the grave of March, the grave of Gwythur,*
> *the grave of Gwgan of the Red-Sword,*
> *it is hard for the world to ponder a grave for Arthur.**

A short-lived British resistance followed Arthur's passing. A mere hundred years later, more territory was in English hands than British ones. But Arthur left behind him the memory of a series of campaigns that had delayed the Saxon advance and maintained ancient alliances with the British kingdoms of the north. After the battle of Chester in 613, this connection was severed, leaving the British kingdoms of Wales and Cornwall isolated from their northern kinsmen, who continued to bear the brunt of the English offensive throughout the following century until their names fell into forgetfulness. The impetus of their struggle is remembered through the deeds and person of Arthur who, in the chapters of legend, bears forward the standard of British resistance. Although he would be memorialized in ways that had little to do with his origins, Arthur is remembered today in a way that heroic British leaders like Urien of Rheged and Cadwallawn ap Cadfan are not.

Arthur's transformation into a heroic medieval king was through a process of mythmaking that began within a few years of his passing. The British battle leader of history was to become a mythic chieftain, riding through time at the head of a war band of unconquerable heroes.

---

*Our translation.

4

Arthur of Myth

Granter of Quests

On the one hand we have the man Arthur . . . on the other
a greater Arthur, a more colossal figure, in which we have,
so to speak, but a torso *rescued from the wreck of the Celtic*
pantheon.

SIR JOHN RHYS,
ARTHURIAN LEGEND (1891)

THE MYTHIC AND BARDIC TRADITIONS

As the days of his military glory receded, the figure of Arthur gradually passed from history into myth. In the stories, poems, and legends that cluster about the formation of the mythic Arthur, mostly gathered up in medieval Wales, one location is continuously mentioned: the realm of Oeth and Anoeth—a place echoed so often by later Welsh storytellers that in the end no one knew its significance or location. It literally means the place of "Wonders and Even Greater Wonders." In *Culhwch and Olwen,* explored below, Arthur's porter, Glewlwyd the Gatekeeper, speaks of the places he and Arthur have been together:

I have been in Caer Se and Asse,
in Sach and Salach, in Lotor and Fotor;
and I have been in India the Great and India the Less;
and I was in the battle of Dau Ynyr when twelve
     hostages were brought
from Llychlyn. (Scandinavia)
And I have been in Europe and in Africa and in the
     islands of Corsica,
And in Caer Brythwch, Brythach and Ferthnach;
And I was present when you once slew the family of Clis
     son of Merin,
And Mil Du, son of Ducum, and when you conquered
     Greece in the East.
And I have been in Caer Oeth and Anoeth, and in
     *Caer Nefenhyr of the nine streams.**

We immediately know here that we have made the passage from history into mythology, for this is a list of fabulous deeds and places, revealing that Arthur's military expansion has either reached megalomaniac proportions or has entered poetic hyperbole. Marged Haycock has suggested that this list of supposed conquests is modeled closely upon a poem from the *Book of Taliesin* dealing with the conquests of Alexander the Great.[1] Certainly Arthur has passed from being a leader of battles into a lord of wonders. Caer Oeth and Anoeth, like "the land of Nod" or some other fantastic location, appears as the otherworldly venue in a story that paves the way for Arthur to become a mythic and folkloric granter of boons and quests.

How did Arthur of the Battles become Arthur of the Quests? Some part of this formation is due to the historical isolation of Wales and the growing strength of the kingdoms of the English. By the early seventh century, the British kingdoms in Cornwall, Wales, and Scotland were completely separated, not only from participation in the English

---

*Our translation.

kingdoms, but from each other. Even the northern alliance between British Strathclyde and Gaelic Dalriada broke down in the wake of the Battle of Chester in 613, which also effectively cut off the northern kingdoms from Wales, despite a brief British alliance with pagan English king Penda of Mercia in 655. The Old North of Y Gogledd and Wales drifted apart, leaving behind a miasmic memory of ancient kinship traditions. It was clear that the old heady days of military glory and smashing Badonic victory were over. The stories about Arthur now show him coalescing into a Welsh prince with his court, before he becomes a Welsh savior in works like the ninth- to tenth-century Welsh prophetic poem "Armes Prydain," or an emperor of the golden age in the Middle Ages, and everywhere else into the heroic genius loci of Britain.[2]

Such became the centrifugal power of the Arthur myth that many historical characters from the Dark Ages were drawn into its engine: rulers like Urien and his son Owain of Rheged and March of Cornwall become Arthur's contemporaries, as do poets like Taliesin and Myrddyn (Merlin), all of whom date from later times. The lode-bearing core of the oral Arthurian tradition resided in the late sixth-century north but was borne forward and nurtured by Welsh poets who often recited their verse as if it had come from the mouths of Merlin or Taliesin to give it a fully heroic resonance.

This mythic material arrived by a different route than that of the semihistorical chronicle sources recorded by clerics and churchmen. The Welsh myths and stories arise from a secular and British-speaking class of storytellers who have no overtly Christian ax to grind. Their stories are not yet the literary masterpieces of the twelfth-century French Chrétien de Troyes nor of the fifteenth-century Sir Thomas Malory; rather, they are for recitation aloud to a live audience, as we can tell if we look at the internal state of texts like *Culhwch and Olwen,* which, though they are written down in early medieval times, still reveal the ancient oral underpinning of a storyteller's "runs"—florid passages where the fluidity of speech and high-wrought formality of image stand out as clearly as a musical cadenza in a concerto.

Gildas spoke slightingly of rulers who, in characteristic Celtic fashion, loved to hear their deeds recited by the household bard. The evident antipathy between clerics like Gildas and the only other comparably educated elite in British society, the bardic community, is evident in *De Excidio Britonum* where he speaks about the poets at the court of Maelgwn Gwynedd who have "mouths stuffed with lies and liable to bedew bystanders with their foaming phlegm."[3] Born out of an oral tradition that set nothing in writing until after the Christian era, poets maintained the living memory of the people, reciting ancient traditions, using themes of battles, heroes, and ancestors for their verse.

Realistically, the best poets made a living from the patronage of noblemen, while the lesser ones made their poetic circuit receiving payment and board wherever they went, but the value of a poet was no small thing for, as *Y Gododdin* tells us: "the bards of the world assess the men of valour" and gave fame to those who were worthy of their remembrance. Yet it is these very poets and their cousins, the *cyfarwyddion,* the storytellers, who bore the oral legend of Arthur forward until its transcription in the early Middle Ages and so down to our own times. Today, the Arthurian corpus of myth is a true survivor of bardic memory, while few now read the disgusted blandishments of Gildas.

One poet who became deeply associated with the mythic Arthur is the late sixth-century poet Taliesin, known to have been the bard to both Urien and his son Owain of Rheged, since many extant poems give eulogies and death songs to his patrons. Both Taliesin and Aneirin, the author of the *Y Gododdin,* were contemporaries; they were the *cynfeirdd*—the "first or earliest poets" of the rapidly contracting kingdoms of Britain that became concentrated into Wales and Cumbria during the late sixth century, in the generations after Arthur's passing. Their contribution to the Arthurian story is not inconsiderable.

If we look at the internal evidences of the poems ascribed to Taliesin, his career would seem to be a long one; for he is said to have been on the ship that brought back the head of the legendary British chieftain, Bran the Blessed—a story set before the Roman conquest—as well as being the chief poet of Arthur! Scholars for whom myth represents some kind of illusion or untruth often scorn such stories as "mere fable," but the truth lies in the nature of the bardic tradition and the way in which ancient traditions were always felt to be vibrantly dynamic. It is an understanding that will help us enter the stream of myth in a more respectful way.

A clue to this lies in *Y Gododdin* where the reciter of the epic says of himself "it is I, yet not I, Aneirin."[4] Yet the poem clearly tells us elsewhere that Aneirin was killed, so how can he recite or remember his poem if he is dead? In the bardic tradition of the Celtic peoples, whoever recited an old poem embodied or invoked the undying soul of its composer, so that, through the cynosure of the poetic vision, the living poet was able to be at one with a dead one. In this context of poetic embodiment, which was almost certainly a feature of actual performance, the next phrase is interesting, for the poet says, "Taliesin of skillful song knows it." Taliesin is invoked here as a witness because he was known by British bards to have been omnisciently present at events throughout the whole of time. In the many extant poems attributed to Taliesin, he frequently gives us instances of his poetic omniscience in poems that begin "I have been" or "I am" and lists people, objects, and landscape features from times and places far distant. This poetic omniscience and embodiment of knowledge dates back to a pre-Christian era in which bards were not mere versifiers, who sang for their keep or for gold and cattle, but poets who had the magical and shapeshifting skills of Druids.[5] Through their poetic vision, they enabled others to "be present at" events long distant in time and place. This is still a major role of performers today. As the preeminent poet of the Old North, who else but Taliesin could be worthy of becoming "Arthur's bard"?

Arthur is remembered several times in the *Trioedd Ynys Prydein* (The Triads of the Island of Britain), transcribed in the early fourteenth century from earlier oral traditions.[6] These terse triadic story lists were useful bardic memory triggers, being encapsulations of much longer stories or traditions, recalling notable events under a single heading, like "the three great enchantments upon the Island of Britain." Unfortunately, many of these references are to stories that have been subsequently lost. The figure of Arthur revealed in the Triads is at odds with the medieval idea, associating him with mythic roles that may stretch back to primordial traditions. They give us intriguing and illusive snapshots of a mythic Arthur who may actually predate the sixth-century war leader. Here, Arthur is revealed as a generous prince, an amateur bard, a bloodthirsty raider, a pig sticker, a palladium of Britain, a betrayed ruler, a prisoner, a retaliatory husband and unfaithful consort, an inept strategist, a bountiful provider, and a mythic guardian. Yet he also appears as a foremost kingly personality, the most worthy model for other great rulers. We have already noted some of these triads as markers along the route by which the faces of Arthur began to coalesce.

HUNTING THE BOAR

The early mythic Welsh material involves Arthur in adventures in which he overcomes monsters, giants, and supernatural assailants as well as initiating quests for fabulous objects that will bring honor to Britain. He does so with the help of his men, a collection of warriors of every stripe and nation, who rally behind him. Here is no round table nor chivalric society, but rather a hall of semicivilized ruffians and their boorishly heroic leader who is more of a raider than a king.

The hunting of the pig Troit was one of Arthur's greatest adventures. The earliest mention of it occurs in Nennius's ninth-century *Historia Brittonum,* in which a list of places associated with wondrous tales includes a rock on a mountaintop that bears a memorial of the time when Arthur chased the monstrous boar Troit.[7] Arthur's dog, strangely called Cafall or Cabal—which is the British word for horse—leaves his footprint upon Carn Cabal, identified as the present-day Carngafallt, a hill near Rhaeadr where three prehistoric cairns are situated.

The principal source for the story, however, is *Culhwch and Olwen,* a catalog of much earlier stories in which heroes, folk stories, and events from many mythic strata have been woven together.[8] The Arthurian parts of the stories are interwoven with a foundation folk-story theme in which a young hero attempts to win a giant's daughter. This ramshackle mix of heroic saga, bucolic romp, and seemingly hopeless love story suggests a series of independent tales told by professional storytellers that have been woven together in a narrative sequence by someone who is partially at odds with his own native lore—an anonymous narrator for whom the material is quaintly antique and with which he can take liberties. His hearers would have had at least a partial knowledge of the stories he sends up, and because this crowd-pleasing combination is recorded in Welsh, we know that it must have been for a British rather than a Norman audience.

The story begins with Arthur's nephew, Culhwch ap Cilydd, falling in love with Olwen, the daughter of the giant Yspaddaden. Not knowing how to win her, the youth goes to the court of his powerful cousin Arthur in order to ask for help. Arthur welcomes him and cuts Culhwch's boyhood locks to signify that he is now a man among men. In the manner of all good stories, Arthur carefully offers to grant Culhwch his boon: "I will grant whatever your tongue may name, as far as wind dries, rain wets, sun revolves and sea encircles and earth extends," reserving only seven of his own possessions, including Prydwen his ship, his mantle, his sword Caledfwlch (Battle-breacher), his lance Rhongomyant (Killer Spear), his shield Wynebgwrthcher (Night Gainsayer), his dagger Carnwenhau (White-Haft)—and, of course, his wife, Gwenhwyfar.

Culhwch requests his boon that Olwen be obtained for him by invoking the names of every person at Arthur's court—a formidable list that includes individuals mythical, historical, and anachronistic, such as the very Gwauthur with whom Arthur is compared in *Y Gododdin,* and Gildas himself, not to mention William the Conqueror and Arthur's traditional enemy, Octha of Kent, son of Aesc, who appears as Osla Big Knife—for not even the Saxons are excepted from the myth. Osla Big Knife is a handy fellow to have around because, whenever Arthur and his hosts come to an unfordable river, they merely lay Osla's knife across the water to form a serviceable bridge.

After a year's search, Culhwch arrives at the giant's house with Cei and Bedwyr, demanding to pay court to Olwen. In order to stall proceedings, Yspaddaden sets Culhwch a list of thirty-nine formidable tasks that will prepare for the wedding. These range in difficulty from the clearing of a wood and the ploughing and sowing of the land with wheat in a single day, to the task of obtaining the otherworldly birds of Rhiannon who can wake the dead and soothe the sorrows of the living. Only a third of the named tasks are recounted in the ensuing story. These tasks are called *anoethu,* meaning "very great wonders" or, from a more realistic perspective, what we would call impossibilities. Some of the tasks are doubled—two giants to overcome and two boars—suggesting that in the compilation of the story, the narrator felt obliged to include variant traditions.

These *anoethu* cannot be accomplished without the help of "the best men in the world," as Arthur calls his followers in the poem "Pa Gur." The function of Arthur's men in this story can be identified with a folk-story motif known as "Six Go Through the World," a theme in which a young hero gathers to him men of extraordinary talents to help him achieve impossible quests. They are here in abundance, from Clust ap Clustfeinad (Ear, son of Hearing), who could hear an ant fifty miles away, to the druidic Menw ap Teirgweith (Little One of the Three Shouts), the maker of illusions.

Among their number are men we will know better from medieval legend: Cei mab Kenyr, literally Path, Son of Way, the longest-lived follower of Arthur's career. As the man who can breathe under water for nine nights and days and go for the same period without sleep, become as tall as the highest tree, or keep any object he holds dry because of his hot nature, he is scarcely identifiable as the medieval Sir Kay he will become.[9] He is continually accompanied by Bedwyr, the one-handed warrior, whose spear returns to him upon the wind and which produces wounds so deep that they do the equivalent damage of nine ordinary spears; he will turn into Sir Bedevere in later legend.

In addition to these men, there are deeply mythical characters of greater antiquity such as Manawyddan ap Llyr, who is cognate with

Manannan mac Llyr, the Irish god of the sea and the otherworld. Then there is Mabon map Modron, who is none other than Maponus, the British Apollo, and Llwch, who is probably the trans-Celtic god Lugh.

The major task incumbent upon Culhwch is the catching of Twrch Trwyth, who is not just any common boar but an enchanted human being called King Tared, who has been turned into a boar because of his sins. He tears across the countryside, causing great devastation and terror. Between his hairy boar's ears are the emblems by which Yspaddaden's power will be toppled: the shears, comb, and razor that will barber him ready for the wedding. These objects and the boar who carries them seem to function as the exterior soul of the giant, who is otherwise invulnerable.[10] When these objects are discovered, the giant will fall. The spell upon King Tared may be in accordance with the nature of his sin, for Twrch Trwyth seems to partake of both sexes; despite being a boar, he is strangely accompanied by piglets, which normally follow the sow not the boar!

One by one, all the tasks are accomplished, including the theft of a certain cauldron from Ireland, which we will explore further (see pp. 158–70). The boar's piglets are killed, and Arthur, who apart from sanctioning the help of his men has played little part of the action, steps into the fray. His men continually urge him to stay home and let them take care of things, so that we see the very earliest hint of the *roi fainént* or the "do-nothing king" of later medieval legend. In one of the final tasks, Arthur wades in to kill Orddu (Very Black Witch) whose blood is needed to condition the tangles in the giant's hair and bring them to straightness. Even though his men feel that grappling with a hag is beneath him, Arthur casts his knife and cleaves her in two while Caw collects her blood.

The boar is finally neither killed nor overcome, although Kyledyr the Wild and Mabon son of Modron snatch the shears and razor from between his ears before Twrch dives into the sea. The comb is also gained with much trouble, although we are not told by whom. With all the tasks fullfiled, Yspaddaden is roughly barbered by Caw the Pict, having his beard, his hair, and the scalp beneath it ripped off, before Goreu ap Custennin beheads him. Finally Culhwch marries Olwen, providing her with a colorful wedding party and an extraordinary dowry of fabulous objects.

The underpinning theme of this compendium of stories concerns the rise of youth and the fall of age, which is symbolized by the gaining of the shears, razor, and comb that are between the ears of Twrch Trwyth. These items are essential for the barbering of Yspaddaden, which signals his downfall: this is balanced, at the beginning of the story, by the hair cutting of Culhwch by Arthur in an act that signals the initiation of the youth into manhood, just as the cutting off of the giant's beard causes the downfall of the strong and mature.

In British magical lore, the comb, scissors, and razor are not merely symbols of hairdressing but emblems of sacred cleansing: the razor or scissors cut away what is no longer needed, while the comb combs away any intrusions. They are the tools of spellcraft and magical protection in folk tradition. When they are in the hands of a woman, the knife or scissors and comb are joined by the mirror by which evil spells or fairy darts are sent back to the sender, in the manner of the spear that Culhwch casts back at Yspaddaden during their first interview. Between the youthful Culhwch and the aged giant Yspaddaden, Arthur maintains his role as the mature man whose order and authority overcome the chaotic ravaging boar and the inflexible giant with the help of his men.

If we set aside the love quest of Culhwch for Olwen, this text can be seen as a tapestry of many stories in which every hero and god is invoked to put down the forces that menace the land. The early Welsh legends frequently focus upon *gormesiaid* or enchantments of astonishing severity that constitute national afflictions: these manifest as transmogrified monsters, symbolizing power that is completely out of control. It is not hard to see in Twrch Trwyth's mad career across the land the upheaval and destruction wrought by the Saxons from "sea to sea," as Gildas puts it. Even the meaning of his name—"the turning boar" or "the boar who urinates"—hints at his territory-defining rampage through Britain. The chaos caused by the boar's career in *Culhwch and Olwen* ceases when Twrch Trwyth seeks the depths of the sea as he is driven from the land.

From Geoffrey of Monmouth's later twelfth-century *Historia*

Regum Britanniae onward, Arthur is known as the Boar of Cornwall, which is how he is identified in the *Prophecies of Merlin*, but his association with matters porcine is clearly a much earlier one. The act of possession or chasing of a pig seems to be anciently connected with the sovereignty of the land in Celtic legend, where pigs are frequently part of kingly or royal foundation stories.[11] Twrch's own name gives us a clue to this. In the eleventh-century Irish glossary of archaic words, *Cormac's Glossary,* the word *torc* is given as not only the term for a young pig but also for a young prince.[12] In our coming-of-age story, Culhwch's name actually means "pig-sty" because his mad pregnant mother gave birth to him in one. This seems like a not-too-subtle bardic joke. The young porker grows up to chase pigs, while his uncle gets to wrestle with a witch to render her blood into a giant's conditioning lotion! *Culhwch and Olwen* is full of such risible, pastiche elements that would have played to a Welsh audience in much the same way that such modern comic retellings as the film *Monty Python and the Holy Grail* still do.

Arthur is depicted here as a hunter and granter of quests, in a story that links back to what Nennius knew of him and his wonders.[13] Arthur is in good company within this story, which features none other than Gwyn ap Nudd, the Lord of the Wild Hunt himself, a specter who runs with his hounds on dark nights, as the leader of a retributive hunt. Gwyn and his rival Gwythyr ap Greidawl perpetually fight over a lovely woman, Creiddylad, in an episode that gives us our first view of Arthur as judge, especially of love affairs. In order to quell the riot that this squabble causes, he judges that Creiddylad must stay in her father's house and that the rival claimants must fight for her every May Day until doomsday and whoever should be victorious would have her. This is an episode that has a bearing on the whole of the Arthurian legend hereafter, as we shall discover.

One further incident from *Culhwch and Olwen* deserves deeper study because it has a bearing on the subsequent involvement of Arthur with the Grail quest, which remains one of the most significant developments of the Arthurian legend, weaving it inextricably with the spiritual aspirations of Christendom. However, it is perhaps best to set aside such considerations as we approach the Welsh underworld in a raid that, though mysterious, has nothing whatever to do with Christianity.

HARROWING THE UNDERWORLD

In *Culhwch and Olwen,* one of the *anoethu* is to fetch from Ireland the cauldron of Diwrnach the Irishman in order to cook the wedding dinner. We are told no more about this vessel, but Arthur enters his ship with a small retinue and sails to Ireland in order to ask for it. Diwrnach refuses to give up the cauldron, but Bedwyr snatches it and puts it onto the back of Hygwyd, Arthur's ceremonial cauldron bearer. An Irishman called Llenlleawg seizes Arthur's sword Caledfwlch and brandishes it. Diwrnach is slain, and the British return home with the cauldron "full of Irish money." Arthur then summons the warriors from the three islands of Britain and also from France, Armorica, Normandy, and the Summer Country to make a further assault on Ireland. Then, restrained from violence upon the Irish by the prayers of saints and appeased by gifts of provisions, Arthur goes as far as Esgeir Oerfel (Seicenn Uairbeoil in Leinster) where he sets upon the boar and its seven piglets. The Irish fight against him, until Twrch lays waste a fifth part of Ireland. The next day, the hosts of Arthur fight with the boar. On the third day Arthur himself fights with the boar for nine nights and nine days, without having killed even one piglet.

The raid is a late remnant of an earlier myth, of which it is clearly a remembrance: its origin is found in the poem known as the "Preiddeu Annwyfn" (The Raid on Annwyfn), which appears in the twelfth-century *Book of Taliesin* but can be demonstrably shown to date from the ninth century. It is certainly a more archaic retelling of the incident above from *Culhwch and Olwen.*[14] Annwfn (modern Welsh Annwn) is the non-world or the realm beneath Earth. The British did not see it as analogous to the Christian hell or the classical Hades, but as a mysterious region from which come pigs, cauldrons, giants, undying warriors, and ancestral beings. As in many of the cauldron myths, which mutated and grew into the later Grail legends, the otherworldly

Annwfn is a womb from which many wonders are birthed, but it is not an adventure for the fainthearted.

> *Predestined was Gweir's captivity in Caer Sidi,*
> *According to the tale of Pwyll and Pryderi.*
> *None before him was sent into it,*
> *Into the heavy blue chain which bound the youth.*
> *From before the reeving of Annwfyn he has groaned,*
> *Until the ending of the world this prayer of poets:*
> *Three shipburdens of Prydwen entered the Spiral City*
> *Except seven, none returned from Caer Sidi.*
>
> *Is not my song worthy to be heard*
> *In the foursquare Caer, four times revolving!*
> *I draw my knowledge from the famous cauldron,*
> *The breath of nine maidens keeps it boiling.*
> *Is not the Head of Annwfyn's cauldron so shaped:*
> *Ridged with enamel, rimmed with pearl?*
> *It will not boil the cowardly traitor's portion.*
> *The sword of Lleawc flashed before it*
> *And in the hand of Lleminawc was it wielded.*
> *Before hell's gate the lights were lifted*
> *When with Arthur we went to the harrowing.*
> *Except seven none returned from Caer Feddwit.*
>
> *Is not my song fit recital for kings*
> *In the four-square Caer, in the Island of the Strong Door,*
> *Where noon and night make half-light,*
> *Where bright wine is brought before the host?*
> *Three shipburdens of Prydwen took to sea:*
> *Except seven none returned from Caer Rigor.*
>
> *I sing not for those exiled of tradition*
> *Who beyond Caer Wydyr saw not Arthur's valour?*

Three score centuries stood upon the wall,
Hard it was to parley with their sentinel.
Three shipburdens of Prydwen we went with Arthur:
Except seven none returned from Caer Goludd.

I sing not for those whose shield-arms droop,
Who know not day nor hour nor causation
Nor when the glorious Son of Light is born,
Nor who prevents his journey to Dol Defwy.
They know not whose the brindled, harnessed ox
With seven score links upon his collar.
When we went with Arthur on difficult errand;
Except seven none returned from Caer Fandwy.

I sing not for those not of our company,
Who know not on what day the chief was born,
Who do not know the hour of his kingship,
Nor of the silver-headed beast they guard for him.
When we went with Arthur of mournful mien:
Except seven, none returned from Caer Ochren.[15]

The "Preiddeu Annwyfn" poem presents a descent into the underworld, a region guarded by eight *caers* or towers:

Caer Sidi	Revolving Tower
Caer Feddwit	Tower of Mead
Caer Pedryfan	Four-Cornered Tower
Caer Rigor	Indomitable Tower
Caer Wydyr	Glass Tower
Caer Goludd	Tower of Riches
Caer Fandwy	Tower of the High One
Caer Ochren	Tower of Keys

Some of these otherworldly regions are known to us from else-where in Welsh legend: Caer Sidi appears in the *Mabinogi* as the abode of Arianrhod, mother of the hero Llew Llaw Gyffes, as well as in the poetry of Taliesin as the place of his own poetic initiation.[16] Revolving towers whose doorways are hidden until the right person approaches them are common in Celtic tradition. Caer Wydyr must have been a well-known location, for it appears in the *Historia Brittonum* in Nennius's description of the coming of Mil the Spaniard and his com-pany to Ireland: "they saw a glass tower in the middle of the sea, and saw men upon the tower, but though they sought to speak with them, they never responded."[17] This same description is also found in *The Voyage of Maelduin,* an Irish story that tells of a voyage to many otherworldly islands. Maelduin and his companions encounter a crystal tower rising from the sea, as well as an island surrounded by a revolving wall whose inhabitants are hard to speak to. There is clearly a common source to these traditions, since stanza five of the "Preiddeu Annwyfn" tells us:

> *Who beyond Caer Wydyr saw not Arthur's valour?*
> *Three score centuries stood upon the wall,*
> *Hard it was to parley with their sentinel.**

This is a clear sign that Arthur's voyage is not merely to Ireland, but to a region of the Celtic otherworld; later legend accords him another such island sojourn in Avalon, from whose confines he is still expected to return.

The mystery of this poem concerns not only the cauldron, which Arthur goes to fetch, but gives us a hint that others have made this attempt and have become famous prisoners. The captivity of Gweir in stanza one may simply be a further reference to the Glass Tower, for it is also the name for Lundy Island, which lies thirty miles from the north Devon coast into the Bristol Channel, and which in Welsh is called Ynys (G)Wair. Lundy, like Grassholm and Bardsey Island off the western coast of Wales, shares otherworldly associations with the

---

*Our translation.

Islands of the Blest. But Gweir is also the mythic name of a primordial prisoner who reappears throughout Welsh legend in the guise of many heroes, including Pryderi, Goreu, and, most notably, Mabon son of Modron, the being that Culhwch and companions must seek before Twrch Trwyth's barbering objects can be won. Mabon has been lost since before human memory can recall, and only the chain of memory formed by the recall of the Oldest Animals can help discover his prison. The youth that was "taken from between his mother and the wall" when he was only three nights old is liberated as a radiant youth whose hunting skills are unparalleled. In this poem Arthur aligns himself with this long chain of heroes who vanish into the otherworld until they are called forth again or liberated. This primordial mythic sequestration found its way into the Arthurian legend to create the powerful myth of Arthur's return, as we shall shortly see.

In "Preiddeu Annwyfn," although three shiploads of men embark on Arthur's vessel Prydwen, only seven return, so the mournful chorus tells us. It mirrors the ill-fated voyage to Ireland in the earlier British myth of Bran the Blessed, whose ship likewise returned with only seven men.[18] The raid on Annwfn is related by Taliesin, who anachronistically accompanies Arthur on this mission: the poet is also significantly said, in the *Mabinogi,* to be one of the seven survivors of Bran's expedition. Here we are presented with the first definitively mythic face of Arthur as the dynamic adventurer on quest.

In *Culhwch and Olwen,* Arthur goes to fetch the cauldron, not from the otherworld, but from an Irish lord over the sea. We are subsequently told, in a fifteenth-century list of the Thirteen Treasures of the Island of Britain, that the cauldron of Diwrnach cannot boil food for a coward, only that of heroes.[19] It is actually a British and more equitable version of the Irish hero's portion, a custom in which the apportioning of the prime joint at any meal was awarded to the preeminent hero of any band—sometimes a tricky call when in the company of celebrity heroes, *all* of whom feel themselves to be the most courageous. But Arthur's motive in seeking the Cauldron of Annwfn is of an entirely different genre. In "Preiddeu Annwyfn" we hear the genuine accents of a much more serious quest, one in which men die by the shipload in order to bring something magical back into their world. The poem continually underpins the necessity for courage and that even its telling is not for the ears of cowards, traitors, or shirkers.

Cauldrons in general have a large part to play in Welsh myth: apart from their obvious ability to provide plenty, they also bestow gifts as various as omniscient wisdom or the restoration of the dead. As a prototype of the Grail, the cauldron's miraculous qualities of plenty, initiation into wisdom, and rebirth are echoed in the mystic vessel's own properties: to give the food most desired, to empower the seeker with spiritual gnosis, and to restore the wasteland and the Wounded King.[20] We notice that, just as in the medieval legends where the Grail is accompanied or borne by female guardians, so here, in the Welsh underworld, it is guarded by nine maidens whose muse-like breath warms the cauldron and keeps it boiling.

Just as "Preiddeu Annwyfn" seems to be the original cauldron quest of Arthur, acting as a source for the cauldron quest in *Culhwch and Olwen*, so a later poem, "Par Gur," seems to be the origin of the list of Arthur's men and more besides. Apart from its connection to the raid on Annwfn, it interestingly takes us back to the northern British kingdom of Manau Gododdin and into the realms of semihistorical remembrance.

THE PORTER AT THE GATE

The poem "Pa Gur" is found in the *Black Book of Carmarthen*, a fourteenth-century collection of earlier Welsh verse.[21] It describes a list of Arthur's men and their exploits in an engagement at or around Edinburgh. The obliqueness of the narrative is obscure to a degree where we are unsure whether it is Arthur who is reporting this account or some other narrator, for the poem speaks of "my fierce servants" at one point and "I had servants. It was better when they were alive," while at another it speaks of Arthur in the third person. The manuscript in which the poem is found unfortunately breaks off at line ninety and the rest is lost to us, but the whole second half of what remains relates the deeds of Cei in some detail, giving us some sense of how much more we have lost.

The poem briefly relates some events that we know about from the quests in *Culhwch and Olwen:* the killing by Arthur of the witch for her blood in the hall of Afarnach (the Sorrowful Place), and much more about Cei, who is the primary object of Arthur's praise in this poem. Cei overcomes a monstrous creature called the Palug Cat, as well as skewering nine witches upon his sword.

The nine witches killed here by Cei appear throughout the Arthurian and Celtic legend; they are none other than a set of nine priestesses who are the mythic precursors of the medieval ladies of the lake.[22] We have already met them as the keepers of the cauldron in "Preiddeu Annwyfn." They were also known to classical geographers and explorers like Posidonius, as well as to Christian saints like Patrick, who prayed along with fellow clerics against "the spells of women."[23] The nine witches also make their reappearance in *Peredur,* the Welsh version of Chrétien de Troyes's twelfth-century romance *Perceval, ou le Conte du Graal,* as the battle trainers of Peredur.[24]

These encounters with cats and witches may mislead us into taking this poem as a mere mythic romp, but embedded at its heart is an account that may have historical foundation. It tells how Arthur's men helped Mabon, Anwas, and Lluch Llawynnauc reclaim their ancestral northern seat from dangerous enemies:

> *Fierce were my servants*
> *in seizing back their rights.*
> *Manawyd brought back*
> *the pierced shields from Tryfrwydd.*
> *And Mabon son of Mellt (Lightning)*
> *Who splattered blood upon the grass;*
> *And Anwas the Winged,*
> *And Lluch Llawynnauc*
> *(Who) were usually defending*
> *Edinburgh's borderland.*
> *A lord would give them refuge,*

And where he could, avenge them . . .
(Arthur) pierced Pen Palach (Club-Head)
In the dwellings of Disethach.
At the mount of Edinburgh
He fought against the dog-heads.
By the hundred they fell,
Every time a century fell
Before Bedwyr the brave.
On the shores of Tryfrwydd
Fighting against Garwlwyd
Of furious nature
*With his sword and shield.**

What arrests us here is the mention of Tryfrwydd, which we have encountered before as Tribuit, the location of Arthur's tenth battle, possibly on the Forth near Stirling (chapter 3). The phrase "pierced shields from Tryfrwydd" appears in several places in Welsh poetry,[25] as if it were a stock phrase to conjure up remembrance, just as the phrase *ground zero* hauntingly does for us today. Again, "perforated was the shield from *trywruyd*," (italic ours) says the poem about the Battle of Arderydd of 573.[26] As we have seen from Arthur's tenth battle, *Tribruit* is a word that itself means "very pierced or broken," possibly identified as a place along the Firth of Forth by which Edinburgh could be defended. "Pierced shields" may seem to imply shields broken in combat, but a reference in *Y Gododdin* to a Votadini hero carrying "a shield with sieve-like open-work in gold" upon its frame suggests another possibility.[27] It is possible that *"the pierced shield from Tryfrwrydd"* is a descriptive name for a crack defensive force of the Gododdin from the Tribuit region: a self-deprecating kind of pun on their garrison of origin, and the shields they carried as a visual reference to this sea-broken coastline. Manawyddan, as lord of the sea, could easily have "brought them back" along the Forth estuary to help defend Din Edin, the old name for Edinburgh.

---

*Our translation.

Mabon, Anwas, Lluch, and others are members of a defensive force who have come to Arthur for help to restore their rights. He has given them refuge and helped them avenge the honor of Din Edin. Bedwyr takes the glory by fighting hand to hand against the enemy leader, Garwlwyd, who appears also in *Culhwch and Olwen*. His full name, Gwrgi Garwlwyd, literally means "Rough-Gray Man-Dog." The character of Gwrgi can be judged from a reference in the Triads, where his death is described as "one of the three fortunate slaughters of Britain" because "Gwrgi used to make a corpse of one of the Cymry every day and two on Saturday, so as not to kill on Sunday." Gwrgi's name seems to imply he is some kind of werewolf figure with a wolf's head and a man's body, hence the *cinbin* or dog heads.* Dog head is employed here like towel head is today, a term of reproach for an enemy, here implying someone less than human. It probably refers to a distinctive tribal force.

We see how "Pa Gur" can be read as an account of Arthur and a detachment of his men seeking to gain entrance to an unknown fortress. When Arthur and Cei beat upon the door to gain entrance, the porter, who identifies himself as Glewlwyd (who is the same porter from Arthur's court in *Culhwch and Olwen*), refuses entry unless Arthur can vouch for himself and his warriors. In response, Arthur describes his men and their exploits and how he has championed them above Hadrian's Wall in the region of Manau Gododdin and how they have fought a group of Picts who were arrayed with their tribal markings on body, shield, or banner. The outcome of the dialogue is unknown to us: it is like a long curtain raiser to an entrance into the stronghold, but the conclusion is lost. However, we can reconstruct an original sequence to these events.

If we examine the dialogue between the porter and Arthur, we realize that this is not just a storyteller's "run," a question-and-answer device that enables the whole audience to join in, but also something far more significant. So famous is this dialogue between Arthur and the porter at the gate that he appears not only in "Pa Gur" and twice in *Culhwch*, but is also graphically depicted upon the eleventh-century

---

*Our translation.

archivolt of Modena Cathedral in Italy, where Arthur attempts to enter a castle and is challenged by a fearsome axe-wielding gatekeeper who tries to keep him out. (See plate 7.)

Returning to *Culhwch and Olwen,* we find this parallel dialogue when Arthur's men attempt to enter the court of another giant, Gwrnach or Wrnach, in order to take his sword in fulfillment of Yspadadden's tasks. This time Cei asks the questions:

"Is there a porter?"

"There is. And if your tongue be not mute in your head, why do you call?"

"Open the gate."

"I will not open it."

"Why not?"

"Knife has gone into the meat, drink into the horn, and there is revelry in the hall of Gwrnach the Giant, unless a craftsman comes bringing his craft, the gate will not be opened tonight."

"Truly, porter," said Cei, "I bring my craft with me."

"What craft is that?"

"I am the best burnisher of swords in the world."[28]

It has been noted by many that the name of the giant, Wrnach, is remarkably similar to Diwrnach, the owner of the cauldron that Arthur and his men fetch from Ireland. What we may have here is an interpolated episode concerning the cauldron taking found in "Preiddeu Annwyfn." After Cei and Bedwyr have tricked their way past the porter and entered Wrnach, the giant's hall, they try their next feat: they get hold of his sword by pretending to burnish and sharpen it; finally, in the act of sheathing the sword, Cei beheads the giant. This episode of entering the castle, enshrined in "Pa Gur," has become detached from its main story, which is nothing less than the taking of the cauldron of Irish Diwrnach, who is the same person as Wrnach the Giant in *Culhwch,* who was originally the Pen Annwyfn or Lord of the Underworld from "Preiddeu Annwyfn." We now see that the dialogue between Arthur and the porter is really about the entrance of his men into the underworld, but in *Culhwch and Olwen,* this quest has been submerged in a welter of other tasks and downgraded from an otherworldly voyage to a mere raid upon Ireland!

We can see this more clearly if we look at the pivotal sword maneuver undertaken in all three stories. In each story, a similarly named man performs a similar action.

Text	Warrior	Sword and Action
Culhwch and Olwen	Llenlleawg Wyddel	Caledfwlch is brandished
"Preiddeu Annwyfn"	Lleawc Lleminawc	Sword of Lleawc flashes
"Pa Gur"	Lluch Llauynnawc and Llachau	Swords of Cei and Llachau "brought battle"

In "Preiddeu Annwyfn" the warrior Lleawc Lleminawc plays a vital part in wielding a sword when it comes to stealing the underworldly cauldron. He is evidently the same person as Llenlleawg the Irishman who, in *Culhwch and Olwen,* seizes Arthur's sword, Caledfwlch, during the raid upon Ireland for Diwrnach's cauldron. In "Pa Gur," from which any cauldron-stealing incident has been lost, the most notable sword bearer is Cei, who is described as "a sword in battle." With his young companion Llachau, together they "brought battle."

Looking at the list above, the eye is dazzled by the similarities between the epithets Llenlleawg/Lleminawc/Llauyannawc and the personal names Lleawc/Lluch/Llachau. Llauyannawc means "Wealthy-Handed One," while Llenlleawg has the connotation of "Veil-Piercer." *Llemenig* is Welsh for leaper and is an epithet used in Welsh verse for one who is not only nimble but a longed-for national savior who will leap over present difficulties to repel occupying forces. *It is the prophetic name of a special hero.*

But the personal name that shines out to Arthurian eyes is that of Llachau, who fights side by side with Cei. Later Welsh tradition makes Llachau Arthur's son and Cei his slayer. There is no extant myth of this incident, which is briefly developed in the thirteenth-century text of

Perlesvaus, where Sir Kay kills Arthur's son Loholt.[29] In "Pa Gur" there is no hint of this slaying: later on in the Triads, Llachau will appear as "son of Arthur," but in "Pa Gur," he does not even have a patronymic. Cei the Fair and Llachau are merely battle bringers here. It is the derivation of Llachau's name from the Welsh root *llach,* meaning "slash," that is of significance here; Llachau is "one who slashes." This is a name fit for a hero, perhaps further strengthened by the fact that the Welsh Llachar is "flashing, glittering, or brilliant." The sword blow that liberates the cauldron shines down the ages. It is clear that in the original cauldron-taking story, *someone's* sword was brandished with all the skill of a martial artist in a feat so stupendous and brilliant that the theft of the cauldron went momentarily unnoticed by its owner.

There are obviously internal connections between the story of *Culhwch and Olwen* and the themes explored in the poems "Pa Gur" and "Preiddeu Annwyfn." Their common features concern difficult entry into fortified or otherworldly regions; combat with monstrous and otherworldly combatants; and loss of life, as well as astounding skills and exploits. *They are all remnants of the same traditional story,* which may have resonances in the historical story of Arthur. From "Pa Gur" we see how Arthur's tenth battle of Tribuit is suddenly given motivation: he is helping "the Pierced Shields of Trwyfwyd" reclaim control of Din Edin and the Forth estuary. Both "Preiddeu Annwyfn" and *Culhwch and Olwen* relate how a cauldron was stolen, while "Pa Gur" gives us links to both texts, as well as confirming Arthur's association with Manau Gododdin. The Welsh Genealogies confirm another extraordinary Gododdin connection, for a man called Llaennawc, perhaps the same Lluch Llauynnawc who is named in "Pa Gur" as part of the defensive force of Tribuit, was the grandfather of the poet Aneirin, the composer of the poem *Y Gododdin.*[30]

If the suggestions of these interwoven myths are set alongside the bare accounts of the written historical material, Arthur appears yet again as a northern warlord but one whose deeds have been conflated with those of earlier, national heroes whose duty has ever been to maintain honor and freedom and to wield objects of otherworldly power at times of need. This mantle of greatness had an immediacy and urgency for the Welsh of subsequent centuries who looked to Arthur as a national rallying point, while their other fellow countrymen settled down under the Norman yoke with the same complacency as the Britons did under the Romans, if we are to believe Gildas. Wales in the wake of Arthur was a smaller, less heroic place: it needed myths to remind its warriors of a greater past and to encourage its people to hope for a better future.

THE STATURE OF SMALL MEN

Welsh myth speaks of the gigantic chieftain of North Wales, Bran the Blessed, a man so large that he is able to wade the Irish Sea and pull his fleet from Wales to Ireland, so tall that his entourage are able to cross dry shod over his body as he lies down over the River Shannon. Such metaphorical gigantism arises frequently in the Welsh mythic name for Britain, "the Island of the Mighty," and harks back to a time in which giants were said to rule over Albion, as Britain was originally known in some accounts.

In the wake of Britain's sixth-century heroic struggle, following the Saxon incursion and the Norman Conquest, this mythic greatness was sorely missed. In the Welsh story of "The Dream of Rhonabwy," found within the collection of stories that make up the *Mabinogion*, Rhonabwy and his companions find themselves in mythic times and presented to Arthur who laughingly inquires, "Where did you find these little men?" When their guide Iddawg asks why Arthur laughs, he responds, "Because it grieves me that men of such stature as these should have this island in their keeping, after the men that guarded it from ancient time."[31]

"The Dream of Rhonabwy" shows signs of having been a folk story worked up into a more sophisticated entertainment, for it moves from a seemingly contemporary standpoint back into the mythic past and uses a welter of such dense description that, the story tells us, it cannot be remembered by anyone other than a bard. The action starts by relating how a ruler of Powys, Madog ap Maredudd (a historical figure who died in 1160), goes seeking for his brother Iorwerth who, dissatisfied with his lower rank, supports himself by making raids into England. The real Iorwerth ap Maredudd, known as the Red, was actually the chief *latimer* or king's translator for Powys and was no doubt part of Henry II's scheme to win over the lords of North Wales with gifts and favors. Iorwerth Goch actually accepted the fief of Sutton in Shropshire through the agency of his position of *latimer,* at some distance from his native lands.[32] The historical context of "The Dream of Rhonabwy" is therefore one of Norman intervention in Welsh affairs, the subversion of Welshmen into the English king's service and dishonorable acceptance of the Norman yoke. Things are at such a low ebb in the Welsh psyche that the anonymous storyteller needs his listeners to draw upon the memory of better times and greater men.

To demonstrate how low morale and the economy had become in Wales, the story relates how Rhonabwy, part of the search party, becomes benighted and forced to seek the miserable hospitality of an impoverished and rundown house. This episode is a sad reflection upon the warm British hospitality expected by the guest. The best thing to sleep upon is a yellow calfskin in which Rhonabwy curls up and begins to dream. But such skin-wrapped sleep was once a druidic method of discovering forgotten knowledge: unknowing of this, in his dream Rhonabwy finds himself and his companions at a ford upon the Severn. Here he is met by a finely equipped youth who declares himself to be Iddawg, the Churn of Britain, the fateful messenger between Arthur and Medrawd whose crooked words caused the Battle of Camlann (see chapter 3).

To his astonishment and awe, Rhonabwy is led to an island below the ford where Arthur sits: the emperor is somewhat less impressed with Rhonabwy and his companions as we have seen above. In a device that will ensure this encounter is recalled later, Iddawg directs Rhonabwy to observe the emperor's ring, which will enable him to remember everything that he experiences in this place.

The timelessness of this dream is now fully evoked as Rhonabwy is informed that many men are gathering here for a rematch of the

Battle of Badon against Osla Big Knife, who is none other than the historical Octha of Kent, son of Aesc! A great press of troops gathers in the Severn Valley as Arthur is brought his sword: when drawn from the scabbard, it shoots forth two flames from the twin serpents engraved upon it. A mantle is also spread upon the ground that has the property of causing whoever stands upon it to become invisible due to its camouflaging effect. Arthur and his nephew Owain sit together upon this mantle and play a magical board game. The historical Owain ap Urien lived at least two to three generations after Arthur, but in this otherworldly scene, time no longer runs. There ensues a remarkable contest, for whenever Owain's gaming men win, then Arthur's actual troops in the field suffer; whenever Arthur's gaming men succeed on the board, then Owain's troops in the field are wounded. On the third finalizing game, Arthur takes the gaming pieces in his hand and crushes them to dust. At this juncture, Osla Big Knife comes to beg a six-week truce. Arthur takes counsel with his men who are listed in almost as much detail as they are in *Culhwch and Olwen;* a truce is granted, and the Badon rematch postponed. As Cei bids Arthur's men be ready to return to Cornwall, the tumult is so great that Rhonabwy awakes to find himself still wrapped in his yellow calfskin. Like the otherworldly feasts of Irish tradition whereby a pig slain for supper is whole and entire again by the next morning, here Badon seems to play round and round in a continuous loop.

Through the timeless otherworldliness of this medieval story, we may discern the faint traces of historical reality about Badon and Camlann. This replay of Badon has the men muster at Rhyd y Groes, the Ford of the Cross, on the Severn River. The troops move off to Kefn Digoll away from the Severn Valley. The troops that muster include those of Arthur's cousin, March (later remembered as King Mark), and other notable Britons, as well as the men of Greece, Denmark, and Norway. Arthur leads his men to below Caer Baddon where he grants a truce to Osla Gyllellfawr or Big Knife. *This is the only time we are specifically told whom Arthur fought against at Badon.* Octha's nickname of Big Knife is a reference to *saex,* or short sword, for which the Saxons were renowned!

In *Culhwch and Olwen,* Osla Big Knife appears in the listing of men at Arthur's court: later in that story he drowns in pursuit of Twrch Trwyth, when his knife is sucked down by lodestones in the Severn and his scabbard fills with water. This sounds as if it might be a distant echo of Octha's defeat at Badon, which is here located somewhere south of Bath, while the drowning of Osla suggests a sea-going battle.[33]

"The Dream of Rhonabwy" also advances our knowledge of Camlann. We have already seen how Iddawg repeated the conciliatory message of Arthur to Medrawd in such a way that offense was given instead, causing the Battle of Camlann. This message was to seek for peace *so that the nobles and princes of Britain should not be slain:* again, this confirms what we have guessed, that Camlann was at heart a civil strife. We also learn another factor from this story, that *Arthur is Medrawd's uncle and foster father* and that the battle lasted three days. These details appear nowhere else. We cannot rest much weight upon these mythically marinaded facts, but they give us another perspective with which to view the last two battles of Arthur.

"The Dream of Rhonabwy" is full of allusions to magical objects. The game that Owain and Arthur play is called *gwyddbwyll,* literally "wood knowledge," a board game wherein the king piece and its companion warriors attempt to get to the edge of the board while the opposing player's pieces try to block or prevent them from doing so. Interestingly, this same action of the gaming board is paralleled in the story upon the field of muster: as Rhonabwy looks upon the host, he sees that the men at the center of the field are trying to reach the edge, while those at the edge are trying to reach the center. Iddawg tells the dreamer that this mêlée is caused by Cei, whose horsemanship is such that everyone is trying to look at him. This is also a coded reference to the Battle of Camlann itself, which entered the Welsh language as *cadgamlan,* a poetic epithet for "a confused rabble."[34]

The gaming board has a way of standing for territorial competitiveness in Celtic tradition, but here the *gwyddbwyll* board of Rhonabwy is clearly part of the special regalia known as the Tri Thlws ar Ddeg Ynys Prydain: the Thirteen Treasures (*thlws*) of the Island of Britain, which constitute the hallows of Britain—items of magical regalia.[35] Arthur is said to own the thirteenth hallow—a cloak of invisibility and omniscient sight: this is the very same mantle that appears in "The Dream of Rhonabwy," where it is called *gwenn* or white. Nothing that is not white can be placed upon it because anyone attired in it will become invisible: the implication being that only the most pure or high minded can wear it. In later Arthurian legend, the cloak that tests virtue is a common theme; if placed about the shoulders of impure women, it shortens to reveal their private parts; if placed about the shoulders of faithful women or virgins, it lengthens to cover their modesty. Arthur's magical cloak conveys the ability to see without being seen, the prime vehicle for a king to test the mood of his kingdom. He inherited this mythic cloak from earlier users, for it is first mentioned in Welsh tradition as being the cloak of Caswallawn, the same chieftain who fought against Julius Caesar.

"The Dream of Rhonabwy" takes us beyond the early mythic material, deep into the disillusionment of historical Norman-occupied Wales. Yet it looks back to a larger-than-life past in which heroism is upheld by honorable men and where warfare resembles a friendly match game more than a battle of gore and defeat. Arthur is the great emperor Arthur, surrounded by the Treasures of Britain and by a panoply of men who never die and are always game for a fight.

The Arthurian legend is perhaps remembered more today for its magic and romance than for its deeds of arms and honor. One of the driving myths is the betrayal of Arthur by his queen and his first knight, which ultimately causes the downfall of Camelot and leads to his death. Let us discover the root of the Arthurian love triangle and its role in the early material.

AND MY WIFE GWENHWYFAR . . .

In granting his nephew's boon in *Culhwch and Olwen,* Arthur promised Culhwch whatever he could provide, carefully exempting all of his own personal equipage and, almost as an afterthought, his own wife,

Gwenhwyfar, whom we know more familiarly as Guinevere. This is the first known reference to Arthur's wife, and she appears only in the mythic material. Gwenhwyfar's name seems to be the British version of a similar Irish name Findabair. Some scholars have detected a possible root derivation from "white phantom or fairy," which has led to speculations about whether Gwenhwyfar was a human or otherworldly woman.[36] In any case, she is a fairly late addition to the Arthurian legend, for none of the triads in which she appears can be dated from earlier than the mid-fourteenth century. In the continental Arthurian writings of the Middle Ages, Arthur's queen takes a larger role in the story because courtly audiences demanded more about the Arthurian women to enhance the conceit of Courtly Love.

Those familiar with the medieval Arthurian legends will know Guinevere as an unfaithful wife and as the lover of Lancelot, but she did not begin this way. Long before Lancelot comes into the Arthurian legend in the twelfth century, there is an earlier tradition about her being abducted by Melwas of the Summer Country, first recorded in the eleventh-century *Vita Gildae* by Caradoc of Llancarfan.[37] This story was independently remembered by the Welsh poets, who have left us their evidence. The tale relates how Melwas takes Gwenhwyfar to his marsh-protected seat of Glastonbury in the Summer Country where he holds her until Arthur besieges him. The abbot of Glastonbury intervenes; Arthur receives back his wife and grants lands to the abbey in thanks. This is the first, but certainly not the last, abduction of Guinevere who, in the words of a high school essay, was "a lady much given to being run away with." This story is reworked by Chrétien de Troyes's twelfth-century tale of *Le Chevalier de la Charette,* where King Melwas becomes Sir Meleagant and where Lancelot becomes her rescuer. The abduction of Guinevere is also graphically depicted upon the archivolt in Modena Cathedral in Italy where she appears as Winlogee. This is the same carving that includes Arthur and the famous porter from "Pa Gur."

In "Ymddiddan Melwas a Gwenhwyfar" (The Dialogue of Melwas and Gwenhwyfar), a Welsh poem from the eleventh or twelfth century, we have an elliptical exchange between Melwas the abductor, Cei the rescuer, and a most unvictimized Gwenhwyfar who mocks her abductor for his youth and small stature.

> Gwenhwyfar: *"Silence your idle tongue, youth!*
> *Unless you're better than you appear,*
> *You'd never stand up to Cei,*
> *Even if you were backed up by eight others."*

> Melwas: *"Gwenhwyfar of the deer's shape,*
> *Don't dismiss me; despite my youth,*
> *I would face up to Cei alone."*[38]

The exchange breaks off with a final insinuation, presumably a reference to Arthur's prowess in bed, as Cei and Melwas come to blows.

> Melwas: *"I hate a grey-beard's smile,*
> *With his sword skewered up under his chin,*
> *Whose desires outstrip his achievement."*

> Gwenhwyfar: *"More hateful still*
> *Is a proud man, a coward save in words."*
> Melwas: *"Take that!"*
> Cei: *"Take that yourself!"*[39]

Here Cei acts as Arthur's representative, while Gwenhwyfar keeps her cool and actively provokes the combat between her abductor and her rescuer.

It is possible to glimpse the roots of this legend if we look at an incident in *Culhwch and Olwen*, where we see the very first love triangle of the Arthurian legend that plays out over eternity. As we have seen above, the original mythic triangle concerns a beautiful woman called Creiddylad who is fought over by both Gwyn ap Nudd and Gwythyr ap Greidawl. Arthur's rather mysterious judgment upon the lovers is that they should fight over her every May Day till doomsday. This seems to imply that either the maiden will never become the possession of either man or else that she goes to the victor every May Day for a year's duration. On a seasonal level, this story enshrines an archaic battle for the Flower Bride, a tutelary spirit of the growing year, by representative antagonists of summer and winter, as the names of Creiddylad's opponents imply: Gwyn ap Nudd, or White, son of Nudd, and Gwythyr ap Greidawl, or Victor, son of Scorcher. Aspects of this myth were still being enacted in South Wales in the nineteenth century as part of the May Day revels, where two rival groups of men attempted to bring home a lone horsewoman representing the Flower Bride. This mythic love triangle is the template for all the love triangles that will come afterward in Arthurian legend, including Guinevere, Arthur, and Lancelot and Isolt, Mark, and Tristan.[40]

In Melwas's abduction of Gwenhwyfar, we can see aspects of this primordial seasonal fight between the rivals of winter and summer, between Arthur or his representative and the abductor of his wife. The implication here is that Arthur, the older husband of a younger wife, is a winter rival for the hand of the lovely Flower Bride of spring, while Melwas, whose realm is the Summer Country, represents the summer rival. This theme percolates right through the Arthurian legend. We clearly see such a pattern in the love judgment that Arthur gives upon Isolt, her husband King Mark, and his nephew-rival Tristan in the Welsh text of *Drustan ac Essyllt*.[41] Here Arthur judges that Drustan shall have Essyllt while the leaves are on the trees, while March shall have her when the trees are bare. At this Solomonic wisdom, Essyllt claps her hands for joy and proclaims: "Blessed be the judgment and he who gave it! There are three trees that are good of their kind, holly and ivy and yew, which keep their leaves as long as they live!"[42] She will have her lover the whole year through and not only in the summer. Arthur's role of "judge of lovers" devolves to Guinevere in the later medieval texts, where it is she herself who arbitrates between lovers, as we see in the *Lais* of Marie de France and in Chaucer's "Wife of Bath's Tale." Hereafter, Arthur confines his judgments to the affairs of men alone.

The early Gwenhwyfar is less human and more otherworldly, perhaps no more so than in a triad that tells us that the three great queens of Arthur's court were all called Gwenhwyfar, the daughters of different rulers.[43] Triplicity is a common feature in Celtic myth, as we see in the triple Brighid of poets, smiths, and healers and the triple battle-crow sisters, Nemain, Badhb, and Macha, collectively known as the Morrighna. Such triplicity suggests a deeper mythic level. It is not without significance that the father of the *second* Gwenhwyfar in this triad is one of the rival men in the primordial and eternal love triangle from *Culhwch and Olwen:* Gwythyr ap Greidawl. This suggests that Gwenhwyfar's role in the Arthurian legend derives from a much earlier mythic understanding: that she shares the self-same allure as her mother, the original Flower Bride. The tradition that Arthur had more than one wife is supported by the mysterious uncovering of the Glastonbury tomb in the twelfth century: the inscription with the burial stated, "here lies buried the famous King Arthur with Guinevere his second wife in the isle of Avalon."

This proliferation of Gwenhwyfars has already been noted in chapter 3, where we examined the tradition of "the blow that Gwenhwyfar struck upon Gwenhwyfach,"[44] which caused the Battle of Camlann. The names Gwenhwyfar and Gwenhwyfach simply mean "Gwennie the Great" and "Gwennie the Small," which is indicated in the suffix of each name: *far/fawr* and *fach,* which mean "big" and "small" respectively. Medieval legend ran with this theme and worked up stories of true and false Guineveres to account for this mythical proliferation and the apparently conflicting natures of Guinevere as both perfect queen as well as an unfaithful wife.

Later tradition jettisons the suggestion that Guinevere might be a goddess and settles for a moralistically Christian association between her unfaithfulness and the downfall of the Round Table: this was explored extensively by the nineteenth-century poet, Alfred Tennyson in his *Idylls of the King.* By keeping his jealousy in check, Arthur maintains face, but as soon as Mordred forces his hand by revealing that Lancelot is Guinevere's lover, Camelot is doomed. The double sin that causes this final downfall in Malory's *Le Morte d'Arthur* is the adultery of Guinevere with Lancelot, and Arthur's act of killing all the young children of Britain in a Herodian attempt to slay the son he begot upon his half sister Morgause, namely Mordred.

Both the French Wace and English Layamon took up this theme of the queen's abduction, making Modred the one who abducted Gwenhwyfar and married her while Arthur was fighting abroad. The abductors change from text to text, sometimes it is the son of Gwyn ap Nudd, young Edern or Yder, sometimes it is Mordred, until we come to Malory's final flowering of the Arthurian legend where we see the return of Meliagrance (the medieval version of Melwas) and Lancelot himself who finally takes Guinevere to his castle of Joyous Garde.[45]

When Gwenhwyfar is not being abducted, she is being insulted. In two other stories from the *Mabinogion,* "Gereint ap Erbin" and "Peredur" (the Welsh versions of Chrétien de Troyes's *Erec et Enide* and *Perceval, ou le Conte du Graal*), a knight insults Gwenhwyfar by striking her handmaidens or by throwing wine into her lap. In the Triads, Medrawd/Mordred himself stands accused of these very actions: he not only pulls Gwenhwyfar from her chair but strikes her as well.[46]

We lack the full evidence to connect Gwenhwyfar with Medrawd in an amorous way, but hidden deep in the list of Arthur's men in *Culhwch and Olwen* is a clue. We read of a certain Medr ap Methredydd (Striker, son of Aimer) who could "shoot a wren through the two legs" in Ireland from the distance of Cornwall. This skill is a mythic one, which the hero Lleu Llaw Gyffes and his Irish cognate Lugh Lamfhada both perform: killing the wren is an act of *lèse majesté,* symbolic of the dethroning of a former king, which both these youths commit in their parallel stories. In the case of Lugh, he finally kills his horrific grandfather Balor in order to succeed as ruler. In these parallel stories, the wren is "hit between the legs," which is symbolic not only of a very exact small target, but also of castration. In both Welsh and Irish folk tradition, hunting the wren was a ritual of midwinter in which the King of All Birds was killed and ritually processed about the region to symbolize the death of the old year.[47]

With this information in mind, let us examine Medr ap Methredydd more closely. *Medr* (striker) is the root of the name Medrawd who, as we have seen in chapter 3, was the striker of a blow against Gwenhwyfar and Arthur. This small reference may be a remembrance of a lost story in which Medrawd's blow upon Gwenhwyfar was symbolic of the attempted toppling of Arthur through the impugning of his virility and the taking of his wife—events that the chroniclers Wace and Layamon take up and develop in the twelfth century. This would put Medrawd, as Arthur's nephew and foster son, in the place of a youthful, virile usurper whose abduction of Gwenhwyfar is part of a much older myth: nothing less than the struggle of the summer and winter rivals for possession of the Flower Bride.

This powerful underlying myth seeded itself throughout the Arthurian legends, but the original motivations became lost as these stories entered the courts of Christendom, by which Guinevere was judged merely as a sinful woman and unfaithful wife. The dying of the Arthurian dream was subsequently portrayed with Arthur and Guinevere completely estranged, no longer in communication, but in three stray and undated verses from the Middle Ages, found in a margin of manuscript copy of the Welsh poem "The Dialogue of Arthur and the Eagle," wife and husband speak intimately together, directly after the strife of Camlann.

> **Gwenhwyfar:** *"Arthur, son of Uthr, of the long sword,*
> *I tell you a certain truth:*
> *Over every strong one there is a master."*

> **Arthur:** *"Gwenhwyfar, my dear little white one,*
> *My love for you has never abated.*
> *Medrawd lies dead: I myself am near death."*

> *"No doctor has ever seen a scar*
> *Where Caledfwlch once struck:*
> *Nine times I struck Medrawd."*[48]

Gwenhwyfar reminds her husband that death comes for everyone, while Arthur responds that no one has ever recovered from a blow from his sword and that Medrawd is most certainly dead as a result. Here at last the rivalry for the Flower Bride is truly ended. Arthur's Pyrrhic victory in the love triangle leads him to enter a long otherworldly sojourn where his deep wounds must be healed before his return from Avalon.

MERLIN, AVALON, AND
THE OTHERWORLDLY ARTHUR

We have seen how northern British characters like Owain of Rheged and his poet Taliesin have become part of the Arthurian legend, but more popular yet is another individual whose name is now synonymous worldwide with both magic and the kingmaking of the Pendragons: Merlin. The interpolation of Merlin into the Arthurian legend is a late development that rests upon two separate older traditions. The first strand is found in Nennius's account of Ambrosius Aurelianus or *Emrys Guledic* as the youthful prophet whose preternatural knowledge overthrows Vortigern. The second strand of the Merlin legend arises from an independent historical figure known as Myrddin Wyllt, or Merlin the Wild. This latter personage was attached to the court of Gwenddolau, a leader of the Maithi, (or Maeatae) a tribe living between the Antonine and Hadrian Walls. At the battle of Arderydd in 573 (modern Arthuret, above Carlisle), Myrddin runs mad into the Caledonian Forest as a result of witnessing the slaughter of his kinsmen and of his patron.[49]

Nennius's source for the fatherless young Ambrosius is unknown. This youthful prophet is clearly a fusion of the British commander Ambrosius Aurelianus and someone from a native story that has been lost. In Celtic tradition, there are numerous accounts of wise boys and liberating youths who overcome oppression: the template for this archetype is Mabon son of Modron whose recovery from the mists of time is a major part of *Culhwch and Olwen*. Nennius's young Ambrosius develops from being a wonder-working and prophetic youth to the Merlin of Geoffrey of Monmouth's *Historia Regum Britanniae* who advises Uther and Arthur. This same writer is responsible for the union of Emrys, with a northern poet named Myrddin Wyllt, and the eventual flowering of the Merlin myth, making him a prime mover in the affairs of the

the son of Ceidiaw of the tribe of Coel Godeboc, a very powerful prince, and they joining their forces met Rhydderch at a place called Arderydd, where upon the first encounter Gwenddoleu was slain, and with him Llywelyn, Gwgawn, Einiawn, and Rhiwallawn, the sons of Morfryn, Merlin Caledonius's brethren; and in the end after a great slaughter on both sides, Rhydderch obtained the victory, and Aeddan fled the country. (Rachel Bromwich, trans.)

Here we once again find reference to Merlin's brethren falling in the battle. Aeddan, who replaces the sons of Ellifer mentioned in the *Annales Cambriae* as the opponent here, is almost certainly Aedan mac Gabhran, a formidable Irish leader who seems to have raided regularly across the sea into Britain at this time.

The reference to the cause of the battle being over a lark's nest is obscure, but there are a number of similar battles listed in Celtic literature that begin over a seeming trifle and end in bloodshed. Nor should we ignore the mention in the Triads to the death of Gwenddolau's birds. Celtic tradition mentions the birds of Rhiannon, which put those who heard them into a trance in which they failed to notice the passage of time. Perhaps there was once a story in which Gwenddolau possessed two miraculous birds, the death of which caused a war to begin—or perhaps the writer simply wanted to point to the way fights can break out over the smallest thing.

In any case, the death of Gwenddoleu at Arderydd is well attested in all of these references, and in the passage by Vaughan, we also have another reference to Merlin Caledonius. Using the title Caledonius or Scot is not without significance, as we shall see.

The name Myrddin, or a version of it, was certainly known as long ago as the eighth or ninth centuries, or possibly earlier, since these references had almost certainly been preserved in oral tradition for several hundred years before this. Up until this time, Myrddin is presented as a warrior, poet, and madman, but there is no mention of his serving Arthur. This is only found in one of the Triads, certainly written after Geoffrey of Monmouth's work, where Myrddin ap Morfren,

Myrddin Emrys, and Taliesin are described as the "Three Skilful Bards of Arthur's Court." But again this makes Merlin a poet not a magician.[50] This reference is the first *Welsh* association between Merlin and Arthur; the identity of Morfren remains something of a mystery, but someone called Morfryn is the father of the three young kinsmen whom Myrddin mourns at Arderydd.

As we shall see, Merlin's role in the Arthurian legend is strictly the work of Geoffrey, who makes him the kingmaker of the Pendragon dynasty. But even as he is gradually interpolated into the wider medieval Arthurian story, Merlin remains somewhat removed from the action rather than fully integrated into Arthur's court. The figure of Myrddin remains within Welsh tradition as a withdrawn figure that continues to oversee the fate of Britain. In legend, he becomes a guardian of the treasures of Britain within Ynys Enlli or Barsdey Island. So strong was this tradition that, in medieval legend, his name became an epithet for Britain itself: Clas Myrddin or Merlin's Enclosure, which the poet Rudyard Kipling in his book *Puck of Pook's Hill* called "Merlin's Isle of Gramarye."

As we trace the development of the Arthurian story, the character of Merlin changes from warrior poet into an easily seduced old dodderer. If we trace the withdrawal of Merlin from Arthurian affairs that traditionally plays out in the medieval story, we find that it is suggested first by Myrddin's deranged sojourn in the Caledonian Forest after the Battle of Arderydd. The next stage is found in Geoffrey's *Vita Merlini* (Life of Merlin), where Merlin's sister, Ganeida, creates for him a forest observatory. The twelfth-century *Didot Perceval* adapts this idea further, drawing a connection between the man and the hawk with whom he shares a name, making Merlin withdraw into his *esplumoir* or moulting cage.[51] Later medieval legend turns Merlin's intentional withdrawal to a sylvan retreat into something more sinister, where the maiden Nimue, having learned all of Merlin's magic, tricks him into a prison from whence he cannot escape.

Merlin's withdrawal into unknown regions is not his only connection with the otherworld. In the *Vita Merlini*, Geoffrey of Monmouth has Merlin recall the time when he and Taliesin bore the broken body of Arthur from the field of Camlann and had him ferried in the boat steered by Barinthus the Navigator to the realm of Avalon, where Arthur's wounds would be healed. This episode incorporates the Celtic *immrama* or voyage myths of heroes to otherworldly islands within the Arthurian legends. The presence of Barinthus, a character who appears in the medieval legend of St. Brendan's *Voyage to the Isles of the Blest,* suggests that Geoffrey was familiar with the many Irish stories about voyages to the otherworld. These tales involve questing heroes sailing to a series of islands on which many wonders may be encountered, some pleasant and some challenging.[52] As we have seen, in his quest for the cauldron of Annwyfn, Arthur is himself among the ranks of heroes who sail to otherworldly regions in search of wonders.

SAILING TO AVALON

Avalon itself makes its first appearance as an otherworldly island as Insula Avallonia (Isle of Avalon) in Geoffrey of Monmouth's work. He may have drawn upon the classical legends of the Fortunate Isles in referring to it as Insula Pomorum, or Island of Apples, but he may also have known the Irish legend of the Apple Island, Emain Abhlach, which is the realm of Manannan mac Lir, god of the sea and of the otherworld. In his realm people find refuge from trouble, understanding for the heart, and renewal of mind and body. Emain Abhlach has been identified as the Island of Arran off the west Scottish coast, but Avalon did not became associated with Glastonbury in Somerset until a tomb, alleged to be Arthur's, was discovered there in the twelfth century (see chapter 7).

The otherworldly associations of Glastonbury were already well established: its British name was Ynys Witrin, or the Isle of Glass, which, as we have seen, is a name that appears in Arthur's descent to the underworld as Caer Wydyr, the Tower of Glass. The Tor at Glastonbury, visible for miles across the Somerset Levels, is now the pilgrimage point for many in search of Avalonian inspiration; few remember that it is the ancient home of Gwyn ap Nudd, the spectral huntsman and rival for the Flower Bride, whom we met in *Culhwch and Olwen.* It may be argued that Glastonbury today is no kind of island, but before the immense dike system was dug in the Middle Ages to drain the Somerset Levels, it stood proud above marshland and floodwaters as an island, and that during the extensive flooding of the area in 2013, it once again became an island.

Something else crucially links the realm of Avalon with the voyage traditions, for it is a region entirely inhabited by women, analogous to the Island of Women, which is a prime location in the *immrama* stories. Geoffrey of Monmouth follows a long Atlantic coastal tradition, which sees a number of islands peopled exclusively by priestesses with gifts of shapeshifting, healing, prophecy, and magic. These habitations are recorded by classical writers such as Posidonius and Strabo, and their female populations are antecedent to the Ladies of the Lake whom we find in later Arthurian tradition.[53] Chief of these ladies in the early legends is Morgen, who will go on to become Morgan le Fay, wife of Uriens. Morgen has all the skills of her ancient sisters, most notably that of healing. She is the daughter of Afallach, king of Avalon, a mysterious figure who appears in several of the Welsh Genealogies.

Morgen's mythical antecedents can be traced back to the Irish battle goddess Morrighan, as well as to the British and Breton traditions of the Washer at the Ford.[54] Morgan would go on to become the preeminent enchantress of the Arthurian legend, while in Europe, her shapeshifting nature is remembered in the mirage effect called Fata Morgana that is seen over the Straits of Messina, between Calabria and Sicily. But in the Avalon of the Arthurian legends, it is the renewing abilities of the otherworldly island and its mistress that are most prominent. *Le Dragon Normand* (The Norman Dragon) by the twelfth-century chronicler Étienne de Rouen, gives us a fresh insight into the nature of Arthur's passing:

> *The grievously wounded Arthur requested healing herbs*
>   *from his sister:*
> *These were kept in the sacred isle of Avalon.*
> *Here the eternal nymph, Morgan, helped her brother.*
> *Healing, nourishing and reviving him, making him immortal.*
> *The Antipodes were put under his rule. As one of Faery,*
> *He stands without armour, but fearing no fray.*

So he rules from the underworld, bright in battle,
Where the other half of the world is his.[55]

Here Arthur becomes not only a denizen of Avalon but a king of the southern hemisphere, which is another way of referring to the underworld. The twelfth-century *Gesta Regum Britanniae* (The Deeds of the British Kings) by William of Malmsbury confirms the nature of Arthur's relationship with Morgen, the royal priestess of Avalon:

> At that same time when Arthur bequeathed the diadem of royalty and set another king in his place, it was (Morgan) who brought him over (to Avalon) in the five hundred and forty-second year after the Word became incarnate without the seed of human father. Wounded beyond measure, Arthur took the way to the court of the King of Avalon, where the royal virgin, tending his wound, keeps his healed body for her very own and they live together.[56]

The relationship between Morgen/Morgan and Arthur is not yet one of vengeful half sister and half brother, as it later becomes in the medieval legends, but one of renewing priestess and warrior, for it is her task to heal him of his wounds. In Avalon, Morgen shows her Celtic antecedents as Morrighan, the goddess who transforms the newly deceased.

With Merlin as a watchful guardian, and the Lady of the Lake as the all-gifting fosterer and healer, we see a powerful pair of otherworldly "fairy godparents," under whose tutelage Arthur comes to manly power and to whom he will return. Merlin and Morgan are not the only ones who live their lives partly in the otherworld. Just as Myrddin seems to enter into an undying condition like Elijah in the Bible, becoming an ever-living guardian of Britain, so Arthur too becomes the once and future king. This is the myth that most people remember about Arthur: that he is not dead but abides in the otherworld of Avalon, ready to return to the aid of Britain. This myth is much older even than the historical Arthur, stretching back to a time when giants roamed Earth and when heroic leaders were buried to maintain an eternal watch upon the land.

PALLADIAN BURIALS

Throughout Welsh myth are traces of a prophylactic ritual against invasion that is based upon an ancient understanding of the ancestral underworld. The ancestral view held that certain people—usually "the mighty dead" whose deeds were the benchmark of honor—could be dispatched to act as ancestral spokesmen and otherworldly sentinels to keep safe the living. This legend leaves its trace in the undying nature of Arthur and the prophecy of his sure return in times of trial.[57]

We see an example of such a rite in the dying words of Vortimer, son of the hated Vortigern. He asked to be buried facing the Saxon Shore—that littoral once so strongly held by Rome and earlier by British ancestors who maintained its defense against Rome itself—so that his presence might repel invasion after death as he had done in life. His burial is remembered in the Triads as one of "three fortunate concealments," and his disinterment by his father, out of love of his Saxon wife, is given as one of "three unfortunate disclosures."[58]

Back beyond living memory, was an even earlier myth about the gigantic Bran, called the Blessed. This story is told fully in the *Mabinogion*.[59] The gigantic Bran has his seat in Harlech, in the western area of North Wales. Bran makes an alliance with the Irish, agreeing to give his sister Branwen in marriage to King Matholwch.

This Irish suit is unwelcome to Bran's brother, Efnissien, who stirs up trouble and insults the Irish to such a degree that Bran has to give many rich gifts in compensation to the king, including a miraculous cauldron with the capability of restoring the dead to life again. Branwen sends messages home that her husband is mistreating her, so Bran prepares a punitive force to deal with this situation.

As his troops attempt to cross a wide river, Bran utters the words "he who would be chief, let him be a bridge"; in a literal realization of his words, he lays down his gigantic length so that his entourage might pass over his body. These words not only became a Welsh proverb, they also lie at the heart of a ruler's responsibility for the land. Bran fights to liberate his sister but receives an unhealing wound. In his last moments he commands his men to sever his head and to bear it to the White Mount, where the Tower of London now stands, where it should be set facing France to repel invaders.

Only seven return from Ireland, bearing Bran's head with them: a sevenfold pattern that has its resonance in Arthur's raid upon the underworld in "Preiddeu Annwyfn." These seven survivors enjoy an otherworldly sojourn wherein the birds of Rhiannon come and sing to them, stretching the time of their funeral feasting to eighty-seven years, until one of their number opens a forbidden door and serial time begins to run again. The seven companions remember the battle, and sorrow falls upon them again as they are expelled from their earthly paradise. During their otherworldly sequestration, they have conversed with the head of Bran, which continues to utter wise words as if he had been living. Now they complete their task of interring his head to be their defense against invasion.

Arthur's own undying sojourn and his enduring Palladian presence rest upon the example of such heroes. Like Bran, Arthur goes across the sea to Ireland to fetch a cauldron and only seven return. Like Bran, Arthur is believed to reside in a hidden, otherworldly place with his companions in more than one location in Britain. Even the unhealing wound of Bran becomes the archetypal origin of the Wounded King theme in the medieval Arthurian Grail legend.

The endurance of the original Bran myth can be gauged from a legend still attached to the six captive ravens of the Tower of London: the White Mount is said to be the site of its central keep, and the ravens, who maintain the inviolate sovereignty of Britain, are namesakes of Bran, whose name means "raven." In the guise of the tower ravens, which are prevented from flying off by having their wings clipped, Bran is still honored at the Tower of London, cared for by a yeoman warder rejoicing in the resounding title of Raven Master. Intriguingly, from the standpoint of eternal guardians who take animal form, Arthur himself is said to embody another member of the crow family, the chough, a yellow-beaked, raven-like bird that lives around the western coasts of Britain.

One of the "three unfortunate disclosures" that cause trouble in Britain includes the time when "Arthur disclosed the Head of Bran the Blessed from the White Hill, because it did not seem right to him that this Island should be defended by the strength of anyone, but by his own."[60] In the mold of Bran, Arthur hubristically attempts to be the chief bridge for his country's future existence.

Because the historical Arthur upheld the honor of Britain, being swift in attack and steadfast in defense as well as victorious over the enemy, his mythic status was assured by his being ranked with leaders like Bran and Vortimer. This hope buoyed up the Welsh nation from the establishment of the Saxon kingdoms of England through to the Norman invasion and its Angevin and Plantagenet dynasties. Talk of Arthur's return was greeted by the Normans with some scorn. The Anglo-Norman metrical text known as *Lestorie des Engles* (The Description of England) written by Master Geffrei Gaimar circa 1145, speaks thus of the Welsh attitude to the land of England,

> *Openly they go about declaring*
> *That finally they will have it all.*
> *Through Arthur they will have it back*
> *And Britain they'll call it once again.*[61]

Even Geoffrey of Monmouth, a Welsh employee of the Norman kings, shows his own bipartisan views when he states in his *Historia Regum Britanniae* that Arthur was mortally wounded but nevertheless is still living, having been taken to Avalon to be healed of his wounds. This paradoxical assertion was perhaps diplomatic in Angevin, England, when to affirm the death of Arthur was the best course if one wished to remain employed. Secretly many of the native British heartily wished for Arthur's return and an end to the occupation.

The legend of the sleeping lord who would come again was current throughout medieval Europe in the Christian legend of the Seven Sleepers of Ephesus, and in the folk tradition of the Holy Roman emperor Frederick Barbarossa, who was said to lie sleeping under

Mount Etna.[62] But it is Arthur's return that continues to capture the imagination. In his sleep he reigns over his waiting men, ready to defend the realm he so victoriously protected in life.

We began this chapter with a consideration of the region of Oeth and Anoeth, the Land of Wonders and Even Greater Wonders: surely this region lies revealed in these ancient myths. When Arthur's doorkeeper Glewlywd speaks of having been with him in "Caer Oeth and Anoeth" and in "Caer Nefenhyr of the nine streams," he is actually drawing upon two extremes of location. From the poetry of Taliesin, we know that Caer Nefenhyr is the "City of the Highest Sky," where the poet draws upon the nine streams of inspiration. But Caer Oeth and Anoeth is its opposite place, a region below the ground where the undying ancestors and heroes are located. The *Stanzas of the Graves* tell us *anoeth bin u bedd Arthur,* which has been often interpreted as "wonderful is Arthur's grave." Such a grave is farfetched because Arthur is not truly dead, for he has become one of the heroes who guard the land.

The world of early Arthurian myth is one in which the hybrids of history and folk story grow in a rich mulch of primordial, British tradition. These are the seedbed of all subsequent Arthurian legends, explaining why they continue to weave between the pseudo-history of Geoffrey of Monmouth and the world of Oeth and Anoeth where ancient archetypes and adventures still teem in its otherworldly regions. These myths provide a remarkably consistent bedrock, used by all subsequent writers as the lode-bearing strata on which to base the weight of their medieval fabrications and chivalric reworkings.

The original British context for the Arthurian legends was about to be transformed by many European writers and by the chivalric ideology of the Crusades, but not before Taliesin, the most original Welsh fabulator of all, had done his work. In the hills of his native land, Arthur and his men were still remembered, blessed by the *Book of Taliesin's* prophecy of British resistance, "Armes Prydein" (The Prophecy of Britain):

> *in wood, in plain, on hill,*
> *a candle in the dark will go with them.*

5

Arthur of Britain
The Making of a King

Everyone who set their eyes on him was full of delight,
And at once started singing about Arthur the King
And about the splendid triumphs which he had achieved.

LAYAMON (LAWMAN),
THE BRUT[1]

THE RED RAVAGER

Given the historical circumstances of the period in which he lived, it would scarcely be surprising if memories of a Romano-British soldier who mounted a valiant last-ditch stand against the Saxons had gradually faded or become a footnote in the history of these islands.* Instead, as we have seen, within a few years of Arthur's passing, stories of his deeds began to circulate and to grow in the telling. Myths sprang up or were imported from even more distant times and places, and over the next decades Arthur became a national hero, a shining beacon of British

---

*Recent historical evidence has emerged suggesting that several British leaders were in regular contact with Rome from an early time and may even have invited the Romans into the country in a manner that echoes Vortigern's later invitation of the Saxons.

hopes, first during the period of Saxon domination and again after the Norman invasion of 1066.

The political situation in Britain had its own part to play in this. Not long after the Normans had subdued and cataloged England in their *Domesday Book,* the ecclesiastical might of Norman archbishops, with the help of kindred lords and barons, began to turn their attention to the lands and monasteries of Wales. In order to justify their continuing tenure, many Welsh foundations had to come up with documentation in the form of charters and land grants or else suffer forfeiture or takeover by their new masters. These documents needed to appeal to cast-iron precedents and the most unimpeachable sources to protect their foundations, and what better celebrity monarch was there to uphold their land grants than the great King Arthur himself, of whom even the Normans had heard?

New lives of Celtic saints such as Cadoc, Carantoc, Illtud, and Padarn, who were believed to have been contemporaries of Arthur, were hastily compiled (some from older works), in each of which Arthur was shown to grant lands to the holy hermits and sanctified saints of Dark Age Britain. In the process, these saintly lives, written down during the tenth and eleventh centuries, before Arthur became established as a heroic medieval king, offer evidence of a very different figure from that immortalized by Nennius or the mythic tales of the *Mabinogion.* Gone is the warrior and warlord, gone too is the courtly and honorable chieftain who grants quests. Instead, we are presented with a lustful, vain, greedy, impious, and sometimes boorish figure who is more often in the wrong than in the right and whose behavior invariably leads to a grant of land to compensate the saint for his insult to their grace or as penance for his misdeeds. This Arthur is reduced to a stock figure of opportunistic selfishness, the butt of pure-living saints who admonish and forgive him with barely a sigh.

Such hagiographies may well be seen as having more to do with the expediencies of twelfth-century survival than as genuine survivals of sixth-century lore, but they are not as simplistic as they seem, for they purposely trade upon the celebrity of Arthur while at the same time reducing his reputation to burlesque status. We have already seen how the saintly Gildas was exonerated for not mentioning Arthur in his *De Excidio* by virtue of Arthur's supposed killing of his brother Hueil (chapter 2). But the main point of the *Vita Cadoci,* in which Gildas becomes a mediator when Arthur besieges Glastonbury, is that he ends up granting considerable territories to the abbey.

Elsewhere, in the *Vita Cadoci,* Saint Cadoc himself is described as the son of King Gwynllyw of Demetia (Dyfed) and of Gwladys, daughter of King Brychan, from whom Brecon is named. Gwynllyw, having been refused by Gwladys, attempts to elope with her and is pursued by Brychan. Meanwhile, on a nearby hillside, Arthur and his two lieutenants, Cei and Bedwyr, are playing at dice and see the lovers riding below. Arthur admits a lustful predilection for the girl, but the men remind their king that "we are more used to helping the poor and distressed."[2] Arthur becomes sullen with disappointment that his companions aren't going to help him carry Gwladys off, but demands to know the identity of the landowner of that place. Gwynllyw claims that he owns it, and Arthur and his men fight on his side against Brychan—once again emphasizing the importance of land rights.

Later in the story and further forward in time, Arthur pursues a warrior called Lligessawc Llaw Hir (of the Long Hand) for having killed three of his own warriors. Lligessawc takes sanctuary with Saint Cadoc who, with the help of the saints David, Teilo, and Illtud, and clerics from across Britain, sets a suitable honor price by way of compensation for the murder. This is intended to be three oxen or a hundred cows, but Arthur unreasonably commutes this settlement to "cows that are coloured red in front and white behind."[3] These same mysterious beasts are described in the same fashion in the *Mabinogion* story of "Lludd and Llefellys"[4] and again in the Welsh folktale "The Lady of Lyn Y Fan Fach." Being unable to obtain such beasts, Cadoc asks that beasts of any color be rounded up and brought to him, whereupon he changes them into the requisite otherworldly shades—for such are the traditional colors of faery cattle. However, the transfer of beasts is to be held at a ford, and as soon as Cei and Bedwyr pull the cattle onto the opposite bank, the cows immediately become bunches of fern. At this display of ecclesiastical magic, Arthur begs to be forgiven and grants Cadoc's cell a more formal status as a sanctuary.

Arthur seems to be constantly in trouble with these men of the cloth, undoubtedly because he is constantly portrayed as trying to steal things that belong to them. In the twelfth-century *Vita Paterni*, the founder of Llanbadarn returns to Britain after a pilgrimage to Jerusalem with a holy relic, a seamless coat clearly intended to be the garment of Jesus. Arthur takes a fancy to the coat on a visit to the saint's cell but is refused. He returns later to steal it and finds himself swallowed up in the earth up to his neck at the command of Padarn. On being released, Arthur takes Padarn as "his eternal patron." The coat of Padarn appears in a medieval list of the Thirteen Treasures of Britain, where it is called "the coat of Padarn Red-Coat." Its singular property is that if a noble man puts it on, it fits him exactly, but if a lowborn man attempts to wear it, it will not fit him at all. This whole tale is said to take place at a time when King Malgun, clearly a doublet for Maglocunus or Maelgwn of Gwynedd, is at war.

The *Vita Sancti Carantoci*, which deals with the life of Saint Carannog, tells how, when the saint was living in a cave in Ceredigion, he received an altar from heaven that also made a useful guidance system for his boat. He used to throw it upon the Severn and follow in his skiff wherever it led him. The saint meets Arthur when the king wanders into the region of Dindraithon in search of a dragon. Arthur obtains the help of Carannog to lure the dragon into the open, with the saint using his priestly stole as a lead and letting it go again afterward. It then transpires that Arthur has stolen the saint's altar and has been trying to make it into a table but with the unfortunate effect that the altar throws off anything put upon it. Arthur restores the altar and grants Carannog land "eternally by a written deed,"[5] as well as twelve measures of the land where the altar came ashore when Arthur found it.

What these documents show is a continuing familiarity with Arthur's name and reputation—here perceived through the lens of ecclesiastical disapproval. Nor would this be unusual, given the frequently recorded instances of clashes between armies foraging over land owned by the church and angry abbots defending their rights. But it was the changing political situation that promoted an increasing interest in the historicity of Arthur among the Anglo-Norman rulers of Britain. Prompted by a desire to claim a dynastic heritage from Arthur—or the even more distant and fictional "Trojan" founders of Britain, who suggested links with Rome and the rest of Europe—knowledge of Arthur suddenly became a necessary part of the Normans' own tenure.

THE GREAT FABULATOR

Norman claims to the throne of England were in fact based on a very shady oath extracted by Duke William (later William I) from the English king Harold, who was tricked into effectively giving away his kingdom when the Norman duke hid sacred relics inside an altar and pressed Harold into swearing an oath of allegiance he could not subsequently repudiate.[6]

Any work that could imply a connection between the famous hero and the new Norman aristocracy was welcomed with enthusiasm, and this probably accounts to a large degree for the popularity of a book written sometime between 1130 and 1138, which not only bolstered such claims but reinvented Arthur in the form of a fully fledged medieval monarch tailored for a Norman aristocratic audience.

The author of this book was an Anglo-Norman cleric named Geoffrey of Monmouth, whom we have already encountered several times in our journey through the early history of Arthur. The *Historia Regum Britanniae* (History of the Kings of Britain)[7] transformed the story of Arthur forever, making him a medieval king and placing him in a setting that most of us would still recognize as "Arthurian" to this day. The story of Geoffrey and of his book is one of the most fascinating chapters in the history of Arthur; it takes us out of the Dark Ages and into a colorful world of medieval chivalry and magic—a realm where Arthur and his heroes have remained. To accomplish this, Geoffrey drew upon existing sources such as Gildas and Nennius, as well as others that are no longer extant. Patching together fragments of lore and legend with a healthy dash of folktale and more than a pinch of his own imagination, Geoffrey reinvented Arthur as something of a latter-day "emperor," in many ways more Roman than the Romans themselves.

Despite his importance to the developing history of Arthur, we know comparatively little about the life of Geoffrey of Monmouth. It is not even possible to say exactly when he was born, though 1100 is sometimes given as a very conservative estimate of his birth. His name appears as a witness on a number of charters and legal documents dating from 1129 to 1151, telling us that he was of sufficient age and reputation by the first quarter of the twelfth century to be regarded as a suitably responsible signatory. Interestingly, he more than once signed himself Galfridus Arturus Monemutensis (Geoffrey Arthur of Monmouth), and most Geoffrey scholars have taken this as an indication that he was born in Monmouth (or at the very least lived there) and that his father's name was in all probability Arthur. On one or two occasions, he added the title *magister* to his name, suggesting either that he wished to be seen as a scholar or was actually a teacher at Oxford, where he spent the period of time in which the *Historia* was written, and where, though the university did not yet exist, several schools were already established, developing around individual teachers.

It is assumed that Geoffrey grew up at a time and place where stories of Arthur the Briton (or the Celt, or the Roman) were already circulating. Some commentators have suggested that Geoffrey may have been of Breton origin, citing as evidence his enthusiastic references to Armorican history. In either case, he would have heard stories about Arthur during his childhood and may well have learned others from his father. This may well have established within him a love of these old tales and a desire to tell them himself.

By 1129 he was settled in Oxford in the secular college of Saint George on the island of Osney, possibly as one of six Augustinian canons who lived and taught there until 1149. Geoffrey seems to have remained there for the next twenty-two years, and it was during this time that he composed the *Historia*. The impetus to do so is clearly stated in the preface to the work:

> While occupied upon many and various studies, I happened upon the History of the Kings of Britain, and wondered why, in the account which Gildas and Bede had given of them, I found nothing said of those kings who lived here before the Incarnation of Christ; nor of Arthur, and many others who succeeded after the Incarnation; though their actions both deserved immortal fame, and were also celebrated by many people in a pleasant manner and by heart, as if they had been written. Whilst I was intent upon these and suchlike thoughts, Walter, archdeacon of Oxford, a man of great eloquence and learned in foreign histories, offered me a very ancient book in the British tongue, which, in a continued regular story and elegant style, related the actions of them all, from Brutus the first king of the Britons, down to Cadwallader the son of Cadwallo. At his request, therefore, though I have not made fine language my study by collecting florid expressions from other authors, but contented with my own homely style, I undertook the translation of that book into Latin.[8]

Geoffrey's intent seems largely patriotic. He wants to encourage the British (specifically the Welsh) to remember their past glories. But there are a number of interesting things about this preface. First, it tells us that Geoffrey knew of and had presumably read Gildas and Bede, both of whom, as we saw earlier, failed to make any direct mention of Arthur. The second point is the way the name Arthur is mentioned. He is not called a king at this point but is spoken of almost casually, with the obvious expectation that everyone knew who was being referred to.

Two other points lead us toward Geoffrey's sources. First, he says that the stories of the British kings "were . . . celebrated by many people in a pleasant manner and by heart, as if they had been written." This suggests that Geoffrey was drawing upon oral tradition rather than written sources. Then he mentions a "very ancient book in the British tongue" given to him by Archdeacon Walter. This statement has given a lot of commentators pause for thought over the years. Was there ever such a book? What was it, and what did it say?

Unfortunately, no such book has ever been discovered, though this is by no means an indication that it did not exist: far more medieval manuscripts perished than have survived, and it may well have been a unique text compiled by Archdeacon Walter himself—a redoubtable scholar if we are to believe Geoffrey's own statements. Another possibility is that it was some version of Nennius's *Historia Brittonum*, perhaps lacking the addition of his name, which may in any case be of doubtful provenance. It is also entirely plausible that Geoffrey invented his source—a device widely practiced by medieval authors who sought to claim prestige for their own work by suggesting it derived from a more fabulous source.

A further suggestion concerns a variant version of Geoffrey's book, which exists in four separate manuscripts. This version differs in a number of ways from the version normally known as the Vulgate and is the more usually edited copy. The variant version can be dated to within Geoffrey's lifetime but gives his name only in a colophon. It lacks the preface and dedications, and there is no mention of the mysterious British book or of the archdeacon Walter. The opening description of Britain is based solely on Bede, without the additional material that Geoffrey drew from Nennius and Gildas. In the sections dealing with Roman history, the variant version includes passages copied almost verbatim from the fourth-century chroniclers Orosius and Landolfus Sagax, where these are paraphrased in Geoffrey's vulgate text. This, along with other details, led the variant version's editor, Jacob Hammer, to believe that Geoffrey was not the original author of the *Historia* but had been given an older version by someone else (Archdeacon Walter?), which he rewrote and edited to create his own book. It seems more likely, however, that the variant version should be seen as a set of working notes, compiled by Geoffrey himself from a mixture of texts and afterward polished and written up to become the version of the *Historia* we know best today.[9]

Beyond this, and his avowed statement that he read Gildas and Bede, Geoffrey seems to have drawn upon oral traditions and even his own imagination; though this is less usual in the medieval period since most writers liked to copy each other to a degree we would find odd today. Internal evidence suggests that he must have looked at no less than two authentic sources predating his own because he records Urien of Rheged as Urianus in the *Historia,* although he also refers to Urbgen—a much earlier form of Urien's name—elsewhere. Either he did not know the difference between the two or had a variety of source material that was subsequently lost.

Archdeacon Walter, the supposed source of the ancient book, appears again in a curiously suggestive colophon from a sixteenth-century edition of the *Brut Tysilio* (Chronicle of Tysilio), which, while being clearly based in Geoffrey's book, offers some intriguing variations. It says: "I, Walter, archdeacon of Oxford, translated this book from the Welsh into Latin and, in my old age, I have translated it from Latin to Welsh."

From this curious statement we may assume that Walter had lost the original version from which he has made his "translation" and was for some reason translating it back. But could this have been the ancient British book? The *Brut Tysilio* dates from the 1500s and thus postdates Geoffrey's book. However, the colophon suggests that an earlier version of the *Brut* existed, and it is possible that Geoffrey made use of this when he was working on his own text. Perhaps the reason why Walter was retranslating the *Brut* was because he had given his only copy to Geoffrey! The ramifications of medieval copying make this hard to elucidate but suggest that the *Brut Tysilio* could be the source of some part of Geoffrey's work, or even that it is the actual "ancient book" of Archdeacon Walter.

As we have seen, the popularity of Geoffrey's book was at least partly due to the fact that his text backed up the claims of the Anglo-Norman kings to rule not only over England but also parts of Europe and that, even more importantly, it implied they were independent from the kings of France whose vassals they nominally were. If, as Geoffrey stated, Brutus of Troy had defeated the rulers of Gaul before arriving in Britain, and if Arthur had conquered France before the age of Charlemagne, then the kings of France could be seen as subject to those of England.

AN ANCIENT HISTORY

As if this were not enough, Geoffrey also made it clear that both the French and the Britons were actually descended from Trojan Aeneas and were thus of the same race. His book begins with a poetic description of Britain based largely on older classical works such as those of the Greek traveler Posidonius. Then he moves briskly into an account of the adventures of the legendary King Brutus (from whom Geoffrey derives the name of Britain), great-grandson of Aeneas of Troy, who, having escaped the fall of the city, established a line of kings in Italy. Forced out of the country by his enemies, Brutus gathers the last remnants of Troy about him and heads off in search of other lands to conquer. A prophetic statue of the goddess Diana directs him toward:

> *An island which the western sea surrounds*
> *By giants once possessed; now few remain*
> *To bar thy entrance or obstruct thy reign.*
> *To reach that happy shore thy sails employ;*
> *There fate decrees to raise a second Troy,*
> *And found an empire in thy royal line,*
> *Which time shall ne'er destroy, nor bounds confine.*[10]

This island is Britain—or as it is then called, after its gigantic founder, Albion. After fighting with giants himself, Brutus does indeed found a line of kings, including a number of semilegendary or wholly mythical characters such as Hudibras, Bladud, Lud, Coel, and Lear, finally leading to Constantine, prince of Armorica, from whom descend two kings: Aurelius and his brother Uther, who is to become the future father of Arthur.

Most of this already existed in a far more sketchy form in Nennius, but Geoffrey vastly elaborates it. He borrows names from Welsh and

Breton mythology for several of his kings, mixing them in with historic personages such as Cassivellaunus. He also fails to mention the fact that the Romans conquered Britain, though he does give a more or less accurate account of the coming of Julius Caesar, adding how the future emperor realized that, since the Britons were descendants of Troy, they are in fact cousins! However, Caesar finds that they have grown "decadent" and decides to come to their aid. Thus, instead of an all-out conquest, Britain becomes a client kingdom, with its kings owing allegiance to the emperor.[11]

There follows a brief account of the rebellion of Maximus, and then Geoffrey reports how the Britons began to suffer from incursions of Picts, Scots, Norwegians, and Danes. Eventually they appealed to Rome and having received some initial help are then told, as in all the previous accounts of this period, that they are effectively "on their own." In a reference to known events, Geoffrey has the archbishop of London, Guitelinus (Vitalinus), appeal to the Roman Agicius (Aëtius), who refuses to help. Guitelinus then turns to the Armorican king Aldroenus. Geoffrey used this opportunity to extol the virtues of the Bretons, leading some commentators to suggest that he may have been of Breton origin.

Aldroenus declares that he cannot help because, effectively, Britain is in too much of a mess to bother with. However, he does agree to send his brother Constantine, who arrives in Britain and promptly marries a British woman and establishes a new dynasty. Ten years later, following a period of uneasy peace, a Pictish assassin murders Constantine, and a dispute ensues over who will succeed him. His eldest son, Constans, is a monk, and two other children, Aurelius and Uther, are still minors. It is at this point that Vortigern appears on the scene. He sets up Constans as a puppet king with himself as adviser, but almost at once begins to plan Constans's death and his own assumption of the crown.

Constantine is probably based on the usurping emperor Constantine III who reigned from 408 to 411 and did indeed have a son named Constans who was murdered by one of his father's generals. Geoffrey may have borrowed the names from two actual British princes,

Aldwr (Aldroenus) and Custennin (Constantine), who are said to have ruled over part of Cornwall in the mid-fifth century. In any case, the dates are wrong enough to show that Geoffrey had only a vague idea of the period he was writing about or was simply drawing on unreliable sources for his own ends.

Having arranged for the monkish King Constans to acquire a Pictish bodyguard, Vortigern easily arranges for him to be assassinated. He then makes a great outcry, has all the Pictish guards executed, and proclaims himself king until Constantine's next son, Aurelius, comes of age. In reality, Vortigern has no intention of giving up his claim to the throne and plans to have both the heirs killed. Fortunately, a loyal nobleman becomes suspicious of the new regent and arranges for the boys to escape to Brittany, where they are made welcome by King Budicius (Budic)—a real king of Brittany who did not come to power until the beginning of the sixth century and is thus too late to fit Geoffrey's increasingly erratic timescale, or indeed the actual events of the time.

With Constantine's two sons safely out of his reach, Vortigern becomes increasingly nervous and unstable, finally inviting the first band of Saxon mercenaries, under the command of Hengist, into Britain. The alliance is further cemented when Vortigern marries Rowena, Hengist's daughter. This is followed by the Treachery of the Long Knives, in which Hengist and his Saxons contrive to massacre most of the nobility of Britain and begin to ravage the country in earnest.

CHILD OF WONDER

Now hated by everyone, Vortigern flees to Wales and attempts to build himself a refuge. It is here that Geoffrey retells the story of the tower that would not stand, and the marvelous boy who confounds Vortigern's magicians by telling them the real reason why. All of this was, of course, borrowed from Nennius, suitably embroidered in Geoffrey's flowery style. At this point he interrupts himself to report how, having reached this point, he was approached by a number of people, including

Alexander, the bishop of Lincoln, to publish Merlin's prophecies.

Geoffrey agreed, with a suitable show of modesty: "The regard which I owe to your great worth, most noble prelate, has obliged me to undertake the translation of Merlin's prophecies out of British into Latin, before I had made an end of the history which I had begun concerning the acts of the British kings."[12]

He now has the young seer launch into an extended series of prophecies, foretelling the coming of Arthur and continuing onward through time to a very apocalyptic ending in which the goddess Ariadne summons the forces of the planetary spheres and brings the world to an end. Arthur is announced as follows: "The oppressed people (the Britons) will prevail in the end, resisting the savagery of the invaders (the Saxons). The Boar of Cornwall (Arthur) will bring relief from these invaders, and shall trample their necks beneath its feet."[13]
Vortigern's own end is predicted and follows soon after.

Though following Nennius's story of Ambrosius closely, Geoffrey makes some interesting changes. Most importantly he calls his wonder-working boy Merlinus (Merlin) and gives him a backstory as the child of the daughter of the king of Demetia, who had been visited by an incubus—an evil spirit* "that lives between the earth and the moon. Part man and part demon they can take the shape of men and in this form have intercourse with women."[14]

Thus, effectively, the character of Merlin with which most of us are familiar today is launched upon the world. Geoffrey did to Merlin what he was shortly to do to Arthur—made him into a medieval figure and armed him with magical as well as predictive powers. The *Prophecies of Merlin* are in fact based on an earlier work, compiled by Geoffrey circa 1130 and now incorporated into his new book to add to the heady brew of mystery with which he cloaked the Dark Age material. Later still he was to write a very different version of the Merlin story, the *Vita Merlini,* which makes it clear that he was familiar with older Welsh

---

*Geoffrey quotes the Roman author Apuleuis from a real text, *De deo Socratis,* that does indeed include a passage on incubi and succubi.

legends of a seer who went mad and lived the life of a wildman in the depths of the forest.

As Merlin had foretold, Constantine's children, Aurelius and Uther, return at the head of a Breton army and, having killed Vortigern, set about destroying the Saxons. Under Ambrosius's inspired leadership, the combined Breton and British forces have some success, and the Saxons are driven back to the shoreline. Ambrosius then sets out to rebuild the fortunes of the country and commands Merlin (who has mysteriously shown up again, just as he is to do so often during Arthur's time) to create a lasting memorial to the murdered British nobles. Discovered at the Fountain of Galbes, where he is said to go often "to recreate himself," Merlin is brought before the newly crowned King Aurelius, who greets him lightly and immediately asks to know about future events. Merlin's response is direct and to the point: "Mysteries of that sort cannot be revealed . . . except where there is the most urgent need for them."[15]

Suitably abashed, Aurelius turns to the subject of the monument. Merlin suggests that a circle of giant standing stones, known as the Giant's Dance, should be brought across the sea from Ireland and reerected near the site of the battle. Aurelius's response is to burst out laughing. "How can such large stones be moved from so far-distant a country?" he asks. "It is hardly as if Britain itself is lacking in stones big enough for the job!"[16] Again Merlin rebukes him:

> Try not to laugh in such a foolish way. . . . There's nothing ludicrous about my suggestion. These stones . . . have properties that are important medicinally. In the past Giants transported them from the remotest confines of Africa. . . . Whenever they fell ill, baths were prepared at the foot of the stones. They used to pour water over them and run this into baths in which their sick were cured. . . . There is not a single stone amongst them which does not posses some medicinal virtue.[17]

Hearing this, Ambrosius is convinced and at once mounts an expedition to fetch the stones. This entails a brief struggle with Gillomaurius, the king of Ireland, but once this opposition has been overcome, they begin considering ways to bring the stones back to Britain. Merlin watches them for a while and then challenges them: "Try your strength young men . . . and see whether skill can do more than brute strength."[18] The artificers struggle with ropes and pulleys but to no avail. Merlin laughs and sets to work, magically moving the stones, which are then floated across the sea to Britain and set up on the Plain of Amesbury.

It seems clear from the description that Geoffrey is actually referring to Stonehenge. However, he repeatedly confuses Amesbury, which has long been associated with Ambrosius, with both Avebury and Stonehenge—both sites of vast stone circles. At this point in time, no one knew how the Neolithic stone circles had been erected or by whom, but the air of mystery surrounding them made them a perfect setting for this first great magical act by Merlin. It may in addition be the seed from which the idea of Arthur's Round Table sprang.

Geoffrey Ashe has argued plausibly that we may be looking at a very ancient memory, indeed, of a godlike builder of the great Henge, remembered through druidic and later bardic lore, who somehow became linked to the name Merlin, possibly through the geographic link between Merlin's hometown of Carmarthen and the site of the Prescelly quarry, from where the blue stones that form the inner ring of the Henge were originally brought to Salisbury Plain.[19] Whatever the truth, the account of the event in the *Historia* established Merlin's already impressive credentials as a worker of wonders. From this point onward, he was increasingly represented as a magician who could change shape at will and had access to unearthly or occult lore.

UTHER AND THE BIRTH OF ARTHUR

Geoffrey now tells us that Aurelius did not live long. Vortigern's son Pascent joins with Gillomaurius, the king of Ireland, still smarting from the theft of the Giant's Dance, to make war on the new king. Soon after, a Saxon spy disguised as a doctor poisons Aurelius, and his brother Uther becomes king. Nennius has a different account of this in which Ambrosius is in fact friendly with Pascent and gives him lordship over Vortigern's old lands, making it unlikely that Pascent would have wanted to attack him. In fact, Geoffrey seems to have confused two men with the same name, one of whom, the son of the sixth-century Urien of Rheged, is mentioned in the *Trioedd Ynys Prydein* as one of the "Three Arrogant Men of Britain"[20] and seems to have been an altogether more warlike character.

Aurelius's death is marked by the appearance of a great comet: "A star of wonderful magnitude and brilliance, darting forth a ray, at the end of which was a globe of fire in the form of a dragon, out of whose mouth issued two more rays, one of which seemed to stretch itself beyond the extent of Gaul, the other toward the Irish sea, and ended in seven lesser rays."[21]

Merlin is summoned to interpret this and having announced that it marks the death of Aurelius declares that Uther shall now be king of Britain and that "the star, and the fiery dragon under it, signifies yourself, and the ray extending toward the Gallic coast, portents that you shall have a most potent son, to whose power all those kingdoms shall be subject over which the ray reaches."[22]

Geoffrey is preparing the way for the coming of Arthur and uses the appearance of the dragon star to explain the title now adopted by Uther—Pendragon—though, as we have seen, the title is far older than this. As for the comet itself, although there are no exact correlatives for the appearance of such a heavenly body at this time, at least three sightings were recorded during the sixth century. One of these, recorded by Byzantine astronomers in 530, was called the Firebrand, while another, observed in 539, was of such prodigious length it was called the Swordfish. A third was seen in daylight during a total eclipse of the sun in 563. Any of these could have provided Geoffrey with a model for his dragon star.[23]

Another theory recently advanced has suggested that several themes in the Arthurian legends, including Arthur's sobriquet Pendragon and the appearance of the battling serpents at Dinas Emrys, may be memories of a comet that is believed to have visited Earth during this period, causing widespread climatic changes. The dendrochronology of the period does indicate some kind of disaster, and this has led to a suggestion that Merlin's more apocalyptic prophecies may have been inspired by this event.[24] The dragon star might also be an early appearance of Halley's Comet, which is visible from Earth approximately every seventy-five years.

Geoffrey's attention now moves to Uther, Aurelius's brother, who succeeds him as king. Uther is mentioned in several texts that predate the *Historia* and may have at one time been an important character on his own (see chapter 2), but Geoffrey is the first person we know of to make him Arthur's father and to give him a central role in the events of the Arthurian period.

At the advice of Gorlois, the Duke of Cornwall, Uther makes a night attack on the Saxons, led by Hengist's son Octa. Taken by surprise, they are quickly defeated, and Octa is captured and imprisoned in London. Uther next sets out on a tour of the northern lands to assess the damage done by the Picts and Saxons. He then returns in triumph to London and decides to hold a great feast to celebrate his victory. It is here that Geoffrey gives us one of the most familiar episodes in the Arthurian saga.

The celebration is attended by both Gorlois of Cornwall and his wife, Ygerna (also spelled Igerna and Igraine), whom Uther lusts after as soon as he sees her. Affronted, Gorlois leaves the banquet, and Uther demands an apology. When none is forthcoming, the king raises an army and begins to ravage the lands of his former ally. Gorlois, unable to raise a large enough force to fight Uther directly, places Ygerna in the comparative safety of Tintagel Castle, while he himself retires within the walls of a castle at Demilioc, to which Uther lays siege.

Pining for Ygerna, Uther summons Merlin and asks for his help. The enchanter suggests that he change Uther's shape into that of Gorlois so that the king can gain access to Tintagel Castle and lie with Ygerna. This he does, and on that night Arthur is conceived. Meanwhile, Uther's army mounts another attack on Demilioc, and Gorlois is killed, thus, by a clever piece of medieval reasoning, making Arthur semilegitimate, since Ygerna's husband is supposedly dead before Uther sleeps with her!

Plate 1. Hadrian's Wall. The sixth-century poem "Kadeir Teyrnon" suggests that Arthur's origins can be traced to the frontier: "From the slaughter of chieftains/From the destruction of armies/From the loricated Legion/Sprang the Guledic/Around the fierce old boundary." (photo courtesy of John and Caitlín Matthews)

Plate 2. Inscription from Podstrana, Croatia, giving a detailed summary of the career of Lucius Artorius Castus, claimed to be "the only historical character with whom Arthur can with any plausibility be connected." (photo by Linda Malcor)

Plate 3. Carving of a Sarmatian warrior on a stele from Tanais on the Don. Artorius's command of a troop of these noted horsemen provides a strong link with Arthur: "A constant feature of the later accounts of Arthur is his use of armoured cavalry carrying long lances." (photo courtesy of Hermitage Museum, Moscow)

Plate 4. Arthur riding into battle under the dragon standard, from a manuscript of Robert de Boron's *Merlin*. The similarity with the battle standard of the Sarmatians offers strong evidence for the association of Artorius with Arthur.
(photo courtesy of Bridgeman Art Library)

Plate 5. Arthur inherited the Roman task of fighting on many fronts to defend the coasts of Britain—one of the greatest challenges he faced was to unite a land, which, as the map included in the *Notitia Dignitatum* indicates, had become increasingly fragmented. (photo courtesy of Bodleian Library)

Plate 6. Ambrosius Aurelianus, "the most able and prominent of the British leaders to try to galvanise resistance after the death of Vortimer" became an important figure in the days before Arthur appeared. From a manuscript of Robert de Boron's *Merlin*. (photo courtesy of Bridgeman Art Library)

Plate 7. Arthurian scenes are carved on the eleventh-century archivolt of Modena Cathedral, Italy. Here we see Artus de Bretani (Arthur) with Isdernus (Yder) riding to the rescue of Winlogee (Guinevere) from the castle of Burmaltus. (photo courtesy of Bridgeman Art Library)

Plate 8. The constellation of the dragon, from a manuscript produced early in the reign of Henry VII. In an ode commemorating Henry's victory at Bosworth Field, he was acclaimed as "the great joy predicted by Merlin" and the bearer of the red dragon standard of Gwynedd, 'the beast from North Wales . . . Bird and bull of the blood of Arthur." (photo courtesy of the British Library)

Plate 9. A mosaic on the floor of the Cathedral of Santa Maria Annunziata in Otranto, Italy, shows Arthur riding a goat and surrounded by astrological and biblical figures. His placement in the center of the mosaic emphasises his importance and semidivine status. (photo courtesy of John and Caitlín Matthews)

Plate 10. Merlin's Grotto was constructed in the gardens of Richmond Lodge, London, in 1730 at the command of Queen Caroline (wife of George II). Designed by the queen's architect, William Kent, it included busts of Merlin and his "secretary," depicted taking down new prophecies. (photo courtesy of John and Caitlín Matthews)

Plate 11. This illustration by Dorothea Braby from the 1952 edition by the Golden Cockerel Press of the medieval poem "Sir Gawain and the Green Knight" is typical of the extraordinary artwork produced in the twentieth century in response to Arthurian literature. (photo courtesy of John and Caitlín Matthews)

Plate 12. *The Lord of Venedotia* by David Jones.
(courtesy of the David Jones estate)

Later stories in which doubts about Arthur's paternity were expressed gave rise to the inclusion of the sword-in-the-stone episode, designed to offer proof of Arthur's legitimacy.

A possible origin for this episode comes in the Welsh Triads, where Uther is said to teach enchantment to Menw son of Teirgwaedd.[25] Menw appears again in the story of *Culhwch and Olwen* where he is described as a shapeshifter. If Geoffrey knew this story, he could have made the assumption that Uther's enchantment was that of shifting his own form to that of Gorlois—perhaps originally without Merlin's help.

Assuming that he was not following an attested source, Geoffrey may have decided to make Uther Arthur's father from a reference in a poem attributed to the sixth-century bard Taliesin, who mentions Uther's son Madog, whose fortress is said to have been a place of "abundance, exploits and jests."[26] Madog himself is described as the father of a "golden-tongued knight" named Eliwlod, who in the poem "Arthur and the Eagle" is a cousin of Arthur's—which would be right if Madog was Uther's son by another woman. There are also references to a Merin (easily transcribed as Merlin) son of Madog and to Myrddin son of Morfryn in the Triads.[27] Any one of these clues could have led Geoffrey to choose the name Uther for Arthur's progenitor.

By choosing Tintagel as Arthur's birthplace—without, as far as we can see, any specific source—Geoffrey established a tradition that continues to this day. The present castle, perched dramatically on the cliff edge above the North Cornish Sea, dates from the thirteenth century and was founded by Earl Richard of Cornwall. The anonymous medieval French author of *La Foli Tristan* said that it had been built by giants and used to disappear every Midsummer Day and midwinter day.[28] However, Tintagel does have Dark Age connections. The remains of a site, dating from the fifth century and originally thought to be the remains of a monastic settlement, were uncovered in the 1930s and subsequently excavated. A significant amount of high-quality pottery was discovered there. Dubbed "Tintagel ware," it was shown to have originated in the Mediterranean. This led to the conclusion that whoever had occupied the site continued to import wine and other goods from the Continent after contact with Rome was officially severed. The suggestion followed that a person of some importance had lived there, and it was assumed that this could have been Gorlois or even Arthur himself. A further series of recent excavations were undertaken at the beginning of the twenty-first century, following a fire that burned off the grass on an adjacent area and revealed the remains of a far more extensive set of buildings. It is now generally considered that the site was an important center for trade (a harbor almost certainly existed there in the fifth and sixth centuries) and a major power center within the kingdom of Dumnonia.[29]

In the summer of 1968, a team of archaeologists from Glasgow University, digging at Tintagel, uncovered a broken piece of slate that had been used as a drain cover. Its orthography could be safely dated to the fifth or sixth centuries. On it was an inscription written in Latin that also included some more primitive British and Irish elements. The inscription, which had been scratched onto the slate, appears to read: *Pater Coli avi ficit . . . Arthognov . . . Col . . . Ficit,* which can be translated as meaning: "Arthognov, father of a descendent of Coll, has had this made."[30] The discovery caused a sensation in the press and was hailed as "the find of a life-time." The fact that one of the names contains the element *Arth* was immediately assumed to offer conclusive proof of Arthur's connection with Tintagel. However, Arthognov is not Arthur; the only point it shares with him is the first four letters of his name. Nor, as a number of commentators have pointed out, does the name Arthognov appear anywhere else as an alternative reading of Arthur.

An alternative and far more acceptable reading, offered by Geoffrey Smith,[31] comes out as "Paternus, descendent of Grandfather Coll, made it"; while the lower part of the inscription, where it is somewhat damaged, may have followed the same pattern to read: "Arthognov, descendent of Grandfather Coll, made it." This suggests that the slate was the work of two people, perhaps intending it as an inscription honoring their grandfather, or that it was a rough version, which would have later been carved on a memorial stone. Of more interest is the fact that a Paternus (or Padarn) and Coll are both recorded in the Dark Age period. Padarn was a sixth-century saint whose encounter with Arthur presents the latter in a less-than-favorable light (see page 195), while Coll ap Collfrewy is mentioned in the mythological poem "Par Gur" (see chapter 4) and in the Welsh Triads as an enchanter and "one of the three powerful Swineherds of Britain."[32] The presence of these two names alongside that of Arthognov is probably no more than a coincidence but leaves the question of the Tintagel inscription open for further investigation.

We should also mention, in passing, the name of Arthur's mother, Ygerna. It is possible that this name derives from the word *tigerna,* which means "lady" in Old Welsh. The masculine *tigern* (Lord) appears in such names as Kentigern (Lordly Hound) and also, of course, in Vortigern (Strong Lord). The mother of the Irish wizard Mongan is named Caintigern, from *cain,* beautiful, and *tigerna*—Beautiful Lady.[33] In Geoffrey's text, Ygerna is referred to as "the most beautiful woman in Britain."[34] Since her name is often written Igerna, the change from *(t)igerna* to this is only a small one. In Welsh versions of Geoffrey's text, Arthur's mother is known as Eigr and she is given an interesting pedigree. In the *Brut y Brenhinedd,* a thirteenth-century collection of Welsh texts that derive from the *Historia,* she is the granddaughter of Cunedda, the fifth-century ruler of the Votadini, and the daughter of Amlawdd Wledig, a semilegendary chieftain.[35] This identification reinforces Arthur's connection with the area of Manau Gododdin and may be genuine, incorporating historical information no longer extant.

The attribution of such wondrous births to heroes is not unusual, since wonderful warriors must be seen to grow from wonderful children. In Irish tradition a similar story is told of the birth of Mongan, a shapeshifter and magician whose mother's name, as we have seen, is not a far cry from that of Ygerna. In all events Uther and Ygerna seem to have been happy, despite the fact that Uther is responsible for the death of Gorlois. Geoffrey says specifically that "from that day forth they lived together as equals, united in their great love for each other; and they had a son and daughter: the boy named Arthur and the girl Anna."[36]

THE COMING OF THE KING

According to the *Historia,* the next few years seem to have passed comparatively peacefully—until the imprisoned Saxon leader Octa is permitted to escape and at once flees back to Germany where he raises an army to attack Britain. Uther, suffering from an unspecified illness, puts the British forces under the leadership of Loth of Lodonesia, who is by this time married to Uther's daughter Anna. Loth appears in later Arthurian romances as King Lot of Lothian, a name that may possibly be the result of Geoffrey's fondness for inventing eponyms based on places.

The war between the Saxons and Britons continues with no outright victory on either side, and Uther, now old and "half dead," orders a litter to carry him to the army, whom he harangues into action. The next battle with the Saxons takes place near Saint Albans, and the Britons are victorious, driving their enemies northward and killing Octa. But the Saxons are not beaten. They send spies disguised as beggars to watch Uther, and having discovered his habit of drinking from a certain pure spring, they poison it. Uther drinks and dies, along with a hundred of his men. He is buried with great honor beside his brother Ambrosius at the Giant's Dance.

Now Geoffrey at last reaches the core of his history—the life of Arthur. Though it was to become the source for virtually every tale told from here onward, it has a leaner, more historical feel to it. Geoffrey convinces us that he is telling a true story, even though we know that barely a third of what he writes bears any relation to the truth.

With Uther dead the Britons meet to decide who shall lead them. They are unanimous in choosing Arthur, Uther's son, though he is only fifteen at the time: "but he was of outstanding courage and generosity" says Geoffrey, "and his inborn goodness gave him such grace that he was loved by almost all of the people."[37]

The Saxons, meanwhile, had chosen a new leader, Colgrim, and began to attack again with increasing strength. Arthur gathers an army and meets the enemy "beside the River Douglas," inflicting on the

Saxons another resounding defeat. Geoffrey's choice of the Douglas suggests that he had seen either Nennius's battle list or its source; however, he thought the Douglas was close to the city of York, which it is not. Colgrim summons reinforcements, and outnumbered, Arthur retreats to London and calls on King Hoel of Brittany for help. Geoffrey says Hoel is the son of Arthur's sister Anna and Budic, the Breton king who had sheltered Aurelius and Uther. This cannot be right as he had previously told us Anna had married Loth of Lodonesia, and if she is the second child of Uther and Ygerna, she would have been younger than her brother and could therefore not have been married before. Later Geoffrey says that Loth had married the sister of Aurelius Ambrosius, which would make more sense. Equally, since the legends supply Arthur with several half sisters, it may have been one of these to whom he is referring.

Hoel arrives at Southampton with fifteen thousand Breton warriors—thus ensuring that Arthur really does fight "alongside the Kings of the Brittones" (Bretons) as Nennius had reported, while still keeping Arthur as overall king of Britain.[38] The combined forces set off, following (more or less) the battle list supplied by Nennius. However, Geoffrey has no idea where most of the battles were fought and mangles the geography. He has his own ideas about some things, and when he gets to the Battle of Badon, he describes the area (*pagum Badonis*) as being in Somerset and makes it clear that he means Bath. (He had previously described the founding of the city by the mythical King Bladud and called it Caer Badum; now he refers to Badon several times as *Bado*.) He also has the Saxons land at Totnes, the landing place for many invaders, from Brutus to Vespasian, as well as Constantine and even Aurelius and Uther. He thus, perhaps deliberately, establishes an iconic arrival point for some of the major characters in his book. A stone bearing the "footprint of Brutus" can still be seen at Totnes.

Interestingly, Geoffrey's description of the battle fits very well with earlier accounts. He has the battle last three days, which fits with the entry in the *Annales Cambriae*. (Geoffrey could not have seen this but may have had access to a text on which the *Annales* themselves were

214 Arthur of Britain

based.) The first encounter is near Badon, and the Saxons are then driven back to the nearby hill—which fits with Gildas's *Mons Badonicus*. Finally, Geoffrey ensures that Arthur alone leads the army. Hoel is sick and remains behind; Arthur's other ally, Cador of Cornwall, son of Gorlois and Ygerna and therefore Arthur's half brother, does not arrive until later.

This suggests that Geoffrey had reached the same conclusion that most commentators have regarding Nennius's statement that Arthur alone slew the enemy at Badon by interpreting it as meaning that he won his great victory without the aid of his allies.

Another indication of Geoffrey's wide reading and access to earlier sources is the description he gives us of Arthur preparing for battle.

> Arthur himself, having put on a coat of mail suitable to the grandeur of so powerful a king, placed a golden helmet upon his head, on which was engraved the figure of a dragon; and on his shoulders he placed his shield called Pridwen, upon which the picture of the blessed Mary, mother of God, was painted, in order to put him frequently in mind of her. Then girding on his Caliburn, which was an excellent sword made in the Isle of Avalon, he graced his right hand with his lance, named Ron, which was hard, broad, and fit for slaughter.[39]

This reads like a typical list of the weapons of a much earlier hero. In fact, it is an almost exact match for *Culhwch and Olwen* the early bardic story (see chapter 4). Here, too, for the first time in any surviving history of his life, Arthur is armed with the sword Caliburnus, an earlier version of Excalibur, which is here said to have been "made on the Isle of Avalon"—an idea that was to grow in the telling throughout the later medieval romances. The final statement regarding the lance reads like a line from the work of a Celtic bard, though Geoffrey treats the word *ron* as a title while it is actually a word referring to a type of long spear and probably derives from *ron-cymmyniad* meaning "spear of command." This is also the first known mention of Avalon, reference to which Geoffrey may have found in earlier sources or simply invented.

Arthur's victory is certainly a great one, though by no means the last of his battles to secure the kingdom. Both Colgrim and his brother Baldulf fall at Badon, and the surviving Saxons, now led by Cheldric, flee back to their boats. There, Cador intercepts them before they can escape and in another battle decimates them, killing Cheldric and forcing the few remaining survivors onto to Isle of Thanet, where they finally surrender. Arthur meanwhile marches north to Alclud, where Hoel has engaged the Picts and Scots. More battles follow until the enemy forces are finally besieged at Loch Lomond—a detail that supports the idea that Arthur's battles were fought in the north. However, before Arthur has time to utterly destroy his enemies, he learns that the Irish king Gillomaurius has landed nearby in an attempt to relieve the hard-pressed Picts and Scots. Meeting this fresh threat head on, Arthur cuts the Irish to pieces, forcing them to return home. He then turns his attention back to the Picts and Scots and decimates them. In Geoffrey's words, "he treated them with unparalleled severity, sparing no one who fell into his hands."[40]

Arthur seems poised to continue deeper into Scottish and Pictish lands, but at this moment, the northern bishops and clergy arrive, *their feet bare and in their hands the relics of their saints,*[41] to fall on their knees and beg Arthur to have mercy. As we have seen, Arthur's relationship with the churchmen of his time was far from comfortable. But here he is persuaded by their pleas and grants a pardon to the defeated peoples.

With most of his enemies dead or crushed into submission, Arthur returns in triumph to York, where he implements a program of rebuilding churches and monasteries and returning lands to those Britons who had been driven out by the Saxons. As we saw in chapter 1, much of the detail of this campaign against the northern tribes parallels that of Lucius Artorius Castus, which took place almost three hundred years earlier. It is possible that Geoffrey had heard stories still circulating of this much earlier event, or that whatever source he was utilizing at that moment had recorded the story of a soldier named Arthur who brought the northern "barbarians" to their knees. It is almost impossible to see the truth or otherwise of this now, because Geoffrey muddled up the geography and conflated more than one version of events. However, it is interesting that we find Arthur operating from a base at York, as this was traditionally the center for the *Dux Britanniarum*—a post briefly held by Artorius. Ultimately, however, what is important here is that Geoffrey's text describes Arthur as a king who is both bold and confident, had strong and dependable allies, and was very much the darling of the people.

Among those honored at the victory celebrations are three northern lords, whom he says are brothers, though they later appear unrelated. These are Urianus of Murefensium, Loth of Lodonesia, and A(n)guselus of Albany. The names are interesting as they all have resonances with earlier characters, some perhaps legendary, others recognizable historically, and two at least remain part of the Arthurian world long after. Urianus is Urien, the real sixth-century chieftain of Rheged (comprising parts of Cumbria and adjacent lands), whom Nennius reports as one of the leaders who continued the battle against the Angles in the north after the death of Arthur (chapter 3). Later he reappears in the *Mabinogion* tales of Arthur and the later medieval romances as one of Arthur's chief supporters, and his son, Owein, becomes a leading knight of the Round Table. The deeds of this historical chieftain were recorded in a number of praise-poems attributed to Taliesin, whom Geoffrey connects with Arthur in his later work *Vita Merlini*. Geoffrey says that Arthur gave Urien the province of Moray; however, the *Brut Tysilio*, another source, makes this Rheged—suggesting either that Geoffrey changed this or that the compiler of the *Brut* had a more accurate source.

Loth makes a powerful reappearance in the later medieval romances, initially as Arthur's ally and only later as his enemy. His association by Geoffrey with the kingdom of Lothian (again in Southern Scotland) may simply have arisen from the similarity of the names, though it has also been suggested that Loth might be identified with an actual fifth-century ruler of Lothian named Leudonus. Geoffrey also makes him the disposed king of Norway, which becomes an excuse for Arthur to attack that country, as we shall see.

The third and final brother, A(n)guselus, may be based on a Dalriadan prince named Angus who ruled over Argyll in 498 and became chief of Islay and the surrounding islands soon after. However, the latter almost certainly had no connection with Arthur, and this may be seen as yet another example of Geoffrey's pillaging of older documents to supply names for his characters. Anguselus however does remain part of the later Arthurian cannon, reappearing in later texts as Angusel and possibly as Anguish of Ireland, who is represented at different times as both as an ally and an enemy of Arthur. The *Brut Tysilio* names him Arawn, a name redolent with mythic connections in Welsh tradition, where he is the lord of the underworld realm of Annwfyn (chapter 4).

Having set the kingdom to rights, Arthur now decides to marry. He chooses someone who is described as "the most beautiful woman in the entire island"[42] and someone who was to become a central figure in the Arthurian legends from here on: Guinevere. We have already examined the mythic antecedents of Arthur's queen in chapter 4; here we should note that Geoffrey says she had been brought up in the household of Cador of Cornwall, who is, of course, both Arthur's ally and his half brother. The *Brut Tysilio,* an adaptation of Geoffrey's book, amplifies this by using a more ancient British form—Gwenhwyfar— and recording that she was "the daughter of Gogfran the Hero." Her mother is also said to be from a noble Roman family.

Despite efforts on the part of some scholars to identify Guinevere with an actual historical woman, there is no conclusive evidence to support this. There are certainly earlier references to those in Geoffrey, most notably in the bardic tale of *Culhwch and Olwen,* which, though its transcription postdates Geoffrey's text by between fifty and seventy years, contains material from a much earlier date. The version in the *Historia* is plausible, since it is likely that Arthur would have known Guinevere as a child, growing up in the court of Cador and might even have fallen for her then—making his choice (other than her renowned beauty and her Roman blood) a reasonable one.

Elsewhere in Welsh tradition, Gogfran (or Ogrfan) is described as a giant, while the Triads name him as the father of one of three queens named Guinevere.[43] The *Brut Tysilio* is alone in calling him a hero and describing him as the father of Arthur's queen. The old name for the town of Oswestry was Caer Ogyrfan, perhaps suggesting that this may have been the hero's home. As ever with these accounts, we are almost certainly seeing a mixture of real and legendary material, so that there may indeed have been a real person named Guinevere, who might indeed have been married to Arthur, even though we have no firm evidence for this.

THE GREAT KING ARTHUR

Geoffrey's chronicle now enters more curious territory. Up to this point he has confined himself within the bounds of possibility, following sources that had at least a basis in actual events. Now he takes flight into the realms of pseudo-history.

Following his marriage Arthur gathers together a fleet of ships and sets sail with his army for Ireland. There he once again encounters Gillomaurius of Ireland and defeats him with ease. Not content with this, the youthful king continues on and conquers Iceland. The effect of this is to bring Doldavius, king of Gotland, and Gunhpar, king of the Orkneys, to sue for peace—presumably before Arthur can attack them!

None of this really makes sense. Assuming for a moment that Arthur did indeed conquer part of Ireland—and Giraldus Cambrensis (Gerald of Wales) does say in the twelfth century that the kings of Ireland paid tribute to Arthur—no one at this time would have been interested in Iceland, even assuming they could have found it. However, the *Brut Tysilio* again offers a possible clue. There, Iceland is called Islont, which may plausibly be Islay, an island in the Southern Hebrides ruled over at this time by the same Angus, who may have given his name to Arthur's ally A(n)guselus. It would be logical for Arthur, having awarded the territory to this chieftain, to have sent men or gone himself to eject the current occupants. Given that Arthur will soon restore Loth to the throne of Norway, there is at least a certain crazy logic in Geoffrey's account. If the "Irish" who Arthur defeats were in fact the Dalriadians of Argyll, who had originated in Ireland, then this shifts the whole scene from Ireland and Iceland to the Scottish mainland and the Hebrides, which certainly makes more sense in the context of Arthur's actual time line.

As to the kings of Gotland and Orkney—this reads like a deliberate mistake. Not long before Geoffrey's time, there had been a considerable dispute between Scotland and Sweden over the sovereignty of both the Orkney and Hebridean Islands, and it may well be simply that Geoffrey wanted to place a recognizable reference into his text. *Brut Tysilio* has Scotland for Gotland, which again seems to fit. If Arthur (or some other Dark Age prince of the north) launched a campaign, which took him into Scotland (fighting against the Irish), then onward to the Orkney and Hebridean Islands (fighting against Danes or Geats), an account of this could well have given Geoffrey the idea of making Arthur the hero of such a tale, thus extending his growing kingdom outside Britain and emphasizing his status as a Roman emperor or medieval-style king.

Another text, referred to in the writings of the Elizabethan magus John Dee, could be a possible lost source for this. The book, known as *Gestae Arthuri* (Deeds of Arthur),[44] may well be another contender for Bishop Walter's "British Book," and as we shall see, together with Geoffrey's book, it became part of a campaign to includes several northern territories within the realm of Queen Elizabeth I.

Geoffrey now took his hero further into the role of monarch. Returning from his conquests and having established an era of peace that was to last twelve years, Arthur settles down for a time. And here for the first time, we catch a glimpse of the Arthur of romance—the great king with his entourage of knights. As Geoffrey tells us:

After this, having invited all those who were most famed for valour among the foreign nations, he began to increase the number of his household, and introduced a code of courtliness into his court, that people of the remotest countries thought worthy of imitation. Soon there was not a nobleman who thought himself worth anything unless his clothes and arms were in the same fashion as those of Arthur's knights.[45]

Word of Arthur's brilliant court and his great deeds soon reached the Continent, and various rulers of kingdoms across the sea began to fear that he would try to conquer them. Town walls were strengthened, towers rebuilt, and new fortresses sited at selected points where it was felt Arthur might attack. Unfortunately, this had the opposite effect to that desired by the foreign kings. When Arthur hears how he is feared, he decides he rather likes the idea of conquering Europe and begins to raise an army.

First, however, he sails to Norway, to restore Loth to the throne. It is only now that we learn that Loth is related to Sichelm of Norway, who had died and left the kingdom to him in his will. The Norwegians, however, were reluctant to accept him as their new king and instead elected a man named Riculf to the throne. After a brief aside to tell us that Loth's son Gawain, then twelve years old and later to be among the greatest of Arthur's knights, has been sent to serve in the household of Pope Sulpicius, who dubbed him a knight, Geoffrey proceeds to relate the attack on Norway, which is so successful that in the end Arthur conquers Denmark as well, adding both kingdoms to his growing empire.

The sources for this, and the following part of Geoffrey's book, are by no means clear—despite his own statements regarding his sources. The mention of Gawain may be drawn from one of the few other surviving Arthurian texts written in Latin. The *De Ortu Waluuanii* (The Rise of Gawain), which dates from the last quarter of the twelfth century and does indeed tell the story of Gawain, who is captured by pirates and sold into slavery before eventually arriving in Rome and becoming one of the Pope's bodyguards. Later in the same text, Gawain returns to Britain to aid his uncle Arthur, who is threatened by attackers from the West.[46]

In one of the most dramatic and colorful episodes of the *Historia,* Arthur decides to conquer Gaul. He finds himself opposed by the Roman tribune Frollo on behalf of the emperor Leo. Many of the

Gauls flock to join Arthur, and after an initial encounter in which the Romans are driven off, Frollo flees to Paris. A siege ensues, and after a month Frollo issues a challenge to Arthur to meet him in single combat on an island in the River Sein. Arthur happily agrees, and the two men meet and fight a long and bloody combat. Despite the fact that Frollo is "of immense stature" (contemporary illustrations of this fight often depict him as a giant), Arthur kills him. The Gaulish army now surrenders, and Arthur sends Hoel with half the army to attack Poitou, Aquitaine, and Gascony, while he himself ravages the rest of Gaul. According to Geoffrey, the continental wars continue for nine years, at the end of which time Arthur is master of all Gaul. Returning to Paris he gives the provinces of Normandy and Anjou respectively to his cupbearer Bedivere and his seneschal Sir Kay.

Much of this is of interest. We have already noted in chapter 1 the campaign led by Lucius Artorius Castus, which echoes Arthur's continental wars (see pages 6–17), and the evidence for Riothamus, who also fought a series of battles in Brittany and Gaul (see pages 84–86).

We should note that the *Historia* does show a distinctly Breton preference. From the Armorican exploits of Riothamus and the late fourth-century usurpers, notably Maximus and Constantine III, who rallied their troops in that region, to the British immigrants who fled from Saxon incursion in such numbers that it came to be called Brittany, or Little Britain, there were strong connections between the two countries. The eleventh-century Breton *Life of St. Goeznovius,* as we may remember, paints a picture of a threatened British church defended by "the great Arthur, King of the Britons" who wins many battles "in Britain and parts Gaul." One authority is unequivocal in his belief that "an early eleventh-century book of Breton origin is the only tenable candidate we have come up with" for Geoffrey's original source for this part of his narrative.[47]

That a passionate Breton interest in Arthur continued well into the medieval period, is indicated in the following passage by the twelfth-century chronicler Alanus de Insulis in his *Merlini Ambrosii Britanni.*

Go to the realm of Armorica, which is lesser Britain, and preach
about the market places and villages that Arthur the Briton is dead
as other men are dead, and facts themselves will shows you how true
is Merlin's prophecy, which says that the ending of Arthur shall be
doubtful. Hardly will you escape unscathed, without being whelmed
by curses or crushed by the stones of your hearers.[48]

Geoffrey's account of the Gaulish campaign once again demonstrates
his familiarity with older sources when he lists Bedivere and Kay as
Arthur's cupbearer and seneschal. As we have seen, these characters have
been with Arthur for a long time and are mentioned in many of the earliest mythological sources—including, perhaps, Breton lays that recalled
the deeds of Arthur. Both Bedivere (Bedwyr) and Kay (Cai) were to
remain part of Arthur's permanent entourage throughout the remainder
of his career in literature. The fact that Geoffrey gives them lordship over
Normandy and Anjou is significant. It seems part of a desire—fueled no
doubt by self-interest—to show that the Norman kings of Britain were
descendants of Arthur and had inherited his authority.

Why else did the Normans adopt Arthur as a major hero—as they
seem to have done from the appearance of Geoffrey's book onward?
Could it have been that the oral Breton lays had made him famous, or
was it because the Normans, who were themselves the conquerors of
Arthur's former English enemies, now aligned themselves with him?
While Geoffrey was attending to the early history of Britain, William of
Malmesbury and Henry of Huntingdon were composing histories about
the English kings and bishops. Geoffrey's decision to discuss the Britons
and not the English comes from his Welsh upbringing, but he drew his
living from Norman patronage. His focus upon Arthur's European campaigns would have increased his readability among the northern French
at home and in England and was later invoked by several English monarchs as a reason for their attempts to conquer lands in Europe.*

---

*For Henry II see page 245; other monarchs, including Henry VII, Elizabeth I, and
James I, also used the example of Arthur's conquests and their own supposed descent
from him as excuses for expansion claims (see pages 307–15).

According to Geoffrey's rather sketchy chronology, Arthur is now in his forties and has been fighting almost constantly over the two decades since he came to the throne. He now decides to return to Britain and to hold a showy celebration at which he will wear the crown. Some commentators have assumed this to be Arthur's coronation, but in fact he had been consecrated by Archbishop Dubricus on first assuming the throne. Here he is simply staging a symbolic tableau in which he will sit in state as a very medieval king surrounded by his powerful barons and lords and greet all those who owe him fealty.

The setting for this magnificent occasion is the City of the Legions (Caerleon upon Usk), which had Arthurian associations stretching back as far as Lucius Artorius Castus. Geoffrey was the first to suggest Caerleon as Arthur's most important seat of power. Possibly he knew the place personally and wanted to sing its praises. He does so in no small measure, describing it in glowing terms and allowing free rein to his imagination—inspired perhaps by the Roman ruins that were still standing in his day. The circular amphitheater, which can still be seen there, may also have influenced the creation of Arthur's Round Table.

The detailed description of the city, with its "beautiful meadows and groves, and the magnificence of the royal palaces with lofty gilded roofs that adorned it, made it even rival the grandeur of Rome,"[49] shows how far indeed we have come from Dark Age Britain.

Kings and chieftains come to Caerleon from all over Britain and much of Europe and from Scandinavia to attend the coronation. All attend mass in the two great cathedral churches, and afterward there is a splendid feast, at which Kay the seneschal, attended by a thousand noblemen dressed in ermine, brings in the food. Geoffrey goes on:

If I were to describe everything, I should make this story far too long. Indeed, by this time, Britain had reached such a standard of sophistication that it excelled all other kingdoms in its general affluence, the richness of its decorations, and the courteous behavior of its inhabitants. Every knight in the country who was in any way famed for his bravery wore livery and arms showing his own distinctive color; and women of fashion often displayed the same colors. They scorned to give their love to any man who had not proved himself three times in battle. In this way the womenfolk became chaste and more virtuous and for their love the knights were ever more daring.[50]

Here we have a medieval Christian court ruled over by Arthur, with its knights and ladies (the former seeking to impress the latter with their prowess in battle), its splendid banquets, and its great churches. For the first time in literature, we see him presiding over a tournament at which the knights bear arms with their own distinctive heraldry. This is not far from the elaborate romances that were to follow, but it is a long way from the smoke-filled halls of the Dark Age Arthur.

The guest list of people who attend this stately ceremonial is drawn from a variety of sources. Some, undoubtedly, show Geoffrey drawing at random from genealogies that mix mythic and historical characters. Uriens is there, as are Cador of Cornwall and Cadwallo Laurh, king of the Venedoti, who has been identified as Cadwallon Lawhir or "Long Hand" of Gwynedd, who ruled from around 500 to 534. Some have suggested that Geoffrey was working from an ancient "king list" here, but for the most part, the names are randomly selected to show that Arthur's rule stretched over the whole of Britain and much of the Continent. Thus when Arthur proceeds to the church to wear the crown, he is accompanied by four kings, hailing from Albany, Cornwall, Demetia, and Venedotia (Gwynedd). The consorts of these kings, who carry white doves to be released at the appropriate moment, similarly surround Guinevere.

Arthur is also presented here as a titular head of the church in Britain. When the saintly Archbishop Dubricus resigns to follow the life of a hermit, Arthur appoints his own uncle, David (whom we have not heard of before and who cannot be identified with any historical figure), to the archbishopric. At the same time, with the approval of Hoel, he appoints Tebaus of Llandaf to the See of Dol in Brittany and appoints new bishops to Silchester, Winchester, and Alclud.

THE ROMAN WARS

During Arthur's ceremony twelve envoys arrived carrying olive branches. They presented Arthur with a letter from the Roman procurator Lucius Hiberius, who takes Arthur to task for failing to pay due tribute to Rome and for attacking and laying claim to territories in Gaul and elsewhere that still belong to the Roman Empire. Arthur is summoned curtly to appear in Rome and face the consequences of this behavior. Failure to do so will bring the wrath of Rome upon him, and Lucius himself will invade British territory in order to restore to Rome what is Rome's.

Arthur's reaction to this is immediate—he responds by declaring that Rome should be paying *him* tribute since his forbears, Constantine and Maximus, had both ruled over the empire. Cador of Cornwall remarks lightheartedly that everyone in Britain was getting far too complacent and that it was time for another war! Arthur then begins to assemble a huge army of 180,000 men and places the kingdom in the hands of Guinevere as regent, with his nephew Mordred as her adviser.

Geoffrey is clearly enjoying himself hugely here. He gives over almost as much space to Arthur's Roman war as he does to the whole of the rest of his lifetime. He invents grandiloquent speeches for everyone and describes the battles in great detail. He also introduces Mordred as the king's nephew—a significant act, as we shall see.

Arthur departs from Southampton with his army, but on arriving in Gaul makes a detour to Mont Saint-Michel to fight a giant who has been devouring maidens. Here, Arthur reverts to the giant-killing status of older bardic tales and the *Vitas* of Saints, and once again Geoffrey throws away any chance that we might take his history seriously by taking us into the world of myth. This done, however, he proceeds to a brisk and racy description of Arthur's great battle against Lucius Hiberius in which the heroes Bedivere and Kay both fall and Lucius himself is killed.

The question must now be asked: Who was Lucius Hiberius? Geoffrey himself seems to get confused as he refers to him four times as emperor, several times as general, and also as procurator, while also referring to him as a servant of the emperor Leo. All this suggests that once again Geoffrey is working from more than one source and paying little attention to details where they do not agree. Lucius is at least a partially invented character since no emperor with such a name is known to have ruled over Rome at this time. There was an emperor Leo I, who ruled over the Eastern Empire from 457 to 474. "Hiberius" could stand either for "of Ireland" or "of Spain" or simply be a misspelling for "Tiberius," a Roman name under which he appears in other texts. The later Norman adaptation of Geoffrey by Wace tells us he was born in Spain and was between thirty and forty when he went to war with Arthur, but we do not know if this comes from another source or was just embroidery. The great Arthurian scholar R. S. Loomis suggested his name was derived from the Welsh Llenlleawc Hibernus (Llenlleawc the Irishman),[51] and following up on this, August Hunt has declared that the entire war is an account of a raid on the otherworld by Arthur, accounts of which are certainly found within the mythic material relating to Arthur.[52]

Geoffrey Ashe in his study of the Riothamus material suggests a puppet emperor named Glycerius, who ruled briefly in 473–474[53] as the original Lucius. A further possibility is that Geoffrey is drawing upon a life of the Frankish leader Clovis, who came to power in 481, aged fifteen (as does Geoffrey's Arthur) and defeated the Roman governor of Northern Gaul (as did Arthur), before going on to pursue a nine year campaign in Brittany (again echoed by Arthur). In 509 he became sole leader of the Franks but died soon after, aged forty-five. The parallels between Clovis and Arthur presented in Geoffrey's book are sufficient to suggest that Geoffrey may have used a life of this figure to create his account of Arthur's continental victories.

Having won this victory over the might of Rome, Arthur now audaciously considers advancing on the eternal city itself. Had he done so, and had he been again victorious, he would have become the ruler of a kingdom at least half the size of the historical empire, but before he can do so, word comes that Mordred has seized power in Britain and has been joined by Guinevere. Arthur gives over command of the Roman campaign to Hoel and returns to Britain. There he finds that Mordred has joined forces not only with the hated Saxons but also with the Picts and Scots, raising an army of eighty thousand men. A battle follows in which Arthur's nephew Gawain and King Anguselus are killed and Mordred's forces pushed back to Winchester. Hearing this, Guinevere flees to the City of the Legions and enters a nunnery.

Two more battles follow, the first at Winchester in which Mordred loses many of his men, and the second at Camlann (Geoffrey says the River Camblan, the *Brut Tysilio* corrects it to Camlann) in which Mordred is killed and Arthur mortally wounded. Geoffrey rather tersely ends his account by telling us that Arthur "was carried off to the Isle of Avalon [Insula Avallonis], so that his wounds might be attended to. He handed the crown of Britain over to his cousin Constantine, the son of Cador Duke of Cornwall; this in the year 542 after our Lords Incarnation."[54]

Geoffrey thus gives us a final end for Arthur but makes it mysterious. Did Arthur die of his wounds or was he healed in Avalon? Later authors were convinced he did not die but lived on in a state of suspended animation until he was called upon to return. One of the most interesting details of this episode is that Geoffrey knows that Arthur and Mordred fell at Camlann, yet the only known early source that mentions this is the *Annales Cambriae*, which he could not have seen.[55] Again we are forced to assume that Geoffrey had access to another source—presumably the ancient British book. Geoffrey's date for these events—one of only three precise dates he gives in the whole book— seems too late, but again we must ask, where did he find it? Gidlow thinks it might be in Bede, since he alone of Geoffrey's known sources used the *Anno Domini* form of dating, and the two dates Geoffrey includes earlier in his book both match those given by Bede. However, *The Ecclesiastical History of the English People* does not mention either Arthur or Camlann. Geoffrey could have looked ahead five years to the arrival of the Saxon king, Ida, in 547 and taken a line backward, but this seems unlikely.[56]

Another interesting detail is that soon after the Battle of Camlann,

Geoffrey describes how Constantine, Arthur's successor, murders the two sons of Mordred in a church. This seems to hark back directly to Gildas, who tells the same story without naming the murdered children's father.[57]

Geoffrey uses the first third of his book to get to the establishment of the first House of Constantine, then gives over almost all the remaining pages of his book to tell us about Arthur's immediate forbears and Arthur himself. The last fifth of the book is a rapid gallop through the Saxon period immediately after Arthur's death—though it is obvious that Geoffrey has lost interest. What really excites him is the story of the great king who ruled over Britain in the time after the departure of the Romans. But this is not the Arthur of Nennius, nor does the "history" bear much resemblance to the accounts of Gildas or Bede, both of whom Geoffrey insists he had read. Instead, we have a wondrous brew, consisting of part mythical and part legendary details, with some real history thrown in, all of it bound together by Geoffrey's racy style and dressed in the costume of his own time.

Two of the many variant versions of the *Historia,* those kept at Bern and Harlech, end with a colophon that is not in the Vulgate version. It shows Geoffrey determinedly holding on right to the end to the idea that he had based his book on a reliable source—though it is possible that a later hand added this.

The Welsh, once they had degenerated from the noble state enjoyed by the Britons, never afterward recovered the overlordship of the island. On the contrary, they went on quarrelling with the Saxons and among themselves and remained in a perpetual state of either civil or external warfare. The task of describing their kings, who succeeded from that moment onward in Wales, I leave to my contemporary Caradoc of Llancarfan. The kings of the Saxons I leave to William of Malmesbury and Henry of Huntingdon. I recommend these last to say nothing at all about the kings of the Britons, seeing that they do not have in their possession the book in the British language which Walter, Archdeacon of Oxford, brought from Wales.

It is this book which I have been at such pains to translate into Latin in this way, for it was composed with great accuracy about the doings of these princes and in their honour![58]

TRUTH OR LIES

The *Historia Regum Britanniae* became a bestseller of its time, with almost two hundred manuscript copies being made and distributed throughout England and the rest of Europe, influencing chroniclers as far distant as Poland. It was widely accepted as a serious work of scholarship, and Geoffrey's veracity as a historian was seldom attacked, even by his near contemporaries. It may seem remarkable to a modern reader that most people of the time took it seriously, but it should be borne in mind that there was very little sense of history as we would understand it today in the twelfth century; to the people of the time, the Dark Ages were so far off as to be virtually mythical. This largely explains how the mythic version of Arthur developed alongside Geoffrey's account of him, with its avowed intention to place Arthur in a more "serious" historical setting—one that helped ratify the claims of the Anglo-Norman dukes of Normandy to be independent from the kings of France.

The *Historia* duly became the standard reference work for British history, giving shape, meaning, and continuity to the past. Yet there were occasional detractors. For example, the twelfth-century traveler and gossip Giraldus Cambrensis suggested a certain degree of doubt when he told the following story in his *Itinerarium Cambriae* (Itinerary of Wales). He recounts the tale of an illiterate seer called Meilerius who lived in the neighborhood of Caerleon (perhaps a distant ancestor of Merlin!) and was known to have recourse to familiar spirits to enable him to foretell the future, tell whether statements were true or false, and even detect untrue passages in books. Giraldus goes on: "It happened once when he was being abused beyond measure by foul spirits, that the Gospel of St. John was placed on his breast; the spirits vanished completely, at once flying away like birds. When it was later removed and the History of the Britons by Geoffrey Arthur substituted for it, by way of experiment, they settled down again, not only on [Meilerius's] entire body, but also on the book itself, for a longer time than they were accustomed to, in greater numbers and more loathsomely."[59]

The suggestion that the *Historia* was largely a work of fantasy was put more directly by Geoffrey's contemporary William of Malmesbury, who referred to him as a "fabulator" and a "writer of lies," while a later chronicler, Ranulf of Higden, in his book *Polychronicon* (ca. 1327) tears into Geoffrey's wilder fancies:

> Many men wonder about this Arthur, whom Geoffrey extols so much singly, how the things that are said of him could be true, for, as Geoffrey repeats, he conquered thirty realms. If he subdued the king of France to him, and did slay Lucius the Procurator of Rome, Italy, then it is astonishing that the chronicles of Rome, of France, and of the Saxons should not have spoken of so noble a prince in their stories, which mentioned little things about men of low degree. Geoffrey says that Arthur overcame Frollo, King of France, but there is no record of such a name among men of France. Also, he says that Arthur slew Lucius Hiberius, Procurator of the city of Rome in the time of Leo the Emperor, yet according to all the stories of the Romans Lucius did not govern in that time—nor was Arthur born, nor did he live then, but in the time of Justinian, who was the fifth emperor after Leo. Geoffrey says that he has marvelled that Gildas and Bede make no mention of Arthur in their writings; however, I suppose it is rather to be marvelled that Geoffrey praises him so much, whom old authors, true and famous writers of stories, leave untouched.[60]

There remains a kernel of truth in what Geoffrey wrote, and despite his flights of fancy, he followed the general outlines of earlier authors whom he believed to be recording the truth. Lewis Thorpe, the most recent translator of Geoffrey's work, compared the relationship between the book and the history of Dark Age Britain to that of the seventeen historical books of the Bible and the history of the Israelites in Palestine.[61]

As we have seen, Geoffrey himself claimed to have drawn upon an ancient book in the British tongue, although no trace of this has ever been discovered, but whether or not such a book existed, Geoffrey succeeded in pulling together strands of oral tradition, historical memory, and pure invention and dressed them in the fashions and settings of the time. In doing so, he created the first Arthurian "novel" and set the seal upon the literary career of his hero for several ages to follow.

THE LIFE OF MERLIN

Encouraged by the success of his first literary excursion, Geoffrey now turned his attention to the second most popular character in the *Historia*—Merlin. The *Vita Merlini*[62] dates from the period between 1148, when its dedicatee, Robert de Chesney, became bishop of Lincoln, and 1151, when Geoffrey himself became bishop of Saint Asaph— perhaps as a result of his literary success. Though the manuscript itself bears neither title nor author, a later scribe has written in the margin *"Explicit Vita Merlini Caledoii per Galfridum Monemutensem"* (Here begins the Life of Merlin by Geoffrey of Monmouth). We have no reason to believe that Geoffrey is not the author, and a careful reading of the two texts that bear his name show a number of stylistic similarities.

Geoffrey's sources were almost certainly a number of poems attributed to the authorship of the Welsh bard and seer named Myrddin, and following up the hints and clues he found in these, along with the story of a Scottish seer named Lailoken, he created a very different tale of the magician he had described so vividly in the *Historia*. It is a picture that we will recognize in part from the mythic materials discussed in chapter 4. As he had done for Arthur, Geoffrey brought Merlin firmly into the twelfth century, establishing him as a character that would remain more or less unchanged throughout the medieval period and on into the seventeenth and eighteenth centuries.

At the beginning of the *Vita,* Merlin is described as a king and prophet of the south Welsh, famed far and wide for his wisdom and power. Then war breaks out between Gwenddoleu, the king of Scotland,

and Peredur, a prince of North Wales. Merlin fights alongside Peredur, together with Rhodarcus of Strathclyde (Geoffrey Latinizes the names throughout, so this is the Rhydderch mentioned in the Myrddin poems). There are also three "brothers of the Prince" who are mighty warriors and slay many of the enemy until they are themselves slain. The effect of this on Merlin is profound. He laments their death movingly and commands a tomb to be raised over them. Finally, the weight of sorrow overthrows his mind, and he runs mad, fleeing from the battlefield into the forest. The wording of the text makes it unclear whether the three young men are Merlin's brothers or perhaps those of Peredur.

When winter comes, Merlin finds it increasingly hard to survive. He complains of this aloud, in verses that show Geoffrey's indebtedness to the older Myrddin poems, until one day a man hears his laments. He is from the court of king Rhodarcus (Rhydderch), who is now married to Merlin's sister Ganeida (Gwenddydd). He reports what he has seen and heard, and a party is dispatched to the forest to capture the wild man and bring him back to court. They send a bard with the soldiers, and it is this man's playing that brings Merlin back to the edge of sanity. Through music he remembers both his sister and his wife—a shadowy figure named Guendoloena—who has almost no part to play in the story, though her existence will contribute to Merlin's story later on.

Much of this is startling, since it makes Merlin a king and even provides him with a family—something no other writer after this was to do. In fact Geoffrey's account is so completely at variance with the description of the wondrous child of the *Historia* that we may be forgiven for thinking that he is dealing with another Merlin entirely. What little evidence we possess suggests that this is, indeed, the case and that the Myrddin of the poems lived in the late sixth or early seventh centuries rather than in the presumed lifetime of Arthur in the fifth century.

Once back at court, the sights and sounds and the large gathering of people drive Merlin back into his shell of madness. He begs to be allowed to return to the woods he has grown to love, but Rhodarcus has him incarcerated until he can be restored to health.

Eventually, Merlin is released and vanishes back into the woods. After a suitable interval in which he is presumed to be dead or permanently insane, Guendoloena plans to remarry. But Merlin has been watching the stars, and there reads of this coming event and feels abandoned by his wife. He summons a herd of deer and, riding on the back of a stag, drives them before him to the court. There, seeing Guendoloena's would-be bridegroom standing in a window laughing at him, Merlin wrenches off the stag's antlers and throws them, killing the man instantly. Officers from the court pursue him and catch him when he falls into a river. He is brought back to the court in chains and on the way twice laughs out loud, apparently without reason.

When he hears of this, Rhodarcus is consumed with curiosity and demands to know the meaning of Merlin's laughter. At first Merlin refuses to explain anything but finally agrees to talk if he is allowed to return to the forest. Rhodarcus agrees, and Merlin explains that the first time he laughed was when he saw a man begging in the street, little knowing that he was sitting on top of a horde of gold. The second time was when he saw a man buying a new pair of shoes, though in fact he would drown in the river a few hours later. When both predictions are proved true, Merlin is set free.

Before he departs, Gwenddydd again begs him not to leave, but Merlin is adamant. "Why, my dear sister, do you strive so hard to hold me back? Neither winter with its storms, nor the chill north wind when it rages with savage blast and lashes the flocks of bleating sheep with sudden hail-shower . . . will be able to deter me from seeking the forest wilderness and the green glades."[63] Then he relents and asks her to build a house for him, with seventy doors and windows, through which he may study the stars and read the future of the nation.

Soon after this the bard Taliesin comes to visit him, and the two wise men fall to talking of the mysteries of wind, weather, and the secrets of creation. Taliesin, who is listed alongside Merlin in the Welsh Triads as one of the most important bards of Britain, is himself a key character of the later Arthurian legends, who shares many of Merlin's characteristics and becomes associated with Arthur as a kind of royal bard.

As Merlin and Taliesin discuss the wonders of creation, Geoffrey introduces an important detail. Taliesin recalls how together he and Merlin carried the wounded Arthur from the Battle of Camlann and, with the help of the mythical ferryman Barinthus, took him to "the Island of Apples," ruled over by a ninefold sisterhood, of whom the first and most famous is named Morgen. This character will later metamorphose into the familiar Morgan le Fay, Arthur's half sister and archenemy in the great medieval epics of the thirteenth to fifteenth centuries. Here she is represented as a goddess-like figure, or perhaps a priestess, well versed in the healing arts, once again suggesting Geoffrey's familiarity with more ancient folklore and myth. This remains one of the oldest sources that connect Arthur, Morgen, and Avalon, and here we learn more of the aftermath of the fateful battle of Camlann and of Arthur's eventual end that we must assume Geoffrey did not know when he was writing the *Historia*. His description of Avalon appears to be borrowed from the writings of the first-century geographer Pomponius Mela, who described the Isle de Sein, off the north coast of Brittany, in similar terms.

Merlin now gives vent to a further outpouring of prophecies, triggered by his conversation with Taliesin. The leaders are concerned with who will follow Arthur. But while the two seers are thus engaged, word comes of a new spring that has broken forth from the ground nearby. They go to view this, and when Merlin drinks from it, his mind is restored. Word of this reaches Ganeida, and the rest of the court and people begin to make their way into the woods to ask Merlin to lead them again. He refuses, pleading old age and a desire to retire from the world and to continue his observances from within his house. Taliesin decides to remain also, and soon after this, Ganeida also comes to join them and finally to express her own prophetic gifts.

This episode offers a clue to the sources upon which Geoffrey drew for his new book. A fragmentary story found in the *Life of Saint Mungo*, which is about the sixth-century Scottish saint Kentigern (also known as Mungo). It describes the saint's discovery of a wild madman known as Lailoken; however "some say he was Merlyn [sic] who was an extraordinary prophet of the British."[64] The account tells how, during a battle—which is described as taking place "between Liddel and Carwannock," both sites in the area of Strathclyde where Merlin's story is mostly set—a heavenly voice rebukes Lailoken for causing the deaths of so many men in battle. As a result, he is driven out into the wilderness and becomes mad. Saint Kentigern eventually heals him, but not before the text describes a series of prophecies that make it clear that Lailoken is either a substitute for Merlin or the original hero of Geoffrey's tale.

It seems likely that Geoffrey had heard the stories as a child and perhaps read the poems attributed to Myrddin, which he then wove into a new story of the increasingly popular figure of Merlin. Kentigern was the original founder of the community of Saint Asaph, of which Geoffrey was later to become bishop, so he would almost certainly have been familiar with the stories surrounding the saint.

Geoffrey gives us an unforgettable portrait of Merlin: intensely human, crushed by the horror of war, yet crafty and cunning as any shaman of the old world. His Merlin is a lover also, capable of experiencing jealousy, yet he harbors an awesome power—the gift of prophecy and seership, which enables him to foretell the future and see the truth hidden beneath everyday events. By presenting him in this way, Geoffrey established a basic pattern for the characterization of Merlin that would be reworked again and again through the ages.

Some aspects of Merlin's life, such as his madness, were neglected after Geoffrey's time, though they remained just below the surface, as his character underwent further metamorphoses into prophet, magician, and sage. However, along with the poems, the brief mentions in the Triads, and the inclusion of Gwenddoleu, Rhydderch, and Gwenddydd, the *Vita Merlini* preserved what is almost certainly the oldest and most authentic narrative of Merlin's life. We see a picture of a sixth- or seventh-century prince, who fought at the historical battle of Arderydd and was driven mad by the horrific carnage. Afterward, he seems to have run off and lived in the wilderness of the forest, with only animals for company. His experiences there changed him, giving him the gifts of prophecy and seership.

From this moment on, there would be two distinct Merlins. One, the wild man of the *Vita Merlini* and the Myrddin poems, would be known as Myrddin Wyllt (the Wild), or in the style of later writers as Merlin Sylvestris (of the Woods). The other, whose star gradually ascended until it all but blotted out the older figure, would be Merlinus or Merlin, the son of a devil who possessed great knowledge and wisdom but who was only half human. According to which version was known to the authors who wrote about him, the story would take on a different course. But it is to Geoffrey that we owe his association with Arthur, which was to continue, unchanged, henceforward.

LAST DAYS

The remainder of Geoffrey's career is soon told. In a separate introduction to the *Prophecies of Merlin* included in the *Historia,* he had referred to Alexander, the bishop of Lincoln, who was among those who had apparently requested that he make the translations of the work. He did this almost certainly in the hope of promotion, and if so he was disappointed. The *Historia* had two dedicatees, one to Robert Earl of Gloucester, the illegitimate son of King Henry I, and the second to Waleran, count of Mellent, the son an important baron named Robert de Beaumont. However, Geoffrey seems to have received no preferment because of this. The *Vita Merlini* is dedicated to Robert de Chesney, who had been a canon of Saint George's in Oxford at the same time as Geoffrey and had succeeded Alexander as bishop of Lincoln when the latter died in 1148.

This time it seems that Geoffrey's dedication found a sympathetic hearing, because in 1151 he became bishop elect of Saint Asaph, in what is now Flintshire. Ordained at Westminster in the following year, he was consecrated at Lambeth a week later by Archbishop Theobald. After this he drops out of sight, and we next hear of him as one of the bishops who witnessed the Treaty of Westminster between Stephen and Henry Fitz Empress in 1153, suggesting either that he spent very little time in his diocese, or indeed may never have visited it at all. In any case, Saint Asaph was regarded as a very insignificant bishopric, which after the victory of Owen Gwynedd over his Norman overlords at Coleshill near Holywell in 1150, was in the possession of the Welsh. An admittedly somewhat unreliable chronicle places Geoffrey's death not long after, in 1155.

In his lifetime Geoffrey had done more to create an impetus for the outpouring of Arthurian literature that was soon to follow. He made Arthur a Christian king ruling over a Christian court and succeeded in embedding him, retrospectively, into a past in which he may or may not have lived. He gives us the first real portrait of Merlin as the magician of the later Arthurian world. He tells us how Arthur was born, with the help of Merlin's magic, in the castle of Tintagel. He gives him a beautiful queen, a glorious coronation, and a fantastic regalia drawn from the world of myth. And he presents him with a mysterious ending on the Isle of Avalon, which leaves the way open for countless other tales and speculations. Very little of this was Geoffrey's own invention, despite the suggestions of some of his contemporaries. Instead, he took fragments from here and there, both historical and fabulous, and melded them into something new—a kind of fantastic history that included both fact and fiction. He is, when all is said and done, one of the most original writers of his time—perhaps a joker who wrote with tongue firmly in cheek, or a serious man with a serious intent who just happened to be more than a little credulous.

THE CHRONICLERS OF BRITAIN

Geoffrey was not alone in seeking to tell the ancient history of the British people. Other chroniclers, such as William of Malmesbury, Alfred of Beverly, and Henry of Huntingdon, all drew upon parts of Geoffrey's text, while writing more accurate—though far less glamorous and hence less popular—accounts of the same period, and the *Historia* itself was taken up and translated from its original Latin into both Anglo-Saxon and Norman French as well as into Welsh and even Old Norse. In the process details were added to Geoffrey's telling, which remain parts of the Arthurian legacy to this day. They include the first recorded mention of the Round Table and the suggestion that Arthur was brought up by elves.

The poet known simply as Wace was born on the Island of Jersey in the Channel Isles sometime between 1100 and 1110. As a child he was taken to Caen in Normandy to be educated and afterward went either to Paris or Chartres to finish his schooling. He almost certainly wrote a number of other works, most with hagiographic themes such as the *Life of St. Margaret* or the *Life of St. Nicholas*. But his longest and most famous poem, written in Norman French, was the *Roman de Brut* (Romance of Brutus) in which he followed Geoffrey's *Historia* closely but introduced new elements from Celtic myth and legend.[65]

Wace's Arthurian poem is much more flowery and romantic in style than Geoffrey's bare-bones history, halfway toward the romance style of the next generation of Arthurian writers. He consistently plays down the violence of Geoffrey's account and adds references to romantic love, chivalry, and honor that are not always present in the *Historia*. But the single most important addition Wace made to the growing Arthurian tradition may have been his own idea or something that he had heard from one of the Breton singers who roamed the country telling tales of Arthur and his heroes. It occurs when Arthur holds his great court at Caerleon to celebrate his victories in Gaul.

> Arthur held high state in a very splendid fashion. He ordained the courtesies of courts, and bore himself with so rich and noble a bearing, that neither the emperor's court at Rome was accounted as aught besides that of the king. Arthur never heard praise spoken of any knight but he caused him to be numbered of his household . . . . Because of these noble lords about his hall, of whom each knight pained himself to be the hardiest champion . . . Arthur made the Round Table, so reputed of the Britons. This Round Table was ordained of Arthur that when his fair fellowship sat to meat their chairs should be high alike, their service equal, and none before or after his comrade. Thus no man could boast that he was exalted

above his fellow, for all alike were gathered round the board, and none was alien at the breaking of Arthur's bread. At this table sat Britons, Frenchmen, Normans, Angevins, Flemings, Burgundians, and Loherins.[66]

Here Wace is attempting to bring the most important factions of medieval Europe to sit at Arthur's table—not only the British knights, but also the kings and lords of the frequently warring European kingdoms. He is also the first writer to explicitly mention the idea of Arthur's immanent return to the world of men—having not died of his wounds but somehow being preserved in a magical realm called Avalon.

Within a few years of his death, Wace's book was translated into Middle English by a writer of whom we know virtually nothing other than his name: Layamon or Lawman, a priest at Arley Regis in Worcestershire. One cannot help but stand amazed that this poet, the descendant of the very race who were Arthur's most implacable foes, should make Arthur the hero of his very English epic. He brought a rich and heroic style to the telling, dispensing with much of Wace's more flowery passages and replacing them with more realistic details—such as that when Arthur fights at Camlann he receives five wounds, the smallest of which one could thrust two gloves into. He also added some vivid details to Arthur's birth, relating that as soon as he was born:

> *Elves took him: enchanted the child with magic most*
> *   strong.*
> *They gave him the might: to be best of all knights.*
> *They gave him more: to be a rich king.*
> *They gave him too, that he should live long;*
> *They gave to him the best of Princely virtues*
> *So that he was the most generous man alive.*
> *This the elves gave him: thus the child thrived.*[67]

He also mentions Taliesin, whom Geoffrey had described in the *Vita Merlini* as taking the wounded Arthur to Avalon, making him a seer and magician who prophesies in a manner more like Merlin. To the story of the inception of the Round Table, Layamon added some details of his own:

> Afterward it saith in the tale, that the king went to Cornwall; there came to him anon one that was a crafty workman, and met the king, and fair him greeted: "Hail be thou, Arthur, noblest of kings! I am thine own man; through many land I have gone; I know of tree-works, wondrous many crafts. I heard say beyond the sea new tidings, that thy knights gan to fight at thy board; on a midwinter's day many there fell; for their mickle mood wrought murderous play, and for their high lineage each would be within. But I will thee work a board exceeding fair, that thereat may sit sixteen hundred and more, all turn about, so that none be without; without and within, man against man. And when thou wilt ride, with thee thou mightiest it carry, and set it where thou wilt, after thy will; and then thou needest never fear, to the world's end, that ever any moody knight at thy board may make fight, for there shall the high be even with the low." Timber was caused to be brought, and the board to be begun; in four weeks' time the work was completed.[68]

This idea—that it was the quarrelsome behavior of Arthur's men that required the creation of a round table where all could be equal—has a ring of truth about it, and we should note that the mysterious builder intends it to be portable.

Wace and Layamon were the first writers to mention a round table, but the idea was to remain at the center of the Arthurian story from here on. To it came knights and heroes from all over Europe, forming a glittering fellowship dedicated to the emerging concept of chivalry. The Round Table was a hub around which everything else revolved. Adventures began and ended there; distressed women came in search of help in the form of a knight strong enough to overcome all foes. Strange adversaries, borrowed from Celtic myth, arrived to test the courage and skill of the knights. The king's peace meant that anyone could travel the length and breadth of the land, laden with treasure, without fear of assault.

In this we see a development of ideas partially expressed in the older tales of Arthur but here given new shape. Companies of Celtic warriors, seated in their halls around a central fire, apportioning prime cuts of meat as a mark of honor to each hero, boasting of their deeds and conquests, had evolved into a courtly fellowship where all were equal; the old spur toward valor was channeled into quests and adventures undertaken at the request of those in need.

Finally, at the end of the work, Layamon has Arthur say, as he is about to depart for the faery realm of Avalon, words that make him seem an almost Christlike figure:

> And I will fare to Avalun, [sic] to the fairest of
>   maidens,
> To Argante the Queen, an elf most fair,
> That she shall make my wounds all sound:
> Make me whole with healing drafts.
> Afterward I shall come again to my kingdom,
> And dwell with the Britons with greatest joy.[69]

Geoffrey of Monmouth and his followers established Arthur as a medieval king with a fantastic retinue of heroic knights. The chronicle style would give way to a new generation of writers, waiting in the wings with a wholly new style of storytelling—the medieval romance. Here the magical and mythic associations that predated all the written versions of Arthur's history could be explored more fully, and tales spun from the gold of ancient legends. These would take the great hero further still from the dark days of post-Roman Britain into a wholly new and wonderful realm of valiant knights, fair ladies, and mystical quests.

6

King Arthur
Lord of Camelot

*What place is there within the bounds of the empire of Christendom
to which the winged praise of Arthur the Briton has not extended.
Who is there, I ask, who does not speak of Arthur the Briton, since
he is but little less known to the peoples of Asia than to the Bretons,
as we are informed by our palmers who return from the countries
of the East. The Eastern peoples speak of him as do the Western,
though separated by the breadth of the whole Earth.*

ALANUS DE INSULIS,
PROPHETIA ANGLICANA MERLINI AMBROSII BRITANNI (1608)

THE DAWN OF ROMANCE

From the middle of the twelfth to almost the end of the fifteenth centuries, scarcely a year went by without the appearance of at least one
new Arthurian romance—usually many more. In addition to those
that have subsequently been lost, more than one hundred major tales
have been identified from countries as varied as France, Germany, Italy,
Spain, Holland, Norway, and England. Curiously, very few of these
featured Arthur in anything but a minor role; he and his Fellowship

of the Round Table had become a sun around which a constellation of adventures featuring the great knights of the courtly world—Lancelot, Gawain, Perceval, Galahad, Yvain, Tristan, and many others—could circle. Arthur himself took an increasingly less active role, acting merely as a figurehead to whom the knights reported the outcome of their adventures in his name. These adventures redefined him, made him into the great king whose legends we know today and whose fame spread across the world. This was the new face of Arthur, replacing the Roman or Dark Age soldier and the powerful monarch of the chroniclers with a courtly, romantic king ruling over a dreamlike land full of giants, demons, black knights, dwarves, and faery women.

Until the beginning of the twelfth century, most written works fell into one of three categories: history, religious works, or manuals, all of which were believed to contain factual material. From the second half of the century, a new category was added: the romance. This was usually a long story told in verse or prose, more often than not dealing with knightly adventures or love. No longer tied by the restraints of truth, it gave the author freedom to openly invent, combine, or re-create the lives and deeds of characters.

The Old French word *romanz* originally meant "the speech of the people" or "the vulgar tongue" and referred to works written in the vernacular rather than in literary Latin. The meaning then shifted from the language in which the works were written to the type of work. Wace's adaptation of Geoffrey's *Historia Regum Britanniae* was known as *Roman de Brut,* and though it is unclear whether this was used in a sense of "the French version" or "the story," from this point onward roman, or romance, began to refer to a particular type of tale, usually involving adventure, magic, and love, where, for the first time, characters were endowed with reason rather than simply reacting to a situation. In Geoffrey's *Historia,* all of the action is told in the form of a chronicle of events; while in the new romances of Arthur and his knights, individual characters debated with themselves and others over what to do before they reacted, and matters of the heart were every bit as important as the ability of the hero with sword or lance.

At first the authors of these romances were clerks—professional writers trained in grammar and rhetoric in the great cathedral schools of Europe. However, as the language slowly changed throughout the twelfth century from Latin to the native tongue of the writer, a new class of storytellers began to appear. Their chosen subject matter fell essentially into two groups (with the addition of a not-inconsiderable list of romances that dealt with the life and deeds of Alexander the Great): the Matter of France, which treated the stories and legends surrounding the great French king Charlemagne (fl. 742–814), and the Matter of Britain, which dealt with Arthur, his knights, and their ladies.

All of these works focused on individual adventures rather than sweeping epics of war and the rise and fall of kings. They also introduced themes that were barely present in Geoffrey's book or its successors—chivalry and romantic love. The concept of chivalry grew out of the idea of knighthood and service to a feudal overlord. It provided a set of rules that governed the behavior of the knight and gave him a code to live by. The virtues of compassion, mercy, generosity, pity, courtesy, and religious zeal were central to the idea of chivalry. Few living men attained it, and it remained an ideal measure against which a knight could measure himself or be measured. In the Arthurian romances, it is central to the code by which King Arthur's knights live, and many of them are presented as perfect exemplars of chivalrous behavior. Love, especially romantic love as demonstrated by the concepts of Courtly Love, was shown to affect the lives of all the knights. They were no longer simply warriors; in the increasingly sophisticated world of the twelfth to fifteenth centuries, they had time to explore their feelings, to fall hopelessly in love with some beautiful lady (or ladies), and to dedicate their adventures to them as much as to King Arthur.

This changed the face of Arthurian literature forever. Less and less often do we read accounts of Arthur's military successes—though there are occasional exceptions to this, as in the case of his early battles against rebellious kings for the crown of Britain or his fatal war with Rome, which continued to resurface throughout the medieval tales. More commonly, we are treated to a vast cycle of individual adventure stories, most of which begin at Camelot, Arthur's glorious city soon to be introduced by the greatest Arthurian poet of the age, whose works take us deep into a magical landscape of forest and valley, lake and ford, where an endless parade of savage knights, beautiful women, and fairy-tale creatures lie in wait of the audacious knights errant. Here King Arthur rules supreme, the heart and soul of a world that, though it never existed in this form, was nonetheless as familiar to the crowned heads of Europe and their gaudy courts as their own world.

As with Geoffrey of Monmouth among the chroniclers, one writer stands out as the progenitor of this new brand of Arthurian romance. His name is Chrétien de Troyes (fl. 1165–1180). He wrote five Arthurian romances in verse, *Erec et Enide; Cliges; Lancelot, ou le Chavalier de Charette* (Lancelot, or the Knight of the Cart); *Yvain, ou le Chevalier au Lion* (Yvain, or the Knight of the Lion); and *Perceval, ou le Conte du Graal* (Perceval, or the Story of the Grail).[1] In these, he created, seemingly from nothing, a wholly new form of fiction. Full of adventure, magic, mystery, and love, these were racy and delightful explorations of themes that have been traced back to both Celtic and classical myth, all written in flowing and evocative language far removed from the dramatic renditions of earlier writers.

As with most medieval authors, we know very little about Chrétien beyond his name and place of birth. He tells us himself that he had written several books, mostly based on the writings of the Roman poet Ovid, before composing his first Arthurian poem, *Erec and Enid,* somewhere around 1155.

He seems to have spent most of his working life at the court of Marie de Champagne, daughter of Eleanor of Aquitaine, though there is some evidence that he may also have visited the court of King Henry II in England. The number of manuscript copies of his works that have survived attest to their popularity during his lifetime.

Erec explores the potential clash between chivalry and love through the adventures of Erec son of Lac, a name of Breton origin that suggests this area as a probable source for the story. But Chrétien, whatever original text, if any, he was following, made it completely his own. He tells us how Erec comes to Arthur's court as a youth and soon distinguishes himself among the Knights of the Round Table. One day, while Arthur is hunting a white stag, he encounters a knight named Yder who insults the queen. Erec takes up the challenge to punish him for this and follows Yder to a town where a contest to win a much-prized sparrowhawk is about to take place. Erec enters the competition and wins, beating Yder and forcing him to make reparation to Arthur and Guinevere. Eric meanwhile falls in love with Enid, the daughter of a nobleman. As a reward for his deeds, he is given her in marriage. At first they are very happy, but Erec becomes so besotted with his bride that he begins to turn way from his knightly duties. Hearing his subjects complaining, Enid is disconsolate. When Erec asks her why, she tells him, and he flies into a fury. Insisting she accompany him, wearing the same dress every day and without servants or guards, Erec sets off on a series of adventures, each of which Enid is forced to watch. Finally, after many near-fatal battles, Erec engages in an adventure known as the Joy of the Court, in which he is victorious. Returning home, he is invested as king of his father's kingdom and despite his cruel behavior lives happily with Enid.

LANCELOT THE LOVER

Chrétien's second tale, *Cliges,* is barely Arthurian, being simply set in Arthur's time but featuring no familiar characters. With his next poem, *Lancelot,* he introduced one of the most important and perennial figures in Arthurian literature. As Arthur began to be joined by individual heroes, knights of great renown who rode in search of adventure (errantry) from his wholly medieval court, new characters had to be created, and this Chrétien did. Before his poem, the most powerful knight at Arthur's court was his nephew Gawain, whose career stretched back to the first Celtic tales of the Arthurian saga; now he was superceded by a new star: Lancelot. As we shall see, Chrétien did not invent Lancelot—though he does seem to have been the first to make him the queen's lover—but he did succeed in making him the most popular knight to sit at Arthur's Round Table.

Various attempts have been made to identify an original Lancelot. Some authorities have pointed out that one of the tribes who supplied warriors to the legions was the Allans of Lot and that this is not a huge leap to the name Lancelot.[2] Roger Sherman Loomis suggested that the name derived from the Welsh name Llwch Llenlleawg, since *llwch* is Welsh for "lake" and Lancelot is known as "of the lake."[3] The second part of the name then went through a number of linguistic changes to form Lancelot. A far more likely idea supposes the existence of an "ur-Lancelot" text, now lost, which formed the basis of several later romances, including Chrétien's and the *Prose Lancelot*.

Chrétien's poem is really only an episode from the great knight's biography, and like *Erec* it is based on older, Celtic material. Essentially the tale is this: A knight named Meleagant arrives at Arthur's court and challenges him to allow Guinevere to enter the forest with only one knight for protection. Kay blusters his way into this task but is defeated, both he and Guinevere being taken prisoner by Meleagant and taken to his castle of Goirre.

At once Gawain and an unnamed knight whom we learn only later is Lancelot set out in pursuit. Lancelot is clearly madly in love with the queen and rides his horse so furiously to get ahead of Gawain that the noble beast falls dead beneath him. The only way Lancelot can travel onward is either by foot or by getting into a passing cart. At this time carts were used to carry common criminals to the gallows, and Lancelot hesitates for two paces before getting in. He is immediately dubbed "the Knight of the Cart" and becomes the subject of public humiliation.

Arriving at Goirre, the two knights discover that the only way into the castle, which is surrounded by water, is by two bridges—one shaped like a sword, the other leading beneath the moat. They also learn that a water fairy raised Meleagant and that he possesses a magical ring that protects him from harm. All of these details point to the fact that Meleagant is actually an otherworldly being and that his home is in fact a form of the Celtic otherworld, generally described as surrounded by water and approached only by a narrow, sword-like bridge. The name

Gorre may well derive from a corruption of the French or Welsh words for glass, *voire* or *gutr*.

This association is supported by the fact that in Welsh tradition, Meleagant is known as Melwas and rules over the Summer Country, an ancient name for the otherworld. As we saw in chapter 4, an episode in the *Vita Caradoci* tells how this same Melwas kidnapped Guinevere and carried her off to his home, from which Arthur himself rescued her. It seems clear that Chrétien had heard of this story and added it into his poem.

He may have also been aware of this whole episode as an ancient theme, the abduction of the Flower Bride, which threads its way through several Celtic tales and reappears in more than one Arthurian romance. This story is the subject of an eleventh-century carving above the northern portal of Modena Cathedral in Italy—an important link in the chain of development in the Arthurian story, as it predates any of the written romances and suggests that the abduction and rescue of Guinevere was known about well before Chrétien composed his poem. The story told on the archivolt appears to be that of Guinevere's abduction, though she is called Winlogee, a probable Breton variant of her usual name, by a giant named Carados at the command of Mardoc (Meleagant). Coming to rescue her are Artus de Bretania (Arthur), Galvagin (Gawain), Che (Kay), and Galvarium (Galahault, a character who appears in later Lancelot stories). The castle where Winlogee is held appears to be a stone tower surrounded by water and reached by a narrow bridge.

It is notable that Lancelot does not feature in the rescue mission, while Gawain does, but this is in line with the gradual shift from Chrétien's time onward, away from Gawain toward Lancelot as the most important knight at Arthur's court. It is likely that by creating the character of Lancelot as he is portrayed in *Le Chevalier de la Charette*, Chrétien borrowed from older tales in which Gawain was the hero and then had the previously nameless hero, now called Lancelot, take over his role. Possibly the fact that Meleagant is described as being brought up by a water fairy may have prompted Lancelot's subsequent history, in which he is brought up by the Lady of the Lake.

Once again this implies Chrétien's wide knowledge of Celtic tales, but as he had done in *Erec,* he adapts these for his own purpose, which is essentially to tell a love story. Chrétien himself says that he was given the subject of his poem by his patroness, Countess Marie de Champagne. Since Marie herself was well read and had a fondness for Arthurian tales, there is no reason to question this.

In the poem Gawain now drops out of the action when he fails to cross the water bridge and almost drowns. Lancelot, however, succeeds in crossing the sword bridge—not without serious wounds—and is greeted by Meleagant's father, Bagdemagus, who heals his wounds. It is suggested that Bagdemagus is a magician, as his name would suggest (magus is an ancient name for a magician), and he is presented as a commanding and powerful figure throughout the work.

Once he is recovered, Lancelot fights with Meleagant and begins to beat him. Bagdemagus requests a truce and arranges for Guinevere to be freed. At first she berates Lancelot for hesitating to enter the cart but eventually softens and forgives him. That night he comes to the window of her chamber and is invited in. Breaking the bars of her prison, he opens fresh wounds, and after a night of passion, spots of blood are found on her sheets. Meleagant accuses the queen of sleeping with the wounded Kay, whose chamber is next to hers. Lancelot fights Meleagant again to prove the queen's innocence, and once again Bagdemagus calls a halt. A third combat is planned to take place at Arthur's court, and Lancelot escorts Guinevere home. A tournament is announced in which Lancelot wishes to fight. Guinevere insists that he prove his undying loyalty to her by fighting badly. He does so for the first day, until Guinevere relents, and on the next day he wins every bout. On his way back from the tournament, Meleagant captures Lancelot and imprisons him in a tower, but Meleagant's own sister releases him, and he returns to Arthur's court in time to stop Gawain from fighting Meleagant in his stead. Disguised in Gawain's armor (a trick that was to feature in many Arthurian romances after this), Lancelot fights his adversary one last time and kills him.

Here for the first time are all the trappings of the great love story that was to become a central part of the Arthurian saga. Chrétien makes it clear that Lancelot and Guinevere are lovers, though some later tales were to gloss over this or find excuses for it. But Chrétien wrote at a time when the cult of Courtly Love, which glorified adulterous relationships and originated rules governing friendships between knights and ladies, was at its height. His text is almost a handbook of how the knight and his *amie* (love) were supposed to behave. He is also the first writer to set Arthur's court at Camelot, a name previously unknown in Arthurian literature. Whether Chrétien invented this name, or borrowed it from elsewhere, we may never know. Henceforward, Camelot became a byword for magnificence and power.

THE KNIGHT OF THE LION

Chrétien's next work (though he may have worked on it concurrently with Lancelot) was titled *Yvain,* and for its hero, he chose someone whose origins lie deep within the Dark Ages. Yvain (or Owein as he is better known) is the son of Urien of Rheged, who featured as one of Arthur's supporters in the *Historia Regum Britanniae,* and both men were almost certainly real people who fought against the Saxons in the sixth century. They are remembered in poems attributed to the sixth-century bard Taliesin, though not in connection with Arthur, and in the Welsh Triads, Yvain's wife, Penarwen, is mentioned as one of "the three faithless wives of the Island of Britain."[4] Geoffrey mentioned Yvain briefly, and in the Welsh tale "The Dream of Rhonabwy" he is shown as a contemporary of Arthur, with whom he plays a magical chess-like board game.

Chrétien's version follows the outlines of the Welsh text of "Lady of the Fountain" quite closely, though he imposes his own unique stamp upon it. It is perhaps the most magical of his poems, borrowing extensively from Celtic mythology.

One day at Arthur's court, Yvain hears another knight talking about an enchanted fountain, which lies in the ancient forest of Broceliande. Deciding to try this adventure for himself, Yvain goes to the forest where he encounters a monstrously ugly herdsman.

His head was larger than a nag's or other beast's. His hair as unkempt and his bare forehead was more than two spans wide; his ears were as hairy and as huge as an elephant's; his eyebrows heavy and his face flat. He had the eyes of an owl and the nose of a cat, jowls split like a wolf's, with the sharp reddish teeth of a boar; he had a russet beard, angled moustache, a chin down to his breast and a long, twisted spine with a hump.[5]

After a spirited exchange with the herdsman, Yvain pours a basin of water over a hollow stone, and this causes a furious storm, with lightning and thunder. Hundreds of birds fly down and sit on the branches of a great pine tree until it is covered with wings and eyes and feathers. Carados, the protector of the fountain, then appears and challenges Yvain. They fight, and Yvain kills the guardian. He then travels to the dead knight's castle where he is trapped between two gates. A servant girl named Lunete rescues him and gives him a ring of invisibility. Thus able to hide in the castle, he watches preparations for the funeral of the dead knight and gradually falls in love with Carados's widow. Lunete manages to convince this lady, whose name is Laudine, to marry Yvain, reminding her of the ancient custom that he who defeats the guardian of the fountain must become its guardian in turn and that therefore Yvain must carry out this role.

Soon after this, Arthur and his knights arrive, and Yvain fights Kay before revealing his identity. Seeking now to return to Arthur's court, Yvain requests leave of absence from Laudine, who allows him to go on the understanding that he will return in one year. Once back at court, however, Yvain loses track of time and overstays his leave of absence until a messenger arrives from Laudine, rebuking him for his failure and renouncing him as her husband. This causes Yvain to go mad, and he roams the hills until servants of the Lady of Norison cure him with a magical ointment made by Morgan le Fay. In return for the healing, Yvain helps the lady to defend her lands against an enemy. He then sets out to return to Laudine. Along the way, he has several adventures, including the rescue of a lion from a serpent. The lion becomes his faithful guardian and refuses to leave his side, and Yvain becomes known as "the Knight with the Lion." Helped by this noble beast, Yvain defeats a giant, rescues prisoners from the Castle of Evil Adventure, and settles a dispute between the daughters of the Lord of the Black Thorn. Finally, he returns to the castle of the fountain, rescues Lunete, who has been imprisoned as a punishment for helping him, and is reconciled with his wife.

There are some fascinating details in this poem. The whole episode of the fountain is full of ancient symbolism and probably derives from a Celtic storm-raising ritual. Fountains or springs of this kind appear quite often in the medieval Arthurian romances and usually indicate a debt to older Celtic material, where fountains or pools were seen as gateways to the otherworld and thus as extremely powerful and magical places. The idea that whoever defeats the guardian of the fountain must become his successor is also an ancient one, which can be traced back to the classical myth of the King of the Wood who guards a spring sacred to the god Zeus at Dodona in Greece and who is replaced each year by a new and younger champion.[6] The giant herdsman who guards the place is perhaps a type of the Green Man archetype, a nature spirit whose head appears carved in churches and cathedrals across Europe and whose origins go back beyond the beginnings of recorded history.[7] In the Welsh "The Dream of Rhonabwy," he is described as a one-eyed, one-legged giant who bangs the bole of a tree with a huge club to summon the animals over which he rules. In other Arthurian romance, the same character reappears in a number of monstrous disguises. Other likely points of origin for this character are the *bachlach* or wild man of Irish mythology, and perhaps even the troll of Norse tradition.

Here Chrétien brings together a whole spectrum of magical events and mysterious beings whose presence in the poem make it a rich and exciting tale. The love story of Yvain and Laudine is, as in all of Chrétien's works, central to the text, and once again we see echoes of his portrayal of the knight as a man torn between home and wife and his life of adventure.

THE STORY OF THE GRAIL

Chrétien's final work, *Perceval, ou le Conte du Graal,* is in many ways the most remarkable of his compositions. It brought a new theme into the Arthurian canon, where it was soon to become perhaps the most important single strand in the sprawling epics of the next century— that of a mysterious object and the quest of Arthur's knights to find it. At this point this object is known simply as "a grail," written with a small *g;* soon it was to become the Holy Grail, a very different object entirely. An entire book would be required to trace the history of this remarkable relic through the ages, and this is not the place to do so, but we must acknowledge the importance of Chrétien in making a link between the Grail and the Arthurian legends and in preparing the way for another writer, Robert de Boron, to take it to a wholly new level.[8]

The story can be summarized as follows: Perceval is brought up by his mother in the forest where, in ignorance of the ways of the world, he happily hunts game with roughly made throwing spears. Then one day he meets three knights in the wood. Thinking them angels because of the brilliance of their armor, he questions them concerning their origin. Learning from them of Arthur's court and the institution of knighthood, he vows to go there in search of adventure, and ignoring his mother's anguished request that he should remain with her, he rides off on an ancient nag to find his way in the world of chivalry. Before he departs, his mother gives him certain advice: always to give help to any women in distress, but to take no more from them by way of reward than a kiss—though if one should also wish to give him a ring, let him take that also. Also if he meets with anyone on the road, he should not part from them without knowing his or her true name, for those who conceal such things are no good to anyone.

Armed with this advice, the first person Perceval encounters along the way is a beautiful woman in a scarlet pavilion, whose ring he takes and whom he kisses, but against her will. He then proceeds to Arthur's court, where he enters in time to witness the arrival of a red knight who spills wine in the queen's lap and carries off her golden cup. Still mindful of his mother's instructions, Perceval pursues the knight, kills him, and returns the cup to the queen.

At the court he seeks training in knightly pursuits and then sets out on further adventures. The most important of these is when he arrives at the castle of the Fisher King, whom he finds presiding over a hall in which are four hundred men sitting round a fire, while an old man lies upon a couch close by. The Fisher King presents Perceval with a sword, which he accepts unthinkingly. A procession passes through the hall, led by a squire carrying a spear from which blood drips upon the ground, followed by two squires each carrying a ten-branched candlestick. After this comes a damsel carrying a grail that blazes with a light so bright that it puts out the light of the candles and of the stars. Following her is another maiden carrying a *talleors* (variously translated as a dish, a bowl, a casket, or a tabernacle). Perceval watches all this but fails to ask its meaning. He retires for the night and on waking finds the castle deserted. He sets out in search of the Fisher King and his people, but no sooner has he crossed the drawbridge than the whole castle vanishes. Perceval then encounters a damsel cradling the body of a knight in her arms and lamenting bitterly. She tells him that the Fisher King has long since received a wound in the thighs, which has never healed, though it might well have done so had Perceval asked about the procession of the Grail. She also informs him that the sword that he was given at the castle will break if he is not careful, but that in such a case he can restore it by dipping it in a lake near which its maker, the smith Trebuchet, dwells.

Returning to Arthur's court, Perceval is upbraided by a hideous damsel who appears from nowhere to mock him for failing to ask the question that would have healed the king and made his country prosperous again. Determined to right this wrong, and to learn more of the mysterious Grail, Perceval sets forth again, and after many adventures meets with a band of pilgrims who reproach him for bearing arms on Good Friday. Five years have passed since he left Arthur's court, and in his eagerness to discover more about the Grail, he has forgotten God. Perceval confesses his sins to a forest hermit and learns from him that his mother died of grief after he left her. He feels great remorse but has still not rediscovered the Castle of the Grail.

The rest of the story deals with Gawain and his quest for a sword that had beheaded John the Baptist. Then Chrétien's narrative breaks off, in midsentence, and there perhaps the story might have ended, but it exerted such a powerful hold over the imagination of medieval Europe that others felt drawn to try to solve the problems left by the unfinished poem. There are three surviving attempts to "finish" what Chrétien began, which jointly extend the original poem by hundreds of lines but in the end leave it as unclear as ever.*

Where did Chrétien find this extraordinary story? In all probability he heard it from the lips of a traveling Breton bard, who may in turn have heard it from the Welsh singers who went from court to court spinning ancient Celtic tales of myth and legend. One surviving text, which we have encountered before and can be dated back to the end of the ninth century, does suggest a clue. The "Preiddeu Annwyfn" is placed in the mouth of the bard Taliesin, though whether he is its actual author or not is uncertain. It describes, in the most cryptic language, an expedition, led by Arthur, in search of a mysterious vessel, which holds the secret of inspiration and perhaps of life itself, from the otherworldly realm of Annwyfn.

As we saw in chapter 4, this is part of a whole mass of mythological material, much of it dateless and some at least very ancient, which suggests the existence of a mythic Arthur, and it is certainly not impossible for Chrétien to have heard some version of this story. What he does with it, however, is to weave an extraordinary tale of mystery around the idea of the mysterious vessel and to be so enigmatic in the process that a succession of writers would attempt to explain what he meant within a few years of his death.

---

*These are, in order of composition, the First Continuation, attributed to Wauchier de Danain (now contested); the Second Continuation, possibly by Gauchier de Donaig; and a third, attributed to a certain Manassier. Another author, Gerbert de Montreuil, complied all of these and wrote his own conclusion. The final total is a staggering 63,550 lines in addition to the 9,234 completed by Chrétien.

Chrétien's contribution to Arthurian literature is enormous. His poems established a new kind of Arthurian story, full of magic, adventure, and wonder. He gave us the first fully rounded portrait of Lancelot and a story of the Grail that became the foundation for numerous later accounts. However, debate still rages over the question of his originality. Three tales (*The Lady of the Fountain, Geraint and Enid,* and *Peredur*) now part of the collection known as the *Mabinogion,* run so closely to Chrétien's *Chevalier au Lion, Erec,* and *Cont du Graal* that some have considered them to be the original sources for his works. Dating is difficult, since these stories were not written down until some time after the first copies of Chrétien's tales. It is just possible that earlier versions of these Celtic tales were available to him and that he used them as the basis for his courtly poems.[9]

A comparison of the two sets of texts shows that the Welsh versions contain far more primitive elements within them. For example, in the Welsh story of *Peredur,* there are many parallels with Chrétien's *Story of the Graal;* however, the Grail in the Welsh text is a dish containing a human head floating in blood rather than the mysterious healing token it is in Chrétien, and Peredur's primary task is to extract vengeance for the death of his uncle.

It is highly likely that versions of these tales existed before either of the written texts was recorded and that just as Chrétien may have heard Norman *conteurs* telling these tales, so the anonymous authors of the *Mabinogion* romances may have heard them told by circuit bards traveling the roads of Britain and Wales. Ultimately perhaps, it does not matter: Chrétien's poems, along with the *Mabinogion* romances, demonstrate the increasing popularity of the Arthurian legends, both in their native land and elsewhere in the courts of France, where they developed, as we have seen, and continued to produce more and more versions over the next two hundred years.

MARIE DE FRANCE

During the period that Chrétien was making a name for himself as the foremost poet of his age, several other, slighter works appeared that added further themes and characters to Arthurian literature. Principal among these were a series of short poems known as *lais,* written by one of the few women writers of the Middle Ages whose works have survived. Marie de France wrote during the second half of the twelfth century and may have lived for a time at the court of Henry II of England. She wrote two Arthurian poems, "Chèvefeuille" (The Honeysuckle) and "Lanval." The former deals with a brief episode from the life of the knight Tristan, whose illicit love for Iseult, the wife of his uncle Mark, became a central theme in the later romances, rivaling the story of Lancelot and Guinevere in popularity.[10]

Marie herself is an interesting figure: she is believed to be the illegitimate daughter of Geoffrey IV of Anjou, founder of the Plantagenet dynasty through his marriage to Empress Matilda, the only surviving child of Henry I. Marie later became abbess of Shaftesbury, in the manner of royal bastards. She tells us her name and that of her native country in one of her verses but nothing else about herself, although a study of the lays shows that the roles of women are strong and authoritative, as befits a royal and consecrated virgin such as herself. Her lays are dedicated to a King Henry and one to a Count William. These are probably her half brothers Henry II and Count William of Poitou, both sons of Geoffrey.[11]

Marie was not alone in fostering Arthurian interests within her family: her half brother Henry II's wife, Eleanor of Aquitaine, had formerly been married to Louis VII who fathered Marie de Champagne before their divorce. It was at Marie de Champagne's court that Chrétien de Troyes flourished. Eleanor herself was the daughter of the *trouvère* poet William IX of Poitiers. Henry II's other half sister, the illegitimate Emma Plantagenet, married Dafydd ap Owain Gwynedd and was the grandmother of a *latimer,* or interpreter, called Wrennoc. As Constance Bullock Davies points out, "the king's half-sisters were respectively, mother in law, aunt, grandmother and great-aunt to royal latimers in Wales."[12]

It appears that a lost work by an unknown twelfth-century French poet may have inspired Chrétien to write a Tristan story, also lost. These works spawned a number of imitators, and at some point Tristan's story was grafted onto the Arthurian saga. Tristan himself may have been a real historical figure named Drustan, who lived in Scotland in the seventh century. His life was probably described in a native story no longer extant, perhaps associated with the early Irish saga of Diarmuid and Grainne, which told of a similar adulterous relationship.[13] In time Tristan was to rival Lancelot as both lover and warrior, but in the earliest poems, such as that by Marie, we are treated to a series of romantic episodes in which Tristan meets Iseult secretly, and they discuss their love for each other. A longer work, the *Tristan* of Thomas, dating from circa 1175, extended the story into a more detailed romance that was then taken up and further embroidered by poets throughout Europe.[14]

Marie's "Lanval" is more Arthurian in nature and tells of the Arthurian knight who met a fairy woman named Triamour, with whom he falls in love. She agrees to become his mistress and provides him with rich armor, weapons, and horses, on condition that he never tells anyone of her existence. All goes well for a time, but when Lanval returns briefly to Arthur's court at Cardiff, Guinevere, who fears him because he sees though her many infidelities, tries to seduce him. When Lanval refuses her on the grounds that he loves a fairy woman whose merest serving woman is fairer than she, Guinevere turns on him, goes to Arthur, and accuses Lanval of making advances to her.[15]

Arthur is predictably enraged and orders Lanval arrested. At the same time, all the rich possessions given him by Triamour vanish. At his trial Lanval is found guilty but given a year to produce his fairy mistress and thus prove his innocence. His goes in search of her but cannot find his way back to their home and returns disconsolate. The court rules that he should be hung. But at this moment, Triamour does appear, and everyone is forced to admit the truth of Lanval's claims. The lovers depart together and live happily ever after.

There are elements of Celtic (especially Breton) legend in this tale, which is unusual for the dark picture it paints of Guinevere. Here there is no doubt of the queen's infidelities, and she is presented as a scheming and promiscuous woman. Among Marie's *Lais,* this was to prove a particularly popular story. It was reprised in the English *Sir Launfal* by Thomas Chestre[16] and in later Arthurian romances where either Gawain or a Breton knight named Graelent are the heroes.

Marie's *Lais* contributed considerably to the Matter of Britain, bringing a strong flavor of fairy tale as well as Norman courtly tradition to the legends.

A VISION OF THE GRAIL

While there was no falling off of interest in tales of adventure and love, another theme was about to enter the skein of the Arthurian saga, adding to the glory of Arthur's rule. At around the beginning of the thirteenth century, an author arrived on the scene who was destined to take the Grail story, first advanced by Chrétien de Troyes, to a whole new level and in the process to change the direction of the Arthuriad yet again. His name was Robert de Boron, and all we know about him is what he tells us in his works—his name and that of his patron, Gautier de Montbéliard. We do not even know Robert's exact dates, though it is possible to estimate when he composed the three verse romances that bear his name. These are known as *Joseph d'Arimathie* (or *Le Roman De l'estoire dou Graal*), *Merlin,* and *Perceval.* Of these only the *Joseph* and the first 504 lines of the *Merlin* have survived in their original form, although prose renditions were made (possibly by Robert himself) shortly afterward.[17]

Gautier de Montbeliard, who commissioned the works, left to join the Fourth Crusade in 1202 and died in the Holy Land in 1212 without returning home. This makes it likely that Robert composed his works before 1202. The text of *Joseph* refers to "the Vales of Avalon," and it is believed that this can be identified with the area around Glastonbury, which has a long association with Arthur; and since bones said to be those of Arthur and Guinevere were discovered there in 1191 (see page 291), the likelihood is that Robert was working on *Joseph* at this date. It is also believed that his work postdates that of Chrétien's *Perceval* and that Robert borrowed details from it.

However, the reason that Robert de Boron deserves to be recognized as one of the most important of the medieval Arthurian writers is his detailed exploration of the Grail *before* it appears in an Arthurian context. In doing so, he made a connection of immense importance—that the Grail of Chrétien's romance was to be identified with the vessel used by Jesus to celebrate the Last Supper—that it was in fact the Holy Grail.

With this one step, Robert changed the face of Arthurian literature forever, directing it away from the secular love stories and magic of Chrétien's courtly poems and instilling it with a spiritual dimension it has retained ever since. Stories would continue to be told that had little or no reference to the Grail, but from this time forward, the central theme at the heart of Arthurian saga was the search for the mystical vessel by Arthur's knights. Not by Arthur himself, we should note: he remains behind when the fellowship sets out on their long journey, bemoaning the fact that never again would all of them sit together at the Round Table.

Robert borrowed heavily from biblical legends of the kind collected in the thirteenth century by Jacobus de Voragine under the title *The Golden Legend*.[18] He also had access to older Christian apocrypha such as The Gospel of Pilate,[19] which tells the story of Jesus's "uncle" Joseph of Arimathea. These works told alternate stories of the early days of Christianity and were a rich proving ground for Robert's imagination. He was not a great poet, but his vision of a unified history with the Grail at its center was fresh and powerful. It influenced several generations of poets and prose writers who took up his story and built upon it a vast structure of Arthurian romances that described the history of the Arthurian period from before Arthur's birth until his death or disappearance.

First Robert tells the story of the Last Supper and the betrayal and Crucifixion of Christ, and then moves on to Joseph of Arimathea, who, together with Nicodemus, acquires Christ's body and the cup with which the first Eucharist was celebrated. While they are preparing the body for burial, some blood flows afresh from the wounds and is caught in the cup by Joseph, thus making it holy forever. After the events of the resurrection, Joseph is thrown into prison, where he is visited by the risen Christ, who gives him the cup (previously hidden in Joseph's house) and instructs him in the mystery of the sacraments. The bread and wine are the body and blood, the tomb is the altar, the platter, its sealing stone, the grave cloths, the corporeal, and the vessel in which the blood was caught shall henceforth be called a chalice. All who behold it shall be of Christ's company and have fulfillment of their heart's desire and eternal joy. Joseph remained in prison, kept alive miraculously by the Grail, until years later the emperor Vespasian, healed of leprosy by the Veil of Veronica, becomes a Christian and frees him—justifiably amazed to find the old man still alive.

Joseph now gathers several of his kin around him, including his sister Erygius and her husband, Brons, and with their followers departs for far-off lands. All goes well for a time, but in one place where they stay, the host's family are dying of hunger. Joseph kneels before the Grail and is instructed to build a table in memory of that at which the Last Supper was held and to send his brother-in-law Brons to catch a fish, to be placed on the table opposite the Grail, which must be covered. Joseph is to sit in the place of Christ with Brons on his right and next to him an empty seat to signify the place of Judas.

The people come, and the single fish feeds them all. Some sit down and are gratified with food and sweetness; others are judged to be sinners when one of their number, Moyes, attempts to sit in the vacant seat and is swallowed up. A voice tells Joseph that only one person will be able to sit there—a great-nephew of Joseph, the grandson of Brons and Erygius. In due time the couple do indeed produce twelve children, of which eleven marry, but one, Alain, remains single. From him we are told will one day issue an heir who will fulfill the purpose of the Grail. Meanwhile, he is to take charge of his brothers and sisters and journey westward.

Another of Joseph's followers, named Petrus, is brought a letter by an angel, telling him to go to "the Vale of Avaron" (Avalon) and remain there until the coming of the Grail winner, whom he is to instruct in the mysteries of the sacraments.

All comes to pass as the voice foretold, while another angel relates that Brons shall henceforth be called the Rich Fisher because he fed the company from a single fish. He is to go westward with Petrus and there await the coming of his grandson, to whom he shall entrust the vessel and at which time the meaning of the Trinity will be made known to everyone. Next day, Brons receives the vessel and is initiated into the secret words that Joseph received from Christ himself while in prison.

Joseph is an occasionally confused story, possibly put together from several disparate sources. At times, however, it is illumined by passages of great beauty and mystery—particularly in the parts relating to Brons, the Rich Fisher, who in later versions becomes known as the Fisher King. Here also we first hear of the mysterious "secret teachings" given by Christ directly to Joseph, which are clearly the inner mysteries of the Grail. The implication is that the teachings may have contained unorthodox ideas, gleaned perhaps from gnostic Christian sources, which offered alternate versions of accepted dogma.

There are other confusions, such as the apparent doubling of the character of Brons (sometimes called Hebron) and Petrus, who is clearly intended to recall Saint Peter, the Rock on whom the Christian church was built. Also notable are the references to the Vale of Avaron, or Avalon, to which Brons and Petrus, but apparently not Joseph, proceed. Later traditions, which have Joseph coming to Avalon (by then firmly associated with Glastonbury), seem to stem from another source or possibly from a misreading of this often-confusing text. One of the most important additions made by Robert is the connection between Joseph, a disciple of Christ, and the family of Brons, who will feature in the later Arthurian romances under a number of slightly different names, and from whose lineage springs no lesser a person than Lancelot. By thus associating biblical apocrypha with the Matter of Britain, Robert brought the Arthurian legend astonishingly close to holy writ.

Robert next turned to retelling the story of Merlin, bringing the figure of the enchanter even more firmly into the fold of Arthur's court by showing him to be the chief architect of the new king's reign. Just as he had done with the Grail myth, now he deepened Merlin's story by adding an account of a plot hatched by hell's devils to produce an Antichrist. Building upon the brief mention of Merlin's demonic birth in Geoffrey's *Historia Regum Britanniae,* Robert extended this into a full-blown episode in which the innocent girl is seduced by the demon and made pregnant. When the child is born, covered in thick black hair, his mother takes him to a hermit named Blaise, who baptizes him and gives him the name Merlin. The black pelt falls away, and the child is redeemed—though retaining all the demonic skills given him by his father, which he will now use for good rather than evil.

The text now follows the story told by Nennius and elaborated by Geoffrey and Wace, with Merlin using his devil-got powers to trick Vortigern's wizards and foretell the destiny of the Britons. The story of Merlin's activities during the reign of Uther is then rehearsed, concluding with Arthur's magical conception. The work ends with the episode in which Arthur pulls the sword from the stone to prove his right to rule, and Merlin prophesies that Arthur's reign will be great.

Robert de Boron thus laid down the basic pattern for the earliest years of Arthur's reign and in the process helped define the kind of king he was and the kind of court he ruled over. He gave us the coming of Merlin, the establishment of the young king, and the founding of the Round Table Fellowship in a new and updated version, making a coherent story from elements borrowed from Christian apocrypha and early medieval chronicles, such as those penned by Geoffrey of Monmouth and Wace. Here for the first time we hear how Arthur was brought up in ignorance of his true identity and how he came to the city of London where a great tournament was to take place to prove once and for all the rightful heir to Uther.

THE DIDOT PERCEVAL

It is possible that Robert's two last books were the source of another important Arthurian Grail work, commonly known (after its nineteenth-century owner, Ambroise Firmin-Didot) as *The Didot*

Perceval.[20] Written somewhere between 1220 and 1225, it follows the outline of Chrétien's story; it takes a line so independent from the rest of the Grail stories that it seems to have drawn upon an entirely different source.

Beginning with a brief prologue outlining the history of Arthur's crowning and the coming of Merlin to court, the story then tells how the great magician gave the Round Table to Arthur. Made by Merlin after the pattern of one constructed by Joseph of Arimathea, which was in turn modeled on the table of the Last Supper, only the best men and women may sit around it, and if any who are false attempt to do so, they are at once swallowed up. One place is always left empty in token of Judas, and only the best knight, a true son of the church and of chivalry, may sit there at the appointed time.

Merlin next describes the Grail, which was given into the hands of the Fisher King to guard. But he is old and sick and will only regain his health when the best knight in the world comes to sit at the table and asks the question: What use is the Grail? At this time "the Enchantments of Britain" will end and a new time of prosperity begin. Merlin departs to his master, Blaise, to have this set down in writing.

The story now turns to Alain le Gros, grandson of Joseph of Arimathea and the inheritor of the Grail lineage. As Alain lies near to death, he is instructed by the Holy Spirit to send his son Perceval to Arthur, who will ensure that he is trained in chivalry until he can journey to his uncle Brons, who cannot die or be cured of his infirmities until he is able to pass on the secret words taught to him by Joseph concerning the Grail.

At court, Perceval outshines all others in knightly pursuits. All say that he should claim the empty place at the Round Table. But when he seats himself there, the earth groans and cracks open. A voice reproaches Arthur for disobeying Merlin's advice and adds that only by the goodness of his father is Perceval spared. Now the best knight in the world must go in search of the Rich Fisher who is old and infirm. Perceval and several other knights vow to set forth immediately. They separate, and the story follows Perceval, who first encounters a maiden weeping over the body of a knight—one of the Round Table Fellowship who was already seeking the Grail. Perceval avenges him on the knight who attacked him and after further adventures meets with his sister, who tells him that he is of the Grail lineage and advises him to visit their uncle, a wise hermit. They do so, and Perceval learns much of the history of the Grail, which he is destined to find—only his sinful nature having kept him from reaching the house of his grandfather Brons.

Vowing repentance, Perceval sets out again, encountering various other adventures and finally coming to a river where he sees three men fishing from a boat. One bids him follow the river downstream until he comes to a house where he will find lodging and shelter. Perceval takes all day to get there but is welcomed as though expected and given a scarlet robe to wear. The Fisher King is carried into the hall on a litter: he wishes to do Perceval every honor as his grandson. A squire comes out of a chamber bearing a spear that drips blood, followed by two damsels bearing silver plates covered in white cloths, then a squire with a vessel in which is Our Lord's blood.

Perceval wonders about this but fails to say anything. Next morning, he finds himself alone. He proceeds on his way and meets a damsel who rails at him for his failure, which might have ended the enchantments of Britain. Perceval seeks everywhere for his grandfather's house, until he is found wandering on Good Friday and sent back to his uncle the hermit, who tells him that his sister is now dead. Perceval does penance and then wanders again until found by Merlin, who reminds him that he is still in search of the Grail. A day later Perceval finds himself returned to the castle of the Fisher King. The Grail appears, together with the other relics, and this time Perceval asks to what use the vessel is put. Instantly, the Fisher King is restored. He asks who Perceval is and on learning that he is his own grandson instructs him in the secret words entrusted to him by Joseph of Arimathea, who in turn had them from Christ himself. Brons then dies, and Perceval remains at the castle. The enchantments of Britain are ended, and at Arthur's court, the seat that cracked when Perceval sat there is restored. Merlin tells Blaise what has happened and takes him to Perceval before continuing to Arthur to tell all that has occurred.

The *Didot* is one of the shortest and most clearly structured of all the Grail stories and is singular in the extent to which Merlin is shown to have played a part in these events. The Grail and the accompanying talismans take on their most Christian aspect, and there is an emphasis on the importance of the color red, which is worn by the Grail knight, perhaps signifying the holy blood.

The significance of Perceval's uncle Brons, who is to be found in Ireland, is not to be overlooked. Brons is a variant of the name Bran, a figure whom we met in chapter 4 as a gigantic, godlike character possessing a cauldron of inexhaustible supply—an early archetype of the Grail.

In this, and the other works that took up the theme of the Grail, we see the spiritualization of the Arthurian saga, which had hitherto concerned itself more with the secular pursuits of warfare and knightly adventure. The adventure is still present, but the love of war and battle is subsumed by a deeper quest—the striving for inner strength and the attainment of oneness with God. This reflects the actual state of human development in the Middle Ages, a world divided between the powers of church and state, between kings and popes. Just as it had at the time of its first recording angels, Geoffrey of Monmouth, Wace, Layamon, and Chrétien, in the hands of Robert de Boron and those who followed him, the Arthurian legends reflect the age in which these authors lived and their own interests and concerns.

THE ENGLISH ARTHUR

In Britain the name of Arthur continued to grow in significance. Henry II used Arthur's name and conquests to boost his claims to European monarchy, while at the same time doing his best to prove that Arthur would not return at any moment (as the Welsh in particular believed) to oust the Normans from the land. He was to be instrumental in the "discovery" of Arthur's grave at Glastonbury in Somerset and encouraged the writing of chronicles that told of Arthur, while establishing a court that rivaled that of Camelot.

English Arthurian romance took a slightly different course from the

French tales, and while many of the works that have survived are either translations or adaptations of these, they show an independent streak by replacing the more courtly elements with a more heroic or otherworldly emphasis—just as Layamon had done in his reworking of the *Historia Regum Britanniae*. Here we find no introspective inquiries about love, or elaborately interwoven lattices of story; instead, the stories are action driven, illustrated with direct speech and narrative energy.

The majority of English Arthurian romances deal with individual knights rather than the wider perspective of the epic cycles of tales emerging from France. Gawain remains the most popular of the Round Table knights, with no less than ten individual stories in which he features as the hero. These include *Gawain and the Carle of Carlisle* (ca. 1400), *The Wedding of Sir Gawain and Dame Ragnall* (ca.1450), *The Jest of Sir Gawain* (ca. 1445), and Sir *Gawain and the Green Knight* (ca. 1370–90).[21] With the exception of the latter, all of these are late entrants into the world of Arthurian literature and are written for the most part in a style of alliterative verse (lines containing internal resonance and assonance) that gives them a sinewy narrative drive. All borrow more from folklore than romance for their themes and have episodes that can be traced back to Celtic myth. *Gawain and the Green Knight* is the best known of these, and the story it tells perfectly illustrates the state of Arthurian literature in Britain from the fourteenth to fifteenth centuries.

At Camelot, as the court is preparing to celebrate the feast of Christmas, a huge and terrible figure crashes into the hall, riding a green horse and dressed in green clothing, even his skin is green. He carries a huge ax and a bough of holly to show that he comes in peace. He offers to play "a Christmas game" (a beheading game) with anyone there and taunts the assembled knights and their ladies when no one comes forward immediately. The object of the game is an exchange of blows, the first to be delivered with the Green Knight's own ax upon himself, the second to be returned in a year's time. When no one appears willing, Arthur himself is about to accept the challenge, until Gawain steps forward and requests that he be allowed to play the game. Hefting the huge ax, he strikes off the Green Knight's head, whereupon the knight picks it up, reminds Gawain to seek him out in a year at the "Green Chapel," and rides off.

The year passes all too quickly for Gawain. He sets out, wandering for many weeks in the wilderness until he comes to the castle of a knight named Bercilak. There he is warmly welcomed and told that the place he is seeking lies only a few miles distant. At supper that night, Gawain sees his host's beautiful wife and an ancient, ugly woman who seems to be her companion and is treated with great courtesy. Next day Bercilak prepares to set out hunting, insisting that Gawain remain behind and rest after his long and arduous search. He proposes that any spoils gained by either man should be exchanged at the end of the day. Once Bercilak is gone, his wife enters Gawain's chamber and attempts to seduce him, though the knight refuses to accept more than a single kiss. When Bercilak returns with the spoils of the hunt, which he offers to Gawain, the hero has only the kiss to offer by way of exchange. The same procedure is followed on the two successive days, with Bercilak bringing more and more spoils, and Gawain gathering first two and finally three kisses from the amorous lady. He retains his chivalrous attitude, however, only on the third day agreeing to accept a gift of another kind—a baldric of green lace that he is told will preserve him from all harm.

Next day Bercilak sends him forth with a guide to take him to the Green Chapel. Resisting the guide's offer to lead him to safety, Gawain reaches a strange place and hears the sound of an ax being whetted against a stone. The Green Knight appears, and Gawain prepares to take the fatal blow. Twice the Green Knight feints, mocking Gawain for flinching; on the third stroke, he nicks the hero's neck, and Gawain springs up declaring that he has taken his blow in accordance with the agreement. The Green Knight now reveals his true identity: he is Sir Bercilak, enchanted into that shape by the old woman at the castle, who is really Morgan the Goddess. It was she who forced Bercilak to test the Arthurian court with the beheading game. Gawain has passed the test with only one failure—that he accepted the green baldric from Lady Bercilak, who had also been constrained by Morgan to seduce Gawain. Chastened by his adventure, Gawain returns to Camelot and tells all that has occurred. The knights all agree to wear green baldrics in token of the hero's honorable and chivalrous behavior.

Here we have all the trapping of a classic Arthurian adventure: mysterious otherworldly beings, knightly honor, and the noble and generous figure of Arthur himself—here seen in a more attractive light than his portrayal in many of the French romances. Gawain is the perfect specimen of chivalrous behavior—refusing the advances of Lady Bercilak with charm and elegance. There is a sophistication here that is every bit as courtly as that to be found in the writings of Chrétien de Troyes but laced with horror (how the Green Knight's severed head rolls and bounces, kicked by the feet of the knights and ladies at the table), humor (Gawain refusing to be played with by the Green Knight), and some powerful descriptions of scenery and details of the hunt, which are seldom to be bettered in the French or German romances. The plot itself marries the ancient theme of the beheading game, which is found in early Irish mythology, with the temptation of the knight by the seductive enchantress, found in numerous Arthurian and non-Arthurian romances of the time.[22]

With the exception of the Gawain poems, and one or two independent tales such as *Sir Launfal* (a version of the *Lai de Lanval* by Marie de France composed in the fourteenth century), English Arthuriana follows the lead of the continental romances. There are versions of *Merlin, Lancelot, History of the Grail,* and a *Mort Artu* (Death of Arthur), though these are cast in a more epic style with the emphasis on heroic and military adventures. The greatest of the English romances of Arthur, *Le Morte d'Arthur* by Sir Thomas Malory, was not to appear until the fifteenth century, when the heyday of Arthurian literature was almost at an end.

IN FAR-FLUNG LANDS

By the end of the twelfth century, the Arthurian legends had spread out across much of Europe. First Italy, then Germany was captivated by the magic and wonder of the Arthurian epic. The German poet Hartman von Aue produced versions of Chrétien's poems of *Erec* and *Ywain* sometime between 1180 and 1198. Hartman was a fine poet in his own right and did more than slavishly follow the lead of his French source.[23]

The Crusades provided the means for the spread of the stories. German princes mingled with French as the vast Christian armies lumbered across Europe headed for the Holy Lands. Trouvères and poets from the greatest medieval courts shared their favorite stories and borrowed from each other. It would seem that when not fighting Saracens, the crusading soldiers regaled themselves with stories of Arthur to keep up morale. Out of this cultural cross-fertilization was born such rich and various tales as Ulrich von Zatzikhoven's *Lanzelet* (1194–1205), which brought a very different story of the birth and deeds of the great French hero, based on more primitive Celtic myths and fairy tales.[24] Other writers followed suit, notably Wolfram von Eschenbach, whose *Parzival* (1200–1210) took Chrétien's basic story of Perceval and fleshed it out with a rich texture of symbolism and meaning, which had been absent in the French.

Adopting the story as told by Chrétien, Wolfram widened and deepened it into a moral allegory of a man's quest for God and truth, roundly denouncing the French author for having got it all wrong and—uniquely in the history of Arthurian literature—claiming a lineage for his poem from Oriental rather than Western sources.[25] Another courtly poet, Wirnt von Grafenberg, claimed an oral French source for his verse romance *Wigalois* (1210–1215), learned, he claimed, while serving in the entourage of Otto I, duke of Meran, one of the leading crusader lords. Wigalois is the son of the famed Sir Gawain, and in Wirnt's world he, rather than Arthur, is the perfect embodiment of chivalry and human valor under God.[26]

Perhaps the greatest German contribution to the Arthurian legends was the thirteenth-century *Tristan* by Gottfried von Strassburg, another author of whom we know almost nothing.[27] Drawing on older narratives concerning a Pictish warrior named Drustan, who lived more or less at the same time as the sixth-century Arthur, Gottfried drew out the story into an elaborate and overheated tale of adultery, forbidden love, and adventure. Tristan, whose mother dies in childbirth, becomes a favorite of his uncle, King Mark of Cornwall (almost certainly a historical figure from the sixth or seventh centuries) and leads an expedition on behalf of Mark to win the hand of an Irish princess called Isolde. Thanks to Tristan's passionate wooing the journey is successful; but on the way back to Britain, Tristan and Isolde drink a love potion intended for the bride and groom and are eternally locked in love. Most of the remaining nineteen thousand lines of the poem are taken up with the efforts of the lovers to spend time together without Mark discovering them, to which end they resort to endless ruses. In the end word of their affair does leak out, and Tristan is exiled to Brittany, where he marries another woman, ironically named Isolde of the White Hands. Their marriage remains unconsummated, however, and when Tristan is wounded by a poisoned blade and sends word to Isolde of Ireland to come and heal him, disaster follows. Having arranged for a ship to show a white sail if Isolde is coming and a black if she is not, the second Isolde lies about the color of the sail, so that Tristan dies of a combination of grief and his wounds.

This story, which was originally unconnected with the Arthurian legends, became extremely popular in the Middle Ages. Most authors made a point of describing the differences between the love of Tristan for Isolde and that of Lancelot for Guinevere. While Lancelot behaves in every way as a noble knight should, foreswearing the court to remain out of reach of the queen, Tristan strives to cuckold his uncle. The love potion was seen as an excuse for this, while the affair between Lancelot and the queen was deemed more natural, with only the knight's will-power preventing him from pursuing his desire.

Many versions of the story were told throughout Europe, and in time Tristan came to be seen as a villain rather than a noble knight. Yet in his heyday, he was one of the most significant Knights of the Round Table and fast friends with Lancelot—in whose castle of Joyous Gard he several times hides with Isolde. Gottfried's account of the life and death of his hero is probably the finest of the half dozen versions that have survived—an enduring work of literature that elevated an otherwise unexceptional story of doomed love to fresh poetic heights.

Only one German author attempted to tell the story of Arthur from birth to death. This was Heinrich von dem Türlin, whose *Diu Crone*

(The Crown), written around 1230, borrowed from just about every extant Arthurian romance—including those of the Grail—and spun from these a wholly new story in which Gawain is the Grail winner and motifs from romance, lay, and fairy tale are brilliantly interwoven with the normal trappings of the Arthurian courtly world.[28] Here Arthur himself is overshadowed by his first knight, and the same is true of his portrayal in several other German Arthurian romances, including the thirteenth-century *Daniel von dem Blühenden Tal* (Daniel of the Blossoming Valley), attributed to Der Sticker, and the anonymous *Wigamur* (ca. 1250), which presented a satirical view of Arthur.[29]

Despite this, more than a third of the German courtly romances from the twelfth to fourteenth centuries that have survived are Arthurian in content or borrow heavily from Arthurian texts in French. Few are original, and when they are, they tend to be wild and fantastic in character, full of monsters, ghosts, and dragons, making Arthur more of a fairy-tale character than the heroic king of French and English stories.

In Italy, Arthur and his knights were the subjects of a number of romances—some based on French originals, others branching out into new areas. The place where aspects of the Matter of Britain did find a home in Italian literature was in the tradition of lyric poetry. Dozens of romantic poems have survived that contain mention of Arthur, Gawain, Merlin, and Tristan. The last named is undoubtedly the most popular character, rivaling Lancelot as both a lover and a warrior. The thirteenth-century *La Tavola Ritonda* (The Round Table), based loosely on the French *Prose Tristan* of the same century, elevated its hero to a high degree by the simple method of downgrading all the other heroes (Gawain in particular) but is both long and dull compared to Gottfried's great work.[30] Most of the other Arthurian tales circulating among the courtly audiences in Italy were copies or reworkings of French and German texts. There is, however, a curious Hebrew version of Arthur, in the form of a poem called *King Artus*,[31] which dates from circa 1279 and was probably adapted from an Italian version of the *Morte Artu*.

Elsewhere the spread of Arthurian romances reached as far as Norway and Iceland, where several striking reworkings of Chrétien's poems were made. *Tristrams saga ok Isondar* (The Saga of Tristan and Isolde), a Norwegian translation of an eleventh-century English poem written by a poet named Thomas, was undertaken at the behest of King Harkon IV of Norway, who seems to have commissioned translations of Chrétien's *Yvain* (which became *Ivan's Saga*) and *Erec et Enide* (*Erex Saga*), as well as several other minor Arthurian works, suggesting that Harkon was himself a fan of the stories.[32] Once again there is a somewhat harsher tone to the passages that relate to Arthur himself—as though he was less popular than his knights. Possibly this goes back to Geoffrey of Monmouth and the other Arthurian chroniclers who made Arthur an invader and king of both Iceland and Sweden. There are versions of the Tristan story, of Geoffrey's *Historia,* and several sagas that feature Merlin as a protagonist, all of which exist in sufficient number of manuscript copies to prove their popularity among the courts of the Scandinavian world.

Among all this flood of Arthuriana, one book became largely forgotten until it was recently revived and partially translated into English. This is a huge, sprawling romance known as *Perceforest,* which is actually a *pre*history of Arthur's time, taking us back to the days of the Trojan adventure into Britain and the visit by no lesser a person than Alexander the Great. This links two of the greatest figures of medieval romance, and Arthur is said to descend from a child of the Greek king and a woman of Britain.

The story is too vast and sprawling to recount here, but it is full of wild magic and the kind of endlessly variegated quest stories so beloved of the medieval public. It presents a previously unknown history of Britain (only some of it borrowed from Geoffrey of Monmouth) in a richness of detail seldom equaled in this time, and creates a lineage for many of the major characters of the legend that serves to add weight and depth to their burgeoning history.

A HIGH HISTORY

Throughout this huge pouring forth of Arthurian literature in the high and later Middle Ages, there is a tendency for Arthur himself to become what the French called a *roi fainéant,* a "do-nothing king." We first see this diminution of dynamic warrior into courtly king in *Culhwch and Olwen,* where Arthur's men exhort him, "Lord, go back, for you ought not to accompany the host on this sort of petty errand," as they set off to obtain the magical objects for Culhwch's wedding. There, despite his first retreat home, Arthur does return as an active exponent of the quest.

In the anonymous thirteenth-century romance known as *Perlesvaus* or *The High History of the Holy Grail,*[33] this tendency to make Arthur no more than a figurehead becomes even more evident. Perhaps the most spiritually developed account of the Grail quest, *Perlesvaus* sits somewhere between the versions of Robert de Boron and the first of the great thirteenth-century cycle of Grail romances known as the Vulgate Cycle. The story it tells, though still following the lead set by Chrétien, differs strongly from other Grail texts in its overtly symbolic references, which owe more to Celtic myth than Christian theology. In particular the work represented the human situation as a quest for a return to a perfect pre-Fall state of being. The Grail becomes a central symbol of Christ's sacrifice, and the humanity of the knights—especially as embodied by Lancelot—was identified with the quest that every soul must accomplish during his or her lifetime.

Everything that had been written so far about the Grail and the involvement of Arthur and his knights in its history seemed to have been preparing the way for a mighty set of books that carry the development of the Arthurian legends into their next (and almost final) stage. Until recently, these were known by the overall title of the Vulgate Cycle, though more recent editors have renamed it the *Lancelot-Grail* in token of the central part played by the eponymous hero. Written between 1215 and 1235, the cycle consists of five roughly sequential texts.[34]

There was probably no single author, though it seems likely that one person may have shaped the overall arc of the story and then handed over the various parts to various individual authors, all of who were probably monks of the Cistercian order. This has led some commentators to suggest that the cycle was written down at the behest of Bernard of Clairvaux, the founder of the Cistercians and one of the most significant spiritual writers and thinkers of the thirteenth century. That Bernard was also instrumental in the founding of the great military order of the Knights Templar, for whom he wrote the Latin Rule, outlining the ideal behavior of a Templar knight, has placed him at the center of a continuing controversy concerning the historical search for the Grail and the accusations of heresy leveled at the Templars at the time of their brutal destruction in 1213. Whatever the truth of this, there are certainly a number of themes and ideas to be found within the Vulgate texts that are broadly similar to those expressed by Bernard in his theological writings.[35]

The Vulgate Cycle consists of *The Prose Lancelot*, a lengthy account of Lancelot's quest for the Grail, in which he fails because of his love for Guinevere; the *Quest del Saint Graal* (hugely expanded from Chrétien's original tale); the *Mort Artu,* which tells of the events leading up to the death of the king; and two other texts, the *Estoire del Saint Graal* and the *Estoire de Merlin,* probably written later and drawing heavily on Robert de Boron's account of the early history of the Grail and the coming of Merlin. An elaborate network of prediction, heavenly intervention, and genealogical history tie these books together into a vast tale, beginning with the creation of man and ending with the death of Arthur. But the king himself is far from central to the story. Here he represents the earthly power of kingship, which, though mighty and laudable, is also weak and tainted with earthly concerns. The monkish writers of the Vulgate texts utterly rejected the Courtly Love ethic and introduced a highly moralistic tone. For example, when the Grail quest begins, ladies are exhorted to remain at home so that the knights can be helped to achieve the quest by remaining chaste.

The lofty tone of the Vulgate Cycle presents us with the weakest face of Arthur—a *roi fainéant,* indeed, whose end is shown to derive directly from his sinful coupling with his half sister and whose doom cannot be prevented even by the presence of the Grail in his kingdom and the quest undertaken by his greatest knights. Of all those who set out from Camelot after the appearance of the Grail, only three (the saintly Galahad, son of Lancelot and Elaine of Carbonek; Perceval, reduced to a secondary figure in this new account of the quest; and Bors de Ganis, Lancelot's cousin) are in any way successful—though even this is clouded by uncertainty, as the all-too-human frailties of the great knights Gawain and Lancelot at times seem to overshadow the mystical victory of Galahad.

The story told in the *Quest del Saint Graal* is a magnificent Christian allegory, weighed down with theology and with homilies aimed at the weak vessels of human frailty. It also contains some of the most powerful imagery to be found anywhere in the literature of the medieval West. It is a far cry indeed from the great epics of war and adventure that had gone before. Here Arthur rules over a Christian kingdom, and the central objective of his knights is to find the Grail and bring the kingdom of God on Earth closer to reality.

The influence of the Crusades is almost certainly to be felt here. From the moment in 1095 when the rallying call went out through the Western world, "Aidez le Saint Sepulchre" (Save the Holy Sepulchre), the Arthurian legends began to change. The city of Jerusalem, long seen as an image of heaven on Earth, had been under Muslim control since the ninth century; now it demanded rescue. The armies of the West began to assemble in answer to the call for a Crusade against the infidels. This was the beginning of one of the most powerful movements in the whole of the Middle Ages, an adventure that swept up most of the able-bodied men in Europe and flung them headlong into unfamiliar lands, where they encountered equally new and unfamiliar ideas. Out of this came new strands in the stories of Arthur, which the crusaders carried with them in their dreams and their literature and returned transformed.

Once the links were established between the Grail and the principal Arthurian legends, Christianity itself carried the new image of Arthur, reshaping it forever and bringing into its frame of reference a new range of meanings and associations. The Celtic cauldrons of life and inspiration were far too powerful to be forgotten, but they could not remain as they were, set in a framework of paganism that was unacceptable to a Christianized Europe. So, as the legends began to grow and develop into ever more complex cycles of stories, chalices replaced cauldrons.

The effect of this process on the symbolism of the Arthurian legends produced an extraordinary blossoming of mystical writing, which delved back into the Celtic past and beyond in order to explore the deepest reaches of the Christian psyche. In the mingling of these streams, the Grail itself found new definitions; its history shifted gear, bringing the sacred vessel closer to the world of everyday spirituality, while at the same time making it an object of eternal search.

This is central to our understanding of the medieval face of Arthur. The Middle Ages had achieved their first flowering, a springing forth of new ideas and beliefs in minds freed at last from the sheer effort of survival. Art, architecture, and literature were in their vernal aspect: Chartres cathedral was still under construction, and complex webs of theology and mysticism were being unwound in both monastery and university. The relationships of mankind with creation, and with God, were among the most important questions of the age, making it scarcely surprising that a new image of the sacred vessel should emerge.

Despite or perhaps because of the fact that literacy was a skill reserved almost exclusively for the clergy, memory was correspondingly stronger than today. The ear, not the eye, was the gateway to the imagination: when it came to storytelling, there were always willing listeners to wonder tales in which semi-divine heroes slew beasts and overcame implacable enemies in order to rescue, and eventually marry, archetypal maidens. The other effect of this was to ensure that links with older stories and sources were kept open and, in many cases, to give a new lease on life for the stories of the Grail.

There was also a stronger sense of conceptual or symbolic understanding than at almost any time before or since. Laborers were known by their implements of toil; the religious by their habit; nobility by their rich apparel; knights by their mounts and weapons. Although the liturgy of the Mass was in Latin, except perhaps for the sermons, which may have been in the vernacular, this did not seem to matter; the actions of the priest at the altar were necessarily mysterious, emblematic of his mediation between heaven and Earth on behalf of the congregation.

Factors such as these helped prepare the way for the new focus of the Arthurian saga, as did the political state of Europe at this time. Prior to the spread of Christianity, the whole of the Western world had been torn apart by war and insurrection; orphaned from its classical roots by the invading barbarians who eventually made the West their own homeland, Europe remained a tangle of petty kingdoms, each one battling for supremacy.

Yet each kingdom, however small, had its own capital. The archetype for these capitals was Jerusalem, the city of the Divine King; mythically, it was Camelot, the stronghold of King Arthur. Indeed, the role of kingship within European society was a significant one: kingship sprang from a divine source as it had from the Goddess of Sovereignty in Celtic times, and kings were anointed with oil in the same manner as priests—emphasizing the sacred nature of the office.

Jerusalem had been in Islamic hands for a long time before the beginning of the Crusades. Pilgrimage to the Holy Land was possible, if hazardous, under the Abbasid caliphate, but toward the end of the eleventh century, the balance of power changed; under the new Fatimid dynasty, permission to enter Palestine seemed doubtful. Nor was it accidental that Pope Urban II should call for a Crusade at the moment he did. His motivations may have been politically as well as spiritually oriented. He feared an incipient split between eastern and western Christendom and knew that the effort to win back the holy city required a united front. Urban therefore proclaimed at the Council of Clermont that to those who would fight to protect Christendom from pagan incursions and go onward to liberate the holy places, he would grant general absolution and remission of all sins. In effect, he was offering a certain ticket into heaven; to those who forsook their promise, he vowed excommunication and eternal damnation.

Urban's clarion call opened the way for Christians to perform their duty in clear and unambiguous terms; he managed, indeed, to call into being the greatest single fighting force to be seen in Europe until World War II and at the same time helped to solve the problem of unfocused strength. It was not long since Christian armies had to be persuaded not to fight with each other without good reason, and some areas of Europe still faced the problem of armies fighting across their fields.

This situation finds a parallel in Arthurian literature. When Arthur came to the throne, he had first to prove his supremacy in battle over the rival kings of Britain. After he had done this, he engaged their services in policing the country. But when all the fighting was done, when there were no more evil barons to discomfit, no more black knights waiting at fords, and when all the dragons were dead, the famous Round Table Fellowship began to be lethargic, to exhibit some of the traits they had vowed to overcome. Then, as the whole court is teetering in the balance, when the scandal of Lancelot's illicit passion for Arthur's queen is about to break, the Grail appears, leading to new and wondrous opportunities for growth and adventure.

So, too, the Crusades were set in motion at the right moment to harness the various forces of Christendom into a single spearhead of power. Unfortunately, the parallel holds good when we look at the subsequent course of the Crusades: great deeds were achieved, but great evils unloosed as well. Crusader armies butchered eastern Christians and Jews, as in the siege of Constantinople in 1204, and in general behaved in a barbaric fashion toward their enemies. Similarly, Arthur's knights, by approaching the Grail quest unworthily, may have wreaked worse damage than by staying at home, since in the end the loss of the knights who perished on the quest heralded the breakup of the Round Table Fellowship. Urban's call to Christendom set up a chain reaction the effects of which can still be seen today. Ownership of the Holy Lands, the division between Catholic and Eastern Orthodox churches, and many other issues that still trouble us may be seen as originating with the Crusades.

THE GREAT BOOK

The Vulgate Cycle spawned at least one more cycle of tales, known as the Post-Vulgate, which elaborated the story of the Grail quest and its connection to the Arthurian world even further. It was also the central source for what remains one of the greatest tellings of the Arthurian saga to date. This is the book known as *Le Morte d'Arthur,* written by the fifteenth-century knight Sir Thomas Malory.[36]

It enters the field late and is really the last great Arthurian romance—at any rate of the medieval period. As such it inherits the sum of all that had gone before. Composed toward the middle of the fifteenth century and published in 1485, it is still the source from which most of what we commonly know about Arthur is derived. Robert Graves memorably referred to it as "an enchanted sea for the reader to swim about in, delighting at the random beauties of fifteenth-century prose rather than engrossed in the plot."[37] T. E. Lawrence took it with him into the desert, along with the *Odyssey* of Homer, and consciously modeled his own life on Arthurian chivalry. It has been quoted, misquoted, paraphrased, bowdlerized, extracted, and retold countless times for virtually every generation since its inception.

And yet, we still know very little about its author and cannot even be sure whether he intended to write a single book—the first real English novel—or a cycle of stories. Even the title is problematical: Malory called it *The Book of King Arthur and His Knights of the Round Table.* William Caxton, who published the book in 1485, with the high-handedness of editors then and now, decided it would sell better if it had a shorter and snappier title. He took one from the final tale in the collection, *The Death of Arthur,* and gave it a French twist so that it became *Le Morte d'Arthur,* by which name it remains known to this day.

The book is vast, sprawling, and at times undisciplined but with a narrative drive that keeps it moving energetically along to page-turning effect, but the question of Malory's use of his sources, and of the degree of originality attributable to him, remains difficult. For many years there was only Caxton's text to go on, until, in 1934, a manuscript was discovered in the library of Winchester College, which turned out to be much closer to Malory's original.[38] Unlike Caxton's edition, it showed that the author had apparently written a series of interconnected tales. The original title, *The Whole Book of King Arthur and of His Noble Knights of the Round Table,* adds to the belief that Malory intended the book to be read as a piece.

Caxton himself was clear about his intentions, as he explained in his original preface to the work.

> After that I had accomplished and finished divers histories . . . and also certain books of examples and doctrine, many noble and divers gentlemen of this realm of England came and demanded of me, many and ofttimes wherefore that I have not made and imprinted the noble history of the Sangrail, and of the most renowned Christian king, first and chief of the three best Christian worthies, King Arthur, which ought most to be remembered among us English men before all other Christian kings. . . . And many noble volumes be made of him and of his noble knights in French, which I have seen and read beyond the sea, which be not had in our maternal tongue, but in Welsh be many and also in French and some in English, but no where nigh all. Wherefore such as have been drawn out briefly into English I have . . . undertaken to imprint a book of the noble histories of the said King Arthur, and of certain of his knights, after a copy unto me delivered, which copy Sir Thomas Malory did take out of certain books of French, and reduced it into English. And I, according to my copy, have done set it in imprint. . . . And for to understand briefly the content of this volume, I have divided it into twenty-one books.[39]

It is not really possible to say, with any certainty, which version most closely reflects the intention of the author. The question also arises as to which of the versions reads most powerfully and satisfactorily. Some of the changes in the Caxton edition make better sense than the original; others make strange reading.

THE KNIGHT PRISONER

But who was Malory? Virtually all we know about him is what he tells us in the book, where a number of colophons are included that appear to have been written by him personally. Thus throughout the Winchester manuscript appear a number of prayers addressed to the readers of the book requesting their attention to the plight of the author. At the end of "The Tale of King Arthur" (Books I–IV in Caxton), we read:

> And this book endeth whereas Sir Lancelot and Sir Tristram
> came to court. Who that would make any more let him seek
> other books of King Arthur and of Sir Lancelot or Sir Tristram;
> for this was drawn by a knight prisoner Sir Thomas Malleorre,
> that God send him good recovery.[40]

Other such pleas follow at the end of "The Tale of Sir Gareth" and "The Tale of Sir Tristram." Finally, toward the end of the book, there is a reference to:

> The Most Piteous Tale of the Morte Arthure Sanz Gwerdon
> par le shyvalere Sir Thomas Malleorre, knight, Jesu aide ly
> puvotre bon mercy (Jesu help me of your great mercy)[41]

This suggests that the author was writing the book in prison, from which he hopes to be released soon. It is these statements that led various scholars to certain conclusions as to the identity of the "knight prisoner," whose name, as was common in the Middle Ages, appears under so many variable spellings.

The earliest suggestion came from the sixteenth-century antiquary John Bale who, in a catalog of famous British writers, declared that Malory was Welsh and that he hailed from a place called Maloria, near the River Dee. This suggestion was taken up by another great Welsh scholar, Sir John Rhys, who in his edition of 1893[42] declared that the alternative spelling that appears in the colophon identified the author as coming from an area that straddles the borders of England and North Wales—Maleore in Flintshire and Maleor in Denbigh. This would make Malory a possible relative of Edward Rhys Maelor, a fifteenth-century Welsh poet.

Another contender, of whom we know considerably more, is Sir Thomas Malory of Newbold Revel (or Fenny Newbold) in Warwickshire. He has proved the longest lasting and most popular claimant, and a huge amount of research has been done into his life. For many, this is the Malory of *Morte d'Arthur* fame—though his life seems at times massively at variance with many of the personal statements contained in the book

H. Oskar Sommer seems to have been the first to mention this Malory in his 1890 edition of the *Morte,* but it was the distinguished Harvard professor George Lyman Kittredge who in 1897 outlined the evidence relating to the Newbold Revel Malory.[43] Deriving most of his information from a book of Warwickshire antiquities by Sir William Dugdale, Kittredge presented this Malory as a soldier and parliamentarian who had fought at Calais with Richard Beauchamp, earl of Warwick, one of the truly great chivalric figures of the fifteenth century, who died in 1471 and was buried at Grayfriars in London.

This created sufficient interest to send several other scholars in search of further documentation, including legal rolls contained in the Public Record Office in London. The information they gleaned revealed a very different figure from that suggested by Dugdale. Most of the records concerning the career of Thomas Malory of Newbold Revel were concerned with his criminal record, which included several periods in jail for crimes that included theft, grievous bodily harm, and even rape. This scarcely seemed to reflect the high chivalric standards suggested from a reading of the *Morte d'Arthur.*

This Malory's parents were Sir John and Lady Phillipa, the former originally of Winwick, the latter heiress to the estate of Fenny Newbold. Thomas, their only son, was born somewhere between 1393 and 1416. According to Dugdale, he became a professional soldier and served under Richard Beauchamp, but even here the dates are vague, and we have no idea how or if he distinguished himself. In 1442 he acted as an elector in Northamptonshire, but in 1443 he was accused, together with one Eustace Burnaby, of attacking, imprisoning, and making off with goods to the value of forty pounds, belonging to a Thomas Smythe, of Sprotton in Northants. Nothing seems to have come of this charge, and shortly after we hear that Thomas Malory married a woman named Elizabeth, who later bore him a son, Robert.

In 1443 Malory was elected to Parliament and served at Westminster for the rest of that year, being appointed to a royal commission charged with the distribution of monies to the poorer towns of Warwickshire. We may judge by this that whatever the truth of the accusations made against him the previous year, Malory remained in the good graces of his peers.

This was to change in 1450, when we learn that Thomas Malory, knight, was accused of lying in wait, along with twenty-six other men, to attack and rob Humphry Stafford, Duke of Buckingham, one of the richest and most powerful men in the country. The reasons for this remain unknown, and the accusations were never proved. Various suggestions have been made, including the possibility of Malory's involvement in a political plot organized by Richard Neville, Earl of Warwick. Whatever the truth, Malory seems to have been bent upon a life of crime from this time onward. In May of the same year, he is accused of exhorting with menaces the sum of one hundred shillings from Margaret King and William Hales of Monks Kirby, and on the August following of engineering the same injury against another neighbor, John Mylner, from who he allegedly stole twenty shillings.

Somewhere between these two events, Malory was accused of an even more serious crime. Around June of 1450, aided by three other men, Malory is said to have broken into the house of Hugh Smyth of Monks Kirby and to have stolen goods to the tune of forty pounds and to have raped his wife. A mere eight weeks later, Malory alone is charged with having attacked the same woman, this time in the city of Coventry. Nine months later, along with nineteen others, an order was made for the arrest of Sir Thomas Malory of Newbold Revel. Once again, nothing seems to have come of this, and in the ensuing months, Malory and his "gang"—which seems to have ranged in numbers between ten and sixty, at one point even rising to one hundred—went on a spree of violent robberies. At one point Malory himself was arrested and imprisoned in Maxstoke, but he escaped almost at once, swimming the moat and rejoining his band at Newbold Revel.

And so the story goes on, with the list of robberies carried out by Malory and his men growing steadily, until finally, on August 23, 1451, the matter came to trial at Nuneaton. The list of charges was extensive and included both Malory and several others who, according to the legal system of the time, may or may not have between present to answer their accusers. In any event, the judgment went against Malory, and by January of 1452 he was imprisoned in Marshalsea prison in London, where he seems to have remained for at least a year.

His response to the judgment against him was to plead not guilty and to demand a retrial with a jury of men from his own county. In effect, this never took place, and Malory was released for a time. In March he was arrested again and returned to Marshalsea, from where he once again escaped some two months later, possibly by bribing his guards. Less than a month later, he was back in prison again, and this time was held until the following May, when he was released on bail of £200—a considerable sum at that time.

However, when the date arrived for Malory to answer for his crimes, he could not immediately be found. The reason for this, it transported, was that he was already in custody at Colchester, where he was accused of still further crimes involving robbery and horse theft. Once again, the very resourceful Malory escaped and remained at liberty until November, when he was apprehended and returned to Marshalsea, this time under the huge penalty, against his escape, of £1,000.

During the next few years, we hear less of Malory. For much of the time he was imprisoned, either in Marshalsea or Newgate, though he seems to have obtained bail on at least one occasion and this time to have returned on the date appointed and been duly locked up again. The worst crimes with which he was accused on this occasion are failure to pay loans made to him by various people to enable him to be at liberty.

In and out of prison again over the next few years, Malory's name finally appeared on a register of captors pardoned by the new king Edward IV in 1461. After this little or nothing more is heard of him beyond the brief record of a grandson, Nicholas, born to his son, Robert, who died shortly after. On March 14, 1470, Sir Thomas Malory, knight, himself died and was buried at Grayfriars Chapel, in the shadow of Newgate prison where he had spent time as a prisoner. The fact that his mortal remains were interred in some splendor suggests that not only were his old misdeeds forgotten, but that he was possessed of some wealth. This may have been the result of his misspent life, or because he had a wealthy patron, whose possible existence has been surmised as a reflection of the number of times he was set free or granted bail. Who this patron may have been, if he existed, is a matter for speculation. It has been claimed that it may have been Richard Neville, the kingmaker himself, and that Malory may have spent time as a spy in his pay, but in a life already crowded with events, this may be stretching the evidence too far.

Malory's grave was lost forever when Henry VIII dissolved the monastery of Grayfriars. His grandson, Nicholas, survived to inherit his lands and was sufficiently respected to be appointed high sheriff in 1502. But of Thomas Malory of Newbold Revel nothing more is currently know. He remains an enigmatic and in some ways unlikely author of *Le Mort d'Arthur,* though in other respects he lived a life every bit as colorful and dramatic as some of the characters in the book.[44]

From Malory we learn how Arthur came to power by drawing the sword from the stone; how his rule was challenged by eleven rebel kings and how he defeated them with the help of Merlin; and how once the wars were over he decided to take a wife, and despite Merlin's warnings that she would one day betray him, he chose Guinevere, the daughter of King Leodegrance of Cameliarde. With her came, as dowry, a great round table, made by Merlin at the bidding of Arthur's father, Uther Pendragon; a table "round in the likeness of the world" at which one hundred and fifty knights could sit, none higher in favor than the rest. On the day of his marriage, Arthur required of Merlin that he should find sufficient knights "which be of most prowess and worship" to fill at least fifty of the seats.

This Merlin did, and fifty more came from Leodegrance, so that a hundred sat down together at the table on that first day. And when they had all done homage to Arthur they returned to the Hall where the Round Table stood and found that on the back of each chair was a name, set there in golden letters. The names were all of those already chosen, and many more that were as yet not come. But two remained blank, and of these Merlin would only say that they would be filled in due course.[45]

Thus the Fellowship of the Round Table, hinted at rather than developed by Wace and Layamon, met for the first time on the day of the king's wedding to Guinevere, and if the seeds were already sown for the downfall of Arthur's great dream, the shadows were still distant on that day. The first adventure of the Round Table Fellowship follows swiftly. As the fellowship sit at dinner for the first time, there comes into the hall a white hart, pursued by a white dog and fifty pairs of black hounds. As they race around the table, the white dog bites the hart, which leaps high in the air, knocking over a knight sitting nearby. This man seizes the dog and departs hurriedly, and in the next moment, a lady rides into the hall and demands that he be brought back, for the dog is hers. Before anyone can answer, a fully armed knight rides up, seizes the lady, and carries her off by force.

Astonishment, and perhaps some amusement, attends these events. But Merlin stands forth and states that the fellowship "might not leave these adventures so lightly." So Arthur sends two of the new knights— his own nephew Sir Gawain and the illegitimate son of King Pellinor, Sir Tor—out after the white hart and the dog, respectively, and sends Pellinor himself, a tried-and-trusted warrior, after the lady who had been stolen away.

So at the outset, this single incident had given rise to three separate adventures, which are then narrated at length. They are to be the first of many such that begin in similar fashion, with the entry of knight or lady into the court, requesting succor or some favor of Arthur and of the fellowship. Nor may they refuse, so long as the request is a fair one and the demand, honest. For at the end of that first, triple quest, all of the fellowship swear an oath:

> Never to do outrage nor murder, and always to flee treason; also, by no means to be cruel, but to give mercy unto him that asketh mercy, upon pain of forfeiture of their worship and lordship of King Arthur for evermore; and always to do ladies, damosels, and gentlewomen succour, upon pain of death. Also, that no man take no battles in a wrongful quarrell for no law, nor for world's goods. Unto this were all the knights sworn of the Table Round, both old and young. And every year were they sworn at the high feast of Pentecost.[46]

These simple rules reflect the ideals central to medieval chivalry. Not all of the knights keep to these demands placed upon them by their king. But despite some failings, they hold true to the honor of the Round Table, and as if in answer to their existence, strange events seem to multiply on every side, seeing to it that they never lack the opportunity of being tested and tried.

Arthur establishes a custom, whereby at any high feast he will not eat until some wonder or adventure has been related to him. And so begins a pattern, whereby the knights ride "at errantry," wandering hither and thither throughout the land in search of wrongs to right or villainy to combat. Brother knights are rescued, as well as ladies; evil knights are overthrown and either killed or sent to Arthur to crave pardon. Many of these become Round Table knights themselves, giving up their former pursuits. But there are always others, always further adventures to attempt, as the great knights on their great horses thunder through the forests of Arthur's realm in quest of their king's dream of chivalry and the perfect earthly kingdom.

All of this was drawn from what Malory referred to as "The French Book"—the Vulgate Cycle augmented by stories quarried from other texts. Malory not only gave readers of English a version in their own tongue, but also created a very different version. No slavish translator, he adapted, pruned, and restructured everything he found. Removing the complex theological commentary that stifled the story at every turn in the Vulgate texts, Malory uncovered the bones of the action and added swift-paced dialogue, tightening and fleshing out the material wherever he felt the need. At a time when it was the custom to adapt rather than originate, Malory may possibly have invented the entire story of Sir Gareth, as no exact source for this has so far been discovered.

Though the setting of the book bears all the trappings of the late medieval period in which Malory lived, one reference shows that Arthur was still regarded as a king from a much earlier time. It occurs when the knights are considering the wondrous golden letters that appear written upon the Siege Perilous—an unoccupied position at the Round Table that can only be filled by the Grail winner. They read that, 454 years after the Passion of Jesus Christ, the siege will be occupied. Lancelot then makes a rapid computation: "Hit seemeth me . . . that thys syge oughte to be fulfilled thys same day, for thys ys the Pentecoste after the four hondred and four and fyffty yere."

The quest for the Holy Grail is thus set to begin in the year 487 AD, giving us a startlingly accurate echo from the lifetime of the historical Arthur. Following Malory, if we take the date of Badon as 516 and the Battle of Camlann as 537 from the *Annales Cambriae,* Arthur would have been either a small child or an adolescent in that year.

Thomas Malory's influence on the Arthurian legends cannot be overestimated. Though he arrived at a time when they were already beginning to be regarded as old fashioned, his book made a fitting climax to almost five hundred years in which the medieval Arthur was familiar across most of the Western world, with literally hundreds of works (many copies or translations of each other) disseminated throughout the courts of Europe.

There are few who will fail to find something to delight and inspire them in Malory's great story. It has everything: love, war, heroism, spiritual striving, comedy, tragedy, mystery—and a huge cast of memorable characters. In Malory's hands it becomes a rich, haunting tapestry, which, more than six hundred years after its composition, remains one of the finest pieces of writing in English.

But if *Le Morte d'Arthur* was a threnody for the end of an age, it was most certainly not the end of interest in King Arthur. Though the next three centuries saw a significant falling away in written works about him and his knights, Arthur's name and pedigree were still invoked for political reasons. He became a point of reference for the dynastic claims and expansionist dreams of more than one English monarch.

7

Arthur of Fable

A Nation's Hero

I, King Arthur, head of the Table Round,
Chief leader of all valorous heart
Wish to receive with sincere will
All noble hearts of virtuous deed.
Powerful princes, noble and brave,
You to whom honour is sovereign,
Follow my deeds and my chivalry.*

INSCRIPTION FROM THE SIXTEENTH-CENTURY
CALAIS EXCHEQUER ROUND HOUSE[1]

THE GLASTONBURY TOMB AND
THE RELICS OF ARTHUR

From the Middle Ages onward, Arthur rapidly became a linchpin for romantic and mythic stories, a reference point for popular culture. Whenever the past was invoked, Arthur was the ambassador of Britain's history; his court, his knights and ladies, his Round Table—all lent

---

*Our translation.

substance and weight to others' verse, storytelling, and tableaux.

But as the literary outpourings from the medieval Arthurian legend continued to flow, the face of Arthur began to change yet again. Successive monarchies invoked his name to support their evolving notions of government, often with dismaying results. As the perfect king, with a band of virtuous knights to support his Round Table, Arthur became a convenient template for chivalric kingship, imperial ambition, and political expediency. His supposed conquest of Europe and his victory over the Romans, as told by Geoffrey of Monmouth and others, became a dangerous precedent for empire building.

Almost from the moment that Arthur vanished from the historic record, he began to attract legends. These stories were subject to continuous, subtle degrees of change. We have seen how the heroic age, which gave us the earliest figure of Arthur, gave way to the mythic dimension and finally to the idea of a chivalric king ruling over an elegant medieval court. None of these literary developments took place in a vacuum. Each Arthurian story both contributed to and sometimes inspired the evolving history of the Middle Ages as later times represented Arthur within a more political framework, often with spurious prophecies, attributed to Merlin, declaring for the latest regime.

Some dynasties, like the Tudors, leant heavily on the mystique of Arthur, incorporating him into their family trees to uphold their claims to.the throne of Britain, while the Plantagenet and Norman kings prosecuted their own complex agendas by invoking Arthur as the model of kingship and good government. In an age of relics and uncritical acceptance, Arthur also began to be increasingly reverenced in a kind of semimystical way as the stories were influenced by the accretion of Christian legend and the search for national identity.

The Welsh believed that Arthur was not dead and would return in their hour of need. King Henry II did his best to prove that Arthur was indeed deceased and was not about to return and restore a rival British line of kings. To what extent Henry was prepared to go to prove this and so quash any possible Welsh disaffection is not known, but it certainly accounts for his personal interest in the supposed discovery of Arthur's bones in 1191 at Glastonbury Abbey in Somerset.

Several versions of this event are recorded. The best is from the pen of the gossipy chronicler Giraldus Cambrensis (Gerald of Wales), who actually left two slightly conflicting accounts. The first, written around 1193, gives what appears to be a firsthand account of the discovery. He tells us that great efforts had been made to locate what must have been Arthur's "splendid tomb," suggesting that rumors to this effect were already circulating. Then he adds that it was King Henry himself who had suggested a more thorough excavation.

> The king had told the Abbot on a number of occasions that he had learnt from the historical accounts of the Britons and from their bards that Arthur had been buried in the churchyard there between two pyramids which had been erected subsequently, very deep in the ground for fear lest the Saxons, who had striven to occupy the whole island after his death, might ravage the dead body in their evil lust for vengeance.[2]

But Gerald is not simply reporting the facts as he knew them. He also wanted to make it clear that any notion of a return of Arthur was completely impossible.

> Many tales are told and many legends have been invented about King Arthur and his mysterious ending. In their stupidity the British people maintain that he is still alive, now that the truth is known, I have taken the trouble to add a few more details in this present chapter. The fairy tales have been snuffed out, and the true and indubitable facts are made known, so that what really happened must be made crystal clear to all and separated from the myths which have accumulated on the subject.[3]

Despite the seeming rationalism of this statement, Gerald goes on to add that, after the Battle of Camlann, the body of Arthur, who had been mortally wounded, was carried off by a certain noble matron, called Morgan, who was his cousin, to the Isle of Avalon, which is now known as Glastonbury. Under Morgan's supervision the corpse was buried in the Churchyard there. As a result the credulous Britons and their bards invented the legend that a fantastic sorceress called Morgan had removed Arthur's body to the isle of Avalon, so that he might cure his wounds there. According to them, once he had recovered from his wounds this strong and all-powerful king will return to rule over the Britons in the normal way.[4]

Having made this clear, Gerald then goes on to describe the finding of the body, which was extracted with some effort:

from between two stone pyramids standing in the burial ground. It was deep in the earth, enclosed in a hollow oak, and the discovery was accompanied by wonderful and almost miraculous signs. . . . A leaden cross was found laid under a stone, not above, as is the custom today, but rather fastened on beneath it. We saw this, and traced the inscription which was not showing, but turned in toward the stone: "Here lies buried the famous king Arthurus with Wennevereia his second wife in the isle of Avallonia."[5]

As if this were not enough to set the pulses racing, remains believed to be those of Arthur's queen were discovered alongside those of her husband.

However, they were separate, since two parts of the coffin, at the head, were divided off, to contain the bones of a man, while the remaining third at the foot contained the bones of a woman set apart. There was also uncovered a golden tress of hair that had belonged to a beautiful woman, in its pristine condition and colour, which, when a certain monk eagerly snatched it up, suddenly dissolved into dust.[6]

The bones were, as one might expect of a great hero, larger than those of an average man:

> The thigh bone, when placed next to the tallest man present, as the abbot showed us, and fastened to the ground by his foot, reached three inches above his knee. And the skull was of a great, indeed: prodigious, capacity, to the extent that the space between the brows and between the eyes was a palm's breadth. But in the skull there were ten or more wounds which had all healed into scars with the exception of one, which made a great cleft, and seemed to have been the sole cause of death.[7]

An alternate version of the story, told by Ralph of Coggeshall nearly thirty years later, describes how a monk digging the grave for a dead brother, who had "urgently desired in his lifetime to be interred there," came across a mysterious coffin, which was quickly identified as the grave of Arthur.[8]

The story is interesting for the light it throws on how Arthur was viewed at the time. The idea that Arthur was somehow held in an enchanted sleep, or some chamber of the otherworld, and that he might one day return to rule over Britain again was rather awkward for Britain's Norman overlords, who were keen for any Welsh hopes sustained by Arthur's return to be abandoned. The discovery of Arthur's bones was thus an extremely satisfying event for Henry II; it caused a sensation and made Glastonbury into an instant pilgrimage site, with hundreds of people coming to stare at the "grave" of Arthur. Neither did the event do any harm to the fortunes of the abbey, which had recently suffered a disastrous fire, destroying the greater part of the building and many of its older relics. Within months of the discovery, the abbot received a grant from the crown to rebuild and to create an appropriate shrine for the bones of Arthur.

Henry himself was not above seeking a direct connection with the British "king" who was even more prestigious than Charlemagne, from whom his French rivals claimed descent. It was no accident that Henry's

eldest son Geoffrey named his son Arthur, perhaps in the hope of rees-
tablishing an Arthurian dynasty. If this was his intention, it was to be
foiled by the death in 1203 of the sixteen-year-old prince Arthur of
Brittany at the hands of his uncle, soon to be King John.

The discovery of Arthur's bones has long since been written off as
an outright fraud, though modern archaeology has indicated that the
site was indeed excavated in the twelfth century and that the inscription
on the lead cross, as it was reported, is much older than this period—
though probably not as old as the sixth century. Hollow log burials,
such as that apparently described by Giraldus, would certainly date
from a far distant time, perhaps consistent with the nearby prehistoric
lake village at Street whose inhabitants may have used what became the
abbey grounds as a pagan sanctuary.

Once again it is Geoffrey of Monmouth who proves to be the link
in establishing Arthur with Glastonbury: his writings revealed the
place where such a tomb might be sought. Geoffrey had described how
Arthur, mortally wounded at the Battle of Camlann, was carried off to
"the Isle of Avalon so that his wounds could be attended to."[9] Later, in
the *Vita Merlini,* Geoffrey added significantly to this by describing how
Merlin and Taliesin took the wounded Arthur to the Island of Apples
(Insula Pomorum), ruled over by the mysterious Morgan (see chapter 4).
This mysterious island, clearly a type of earthly paradise, shortly after-
ward became identified with the small town of Glastonbury.

Glastonbury is first mentioned in an Arthurian context in the *Vita
Gildae* in the story of the abduction of Guinevere by King Melwas,
which seems to have encouraged the town to cultivate its links with
Arthur. In his account of the discovery, Giraldus indulged in his own
bit of philological reasoning:

> What is now called Glastonbury was in former times called the
> Isle of Avallon, for it is almost an island, being entirely surrounded
> by marshes, whence it is named in British Inis Avallon, that is the
> apple-bearing island, because apples (in British aval) used to abound
> in that place. . . . It used also to be called in British Inis Gutrin, that

is, the isle of glass: hence the Saxons called it Glastingeburi. For in their tongue *glas* means glass, and a camp or town is called *buri*.[10]

There is no doubt that some kind of grave was found: because it ought to be Arthur's, so it was seen to be. The inscription on a lead cross found with the burial read: "here lies the famous king Arturius, buried in the isle of Avalon," according to Ralph of Coggeshall, writing thirty years after the event in his *English Chronicle*.[11] Gerald, who saw the cross at firsthand, quotes the inscription as: "Here lies buried the King Arthur with Guinevere his second wife in the isle of Avalon."[12]

There is something not quite right about these two reports: although the later medieval Welsh Triads speak of Arthur as having three wives all called Gwenhwyfar, no one before Geoffrey in the early twelfth century knew of Insula Avallonia. Nor had the false Guinevere story yet been written in the *Vulgate Merlin*. Thus, the descriptions of the lead cross must clearly be post-Geoffrey, leading us to suppose that it was the latter's description of Avalon that led to this association.

When the body was reburied in 1278 under a suitably magnificent black marble slab ordered by Edward I, the lead cross was displayed upon it. When the tomb, its contents, and most of the structure of Glastonbury Abbey were dispersed during the Reformation, the lead cross apparently survived. At least, in his *Britannia* of 1610, the antiquary William Camden claimed to have seen it and included an engraving along with his transcription of the inscription as "*hic jacet sepultus inclitus rex Arturius in insula Avalonia*," or "here lies buried the tomb of the renowned King Arthur in the Isle of Avalon" (our translation).[13] However, this inscription is dependent on Geoffrey of Monmouth's citation of Glastonbury as the "Isle of Avalon," which, as we have seen, had no prior existence in the Dark Ages. The cross itself was last said to have been in the possession of an official of Wells Cathedral, one William Hughes, who lived in the early eighteenth century. In 1981 a lead-pattern worker named Derek Malone claimed to have found the original lead cross in a lakebed in Enfield, Middlesex. After showing it to British Museum staff, he subsequently refused to give it up for further examination, was imprisoned, and finally took his own life.[14] It is now thought that the cross was a copy, which Malone could easily have fabricated, given his occupation. The immense excitement caused by this incident demonstrated that the thirst for Arthurian relics had not yet expired.

The obsession of medieval Christians with relics was an attempt to sacralize daily life by proximity to the divine: relics brought healing, conferred blessing, and wrought a special magic. Relics of the Last Supper and the Crucifixion were the most sought after, since the Savior himself had touched them. As we have seen, the Holy Grail, which was variously described as the vessel used to celebrate the Last Supper, or as the vessel that caught Christ's blood at the Crucifixion, became one of the greatest relics—but not only in religious terms. Through the medieval Grail stories of Robert de Boron and others, the last days of Christ upon Earth had become irretrievably connected with the Arthurian legends, and now with Glastonbury, creating a national link with the Christian story.

Considering this, it is hardly surprising that relics of Arthur and his men were sought after as eagerly as those of Christ and the saints. William Caxton, in his 1485 preface to *Le Morte d'Arthur,* mentions several of the most famous, which he said could then be seen—the round table, which hung on the wall of Winchester Great Hall; the skull of Gawain, proudly displayed at Dover Castle; an imprint of Arthur's seal; Lancelot's sword; and the mantle of Carados. There were other relics, notably Arthur's crown and even his sword. How the latter was recovered from the bottom of the lake where Bedivere threw it was never explained, yet Richard the Lionheart is said to have given it to Tancred of Sicily in 1191. Benedict of Peterborough reports that "the King of England also gave to (King Tancred of Sicily) the best sword of Arcturus (sic), which the Britons call Caliburn, he who was once the noble king of Britain" (our translation).[15]

In a later act of cultural appropriation, Edward I took the royal treasures of Wales and Scotland into his own treasury, treating them as venerable objects. The *taliath* or battle diadem owned by the last Prince of Wales, Llywelyn, killed at Builth in 1282, was given to Edward I.

This diadem, also known as King Arthur's Crown, remained in the royal treasury, though it subsequently disappeared: it is thought that it was taken during the 1303 burglary of Westminster Abbey's treasury, or was perhaps given to the ever-rapacious Piers Gaveston, the erstwhile favorite of Edward II, sometime before his coronation in 1311. It was well known that this Edward did not share his father's enthusiasm for the Arthurian legend and might have been indifferent to the dispersal of this particular relic.

Arthur's tomb was not the only burial that excited medieval interest. William of Malmesbury in his *Deeds of the Kings of Britain* (ca. 1125) describes the discovery of the grave of Gawain (Walwen), Arthur's nephew, during the reign of William the Conqueror (1066–1087):

> At this time there was found in the province of Wales called Ros the grave of Walwen, the scarcely degenerate nephew of Arthur by his sister. He reigned in that part of Britain now called Walweitha: a warrior most renowned for his valour, but who was driven out of his kingdom by the brother and nephew of Hengist, of whom I spoke in the first book, though not before he had avenged his exile by inflicting much harm on them. He deservedly shared his uncle's fame, for they averted the ruin of their country for many years. But the tomb of Arthur is nowhere to be seen, for which reason the dirges of old relate that he is to come again. But the tomb of the other, as I have said, was found in King William's time on the seashore, fourteen feet long; whence some assert that he was wounded by his enemies and washed ashore in a shipwreck, some that he was killed by the citizens in a public banquet. The truth is therefore in doubt, though neither story would damage his reputation.[16]

The material relics of Arthur's reign were not the only remains to inspire the kings of England. Given the state of Britain from the Norman Conquest onward, Arthur's reputation for creating unity out of disparate factions had an appeal that seemed to intensify as the medieval centuries wore on. The symbol of that unity was the Round Table, at which all knights sat in equality about their lord.

ROYAL FOLLOWERS
OF THE ROUND TABLE

It is ironic that the very king who was responsible for the sublimation of the Welsh and the battering of the Scots should have himself fallen under the spell of the greatest defender and uniter of the ancient British. Known as the Hammer of the Scots, Edward I (1272–1307) certainly believed in the story of the discovery of Arthur's bones; he had them transferred to a magnificent black marble tomb in front of the High Altar in Glastonbury Abbey, where the remains were personally wrapped and reinterred by Edward and his queen, Eleanor of Castile, in 1278. But Edward was something of an Arthurian fanatic, visiting Glastonbury on a number of occasions, collecting Arthurian texts, and dressing in clothes embroidered with images from the Tristan stories. He also encouraged the organization of pageants known as Round Tables.

Edward's fascination with Arthur is most clearly seen in the elaborate tournament held at Winchester in April 1290, as reported by the Brabançon chronicler Lodwijk van Velthem. The theme of the tournament and the feast that followed it were Arthurian in character. A dramatic scenario was told, with an English squire appearing to demand restitution against some rebellious Welshmen who had attacked him and stolen his goods. A second squire then appeared, bound hand and foot, proclaiming that Irish rebels were guilty of imprisoning him and that their "king" had issued a challenge to "Lancelot." Finally a squire dressed as the "Loathly Lady," straight out of the Gawain and Ragnall story, entered and announced that the duchies of Leicester and Cornwall had rebelled against their king and demanded that "Perceval" and "Gawain" should be dispatched to deal with them. All of this took place in the hall before the beginning of the banquet and the jousts, suggesting that this may have been one of the earliest staged dramas in Britain.[17]

It was probably Edward I who had constructed what is now known as the Winchester Round Table. There is no evidence that he made any claims that this was *the* Round Table, but its symbolism for Edward's claims to the throne of Britain and Scotland would not have been lost upon his guests. The underlying assumption that the Welsh and the Scots were troublemakers was, of course, the whole point and was doubtless a topic of more serious conversation at Edward's Round Table.

Records show that Edward spent a good deal of money refurbishing Winchester Castle in preparation for the installation of the Round Table and that he subsequently held Arthurian-themed tournaments throughout his realm. But while the king lived out his Arthurian fantasy, the peoples of Wales suffered under his campaign of genocidal and cultural erosion without rulers of their own. Edward either killed or imprisoned for life the descendants of Prince Llywelyn of Gwynedd and swiftly incorporated Wales into the English legal framework by 1284, giving the Welsh "their own Prince of Wales" in 1301 in the shape of Edward of Caernarvon, the future Edward II. It is from this time onward that the English male heir apparent has been invested with the title Prince of Wales.

After the failure of his plan to marry his son to the heiress to the Scots throne, Margaret of Norway, who drowned at sea, Edward prosecuted his claims to the overlordship of Scotland through a series of catastrophic wars that took advantage of the Scots' weakened and disputed leadership. Just as Edward had acquired the symbols of Welsh sovereignty for his treasury, so he now took the ancient Stone of Scone upon which Scottish kings were inaugurated for his own, removing it to the sanctuary of Westminster Abbey, where he commanded a coronation chair to contain it. Upon this stone all subsequent English monarchs have been crowned; it remained in England until its return to Edinburgh Castle in 1996, save for its brief absence in 1950–1951 when four Scottish students stole it away back to Scotland, to great national rejoicing.

In seeking to condone his wars upon Scotland and establish himself as its overlord, Edward, in a letter to Pope Baldwin VIII in 1302, showed that his clerks had ransacked chronicles and Arthurian legends in order to give precedence to his sovereignty. As a complement to his master's union of the independent kingdoms of Britain, the chronicler Pierre de Langtoft compared Edward to Arthur:

> *In ancient histories we find written,*
> *What kings and what kingdoms King Arthur conquered,*
> *And how he shared largely his gain.*
> *There was not a king under him who contradicted him,*
> *Earl, duke or baron, who ever failed him*
> *In war or in battle, but each followed him.*[*][18]

This piece of wishful flattery to Langtoft's master is entirely at odds with the manner in which Edward's adversaries in Wales and Scotland either felt or behaved. In a response to Edward and his son's attempts to impose English kingship upon them, the Scots appealed to Pope Baldwin VIII with a dignity and self-possession that won the day for them, for the pope finally upheld their legitimate claims for an independent Scottish kingship. The Declaration of Arbroath was drawn up on April 6, 1320, and signed by thirty-eight most eminent Scottish lords, enshrining the plea that "for, as long as but a hundred of us remain alive, never will we on any conditions be brought under English rule. It is in truth not for glory, nor riches, nor honours that we are fighting, but for freedom—for that alone, which no honest man gives up but with life itself."[†]

In admiration of this *pax Arthuriana,* achieved by his legendary mentor, Edward had expected the princes of Wales and the kings of Scotland to bow meekly to his sovereignty, thus making one realm. His brutal attempted unification of England, Wales, and Scotland may be seen as a direct corollary of his understanding of the Arthurian legends: his attempt to impose the principles of the Round Table was taken to such cruel and coercive lengths that he merely succeeded in shattering cultures and terminally disaffecting neighboring kingdoms. This would lead to years of rebellion and guerrilla warfare into the reign of Edward's successors, down to the sixth generation. Edward was not the

---

[*]Our translation.
[†]Our translation.

last to attempt national unification for the peoples of Britain: the Stuart dynasty would make its own attempt, not without war and rebellion.

As the inheritor of his grandfather's romantic view of Arthur, Edward III (1312–1377) was also fired by the idea of a Round Table; he invoked the more peaceful side of Arthur in the founding of a new and important chivalric order, the Knights of the Garter. According to Elias Ashmole, who wrote a history of the order in 1711, the king, in a manner very like that recorded of Arthur himself, "*did thereupon first design (induct'd by its ancient fame) the restoration of King Arthur's Round Table, to invite hither the gallant spirits from abroad, and ender them to himself*."[19]

This was not an actual table but a splendid building made either to house the table built at the behest of the king's grandfather, or more simply as a hall in which banquets and chivalric sports could take place. Exactly like the seasonal courts summoned by Arthur in legend, on New Year's Day of 1334, the king issued letters of self-conduct to various knights, earls, barons, and gentlemen from several countries, inviting them to attend a splendid celebration on the Feast of Saint Hilary (January 13) at Windsor Castle.

On the day of the great event, the king himself ushered the female guests to their places, seating them in order of rank within the hall. Present were the king himself, his queen, Philippa of Hainault, his mother, Isabel of France, and Edward's daughter, along with nine countesses and a throng of ladies of the court sufficient to fill the great hall, while the Prince of Wales and the male guests dined in a tent outside the hall. Adam of Murimuth, a canon of Hereford and Saint Paul's, who was a guest, described the event in a sparkling manner:

> At the costly banquet the most alluring drinks, enough and to spare. The lords and ladies failed not to dance, mingling kisses with embraces. Many entertainers made the most charming melody and sundry other diversions. The joy was unspeakable, the comfort inestimable, the pleasure without murmuring, the hilarity without care.[20]

The feast was followed by a three-day tournament in which the king himself took part, winning three out of the six prizes on offer. On the fourth day, he summoned everyone to a solemn ceremony at which Edward entered wearing his crown and a mantle of velvet. After Mass the king inaugurated the Round Table hall personally, receiving oaths from several high-ranking knights and lords at the same time. A contemporary account describes what took place:

> The King and all the others at the same time stood up, and having offered the Book [the Bible] the Lord King, after touching the Gospels, took a corporeal oath that he himself, at a certain time limited to this, whilst the means were possible to him, would begin a Round Table, in the same manner and condition as the Lord Arthur, formally King of England, appointment, namely to the number of 300 knights, a number always increasing, and he would cherish it and maintain it according to his power.[21]

Work began at once, and the royal accounts rolls for the year show a considerable outlay of money to employ builders, carpenters, and stone carvers—the number of the latter suggesting the building was to be highly decorated. Later speculation put its size when finished anywhere between 200 and 600 feet in diameter, though recent archaeological investigation indicates that 200 was nearer the mark. Records are scarce and fragmentary, and work seems to have ceased somewhere around November or December of 1334, possibly because of the weather. The indication is that the building was subsequently abandoned. The reasons for this could be simply that the building of a permanent site to be used solely for banqueting may have been considered too frivolous for the time, or it may be that the king's vision shifted as he began to make plans for the setting up of the Order of the Garter. Another possibility is that Edward decided his funds were better used to further his campaigns in France. In either event, the Windsor Round Table was demolished somewhere between 1356 and 1357, and no trace of it remained until its foundations were uncovered in 2006.

Having promised to renew King Arthur's fraternity of knights and uphold the knightly virtues by the foundation of an Order of the Round Table, Edward III's ambitious plans had to be revised as renewed war with France intervened. The origins of the Most Noble Order of the Garter, which replaced Edward's earlier idea, arose from a combination of motives: from emulation of Arthurian chivalry and in order to reward loyalty and military merit; in honor of Saint George, the patron saint of soldiers and also of England; and Edward's claim to the French throne. The origin of the blue garter, which is bound about the left knee of knights of the order, is obscure. A French story tells how, at an assembly in Calais, Joan Countess of Salisbury dropped her garter, and the king himself picked it up and bound it about his own leg. He spoke the words that are the order's motto *Honi soit qui mal y pense,* or "Evil to him who thinks evil." The Order of the Garter was originally planned to consist of twenty-four knights, but the number fluctuated. Today it consists not only of knights but also ladies.

In 1350 it comprised Edward III and twenty-five Knights Companion, one of whom was the Prince of Wales, the Black Prince. The "founder knights" were all skilled in battle and tournaments, some having served in the French campaigns, including the battle of Crécy, while three were foreigners who had previously sworn allegiance to the English king, making twenty-six knights in all. The Order of the Garter remains the oldest and preeminent order of chivalry in Britain, with knight companions from across the world assembling every June on Garter Day.

Apart from the proposed but unfinished Round Table Hall at Windsor, it was probably Edward II who ordered the huge round table, created by his grandfather, to be hung on the wall of the restored Great Hall in Winchester, which had ceased to be a royal residence after the Royal Apartments were destroyed by a fire in 1302. A medieval round table has hung there from 1348–1349 to this day, although it has been subsequently repainted. People have frequently mistaken its age and provenance, believing it to be the actual Round Table of Arthur, rather than a royally commanded copy to enhance the Plantagenet dynasty.

Dendrochronology dates the timbers used in the table's construction to Edward I's time and no earlier.[22]

Between the reigns of Edward III's descendants and the coming of the Tudors, a most unchivalric outbreak of civil war, known as the Wars of the Roses, was to throw into sharp relief the overlap between Arthur's Britain and the civil strife of this turbulent period in which Malory was writing *Le Morte d'Arthur*. Embedded within his Arthurian narrative, we see reflections of the acrimonious wars of the fifteenth century: brother fights and kills brother, unprotected widows are fleeced by usurping strong-armed lords, maidens are raped and imprisoned, young men are attacked and left for dead, properties are sacked or besieged—a weak and powerless king, a terrible wasteland. From the civil chaos emerged a strong and dynamic leader, the magnificently virile grandfather of Henry VIII, Edward of York.

King Edward IV, who came to the throne in 1460, was equally fascinated by the stories of Arthur. After his accession, the prophecies of Merlin from Geoffrey of Monmouth were reworked to fit a proposed glorious future for Edward, featuring his recovery of the true cross and his restoration of the Holy Land![23] Elaborate family trees and horoscopes were drawn up to prove his descent from Arthur, via his Mortimer forebears and the great Cadwaladr. But the Yorkist dynasty was short-lived. It died in 1485 at Bosworth Field, where Edward's brother, Richard III, lost his life, and an obscure Welsh nobleman named Henry Tudor became Henry VII. In that same year Caxton published his edition of Thomas Malory's *Le Morte d'Arthur*. As he prepared for this edition, Caxton published an episode from the book about the dream experienced by Arthur before his Channel crossing to fight Emperor Lucius: Caxton drew contemporary parallels between Richard III, cast as Mordred, and Henry VII, cast as Arthur. In the dream the emblem of the bear is overcome by the dragon, but Caxton foresightedly switched his allegiance overnight from York to Tudor, turned the bear of Arthur's dream into a boar, which was the emblem of Richard III.[24]

"Arthur's world was always one of loss and the hope of recovery," wrote Robert Rouse and Cory Rushton,[25] but now the Wheel of Fortune turned in ways unguessed even by the pseudo-prophecies attributed to Merlin throughout the Middle Ages. With the demise of the Plantagenet line, the legacy of Welsh and Scottish sublimation begun by Edward I finally drew to its ironic conclusion. Both Tudor and Stuart dynasties replaced the Plantagenets, reintroducing first their Welsh then their Scottish blood to the English monarchy. With the rise of these dynasties, Arthur was drawn even more closely into the dream of a greater Britain.

CLAIMING ARTHUR'S SEAT

The Tudors were also determined to prove their right to the kingdom by claiming descent from its premier king. Henry VII (reigned 1485–1509) supported his claim to the English throne by proving his descent from Cadwallader, who according to Geoffrey of Monmouth was the last of the British kings, and through him from Arthur himself. The Welsh acclaimed the accession of Henry VII as a deliverance from the English yoke, for he was one of their own.

Henry, Earl of Pembroke, as he was before he beat Richard III on Bosworth Field, was the direct descendant of Owen ap Meredith ap Tudor, the Welsh gentleman who married Catherine of Valois, widow of Henry V, without the consent of the crown: on the other side, he was descended from the line of Edward III via John of Gaunt's union with his mistress Katherine Swynford. But this double illegitimacy proved to be no disablement. In an ode to commemorate Henry's victory at Bosworth, the Welsh poet Lewis Glyn Cothi acclaimed him as "the great joy predicted by Merlin" and as the bearer of the red dragon standard of Gwynedd, "the beast from North Wales. . . . Bird and bull of the blood of Arthur."[26] In some sense, there was a real return of the Welsh blood, for Henry VII's wife, Elizabeth of York, was herself descended from Llewelyn ap Iorwerth, known as "the Great." In the wake of the Wars of the Roses, Henry was welcomed as one who united the disparate factions of war-ravaged Britain. Nevertheless, he and his son Henry VIII pursued a policy of dynastic genocide by eradicating all Plantagenet Yorkist heirs, clearing away any dissidents and royal claimants for the Tudors' unimpeded success.

To make good his claim and to reinforce his links with Arthur, Henry saw to it that his wife, Elizabeth, was confined at Winchester for the birth of their first child. There, in the city believed by many to be the site of Camelot, the queen gave birth to a son, who was promptly christened Arthur, with the express wish that "there might be another king of that name in Britain." Henry's astrologer had drawn up a horoscope and noted that the star Arcturus was significant of an Arthurian second coming; it was in this guise that King Arthur was supposed to have been embodied as the sun of Britain according to the writings of John Lydgate.[27] As we saw earlier, the association of Arthur and Arcturus dates back at least to the seventh century. Unfortunately for Henry VII's plan, the young prince proved as ill fated as that earlier Prince Arthur, who died at the orders of King John. Arthur Tudor died in 1502, leaving his younger brother, Henry, to become king and eventually inherit his brother Arthur's wife, Katherine of Aragon: an event that subsequently brought in its wake the Dissolution of the Monasteries and hastened the Reformation that swept away so many Arthurian as well as religious relics.

Like his ancestors, Henry VIII (reigned 1509–1547) continued to trade upon his descent from Arthur. In 1511 he spent the vast sum of more than £4,000 in the organization of a huge tournament at Winchester, in which he himself took part dressed as Arthur. The event was intended to celebrate the birth of a son, the third prince to bear the name Arthur, but the infant son of Katherine of Aragon lived only fifty-two days. A few years later, when Henry confronted King Francis I of France at the bombastic and nonhostile event known as the Field of the Cloth of Gold, Henry's banners depicted Arthur as conqueror of the world—the implication being that Henry could lay claim to lands all over Europe if he so chose. Over the portal of a banqueting house, Henry had erected a statue of Arthur, with the device *Cui adhereo preest,* or "Whom I support, wins," engraved beneath it, revealing the depths and faith of his Arthurian connection.[28]

Henry also had the Winchester Round Table repainted with himself depicted as Arthur in the center, ready for the occasion when he hosted Philip of Burgundy, king of Castile, at Windsor in 1522. The two monarchs signed a treaty of friendship between England and Spain, and King Philip was admitted to the Order of the Garter. They dined at a round table that was almost certainly the same one created by Edward I. Later that same year, Henry entertained Charles V, the Hapsburg emperor elect of the Holy Roman Empire, once again dining at "Arthur's Table." Henry's own ideas of European expansionism seem to have been pipe dreams, based upon Arthur's successes against the Romans recorded by Geoffrey of Monmouth.

But the brilliant young king whose stamina had left his courtiers struggling to keep up with him, began to show another side of his character. With the same ruthlessness as his father, Henry had a young nobleman named Rhys ap Griffith beheaded in 1531 for daring to call himself "FitzUrien in commemoration of his ancestor Urien (of Rheged), the companion of Arthur and Lancelot."[29] This act showed not only Henry's exclusivism in regard to Arthur, but also his insecurity about an heir: by using the term *Fitz,* young Rhys seemed to be laying claim to the English throne, and by the same Welsh descent as Henry himself.

Popular Arthurian enthusiasm began to die out or be severely questioned as Henry faced up to the possibilities of Reformation. He put his romantic youth behind him as the serious matter of the succession brought England to face new and unpleasant changes. In the wake of the Reformation and Renaissance influences, a more critical and searching view was brought to the matter of Arthur's existence. What had once been uncritically accepted as historical truth was now put under the glass of humanist scrutiny. The Italian Polydore Vergil (1470?–1555) brought an unwelcome perspective to popular Arthurian belief. He had been on the scene during the years of Henry VII's reign when he had begun his *Anglica Historia,* or English History, in 1506–1507 to help support Henry's claim to the throne. However, the book was not published until 1534. In this work Virgil drew upon early accounts such as Gildas and Bede; he frankly doubted the historicity of Geoffrey of

Monmouth's narrative, damningly concluding that Arthur was nothing but a man about whom legend had woven "such gestes, as in our memories emonge the Italiens ar commonlie noysed of Roland, the nephew of Charles the Great."[30]

To refute this work, John Leland (?1503–1552) who had been appointed king's antiquary by Henry, dedicated to his master a work titled *Assertio inclytissimi Arturii Regis Britannianiae* (An Assertion of the Renowned Arthur, King of the Britons) in 1544. In this and in another work defending Geoffrey of Monmouth as historian rather than fabulist, Leland saw Virgil's attack as not merely one wrought upon a fellow historian but also upon the English nation and *noster Arturius Britanniae,* "our British Arthur." But his partiality did not blind him to fabulations that had crept into the Arthurian story. To his credit, Leland attempted not only a written defense of Arthurian matters but also was the first antiquary to explore Britain itself and to research the evidence and etymologies of land features; he drew also upon the testimony of local people—material that we would recognize today as folklore.

Both Henry VIII and his daughter Elizabeth I cited early Arthurian chronicles in legal documents relating to their use of the term *Imperial Crown.* John Coke who, as "clearke of the kynges recognysaunce," published *The Debate Between the Heralds of England and France* in 1550, modeled this upon Charles d'Orléans's *Le Débat des Hérauts* and promoted this imperial conceit.[31] It spoke of Arthur as the conqueror of every European country from Iceland to Portugal and from Ireland to Italy. In an age of New World expansionism, such rhetoric promoted English imperial dreams without doing anyone much harm. But it was not until the reign of Elizabeth that such aims began to be in reach as privateers and adventurers made the westward passage to the Americas and beyond. Drake's feat of circumnavigating the globe in 1577–1580 resounded to Elizabeth's Arthurian credit as well as to the superiority of English seamanship.

The argument of imperial sovereignty was resurrected again during the years leading up to the Spanish Armada to bolster Elizabeth's authority and sovereign right to the British Empire. Elizabeth's minister Lord Burghley conferred with the queen's magician, John Dee, on this very matter. Dee's book *General and Rare Memorials pertayning to the Perfect Arte of Navigation* (1577) spoke of "that Triumphant BRYTISH ARTHVR," invoking him as the model for an imperial navy. Dee's diary of November 28, 1577, relates, "I declared to the Quene her title to Greenland, Estetiland and Friseland": the precedent for this rested upon the fact that "Kyng Arthur . . . did conquer Gelindia, lately called Friseland."[32]

Dee later extended these ideas into another book, *The Limits of the British Empire* (1578), in which he based his evidence for Elizabeth's claims on a now lost book called the *Gestae Arthuri* (Deeds of Arthur). In the same book he coined the phrase *British Empire,* which soon entered common usage. Thomas Churchyard, in his book *The Worthiness of Wales* in 1587, wrote of the queen as:

> *She that sits in regall Throne,*
> *With Sceptre, Sword, and Crowne.*
> *(Who came from Arthur's rase and lyne).*[33]

Although Elizabeth never publicly emphasized her connections to Arthur, despite having genealogical documents drawn up to prove her Arthurian antecedents, she certainly loved the stories, and on one occasion, while on one of her famous progresses through the country, she attended a pageant at Kenilworth Castle in which her lover, Robert Dudley, played Arthur and which depicted the story of his love for the Lady of the Lake.

The courtly adoration of Elizabeth as the Virgin Queen took many extravagant turns during her reign. One of the mostly outstanding tributes to her was that paid by the poet Edmund Spenser (1552–1599), who began work on his monumental epic poem *The Faerie Queene* sometime in the 1570s, a century after the publication of Malory's *Le Morte d'Arthur.* Spenser's poem plundered the myth for names and incidents that would support his elaborate courtly conceit. The first three books of *The Faerie Queene* were printed in 1590 and the next six in 1596; it was still only half finished when he died, having been planned as a work in twelve parts, each focusing on the virtues of a different knight. We may note with interest that, in genealogical documents drawn up before the poem's publication, Elizabeth's Welsh antecedents were given as proof of her as "a continuator of the Welsh faery blood."[34]

The Faerie Queene is complex and at times rambling, but it is founded on a rich and often profound use of allegory and symbolism. The hero of the poem is called Prince Arthur and is clearly based on a somewhat confused knowledge of original Arthurian texts, but there the resemblance ends. Spenser used the figure of Arthur to represent an image of the perfect knight, and after some brief references to Uther Pendragon being attacked by Hengist's son Octa and his kinsman Eosa, he sends his hero forth on a series of extravagant adventures in search of Gloriana, the Faerie Queene, whom he has seen in a dream and with whom he has fallen hopelessly in love. Along the way, Arthur encounters numerous symbolic beings—including the female knight Una—who test and try him in various ways, always with a view to making him a better knight and a fit consort for the queen. Merlin makes a brief appearance, described as a magician of great power who had built a wall of brass around the old kingdom. Of Arthur's original knights, only Tristan is briefly included in the huge cast of characters.

Had Spenser lived to complete the work, he would presumably have united Arthur with Gloriana, a thinly disguised version of Queen Elizabeth herself, strengthening the avowed tie between the Tudor dynasty and Arthur. In the poem the Fellowship of the Round Table and the Order of the Garter are replaced by the Order of Maidenhead—an obvious reference to the Virgin Queen. Throughout the poem Spenser makes it clear that he regarded the Tudors as the proper descendants of Arthur and the inheritors of his crown and that Elizabeth embodied all the qualities of the great king. The rise of the Tudor monarchy represented the return of Arthur and the restoration of England's glory days.

However, imperial dreams have a way of laying waste to the sovereignty of other nations. Spenser's *A View of the Present State of Ireland,* written in 1595, was suppressed due to its inflammatory content and not published until 1633. It presented a grim picture of Ireland and made suggestions as to how it might be brought to English heel. In it Spenser advocated the pacification of the Irish by a scorched earth policy by which the natives would be reduced by famine and tamed by the erosion of their native tongue and cultural customs. Spenser drew upon the old imperial argument of Arthur as justification for the English suppression of Ireland, but as someone who had served eighteen years on and off in Ireland in the English administration in onerous and sometimes dangerous service, Spenser was glad of some Arthurian diversion. He wrote of his appreciation of his companions in the Society of Archers, a kind of round table sports club, where each member took an Arthurian name in addition to some healthy toxology.[35]

How seriously the Arthurian justifications for English kingship were to prevail can be seen in the reign of Elizabeth's successor, James I, in whom it seemed all the right elements were met for an Arthurian-style reunion of the disparate kingdoms of Britain. If Arthur had been invoked for the Tudors, now it was the turn of the Stuarts to call upon him to legitimize a new dispensation. At the beginning of his reign, James was hailed, in a very well-informed pageant, as "a second Brute sent to redeem the political sin committed when the first king divided Britain."[36] This was a direct reference to Geoffrey of Monmouth's *Historia Regum Britannae* in which the descendant of Aeneas of Troy, Brutus, became Britain's first king, thereafter dividing the island between his three sons: Albanactus, Kamber, and Locrinus—who gave their names to the romantic titles of Alba for Scotland, Cambria for Wales, and Logres for England.

James, called "the wisest fool in Christendom," had many entrenched notions, but it is intriguing to see how clearly his attempt to reunite Britain as one kingdom was driven by the writings of Geoffrey of Monmouth. The Commons [i.e., those representing the common people in the House] resisted his ambition to reunite Britain, a political tussle reflected in three plays of the time, Shakespeare's *King Lear* (1606) and *Cymbeline* (1609–1610) and Thomas Heywood's *Troia Britanica* (1609). In *King Lear,* we see the catastrophic threefold division of the land among his daughters, while in *Cymbeline,* Shakespeare dived further back in time, exploring how the ancient Britons rebelled against paying Roman tribute. Heywood's *Troia Britanica* gave what would be the last serious portrayal of Arthur as a noble king on the British stage for many generations.[37]

Nevertheless, on October 20, 1604, James I proclaimed himself as king of Great Britain, France, and Ireland. He drew upon both the justifying myth of Brutus and of Arthur in pursuing his desire to make the "Great Marriage" between Scotland and England. But it was not until the reign of his great-granddaughter, Queen Ann, that this idea was fully realized with the Act of Union of 1707 when the independent Scottish parliament was dissolved and made one with the English house. One of James's many schemes still haunts the British and Irish psyche: his Plantation of Ulster. James displaced the inhabitants of Northern Ireland with his "New English"—mostly Scots Protestants. But it was James's theory about the divine right of kings that was to prove most immediately injurious to his own heirs.

In 1610 the playwright Ben Jonson wrote a pageant called *The Speeches at Prince Henry's Barriers,* in which the Lady of the Lake announces:

> *Now when the island hath regained her fame*
> *Intire and perfect in the ancient name,*
> *And that a monarch equal good and great,*
> *Wise, temperate, just and stout, Claims Arthur's Seat.*[38]

Jonson's masques are full of such allusive anagrams as "Claims Arthur's Seat," which translates into James I's baptismal name, Charles James Stuart. "Arthur's Seat" refers to the great crag of this name that rises above the city of Edinburgh. No one before the Scottish chronicler John Major in 1521 is known to have made the connection between Arthur and Edinburgh as his seat.[39] Nevertheless, as the new king of

Scotland and England, it was doubly important for James to produce evidence to support his claims; descent from Arthur was just such a proof.

In Jonson's masque *For the Honour of Wales,* two Welsh gentlemen speak in dialect of James's claim:

JENKIN: "We have his prophecies already of your madesty's name . . ."

EVAN: "You mean his madesty's anagrams of Charles James Stuart."

JENKIN: "Aye, that is "Claimes Arthur's Seat," which is as much to say your madesty should be the first king of Gread Pritain, and sit in cadair Arthur, which is Arthur's chair. . . . And then your son Master Charles his, how do you call him? Is Charles Stuart, "Calls True Hearts," that is, he calls us, the Welsh nation, to be ever at your service."[40]

The death of James's eldest son, Prince Henry, completed the cycle of catastrophic deaths of the firstborn son that seemed to bedevil the Tudors and Stuarts. But worse followed when James was succeeded by his second son, Charles I. James's notions on the divine right of kings ultimately brought Charles to the scaffold and Britain to a temporary, kingless Commonwealth in which Arthur and the old customs of England were fogged over by Puritanical disapproval. James I had written that "it is an undutiful part in subjects to press their king";[41] but when so pressed, his inflexible son Charles I had merely assumed the godlike status of a divinely appointed monarch, infuriating his subjects to the point of civil war and regicide. If one king could be beheaded and his son exiled, it was consequent that Arthur himself should also suffer dethronement and a long exile of neglect.

THE ANTIQUE ARTHUR

The swiftly moving current of the seventeenth-century world left little or no room for the fantastic world of medieval romance. Authors and

316 Arthur of Fable

artists turned for inspiration instead to the classical world. However, the figure of Arthur did not entirely disappear. No lesser a writer than John Milton (1608–1674) considered the Arthurian legends as a suitable theme for his own epic poetic intentions, writing in his *Epitaphium Damonis:*

> I hesitate too lest I seem conceited, yet I will tell the tale—give place then, O forests. Go home unfed, my lambs, your troubled master is not free to tend you. I would tell of Dardanian ships along the Rutupian Sea, and of the ancient realm of Imogen, Pandrasus's daughter, of the leaders Brennus and Arviragus, and old Belinus, and of colonists in Armorica under British laws; then I would tell of Igraine pregnant with Arthur by a fatal fraud, of the seeming face and counterfeit arms of Gorlois, Merlin's artifice. Ah! then if life remain, you, my pipe, shall hang on some aged pine far off and forgotten, unless forsaking your native songs you shrilly sound a British theme. Why not a British theme? One man cannot do all things, cannot hope to do all things. Sufficient my reward, my honours ample—even if I am for ever unknown and wholly without fame in foreign parts—if yellow-haired Ouse reads me, and he who drinks the waters of Alaun, and Abra full of eddies, and all the woods of Trent, and above all my own Thames, and Tamar stained with metals, and if the Orkneys and their remotest waves but learn my songs.[42]

However, given the Puritan climate of the times, Milton opted instead for the more sober and morally appropriate subject of the fall of humanity.

With the return of Charles II, the political application of Arthur's fame was introduced once more in Henry Purcell's opera *King Arthur, or The British Worthy*. With its libretto by the Catholic poet John Dryden, it was originally written in 1684 as a complement to Charles II's victory over the Whigs. Their dispute had been over an exclusion bill that would bar Catholics from holding public office, thus also excluding Charles's brother James from the succession. By the time the opera was finally performed in 1691, the country had seen the Monmouth Rebellion and the execution of Charles II's bastard son, as well as the Glorious Revolution, which brought about the deposition and exile of James II.

Under the joint rule of William of Orange and Mary, daughter to James II, the establishment of a constitutional monarchy, by which Parliament kept the balance of power, rather eroded the majesty of monarchy. The glory days of Arthur were also over, for he had lost his political mileage. It was left to a far lesser poet than Milton to present Arthur to the seventeenth-century world. The poet and physician Sir Richard Blackmore (1654–1729) wrote two huge and largely unreadable poems in the style of Milton called *Prince Arthur* (1695) and *King Arthur* (1697), in which he mixed Geoffrey of Monmouth and Virgil in a strange mishmash of political and romantic verbiage. The first poem sets out to allegorize the triumphal rule of William of Orange, while the second used Arthur's Gaulish victories to celebrate William's defeat of the French King Louis XIV.

The eighteenth century was less interested in the legends of Arthur than any previous century. Under the new Hanoverian monarchy, one of the strangest echoes of Merlin's prophetic role took an unlikely form. In 1732 Queen Caroline, wife of George II, commanded an ornamental building to be constructed in Richmond Gardens in London. Called the Hermitage, it included a series of busts of leading scientists and philosophers. Such was the success of this building, which was open to the public, that the queen gave orders for an additional building to be erected called Merlin's Cave, which depicted a tableau of scenes from the prophet's life and contained statues of Merlin and his "secretary," who was depicted taking down new prophecies. The cave and the extraordinary architecture of this site—a weird mixture of Gothic, Palladian, and Rustic—captured the imagination of the public, though the queen's political opponents were quick to make fun of it at her expense. Her reasons for building the cave remain obscure, but she may well have been suggesting, as had so many monarchs before her, a tenuous descent from the lineage of Arthur.

While Arthur may have been relegated as an appropriate subject
for literary works, there was another area in which he gained increasing favor, incidentally preparing the way for the explosion of Arthurian
writings in the nineteenth century. This was the work of a new breed
of antiquaries, gentlemen scholars who roamed the libraries of stately
homes in search of clues to the past and who focused their interest
on the rediscovery and dissemination of vernacular texts—everything
from ballads to romances. These included, of course, Malory, Geoffrey
of Monmouth, various other chroniclers, and a vast number of native
British ballads.

Many of these researches were collected in a hugely influential set of
books published in 1765 and graced with the resounding title *Reliques
of Ancient English Poetry: Consisting of Old Heroic Ballads, Songs, and
Other Pieces of Our Earlier Poets (Chiefly of the Lyric Kind) Together
with Some Few of Later Date.*[43] The three volumes that made up this
collection were edited by Bishop Thomas Percy (1729–1811), a scholar
and churchman whose love of the ancient British traditions probably
saved a number of older texts from disappearing altogether. The collection includes several English Arthurian verse romances (described by
Percy as "ballads"), including *The Marriage of Sir Gawain, The Boy and
the Mantle,* and *King Ryance's Challenge,* all late versions of medieval
works. Most importantly, Percy outlined in his introduction the virtues
of these ancient works and found them comparable to classical epics.
Though he described the poems as "full of the exploded fictions of
Chivalry," he also found that "nature and common sense had supplied
to these old simple bards the want of critical art, and taught them some
of the most essential rules of Epic Poetry."[44]

Gradually the old-fashioned medieval writers seemed less dull and
fantastical, and several poets seized upon them as sources for their own
work. The influential author Sir Walter Scott, who had himself begun
to collect old Scottish ballads and was later to edit the first modern
edition of a romance of Tristan, included an Arthurian episode in his
poem *The Bridal of Treirmain* (1813); while William Wordsworth published his own attempt at an Arthurian romance, *The Egyptian Maid,*

in 1835.[45] Today, this reads as somewhat absurd, with an Egyptian princess arriving in Britain to marry one of Arthur's knights in return for aid given to her father. Merlin intervenes for no other apparent reason than his "freakish will" and causes her ship to flounder. Surviving, she consults Nina, the Lady of the Lake, on ways to counteract Merlin's arbitrary magic, and the poem then becomes an exploration of the appropriate uses of power.

Meanwhile, Arthur featured in popular entertainment in the form of ballad, pantomime, and broadsheet, which contained a strange mixture of folklore and half-remembered story. Arthurian characters developed a burlesque aspect, making impromptu appearances in stories such as *Tom Thumb,* where the diminutive hero becomes a mascot of the king. Arthur himself sinks to the level of stock character, joining the cast of pantomimic figures of popular theater in the eighteenth and nineteenth centuries. In popular ballads he is largely a figure of fun or a cuckold, as in the ballad *King Arthur and King Cornwall:*

> *Then bespake Cornwall King againe,*
> *These were the words said he:*
> *Sayes, 'Seuen yeere I was clad and fed,*
> *In Litle Brittaine, in a bower;*
> *I had a daughter by King Arthurs wife,*
> *That now is called my flower;*
> *For King Arthur, that kindly cockward,*
> *Hath none such in his bower.*[46]

The image of the heroic defender of Britain seems to have been forgotten, but the romantic revival saw the emergence of a new visionary, whose mystical insights into the Arthurian legend evoked an earlier age. The poet and artist William Blake (1757–1827), inspired by the recent druidic revival that had seized the country, saw deeper into the strata of time and created pictures that would bring Arthur to memory. In his *Descriptive Catalogue* of his artistic works, published in 1809, he described a (now lost) work in which the three heroes who escaped from the Battle of Camlann are shown in the Welsh mountains, replete with dying warriors, bards, and Druid temples: "There they dwell in naked simplicity; happy is he who can see and converse with them above the shadows of generation and death. . . . The stories of Arthur are the acts of Albion, applied to a Prince of the fifth century, who conquered Europe, and held the Empire of the world in the dark age, which the Romans never again recovered."[47]

In his radical and mystical way, Blake saw Albion not only as the name for Britain but also as a primal ancestor and as the spirit of a politically awakened Britain. For Blake, this belief was almost a creed: "All the fables of Arthur and his round table; of the warlike naked Britons; of Merlin; of Arthur's conquest of the whole world; of his death, or sleep, and promise to return again. All these things are written in Eden."[48]

Impatient with the historians of his own age, who passed over their native remains without either imagination or interest, Blake pleaded for "the antiquities for every Nation under Heaven" to be seen as "no less sacred than that of the Jews."[49] Fortunately, there had been some imaginative historians and antiquaries before him for whom the land itself had sustained remembrance of Arthur.

THE SLEEPING LORD

Outside the arena of political manipulation and literary representation, Arthur remained unchanging as a guardian of the land itself. We have already seen how, in the ninth-century *Historia Brittonum* of Nennius, Arthur exists in a dual state, both as a warlord and as a legendary denizen of the land. Thus his dog leaves a footprint upon a stone near Builth while Arthur hunts for Twrch Trwyth. This stone cannot be removed: its fellow wonder, Llygad Amr, the tomb of Arthur's son Amr, has another strange property, for it cannot be measured.[50]

These remembrances within the land scatter the length and breadth of Britain. Ancient monuments, megaliths, and earthworks of every era join many land features as King Arthur's bed, table, chair, hall, or stone.

These mighty stone circles, earthworks, and elementally sculpted hills were regarded by the people as the work of giants. The one who had frequently overthrown giants in legend was, of course, King Arthur; these mighty works were therefore associated with him. The impossibility of dating most of these ascriptions may indicate that these were merely popular titles based upon notable landmark features. The early importation of Stonehenge into the Arthurian story by Geoffrey of Monmouth as both a memorial for murdered British nobles and as stones erected by Merlin doubtless led to similar ascriptions.

One such monument, recorded earlier than Geoffrey, is in the *Liber Floridus,* written in 1120 by Lambert of Saint Omer. Lambert tells us that "in the land of the Picts in Britain there is a palace belonging to Arthur the Soldier, built with wondrous art and variety, in which can be seen all his deeds and battles sculpted."*

This may to refer to Arthur's O'on, a structure with a dome that once stood in Carron Valley in Stirlingshire until its demolition in 1742–1743. As early as 1293, it was known as *furnum Arthuri,* "Arthur's Cooking Place." Lambert goes on to relate that when the Saxon Octha came down from the north to Kent, there was a man called "Arthur, leader of the Picts, who ruled the kingdoms of British interior. He was mighty in strength and a fearsome soldier. Seeing that England [sic] was being attacked in this way, and that wealth of the land was being despoiled and many people captured and ransomed and expelled from their inheritances, he attacked the Saxons in a ferocious assault, with the kings of the Britons, and rushing against them fought manfully, being dux bellorum twelve times as written above."[51]

We have no idea what this structure's original purpose might have been, unless it was some kind of memorial or storage facility built by the Romans, but its location is puzzling. The ascription of an oven to such a building is not so surprising, however, for within the parallel Irish tradition of the hero Fionn Mac Cumhail and his roaming *fianna,* many such sites are designated and recognized as "the cooking place of

---

*Our translation.

Fionn."[52] The various "Arthur's Ovens" around the land—in Stirling and in Cornwall—remind us of Fionn's *fulachta* or cooking places. It is not until the medieval texts that we discover the sites of Arthur's supposed court; these are as various as Kelliwig in Cornwall, Caerleon in South Wales, and Carlisle in Cumbria. But the court most remembered by legend is Camelot, a name that first appears in Chrétien de Troyes's *Lancelot* in the twelfth century.

One of the most enduring ascriptions of Arthurian occupation concerns the Iron Age hill fort of South Cadbury in Somerset. Local tradition has long held that this was the original site of Arthur's Camelot—to the extent that when an early archaeological dig was underway, a local man approached the archaeologist anxiously wanting to know if they had "come to dig up the king." No king was found there, and it was not until the 1960s that a much-publicized dig explored Cadbury camp, with interesting results.[53] Though it could not be proven beyond question that this was Camelot, it was clear that the site had been reactivated sometime in the fifth or sixth century, its walls rebuilt and strengthened and what appeared to be the remains of a large timbered hall and even a possible cruciform church built within the surrounding bank and ditch. Many believed then that this was a clear indication of the reality of Arthur and firm evidence that his headquarters lay in Somerset.

More than three hundred years earlier, John Leyland, one of the first of these great antiquarian researchers, found his way to Cadbury and reached a similar conclusion. In his *Itinerary,* written in the 1540s, he stated:

> At the very south end of the church of South-Cadbyri stands Camallate, sometime a famous town or castle, upon a very tor or hill, wonderfully enstrengthened of nature. . . . The people can tell nothing there but that they have hard say that Arthur much resorted to Camallate. . . . The hill and the ditches keep well now 70 sheep. All the ground by southwest, and west of Camallate lieth in a vale, so that one or 2 ways it may be seen far off.[54]

The reality was that the older name for the village, dating back as far as the tenth century, was Cantmael. It only received the name Queen's Camel after Eleanor of Castile was granted title to the village by her husband Edward I in 1284. But Leland, with that remarkable providence that seems to attend all points of cultural fracture where things become lost forever, managed an itinerary of British sites of notable folkloric and historical interest just prior to the Dissolution of the Monasteries, thus providing us, among other sites, with one of the last eyewitness accounts of Arthur's tomb at Glastonbury Abbey before its destruction.

If Arthur had his political uses, he was also the subject for a whole legion of new scholars, the antiquaries who began to explore the ancient past of England and to seek explanations for the mysterious objects that littered the landscape. Who had really built Stonehenge? Was it Merlin, as the myths told, or someone else? And what of the other great stone circles and mysterious places that carried a freight of mythic references? A multitude of places bear Arthur's name still, and Tintagel and Glastonbury still draw thousands of pilgrims every year. But there is another reason why Arthur's name is so resonant throughout every rock of Britain. It concerns the ancient myth of the Sleeping Lord, a gigantic being who was somehow part of the land.

The motif of the Sleeping Lord, the king who will return when the time is right, is clearly of great antiquity, preceding even the historical Arthur. It may explain why, in Nennius, Arthur is already seen as partaking both of history and of myth. Even the first-century Greek historian, Plutarch, speaks of an antique British tradition that he received from the Carthaginian antiquarian, Sextus Sylla:

The natives have a story that in one of these (islands) Cronos has been confined by Zeus, but that he, having a son for gaoler, is left sovereign of those islands. Cronos himself sleeps within a deep cave resting on rock which looks like gold. . . . birds fly in at the topmost part of the rock and bear him ambrosia, and the whole island is pervaded by the fragrance shed from the rock.[55]

This tale is further supported by a report from a Roman official called Demetrius who visited Britain and learned many of its ancient traditions, including the following: "There is one island there where Cronos is a prisoner guarded by Briareus in his sleep—sleep was the fetters designed for Cronos and many daimones lie around him as servants and followers."[56]

In Classical myth, Cronos and the other Titans are overthrown by Zeus, but Cronos lives on, ready to usher in the golden age. But the being whom both Sextus Sylla and Demetrianus report as being like Cronos is a native titan of British, not Greek, origin: he is none other than the Sleeping Lord, a being like the gigantic King Bran the Blessed, but perhaps of even hoarier antiquity than either he or Arthur, who has subsequently succeeded to this mythic role.

Whatever is written about him, no matter to what political or mystical purposes his name is subscribed, as the Sleeping Lord, Arthur remains firmly associated with the island of Britain, waiting for the time when he will return again. As king of fable and chivalry, he abides in the otherworld realms:

> *He is a king crouned in Fairie,*
> *With sceptre and with his regally*
> *Shall resort as Lord and Soveraigne*
> *Out of Fairie and reigne in Britane.*[57]

8

Arthur Everywhere

Rex Quondam, Rexque Futurus

Thus Arthur had himself borne to Avalon and he told his people that they should await him and he would return. And the Britons came back to Carduel and waited for him more than forty years before they would take a king, for they believed always that he would return.

DIDOT PERCEVAL (CA. 1202)

THE NEW ARTHUR

Most people today know about Arthur through literary fiction, TV, or film. This has made him, if anything, more elusive than ever. So many new historical theories have been proposed in the last few decades that it is harder than ever to discern the real face of Arthur, while the legion of fantastic stories appearing every year have more than outstripped the entire corpus of medieval tales. Arthur no longer possesses a single face—if, indeed, he ever did. His latest face could be described as one of the imagination, conjured up to enable us to understand him in all his aspects.

Throughout his long history, Arthur has been repeatedly

mythologized as well as being the object of historical scrutiny. The most frequently asked question whenever the topic of Arthur is raised is whether or not he actually existed, and it makes for widely differing opinions. Arthur is loved or mocked today as he was feared or venerated in the Middle Ages and earlier. These responses derive from the fact that Arthur is once again seen, as perhaps he was at the beginning of his career, as an archetype. Arthur is, quite literally, everywhere and has become so ubiquitous that his legends are perceived as important as those of the classical world.

How this happened is every bit as fascinating as the story of Arthur's rise from soldier to king to national hero. As we have seen, although the legends still lived in the national memory over the three centuries following the publication of Malory's Le Morte d'Arthur in 1485, interest in Arthur faded. Following this lengthy hiatus, a revival began at the height of the Victorian age and in the midst of the Industrial Revolution in the form of a series of dramatic, narrative poems published between 1842 and 1885 under the title Idylls of the King. They were written by Alfred Lord Tennyson (1809–1892), the poet laureate to Queen Victoria, who turned Arthur and his Knights of the Round Table into Victorian gentlemen and the women of Camelot into Victorian ladies. Together with the work of the Pre-Raphaelite Brotherhood of painters, who drew inspiration from the poems, Tennyson's works began a tidal wave of fascination for the Matter of Britain that continues to this day.[1]

At first glance, the Victorian era may seem an unlikely place to find a resurgence of Arthurian works. Yet for all its intense industrial growth and scientific activity, an underlying love of romanticism and sentiment invoked a very idealized view of the Middle Ages and found, in the nobility and moral strength of Arthur and his knights, a subject that was deemed fitting for poetry and the arts. In addition, the publication in 1817 of the first new edition of Le Morte d'Arthur since 1634, edited under the aegis of the poet Robert Southe with the title The Byrth, Lyf, and Actes of King Arthur, generated a huge amount of interest among the Victorian intelligentsia.

Victoria's unusually long reign, which stretched from 1837 to 1901, provided a sense of continuity and stability that created an underlying ground note for a period of expansionism throughout the British Empire and an array of social reforms and scientific discoveries such as had never been seen before this time. The Industrial Revolution, which began in the late eighteenth century, brought its attendant social ills, transforming not only the countryside but also affecting the distribution of wealth. Out of this came the desire of a new middle class to establish its own cultural presence.

One way in which this could be demonstrated was by way of a general espousal of art and literature. People whose ancestors, only a few generations earlier, had been part of the lower-middle class and sometimes barely able to read, now flaunted paintings and books in their homes and related social standing to cultural appreciation. Out of this was born a nostalgia for a semimythical past, especially of the medieval period, in which men and women lived in a dream-like world filled with magical castles and knights in armor, who regularly rescued fainting damsels in distress and defeated evil knights without acquiring a scratch. It was a view of the Arthurian world seen through a distorting mirror, with all the darker parts omitted and the savagery of medieval life glossed over.

The Gothic revival in architecture made everything antique appear quaint and fashionable. All that was required to parallel this in literature and the arts, and to set the revival of the old legends in motion, was a writer whose charismatic character and love of the Arthurian legends would become a vehicle for generations of people. Alfred Tennyson was just such a writer, and his works inspired enough imitators (usually inferior) to ensure that interest in all things Arthurian was sustained throughout Victoria's reign.

Tennyson, born in 1809, first encountered the Arthurian legends through Malory, whom he discovered, according to his own account, while "little more than a boy." From his twenties onward, he was preparing the way for what he already knew would be his magnum opus, drafting various outlines until he felt he had found the right way to retell the story of Arthur. Malory remained the most important influence on everything Tennyson wrote about Arthur, and though his interest in or knowledge of the historical background remained sketchy, he continued to read widely, studying many of the major medieval texts, including the first English version of the *Mabinogion,* published in 1849.

Tennyson launched his grand Arthurian vision on the world in 1842 with a long poem called "Le Morte d'Arthur," which would later reappear in a revised form as "The Passing of Arthur" in the sequence of *Idylls.* Already a popular poet, his reputation grew steadily until the 1850 publication of "In Memoriam." This poem, a sentimental meditation on the death of his friend and mentor Arthur Hallam (whose name may well have influenced Tennyson's choice of King Arthur as a subject) made Tennyson into something of a poetic superstar, with each eagerly awaited new collection selling thousands of copies. It coincided with his acceptance of the office of poet laureate, while the admiration of both the queen and Prince Albert was widely known and well publicized and added to Tennyson's success. After the early death of the prince in 1861, the poet dedicated the *Idylls* to his memory.

Tennyson makes the central theme of his retelling the adulterous love of Lancelot and Guinevere, which casts a shadow over Arthur's court. The downfall of Merlin at the hands of the wily sorceress Vivien (Nimue) is attributed to the despair he feels at the darkness engendered by the affair at the heart of Camelot. Tennyson had debated calling the collection *The True and the False,* a title that reflected his desire to contrast the various kinds of love described in the poems. He chose *Idylls of the King* in the end as it suggested a more dreamy and romantic vision.

The sequence, written over the next twenty years, includes "Merlin and Vivien," "Lancelot and Elaine," "Lancelot and Guinevere," "Geraint and Enid," "Gareth and Linette," and "Balin and Balan," after which came "The Last Tournament," in which the poet explored the decay at the heart of the Arthurian world—a world torn between desire and duty—a favorite theme of much Victorian poetry and drama. Finally came "The Holy Grail," in which Tennyson explored the differences between the various knights who undertook the sacred quest—the failure of the fallen Lancelot and the success of the saintly Galahad. The growing sense of responsibility, which social reform attempted to inculcate among landowners and industrialists of the mid-Victorian era, is clearly echoed in Arthur's concern for the well-being of the land.

The last poem of the sequence, "The Passing of Arthur," is a long drawn-out threnody for the death of love and the tarnished glory of Camelot. It contains some of the most powerful verse written in this time and reflects the themes of faithfulness in love and marriage that were epitomized by the family life of Victoria and Albert.

Queen Victoria herself became a champion of Tennyson's work—a fact that certainly furthered his success and helped make the Arthurian legends a popular subject for all of the arts. In 1847 Prince Albert had commissioned William Dyce to decorate the queen's Robing Room at Westminster with themes from the Arthurian legends. Dyce drew on Tennyson's writings rather than the original medieval works and produced some striking work that can still be enjoyed today.[2]

Conversely, the historical researchers of the time were less certain about Arthur. The two great Victorian historians, Thomas Babington Macaulay and John Mitchell Kemble, both rejected Arthur as an unlikely hero of a period so dark that it was virtually impenetrable. Kemble's view, written in 1849, was that once the Saxons had overwhelmed them:

> The vanquished Britons found a melancholy satisfaction in adding details . . . [of the glorious past; however,] the spells of Merlin and the prowess of Arthur, or the victorious career of Aurelius Ambrosius, although they delayed and in part avenged, yet could not prevent the downfall of their people.[3]

Most histories of Britain from this time until as late as the 1950s passed over these Dark Ages, jumping from the Romans to the Anglo-Saxons with barely a mention of the Arthurian period. Even Charles Dickens, who wrote the famous *A Child's History of England* in 1851, was uncertain whether Arthur was real or not. In the chapter on Celtic

Britain he came remarkably close to the truth when he remarked: "Among the histories of which they [the Celts] sang or talked, there was a famous one, concerning the bravery and virtues of KING ARTHUR, supposed to have been a British Prince in those old times. But, whether such a person really lived, and whether there were several persons whose histories came to be confused together under that one name, or whether all about him was invention, no one knows."[4]

THE GREAT REVIVAL

All of these writers, including Tennyson, would have been aware of the greater appreciation of early Celtic myth and literature that had begun in the late eighteenth century. George IV's ceremonial visit to Scotland in 1822 had legitimized a Scottish revival after the savage repressions following the Jacobite rebellions of 1715 and 1745. The revival of interest in Arthurian matters during the nineteenth century was in no small measure due to another kind of revival, one that has at times been referred to, rather unkindly, as the Celtic Twilight. The Saxons against whom Arthur fought brought their own culture, which did much to dilute the original Matter of Britain and the poems and stories of the Celtic bards. Later, when the Normans invaded England, they imposed a feudal rule over their subject peoples. Ireland was conquered soon afterward, losing its autonomy; Wales was unified with England in 1543. The Act of Union finally incorporated Scotland, after centuries of acrimonious combat, into England in 1707. The language, ideas, and vision of the conquered Celtic peoples were devalued as less important than the predominant English vision of conquest and empire.

The eighteenth century saw the first stirrings of a Celtic revival. The fires of tradition began to burn again with a new fierceness, aided and abetted by a new generation of writers. Rendered politically harmless by the failed attempts of the Old and Young Stuart Pretenders to reestablish their dynasty, Scotland lay in shock. The clan leaders were either dead or had become more English than the English. But Gaelic was still spoken in the Highlands and islands, and the old stories and songs were still told. The work of writers like James Macpherson (1736–1796) in Scotland and Iolo Morganwg (1747–1826) in Wales helped illuminate Celtic tradition for a new generation.

Macpherson, who wrote poems attributed to the mythic figure of the Irish bard Ossian, signaled the beginning of this revival, while Matthew Arnold's influential essay, *The Study of Celtic Literature* (1868), gave it further incentive.[5] Arnold, an English poet who spoke none of the native Celtic tongues, wrote passionately of the beauties and subtleties of the ancient literatures of Ireland, Scotland, and Wales. His work prompted a wave of revivalist concern for the "lost" literature of the Celts—which had never really been lost at all but which now, under the banner of "rediscovery," flourished again. Much of this was Arthurian in content and added to the revival of interest in all things deemed "ancient" and "mysterious."

At the same time archaeologists and antiquaries began to study the artifacts of the Bronze Age. Coins and inscriptions, as well as early texts, were studied and the findings published in newly founded journals like *Revue Celtique, Scottish Gaelic Studies,* and *Y Cymmrodor.* New translations of the ancient bardic works began to appear. Many, like those of Iolo Morganwg, were either inaccurate or downright forgeries. Some, like the works of Celticists such as Kuno Meyer, Whitley Stokes, and Douglas Hyde, were carefully researched and scholarly. Other writers, such as Fiona Macleod (William Sharp), AE (George Russell), James Stephens, Ella Young, and Kenneth Morris, drew upon the words of the traditional Celtic bards and mythmakers to create new visions.[6]

For the poets, writers, painters, and visionaries who together brought into being the renascence of the Celtic spirit, the land and the ancient mythologies that grew out of it were of central importance. They turned to the myths of ancient heroes like Arthur in order to rediscover for themselves the powerful spirit of the Old World, which they renewed for their generation and those that followed. Without them, and the romantic revelations of Tennyson, there might have been no rediscovery of Arthur, and we might now be singing the praises of the Saxon king Alfred, whose life was just as much a source of inspiration to Victoria and Albert.

ARTHUR AND THE PRE-RAPHAELITES

Tennyson's richly descriptive work gave inspiration to some of the greatest artists and writers of the time. In particular the group of painters known as the Pre-Raphaelite Brotherhood took subject after subject from the Arthurian legends. Pledging themselves to the idea of producing art that was freer in form than the more stilted and formal style of leading academicians of the time, they sought romantic and erotic themes for their work. Many of their paintings are characterized by a jewel-like palette and exquisite detail, mostly drawn from life—a style that lent itself easily to the fantastic world of Arthur.

The leading lights of this loosely knit society were William Morris and Edward Burne-Jones. Morris (1834–1896) discovered Tennyson while still at university and shortly after found Southey's edition of *Le Morte d'Arthur,* which he drew to the attention of his friend Burne-Jones (1833–1898). Morris himself wrote several Arthurian poems at this time, including *The Defence of Guenevere,* published in 1858, which was something of a riposte to Tennyson's dour account of the adulterous queen. Here, Morris has Guinevere pleading to be understood even as she faces death at the stake, her passion for Lancelot memorably rendered.

Unlike Tennyson, whose approach to the stories was both romantic and sentimental, Morris's account is powerful and moving in its realism. Morris showed himself to be far more in touch with human emotion than his more famous fellow poet. But it was in the paintings that he, Burne-Jones, and their fellow Pre-Raphaelites, William Holman Hunt, John Waterhouse, and Dante Gabriel Rossetti among others, produced in the succeeding years that places them among the first rank of Arthurian storytellers—for it was to the stories they turned, as depicted by both Tennyson and Malory, for their inspiration, and their paintings tell some of the greatest Arthurian tales as visual poems.

In the summer of 1857, Rossetti visited the Oxford Debating Hall (now the Oxford Union building, then home to the atheistic Oxford

Movement), recently designed by Benjamin Woodward. Rossetti offered to recruit a group of young artists to decorate the ceiling of the hall, free of charge. He had met Burne-Jones and Morris in 1856 and immediately liked them. They shared a passion for Malory and the Arthurian legend and sought to express this in the murals they worked on for the next two years.[7]

For the Oxford Movement as a whole and for painters like Rossetti, Burne-Jones, and Morris, Arthurian legend, and especially the stories of the Grail quest, offered a tangible alternative to the organized religion they had rejected. Burne-Jones especially found the ideas of the Grail story attractive, while Rossetti himself sought to explore his feelings around love and sex through painting the story of Lancelot and Guinevere.

The three artists set out to tell the whole story of Arthur from his birth to death, and as the project grew more extensive, other painters joined them, including Arthur Hughes, John Hungerford-Pollen, Val Princep, and Rodham Spencer-Stanhope. However, problems of finance and disagreements among the artists soon sprang up, and in the end, although ten pictures were completed, only seven of these were by the original artists. Morris and Briton Riviere were later employed to complete the gaps left when the original group broke up.

Looking at the titles of just some of the pictures produced by the Pre-Raphaelite painters, one can see how wide their range was. Among those executed by Burne-Jones are *The Death of Merlin* (1857), *Sir Galahad* (1858), *The Beguiling of Merlin* (1874), and *The Sleep of King Arthur in Avalon* (1898). In addition, he illustrated a rich and beautiful edition of *Le Morte d'Arthur*. Morris completed *Queen Guenevere* (1858), *The Recognition of La Belle Isoude* (1862), and the famous tapestry *The Vision of the Grail* (1891–1894), while Rossetti's major contributions were *King Arthur's Tomb* (1854), *How Sir Galahad Sir Bors and Sir Percival were fed with the Greal,* (1864) and *Queen Genevere* (1858). In many of these works, the artists left Tennyson and Malory behind, striking out on their own to produce works of real originality on themes and incidents not recorded in the original texts. Although the brotherhood lasted less than ten years formally, it had a huge impact on the iconography of the Arthurian legends, anchoring them at once in both the medieval and Victorian worlds.[8]

Tennyson's words not only inspired painters to re-create some of the greatest scenes from his works. The great French engraver Gustave Doré produced some powerful illustrations to the *Idylls of the King,* while themes from the poems were photographed with carefully composed images of costumed people portraying Arthur and Merlin or Lancelot and Guenevere. The person responsible for this unusual treatment of the legends was Julia Margaret Cameron (1815–1879), one of the first people to take photography out of the everyday recording of events and into the realm of art. Cameron was a personal friend of Tennyson, and it seems to have been he who first asked her to illustrate the *Idylls* photographically in 1874. Using family members as well as people off the street and on some occasions the poet himself, Cameron produced a series of striking pictures, which were then reproduced as wood engravings and used to illustrate one of the volumes of a limited collectors edition of Tennyson's works published by Henry S. King and Company of London between 1874 and 1876. The success of these volumes, along with a feeling of dissatisfaction with the woodcuts, prompted Cameron to publish two books containing the photographs along with excerpts of Tennyson's text. She chose scenes depicting Gareth and Lynette, Geraint and Enid, Merlin and Vivien, and Lancelot and Guinevere, among others. Not surprisingly perhaps, she focused on the female characters in each, showing them as powerful and assertive against the rather passive male figures. Cameron is reckoned today as one of the great early photographers, and the images she produced reveal, in their moody romanticism, the way in which Arthur and his knights and their ladies were perceived in the Victorian age.[9]

IMAGES OF EMPIRE

Until the early nineteenth century, Arthur had been wholly a figure of literary folklore or a representative of national heroism and chivalry.

During the reign of Victoria, he began to be portrayed as a paradigm of the British Empire. These ideas, especially those inspired by Tennyson, have remained among the most enduring portrayals of Arthur. In the work of the Pre-Raphaelite Brotherhood and the photographs of Julia Margaret Cameron, we see the romance of both chivalry and love. The impact of these images inspired fresh outpourings of national sentiment as well as providing models for the rising number of cheap illustrated books that took Arthur as their subject. This is especially true of children's books, which began to appear in greater numbers during the late Victorian and early Edwardian periods. Images from these books brought the visual impact of Arthur to a new audience, giving the legends a fresh impetus.

Arthur also became the inspiration for the late-Victorian revival of esotericism. In a more chivalric vein, the establishment of the Round Table Hall, built at Tintagel by the custard millionaire Frederic Thomas Glasscock (1871–1934), allowed people to enter into the spirit of the Arthurian adventure by becoming knights and ladies of his semi-Masonic order. Initiates were given certificates and invited to gatherings in the impressively decorated hall in the small north Cornish village. Such was the influx of visitors into the region that a massive hotel, built in a mock-Gothic style with crenelated battlements and Arthurian shields on the walls, was built at Tintagel Bay, overlooking the castle, which had been made famous by Tennyson as the birthplace of Arthur.[10]

With the end of the Victorian era and the rise of Edwardian England, Arthur as the upholder of empire began to seem as antiquated as Elgar's *Pomp and Circumstance Marches* or Rudyard Kipling's patriotic verses do today. The erosion of chivalric ideals began with the First World War, where ancient skills of hand-to-hand combat and the use of horses were replaced by long-range shells and mechanized warfare. In the face of such massive casualties, chivalry and honor turned their faces to the wall. The leveling of entire countries by warfare was echoed throughout Europe by the leveling of social distinctions between classes as the twentieth century wore on.

ARTHUR IN THE MODERN AGE

In our own time, we have witnessed the return of Arthur by way of an extraordinary proliferation of literature, film, and the arts, with literally hundreds of novels, plays, films, and short stories—not to mention legions of poems—exploring and reshaping the ancient tales and characters, at times almost beyond recognition. Arthur has become a subject of worldwide interest and has regenerated in an extraordinary way.

The International Arthurian Society, founded in 1948, which counts more than two thousand members worldwide, produces an annual bibliography, listing several hundred new titles, including articles, books, and monographs, every year—indicating the continuing scholarly and popular interest in the subject. Contemporary fictional and poetic accounts of Arthur abound and range all the way from great works of literature, such as T. S. Eliot's *The Waste Land* (1940) and David Jones's *In Parenthesis* (1937), to popular works, such as *The Mists of Avalon* by Marion Zimmer Bradley (1982) and Dan Brown's *The Da Vinci Code* (2001).

So much good Arthurian fiction has been produced over the last few decades that it is difficult to select even a few to mention here. In the 1950s T. H. White published a quartet of books under the overall title of *The Once and Future King* (1958).[11] In these books he set out to retell the story as Malory had given it, but with a modern spin. The first book, *The Sword in the Stone,* tells the story of Arthur's childhood and training at the hands of Merlin—or rather, as White spells it, Merlyn. This rather comical old gentleman, who lives backward and is thus enabled to see the future, seems a far cry from the Merlin of earlier times. Yet his magic is no less potent. Like Taliesin in the *Mabinogion,* Arthur learns the things that he needs to fit him for the great task ahead by taking the shapes of bird, beast, and insect, each of which shows him the foolishness of the ways of men.

This lighthearted beginning became gradually darkened in the books that followed. *The Queen of Air and Darkness* concentrated on the figure of Morgause and the childhood of her sons Gawain, Gareth,

Gaheries, and Agravain and culminates in the birth of Mordred, whose coming is to spell destruction for the Arthurian world. The third, *The Ill-Made Knight,* tells the story of Lancelot and Guinevere with a degree of passion and psychological realism seldom attained before or since. Finally, *The Candle in the Wind* relates the story of the downfall of the Round Table, the war against Lancelot, and the doom-laden ending of the tale. A fifth volume, left unfinished by White at his death, was published posthumously as *The Book of Merlyn* (1977). It tells what happens when the old wizard returns to Arthur's tent on the eve of the Battle of Camlann, as he takes his protégé through a further series of transformations that equip him for a new beginning *after* his time in Avalon. It is marred by White's bitter response to the imminent war with Germany, but it nevertheless contains some of his finest writing, taking Arthur beyond the darkness in which his dream ends toward a new source of light.

Arthur is very much a myth-laden being for our time. Magic and mystery, Druid craft and wizardry dominate the pages of books like *The Mists of Avalon* by Marion Zimmer Bradley, subsequently filmed for TV (2001). Bradley tells her story from the viewpoint of Morgain le Fay, whom she substituted for Arthur's other sister Morgause, making Morgain the mother of Mordred. Bradley invoked a rich vision of Avalon as a fairy world gradually floating away from the historical realm of Arthur. She also invokes the shadow of Atlantis in the early part of the book, making Arthur's mother, Igraine, one of the few who escaped (along with Merlin) from the drowned continent, bringing with her the bloodline and magical knowledge of the most ancient and advanced civilization on Earth. *The Mists of Avalon* influenced a generation of readers and writers, with many elements first introduced by Bradley now widely accepted as genuinely ancient.

A. A. Attanasio's Arthor series (*The Perilous Order of Camelot*), written between 1995 and 1999, and Peter Vansittart's *Lancelot* (1978) and *Parsifal* (1988) follow Arthur deeply into the mythic forest of the ancient premedieval Arthurian world. Attanasio's vision remains the most cosmic to date—set in a time outside time, representing Merlin as a being of uncounted age, fighting against overwhelming powers of evil, with Arthur as the central pawn in a vast cosmic chess game. His books are wild and rambling in the way few modern authors have allowed themselves to be. Indeed, it is as though the compilers of the Vulgate Cycle had returned, having absorbed the zeitgeist of twentieth-century living and re-created their vast cycle of tales in utterly contemporary terms.[12]

Vansittart dips into the deepest and darkest cauldron of myth for his books and paints a picture of a stark and powerful world in which mythic characters rub shoulders with figures from history. *Lancelot* retells the tale of the hero in terms of the sixth century, with Lancelot (known as Ker Maxim) a follower first of Ambrosius and later of Artorius at a rough and savage court full of larger-than-life characters. *Parsifal* follows the story of the eponymous hero but takes it through five periods of history—from pre-Roman Britain to the Germany of Hitler and Wagner. Throughout these books, as in his many other historical novels, Vansittart explores themes of memory, storytelling, morality, and death, making use of the characters of Arthur, Gawain, and the rest as doorways into the mythic depths of human consciousness.[13]

Despite these rich flights of fantasy, the historical Arthur has not been neglected either, indeed in many instances it is hard to tell where the history ends and the fantasy begins. Edward Frankland wrote one of the most direct and unsentimental accounts of Arthur in his book *The Bear of Britain*,[14] and this was followed by such works as *The Great Captains* by Henry Treece,[15] which told the story from the viewpoint of Mordred; and *Porius* by John Cowper Powys,[16] a vast sprawling romance worthy of the best of its medieval forbears but wholly contemporary. Perhaps best of all is *The Sword at Sunset* (1961) by Rosemary Sutcliff, which evoked a totally human sixth-century Arthur, struggling to keep the light of Rome burning in Britain.[17]

More recently than any of these, Bernard Cornwell's rendition of a Britain devoid of magic but full of heroes made bestsellers of his *Warlord Chronicles*. The hero and storyteller of these books is Derfel Cadarn, who is mentioned in early Welsh tradition as the founder of the monastery of Llanderfel in Gwynedd and is listed in the Triads as one of the survivors of Camlann. The three books—*The Winter King* (1995), *Enemy of God* (1996), and *Excalibur* (1997)—are perhaps the best researched of the recent portraits of Arthur. Cornwell turns many of the traditional themes upside down with Arthur as protector of the child Mordred, here the rightful king; Guinevere as an ex-prostitute; and Morgan as a witch who converts to Christianity! The Battle of Camlann is fought between Arthur and Mordred but with Arthur as the rebellious aggressor.[18]

Merlin also has seldom been far from the center of action in recent times. Mary Stewart's trilogy of novels, *The Crystal Cave, The Hollow Hills,* and *The Last Enchantment* (1970–1979), presents a portrait of the old enchanter who is more of a modern occultist than the visionary and seer of earlier texts. Yet he is still a recognizable descendant of Geoffrey of Monmouth's Merlin Ambrosius, who falls into inspired trances and suffers the terrible agonies of the visionary but is helpless to do more than watch as the kingdom he helped to create falls back into the darkness from which it emerged.[19]

In the early twenty-first century, the late Robert Holdstock produced a series published under the generic title *The Merlin Codex*. The three volumes, *Celtica* (2001), *The Iron Grail* (2002), and *The Broken Kings* (2007), take us deeply into the world of ancient mythology, bringing in characters from the classical world alongside heroes, shamans, witches, and, of course, the figure of Merlin himself—perhaps here most memorably depicted as a unique, half-mad genius who may be as old as time but cannot remember his own past and who is born to walk the paths of the world with enchantment thicker than blood in his veins. Accompanied by the semimythical Greek sailor Jason, Merlin embarks on a wild and wonderful series of quests, leading him steadily nearer to the world of Arthur, journeys that will lead him deep into an otherworld described with such vivid power one may be forgiven for believing that the author had spent time there. Peopled by mythic reinterpretations of familiar Arthurian figures, this is the boldest and most entrancing of the recent retellings of the Arthurian saga—brilliantly written and astonishingly inventive.[20]

Recently we have seen the appearance of a lost Arthurian classic *The Fourth Gwenevere,* by the eccentric Welsh writer John James. James wrote a whole series of Dark Age novels in the 1970s, displaying an encyclopedic knowledge of the period and an ability to get into the minds of the people of the time that is unequaled by any other contemporary writer. The manuscript, unfinished at the time of James's death in 1993, lay forgotten until 2013, when it was uncovered, brought forth, and finally completed.

The Fourth Gwenevere may seem a strange title to anyone not familiar with the older Arthurian legends, until we remember that the Welsh Triads describe Arthur having three previous wives, all called Gwenevere. In this book, the personal name is merely a title, and the fourth lady to bear it becomes the dynastic cement between rival factions, offering a hoped-for birth of a future ruler acceptable to both British and Saxon.

The book is narrated by Morvran map Tegid, who is also mentioned in the Triads as one of the three survivors of the Battle of Camlann. James's Morvran is a seasoned campaigner, the King of Gwent, one who once ruled in Lindsey until the heathen forces overran his realm and killed his kindred. Despite his limp and his ugliness, both tokens of that conflict, Morvran has more intelligence than the rest of the British kings put together. It is he who uncovers the truth behind the fall of Arthur and who is left to sort out the consequences of a secret plot so complex that only the emperor of Byzantium could have set it in motion.

The humor and understatement of the novel juxtaposes the accustomed isolationist ways of the British with the barbaric but determined incursions of the heathen invaders; this theme is drawn out further when Britons meet continentals during Morvran's quest into Gaul; foreign foodstuffs and different modes of discourse throw them into confusion. James's Dark Age world sports fairies, ancestors, and mythic beings that are as real as the other characters in this book. The conclusion of the novel is a fictional redepiction of the tenth-century Welsh poem, "Armes Prydein" from the *Book of Taliesin,* in which the hopes of the British for the future envision a united, rather than a warring people, who will sweep the Anglo-Saxons from the land.

THE POETRY OF ARTHUR

Poets also have not neglected the traditions of Arthur. John Masefield, poet laureate from 1930 to 1967, produced a series of powerful lyrics in *Midsummer Night* (1928),[21] mingling the heroic and the romantic elements of the old stories. T. S. Eliot, in his hugely admired poem "The Waste Land" (1925), used Arthurian themes to reflect the fractured state of twentieth-century society.[22]

Among those who have found new depths in these old tales is the poet and painter David Jones (1895–1974), whose artistic contribution to the landscape of Arthur is considerable. In his long poem *In Parenthesis* (1937),[23] he portrays World War I soldiers fighting side by side with Arthurian heroes, and in the work that followed it, *The Anathemata* (1952),[24] he created an evocation of Britain from its geological past to a semimythic eternity, bringing in the themes of Arthur and the Grail with tremendous force and vitality. His short, unfinished poem "The Sleeping Lord," which was published shortly before his death, portrayed an Arthur whose mythic connection with the land was such that he is more than its king. Here he hunts the great boar Twrch Trwyth, familiar from the *Mabinogion* story of Culhwch and Olwen (see chapter 4). The whole of the work is in effect a huge single image. The Lord, whether we see him as Arthur or Christ or Bran the Blessed, sleeps beneath the land. He is the land. He is invoked in the name of all the "many, many more whose names are, for whatever reason, on the diptycha of the Island; and vastly many more still, whether men or womankind, of neither fame nor recorded nomen, whether bond or freed or innately free, of far back or of but recent decease, whose burial mounds are known or unknown or for whom no mound was ever raised or any mark set up of even the meanest sort of show the site of their interment."[25]

Thus the Sleeping Lord becomes a container of memory, a living anamnesis who recalls, within himself, the history and myth and story of the land that gave birth to Arthur.

Another poet who understood the original Arthurian legends with great depth is Charles Williams, one of the literary group known as the Inklings, which included J. R. R. Tolkien* and C. S. Lewis—both of whom toyed with the Arthurian legends, though only Lewis published anything on the subject in his lifetime.[26] Williams wrote what is still the most powerful and magical series of poems on the theme of Arthur and the Grail. No simple account can give any real idea of the complexity and beauty of these poems, which appeared in two volumes *Taliessin through Logres* (1938) and *The Region of the Summer Stars* (1944), but a brief sample must suffice to show Williams's vision.

In the poem titled "The Calling of Taliesin," Merlin and his twin sister Brisen, who stand for time and space in Williams's universe and the offspring of Nimue (Nature), enact a magical operation to assist in the founding of the Arthurian kingdom.

> *Between wood and waste the yoked children of Nimue*
> *opened the rite; they invoked the third heaven,*
> *heard in the far humming of the spiritual intellect,*
> *to the building of Logres and the coming of the land of*
> *   the Trinity.*
> *which is called Sarras in maps of the soul. Merlin made*
> *   preparation . . .*
> *He lifted the five times cross-incised rod*
> *and began incantation; in the tongue of Broceliande*
> *adjuring all the primal atoms of earth*
> *to shape the borders of Logres, to the dispensation*
> *of Carbonek to Caerleon, of Caerleon to Camelot, to the*
> *   union*
> *of King Pelles and King Arthur*[27]

---

*The posthumous publication of Tolkien's meditative poem *The Fall of Arthur* in 2013 showed the creator of *The Lord of the Rings* attempting to restore the legend of Arthur to an earlier time.

Williams was, for a time, a member of the esoteric group known as the Fellowship of the Rosy Cross, instituted by the leading esotericist of the time, A. E. Waite, which numbered among its members W. B. Yeats and the notorious magician Aleister Crowley. This poetry reflects a deep awareness of spiritual forces at work in the world, as Williams seeks to bind Christianity and paganism into a single mythical realm that transcends both sacred and secular.

The distinguished British poet John Heath-Stubbs wrote of Arthur in a wide-ranging epic titled *Artorius: A Heroic Poem in Four Books and Eight Episodes* (1973) in which he combined myth, romance, and the heroic in a subtle blend of wit and erudition. Each of the poem's twelve parts is related to a sign of the zodiac, and the forms vary from pseudo-historic lectures to highly wrought Virgilian epic poetry, ironically cast in the mode of Anglo-Saxon verse styles. The twelve sections follow the pattern of the unfolding year from spring to winter, from Arthur's victory at Badon to the grim ending of the Arthurian dream at Camlann. Heath-Stubbs used the traditional themes as a means to comment on the nature of justice and power in our own time as well as the days of Arthur.[28]

ARTHURIAN ART AND MUSIC

The presence of Arthur in the visual arts has varied greatly since the Pre-Raphaelite Brotherhood rediscovered him through the writings of Tennyson.

The poet David Jones, as well as his long Arthurian works, also painted a number of pictures on Arthurian themes, including the *Grail Mass,* which shows a Mass taking place in a bombed-out chapel in the middle of the new wasteland of the western front, where he himself had fought, or the ship carrying Tristan and Isolt from Ireland. In paintings such as *Lancelot in the Queen's Chamber* (ca. 1916), *The Four Queens Find Lancelot Sleeping* (1941), *The Lord of Venedotia* (1948), and *Trystan ac Esyllt* (ca. 1962), Jones distilled virtually the whole of the Matter of Britain, drawing for his inspiration upon everything from Welsh myths to Malory. In so doing, he also showed how the Arthurian world fitted within the pattern of a greater whole, the heritage of Western spirituality and history and the literary heritage of the Middle Ages.[29]

Jones's work forms a bridge between the more representational styles of prewar culture and artworks that emerged after the 1930s and '40s. Though the British Neo-Romantic School, which included such artists as John Minton, John Craxton, Michael Ayrton, and others, continued to represent more traditional styles, most contemporary art has found less interest in Arthurian matters, though artists such as Anselm Kiefer and Harold Hitchcock have found inspiration in the people of Camelot.

Kiefer (1945–) has struggled to come to terms with postwar German culture and expresses the shadowy presence of Nazism and the Holocaust in much of his work. A series of paintings on the subject of Parsifal depict a bare attic room in which various objects are placed and where certain words or fragments of text can be seen. In *Parsifal I* (1973), a crib is placed before a window showing a clear blue sky. To one side is written the name Herzeleide, the name of Parzival's mother in Wolfram von Eschenbach's medieval poem. The suggestion is that the crib represents Parsifal himself, the child of the future time, who comes into the world in a place of loss and separation, hidden from the world of chivalry and adventure. The dark space of the loft perhaps represents the dark forest surrounding the house where Parsifal was born. Other paintings in the series, some executed in paint and blood, are even darker, expressing a nihilistic worldview pierced by the possibility of Parsifal's quest for the Grail.[30]

Hitchcock (1914–) is a prolific painter in a moody postromantic style reminiscent of William Turner. Among his many works are *Camelot* (1969), which seems to invoke Tennyson's view of Arthur's city as a high and perfect place full of splendor and power. In Hitchcock's painting, a group of shadowy figures stand on the shoreline beneath the towering Gothic arches of the castle while amber-sailed ships approach the harbor. The mood is one of transcendence and wonder tinged with a questioning thread of doubt. Another canvas, *Arthur and Guinevere at Avalon* (1971), place the almost insignificant figures of the king and queen against a backdrop of exotic buildings from many different periods and a blaze of colorful flowers, all set in a dream-like landscape. In *Isle of Merlin* (1983) a strange twilight place is revealed in which two figures—perhaps Merlin and Nimue—are surrounded by a dense forest through which is glimpsed a bucolic English landscape.

For Hitchcock, who brings a mystical dimension to his work, it is nature and in particular plants that are important, expressing "not only the beauty but the thoughts of God's world."[31] There is more than a hint of surrealism in Hitchcock's vision, but above all he has tried to capture the mystical and the strange in the Arthurian world in a way that is somehow quintessentially English.

It is the work of book illustrators that many of the finest representations of Arthurian themes have appeared in recent times—along with the varied styles of comic-book art. Here, the marriage of word and image has produced some of the most memorable ideas of Arthur and his times. Artists such as Edward Bawden, Françoise Taylor, and Anna-Marie Ferguson, all of whom have produced memorable artwork for *Le Morte d'Arthur,* have followed the strange and idiosyncratic illustrations designed by Aubrey Beardsley for the 1893–1894 edition of *Le Morte* and those of Dorothea Braby for the Golden Cockerel Press edition of the *Mabinogion* in 1935.[32]

More recently, Alan Lee, best known for his romantic and detailed drawings for J. R. R Tolkien's *Lord of the Rings,* also illustrated the *Mabinogion.* Lee's sense of place and character and his deep knowledge of the Celtic world make these images unique windows into the past. His large-scale drawing of *Merlin* (1999), executed on vellum, depicts a wild and ragged shamanic figure virtually crucified among the entangled branches of the ancient forest landscape of Dartmoor.

All of these artists, as well as legions not mentioned here, and including the varied styles of modern comic-book art, have kept alive the visual presence of Arthur, drawing upon every aspect of his many faces to produce works of outstanding beauty and richness.

The presence of Arthurian legend and story in music has also been important from the Middle Ages onward. Some of the oldest of the Arthurian stories were intended to be sung by the wandering troubadours who carried the ancient Celtic tales across Europe. Though few songs that could properly be called Arthurian have survived, performers of early music have reconstructed a number of those—especially dealing with the Grail—to admirable effect. The early opera *King Arthur, or The British Worthy* by Henry Purcell (1691)[33] used the return of one king to celebrate the coronation of another (see chapter 7). After this, with the possible exception of Thomas Arne's *The Opera of Operas or Tomb Thumb the Great* (1733),[34] which is barely Arthurian, there are no significant musical adaptations of an Arthurian story until Richard Wagner's *Parsifal* (1882), held by many to be his finest work. This dramatic and mystical retelling of the Grail displays Wagner's profound understanding of myth and of the nature of the Grail, and though he made use of Wolfram Von Eschenbach's *Parzival* as a main source, he also borrowed from many other texts to create what is, in effect, a new version of the Grail story. Wagner's other opera *Tristan and Isolde* (1859) drew primarily from the great medieval poem of Gottfried von Strassburg (see chapter 5).[35]

Other works worthy of mention here are Isaac Albeniz's Wagnerian opera *Merlin* (1901), which is almost forgotten today. Even the great French composer Claude Debussy (1862–1918) began a Tristan opera, but abandoned it after two years of work dogged by squabbles over the licensing of the text written by Joseph Bedier. In Britain the eccentric composer Rutland Boughton (1878–1960) organized a festival at Glastonbury and planned a cycle of five Arthurian operas based on episodes from Tennyson and Malory. Only these three were ever performed, while the squabbles surrounding the organization of the festival became the subject of John Cowper Powys's novel *A Glastonbury Romance* (1932).

In more recent years three important operas have drawn on Arthurian themes. Richard Blackford's *Gawain and the Green Knight* (1978–1979) and *Gawain and Ragnall* (1984) are full of energy and stick close to the original versions of these stories; while Sir Harrison

Birtwhistle also chose to retell the medieval poem of *Sir Gawain and the Green Knight* in his 1991 opera of that name, which is a powerful reworking of the story admirably suited to Birtwhistle's characteristically sinewy style.

The existence of even this much Arthurian music (and there is a great deal more in the archives of less important compositions) is just another indication of the importance of Arthur to the national and international world of the arts, which in its turn reflects the deeper resonances of the Arthurian saga in the cultural and imaginative landscape of the west.[36]

ARTHUR OF THE SILVER SCREEN

Arthurian cinema is to all intents and purposes a subgenre within the world of film, with a large number of movies appearing since 1910 when the French director Albert Cepallani released his *Tristan et Yseult*, followed soon after by the American Emmet J. Flynn's version of *A Connecticut Yankee at King Arthur's Court* (the first of many) in 1920.

Since then over a hundred Arthurian movies have been made, some good, some bad, some indifferent. Among the best (and worst) of these are John Boorman's *Excalibur*, released in 1981 and still one the best Arthurian films to date, despite a few minor flaws; Terry Gilliam's *The Fisher King* made in 1991; *Sword of the Valiant* (1983) directed by Stephen Weeks (a remake of his own earlier film *Gawain & The Green Knight*); *First Knight* (1995) with Richard Gere as Lancelot and Sean Connery as Arthur; and the TV epics *Merlin* (1999) and *The Mists of Avalon* (2001).[37]

Among the strangest additions to this list are *The Knights of the Square Table*, directed by Alan Crossland and released in 1917 with the support and backing of the Boy Scout Movement; *Monty Python and the Holy Grail* (1975) again by Terry Gilliam; and Barry Levinson's *The Natural,* (1984) based on Bernard Malmoud's novel of the same name, which dealt the idea of a baseball player whose life reflects that of Sir Perceval. There is also, most curiously of all, a Russian adaptation of Mark Twain's *Connecticut Yankee,* which was released in 1987 in the Soviet Union as an anti-American rant.

Excalibur, directed by John Boorman, with a screenplay by Rospo Pallenburg, was released in 1981. It gives a marvelously rich account of the whole cycle from Arthur's birth to his last battle. The subtext of the film has a unity rare in any Arthurian work. It makes significant use of the symbolism of the Grail quest and successfully demonstrates the links between Arthur and the Wounded King who, in this version, are one and the same. It also contains the best portrayal of Merlin to date, as a wise, quirky, sorrowful figure (played by Nicol Williamson) who draws upon the immense power of Earth to bring about his magical operations. The familiar tale of Malory's Arthur is told against the backdrop of a mythical Camelot.

French cinema has also done well by the myths. There have been several versions of the Tristan story, as well as Robert Bresson's curious *Lancelot du Lac* (1974) and *Perceval le Gallois* by Eric Rohmer, certainly one of the most interesting attempts to capture the Grail story on film. Released in 1978, it adapts Chrétien's *Perceval, ou le Conte du Graal,* using Rohmer's own translation of the text and following it almost word for word. Through this, Rohmer observes Perceval's educational odyssey with an ironic wit. Rohmer's vision is unique in that he rejects the usual Hollywood image of the Middle Ages and opts for highly stylized sets.

The latest movie version of the Arthurian legends to emerge from Hollywood deals with a group of Sarmatian knights stationed on Hadrian's Wall in the fifth century, led by the charismatic Arthur Castus, a descendant of the original leader of the Sarmatian warriors imported into Britain by the emperor Hadrian (see chapter 1). *King Arthur* (2004), produced by Jerry Bruckheimer, directed by Antoine Fuqua, and written by David Franzoni, gives an authentic picture of the Dark Age Arthur, stripped of magic and medieval romanticism and shown in all its powerful savagery. Clive Owen makes a strong and thoughtful Arthur, and the British star Kiera Knightly plays Guinevere, here a Pictish princess. The "knights" are represented by the Sarmatian warriors, though retaining the traditional names of Lancelot, Tristan Bors, and Dagonet. Once again the struggle between the Romano-British and the invading Saxons is played out against the background of a stark northern landscape. After decades of films portraying Arthur as a hero of medieval splendor, this movie points the way toward a revisioning of the character in more authentic terms.[38]

TV also has had its share of Arthurian series and associations. Aside from specific stand-alone films already mentioned, the original series of *Star Trek* (1966–1969) told of the adventures of a band of latter-day knights under the leadership of a futuristic Arthur in the guise of the impulsive Captain James Tiberius Kirk, assisted by the very Merlinesque Mr. Spock. Their starship, the USS *Enterprise,* came to embody a Camelot among the stars, whose mobile Round Table and multiethnic crew came to serve the same force of goodness and justice as their medieval counterparts. With this strong yet subtle rooting in myth, it is not surprising that the TV series and its film spin-offs have found a place in the landscape of human imagination. In a similar way, George Lucas's *Star Wars* saga borrows from many myths, including those of Arthur, for its richly populated universe. Jedi master Obi-Wan Kenobi is characterized with overtones of Merlin, and the Jedi knights themselves, who protect the universe from evil forces, can be seen as futuristic Round Table knights.

More recently *Babylon 5* (1993–1998), a dramatic space opera created by Michael J. Straczynski, has drawn heavily on the myths of Arthur. Here the quest for the Grail continues into the twenty-second century, as we learn in the episode titled "Grail," written by Christy Marx. In this a wanderer named Aldous Gajic arrives on the *Babylon 5* space station. He describes himself as belonging to an order though it is given no name, and he is in search of the Holy Grail, which he describes as "a sacred vessel of regeneration," also known as "the Cup of the Goddess."

Several other episodes of the series feature Arthurian themes, including "A Late Delivery from Avalon," in which Arthur does indeed return, if not in the way anyone might have expected. Other Arthurian characters whose outlines at least may be discerned in the series are The Lady of the Lake, Perceval, and Merlin. As a whole *Babylon 5* represents the most extensive treatment of the Arthurian legend set in the future, though there are, of course, numerous novels that do so—mostly without great success.

Arthur, Merlin, and Morgan le Fay also feature in curiously distorted versions of themselves in the multiuniverses of *Stargate SG-1* (1997–) devised by Brad Wright and Jonathan Glassner. Episodes such as "Quest," "Arthur's Mantle," "Avalon," and "Camelot" present us with an alien Merlin who has lived through time, counting his years with Arthur as only one among many incarnations, while the contemporary heroes and heroines of the series echo the characters of Arthur and his knights as they search for the Grail—here visualized as a weapon that will help defeat an alien enemy. Most recently the TV series *Merlin* (2008–2012), aimed at a mostly teenage audience, created a world poised somewhere between the Dark Ages and the Middle Ages, featuring a young Arthur struggling to learn how to be a king, assisted by a young Merlin. Their world is filled with magical people, including witches, dragons, and creatures from Celtic myth, and familiar characters such as Uther, Morgain, and Lancelot appear in largely untraditional guise.

ARTHUR IN SCIENCE FICTION AND FANTASY

It is perhaps inevitable, given the otherworldly associations that have always been a part of the legend of Arthur, that in our own time he has found a new home in the science-fiction and fantasy genres, in both film and literature—though the physical presences of Arthur and his knights do not inhabit these realms so much as their ghosts. The age-old concepts of chivalry, the eternal quest, and all the endlessly varied themes of the Matter of Britain that can be traced back to Malory, Chrétien de Troyes, Wolfram von Eschenbach, and the rest, have undergone their most radical reworking here. As Richard Monaco,[39] responsible for some of the most enduring Arthurian fables of recent years, including *The Grail War* (1979), *The Final Quest* (1980), and *Runes* (1984), has written: "The strongest Arthurian tales aren't involved with literal and semiliteral history as much as with metaphor. They are anything but 'pure adventure' stories. They are images of initiation; spiritual alchemy; journeys into the secrets of the soul and the actual world."[40]

Such metaphysical journeys represent the particular power of the best sience-fiction writing. The Arthurian mirror is held up to the future world again and again, the heroes of Camelot transcending time and space to awaken in surprising guises amid a clutter of robotics, ships, aliens, and villains as strange as any encountered in ancient quests.

The idea of eternal champions seems to have been around for as long as myths have been formulated. The Nine Worthies, the Seven Sleepers, and the King under the Hill are age-old concepts, and all have been revived in recent years by science-fiction writers. Michael Moorcock, one of the great chroniclers of the ultimate quest, has drawn much of his inspiration from the mythos of Arthur—even though Camelot has not featured much in his pages in an overt sense. Writing of his series of novels and stories relating to the albino champion Elric of Melniboné, Moorcock discusses the importance of the quest. When Elric's object of search, "the Dead God's Book," supposed to contain all knowledge, finally crumbles to dust at his touch, Moorcock comments: "'The Dead God's Book' and the 'Golden Barge' (from the book of the same name) are one and the same. They have no real existence save in the wishful imagination of mankind. There is, the story says, no Holy Grail which will transform a man overnight from bewildered ignorance to complete knowledge—the answer clearly is within him, if he cares to train himself to find it."[41]

In *The War-Hound and the World's Pain* (1981), Moorcock takes this a step further. His hero, Graf Ulrich von Beck, is a brutal soldier of fortune hardly in the Arthurian mold, yet he is singled out by no less than Lucifer to go in quest of a cure for the world's pain—which is, not surprisingly, the Grail. Lucifer's desire is to be reconciled with heaven, perhaps take up his former position there; but not all of hell's denizens share this wish, and before Beck's quest is over, he must face the legions of the damned. Beck does indeed find the Grail and gives it to Lucifer, but it is insufficient to heal the breach between heaven and hell—Lucifer is still not welcome in heaven. Instead, he is given the task of redeeming Earth and of learning the true nature of the Grail.

The original Arthurian cycle ends in defeat at the hands of Mordred's followers, yet there is also another kind of victory: Arthur lives on in Avalon and promises to return in the time of his country's need. In a neglected epic by Martyn Skinner, *The Return of Arthur* (1966),[42] the king does indeed return to set things right in a future world of satanic evil. Malice is reborn in the shape of Morgan la Fay, bringing Arthur out of otherworldly sleep when the world needs him. This theme is explored in several science-fiction novels, including *The Drawing of the Dark* by Tim Powers (1979) and *A Midsummer Tempest* by Poul Anderson (1974). Both are alike in attributing to Arthur the abilities and desire to reaffirm what is threatened by destruction or undermined by evil.[43]

The idea reaches perhaps its purest expression in the graphic novel sequence *Camelot 3000* (1982–1985), where Arthur is revived from an age-long sleep beneath Glastonbury Tor to help Earth against alien invaders. Merlin, Lancelot, Guinevere, Gawain, and Tristan follow, reincarnating rather than being revived. But with the reawakening of Arthur, other ancient powers stir again to combat him. Morgan la Fay, after unsuccessfully trying to combat the powers of Merlin, leaves Earth and drifts through astral realms across the galaxies until she discovers the home planet of the aliens and makes them into her new army with which to conquer Earth. In the guise of science fiction, an age-old battle continues unabated. Even the evil president of Earth's security forces turns out to be a reincarnation of Mordred, who in a twist of the original story becomes the Grail thief and constructs out of it a suit of armor that makes him invincible.[44]

Those works where the Grail appears produce a synthesis of the ageless myth represented by the Arthurian ethos, and what might legitimately be called the new mythology of science fiction. Sometimes, as in Roger Zelazny's *The Last Defender of Camelot* (1979), the mystery will almost be explained away—only to be replaced by another and greater one. Here it is Lancelot, preserved through time, who features as a representative of cosmic chivalry. Meeting Morgan la Fay in an astrological emporium, he discovers that the reason for his preservation is the power of Merlin, whose last action before falling into enchanted sleep was to ensure that when he awoke, millennia later, the strongest knight in the world would be on hand to serve him. Morgan also implies that it could only mean the greatest harm for mankind if Merlin were once again at liberty to use his virtually unlimited power; his desire to right wrongs alone would upset the precarious balance of world power.

Merlin is mad anyway, Morgan says, though Lancelot predictably finds this hard to believe. It was Merlin who "arranged" the vision of the Grail to give fresh impetus to the failing energies of the Arthurian court. This shakes Lancelot, who believes that his preservation is a direct result of his ancient "sin" with Guinevere. Now he believes he must still achieve the Grail before he can be redeemed. Setting out for England he arrives to find Merlin awake and the madness predicted by Morgan to be true. Lancelot then becomes the "last defender," fighting a desperate battle against Merlin's magically operated "Hollow Knight" (a kind of robot) amid a ghostly Stonehenge. Watching Merlin and Morgan, locked in sorcerous combat, vanish forever between the worlds and beginning to age, Lancelot sees a vision of the Grail and follows it to his proper end—the end, Zelazny seems to imply—of the Arthurian quest for all time and the death of magic.[45]

This theme is much used by science-fiction writers who seek a paradigm of hope for the future out of the past and turn to the mythos of Arthur and the golden age of knights and ladies, magic, and wonder when the doors between the worlds were open without need of space flight and computer circuitry.

Good generally triumphs in the end, the aliens are routed, and the old order, though broken, triumphs. Once again we see, in the Arthurian past, a world that can be transported into the present—though sometimes at great cost.

Perhaps here we have the kernel of the use made by science-fiction writers of the Arthurian legends. It is possible to look back to the age of Arthur with nostalgia for what once was, or to stare forward into the infinity of the future as a pattern upon which to build a stable society or a workable world.

Beyond these reworkings of the stories, Arthur's appearances in popular culture are considerable. Though they lie outside the scope of this book, one final example of the way in which the story of Arthur has informed recent history is worth mentioning.

In America, during John Fitzgerald Kennedy's presidency,[46] the White House became known as Camelot, and Kennedy himself identified with Arthur. Regular performances of the Learner and Lowe musical *Camelot* (1960) were requested by the reigning king and queen of the White House. While this was doubtless a piece of political opportunism, the myth survived Kennedy's assassination and even gave rise to a rumor that he had not died as a result of his injuries but remained in hiding in a vegetative state—the implication being that, like Arthur, he would one day return.

Here we see something that has happened countless times in the long history of Arthur—where his name is invoked as a symbol of enduring greatness. The stories, like the king himself, endure all that we do to them without losing any of their original power to move and inspire. From their beginnings in the days when the Romans first arrived in Britain, or perhaps earlier still in the mist-laden realms of Celtic myth, the legends of Arthur have followed us through history.

Arthur himself has brought light out of darkness, becoming a beacon of hope and strength where none existed. He has been bought, borrowed, and reshaped into countless new aspects, for every reason from politics to mysticism. His history has been reshaped countless times: rejected, restored, refurbished, neglected again, then dusted off to furnish us with new evidence of his existence and the times in which he lived. Yet Arthur has never left us; he remains a once and future king who continues to reign over our hearts and minds. The many faces of this once and future hero have merged into a single archetypical Arthur who, in words appended to a fifteenth-century manuscript listing the Knights of the Round Table, has "triumphed over everyone, and in every deed, and over every nation in the world; through the strength of [his] powerful spirit, and the faith and hope that were in his heart."[47]

"The Sovereign's Chair"

We give here the full text of this most important poem, in a new translation, since it offers evidence for a continuing memory of Arthur though the centuries.

The Sovereign's Chair
(Areith Awdyl Eglur)

Declare the clear awdl.	[epic poem]
In awen's *own metre.*	[inspiration]
A man sprung of two authors,	
Of the steel cavalry wing,	
With his clear wisdom,	
With his royal rule,	
With his kingly lordship,	
With his honour of scripture,	
With his red lorica,	
With his assault over the Wall,	10
With his poet-praised seat,	
Amongst the defenders of the Wall.	
He led from the enclosed Wall	
Pale saddled horses.	

❖

The venerable lord,
The nurturing cup-bearer,
One of three wise ones
To bless Arthur.
Arthur the blessed,
In harmonious song,   20
In the forefront of battle,
Trampling down nine.

Who are the three stewards   25
Who guarded the land?
Who are the three storytellers
Who kept the portent?
Who will come eagerly
To welcome their lord?

Noble is the virtuous embankment,
Noble is the tall, tree-like man,   30
Noble the horn that's passed round,
Noble the cattle in their midday
  resting,
Noble is truth when it shines forth,
Nobler still when it is spoken,
Noble when came from the cauldron
The three spears of awen.   [The three drops of
                                    inspiration]

I have been a torquated lord,
With horn in hand.
Unworthy of the chair,
Is he who spurns my word.   40
Bright is the contested chair!
Eloquence of awen's excellence!

❖

What are the names of the three
  Caers   [fortresses]
Between flood and ebb?
No-one knows nor importunes
The nature of their stewards.
There are four Caers
In Britain's regions;
Tumultuous nobles.
From nothing can nothing be,   50
Nothing can come from nothing.

Fleets will come.
The wave covers the shingle,
Dylan's country, the sea, is inevitable.   [Dylan, god of the sea.]
There will be neither shelter nor
  refuge,
Neither hill nor dale,
Nor any refuge from the storm
From the wind when it rages.

The sovereign's chair:
Skilful the leader who preserves it,   60
Let the candidate be sought,
Let his generosity be sought.

Those pierced and lost,
Like such an array,
From the slaughter of the chieftain,
From the radiant ranks,
From loricated Lleon,   [City of the Legions/Carlisle?]
Will arise a king
For the fierce border.

❖

The braggart's *froth shall disperse*   70   [drink of ale and honey]
—Fragile by nature—
Noisy for a while,
At the disputed border.

Strange accents flow,
Eloquent assaults,
Of sea-farers.
From the children of Saraphin   [the snake-armoured ones]
The cursed folk of the wicked world,
Let us release Elphin.   [Taliesin's patron, who
                                               was imprisoned]

(Translated by Caitlín Matthews from the *Llyfr Taliesin* (*Book of Taliesin*)
Early Fourteenth Century)

Notes

Brief citations are given here. Full details will be found in the bibliography under 1: Primary Sources, 2: Secondary Sources.

CHAPTER I. ARTHUR OF ROME:
COMMANDER OF LEGIONS

1. Zimmer, "Gottingische geleherte anzeigen" (1890) 818, note 1.
2. Bruce, *The Evolution of Arthurian Romance,* vol. 1, 3.
3. Jackson, "Once Again Arthur's Battles."
4. Mommsen, *Corpus Inscriptionum Latinarum,* inscription no. 1919.
5. Ibid., inscription no. 12790.
6. Nickel, "Wer waren Koenig Artus Ritter? Über der geschichtliche Grundlage der Artussagen"; Nickel, "The Last Days of Britain and the Origins of the Arthurian Legends."
7. Littleton and Malcor, *From Scythia to Camelot.*
8. Malcor, "The Campanians of the Round Table."
9. Slavitt, *Ovid's Poetry of Exile.*
10. Personal communication from A. Hunt.
11. Richmond, "The Sarmatae, Bremetennacum Veteranorum and the Regio Bremetennacensis."
12. Dio Cassius, *Roman History,* book 71.
13. Malcor, "Lucius Artorius Castus 1."
14. Malcor, personal communication.

15. Richmond, "The Sarmatae, Bremetennacum Veteranorum and the Regio Bremetennacensis."

16. Dio Cassius, *Roman History,* book 71.

17. Malcor, "Lucius Artorius Castus 2."

18. Ibid.

19. Jackson, "Once Again Arthur's Battles."

20. Ibid.

21. Ibid.; Malcor, "Lucius Artorius Castus 2."

22. Hunt, *Shadows in the Mist.*

23. Geoffrey of Monmouth, *Historia Regum Britanniae.*

24. Malcor, "Lucius Artorius Castus 2."

25. Ibid.

26. Ibid.

27. Kennedy, *King Arthur.*

28. Personal communication from L. Malcor.

29. Nickel, "Wer waren Koenig Artus Ritter? Über der geschichtliche Grundlage der Artussagen."

30. Castleden, *King Arthur.*

31. Malcor, "Lucius Artorius Castus 2."

32. Malcor, "The Campanians of the Round Table."

33. Dumézil, *Legends sur les Nartes;* Littleton, "The Holy Grail, the Cauldron of Annwn, and the Nartyamonga."

34. J. Matthews, *King Arthur: Dark Age Warrior to Mythic Hero.*

35. Wadge, "King Arthur: A British or Sarmatian Tradition."

36. Sulimirski, *The Sarmatians,* 171.

37. Rolfe, *Ammianus Marcellinus.*

38. Herodotus, *The Histories.*

39. Nickel, "Wer waren Koenig Artus Ritter? Über der geschichtliche Grundlage der Artussagen."

40. Wadge, "King Arthur: A British or Sarmatian Tradition."

41. Moffat, *Arthur and the Lost Kingdoms.*

CHAPTER 2. ARTHUR OF THE SHADOWS: A HERO IN THE MAKING

1. Rudgley, *Barbarians: Secrets of the Dark Ages.*

2. Gildas, *De Excidio Britonum* [The Ruin of Britain], 18:1.

3. Ibid., 18:2.

4. Ibid., 20:2.

5. Bromwich, *Trioedd Ynys Prydein*, 35.

6. Gildas, *De Excidio Britonum*, 19:2.

7. Mattingly, *An Imperial Possession*.

8. Gildas, *De Excidio Britonum*, 19:4.

9. Tolstoy, "Nennius Chapter 56," 129.

10. Dark, *Britain and the End of the Roman Empire*, 146–48.

11. Nennius, *Historia Brittonum*, 36.

12. Oppenheimer, *The Origins of the British*, 379.

13. Dark, *Britain and the End of the Roman Empire*.

14. Snyder, *An Age of Tyrants: Britain and the Britons*.

15. Nennius, *Historia Brittonum*, 24.

16. Ibid.

17. William of Malmesbury, *The Kings before the Norman Conquest*, 10.

18. Morris, *The Age of Arthur*.

19. Coe and Young, *The Celtic Sources for the Arthurian Legend*, 5.

20. Gildas, *De Excidio Britonum*, 10:2.

21. Gidlow, *The Reign of Arthur*, 76.

22. Gildas, *De Excidio Britonum*, 4:4.

23. Ibid., 27–36.

24. Ibid., 23:1–2.

25. Ibid., 6:2.

26. Ibid., 25:3.

27. Hosea 8:4; Gildas, *De Excidio Britonum*, 109:4.

28. Gildas, *De Excidio Britonum*, 1:2.

29. McKee, "Gildas, Lessons from History."

30. Higham, *King Arthur: Myth-Making and History*, 59.

31. Bede, *A History of the English Church and People*, 15.

32. Nennius, *Historia Brittonum*, 31.

33. Gildas, *De Excidio Britonum*, 50:1.

34. Nennius, *Historia Brittonum*, 31.

35. Ibid., 40–42.

36. Ibid., 73.

37. Ibid., 56.

38. Ibid., 62.

39. Ibid., 45.

40. Ibid.

41. Coe and Young, *The Celtic Sources for the Arthurian Legend*.

42. Gidlow, *The Reign of Arthur*, 118.

43. Rowlands, "Warfare and Horses in the Gododdin and the Problem of Catraeth," 31.

44. Koch, *The Gododdin of Anerin*, xi.

45. Ibid., 35.

46. Ibid., recension B²29.

47. Ibid., recension B²38.

48. Ibid, 147.

49. Griffen, *Names from the Dawn of British Legend*.

50. Bartrum, "Arthuriana from the Genealogical Manuscripts."

51. Coe and Young, *The Celtic Sources for the Arthurian Legend*.

52. Anderson, "The Dating Passages in Gildas's Excidium."

53. Gildas, *De Excido Britonum*, 32.

54. Padel, "The Nature of Arthur," 24.

55. Barber, *The Figure of Arthur*, 37–39.

56. Ashley, *The Mammoth Book of King Arthur*.

57. Ashe, *The Discovery of King Arthur*.

58. Jordanes, *The Origin and Deeds of the Goths*.

59. Sidonius Apollinaris, *Letters*.

60. Gregory of Tours, *The History of the Franks*, vol. II, 25.

61. Sidonius Apollinaris, *Letters*.

62. Bromwich, *Trioedd Ynys Prydein*, triad 1.

CHAPTER 3. ARTHUR OF THE BATTLES: DEFENDER OF THE LAND

1. Nennius, *Historia Brittonum*, 73.

2. Barber, *The Figure of Arthur*, 96.

3. William of Malmesbury, *The King before the Norman Conquest*, 11.

4. Matthews and Matthews, *Taliesin*.

5. Ibid.

6. Koch, *The Gododdin of Aneirin*, 194.

7. *Gallic Chronicles*, quoted in Snyder, *An Age of Tyrants*, 233.

8. Gildas, *De Excidio Britonum*, 1:14.

9. Snyder, *An Age of Tyrants*, 107.

10. Byrne, *Irish Kings and High Kings.*

11. Snyder, *An Age of Tyrants,* 312.

12. Koch, *The Gododdin of Aneirin,* xlvii.

13. Chadwick, "Bretwalda-Gwledig-Vortigern," 228.

14. Ibid.

15. Gildas, *De Excidio Britonum,* 27.

16. Snyder, *An Age of Tyrants,* 54.

17. Ibid., 71.

18. Ibid., 349.

19. Bede, *A History of the English Church and People,* 1:1.

20. Nennius, *Historia Brittonum,* 37.

21. Oppenheimer, *The Origins of the British,* 380ff.

22. Bede, *A History of the English Church and People,* 1:1.

23. Tacitus, *The Agricola and the Germania,* 30.

24. Gildas, *De Excidio Britonum,* 19:1.

25. Carr, "Woad, Tattooing and Identity in Later Iron Age and Early Roman Britain."

26. Coleman, "Launching into History."

27. Koch, *The Gododdin of Aneirin,* 72.

28. Dark, *Britain and the End of the Roman Empire,* 25.

29. Marren, *Battles of the Dark Ages,* 32.

30. Snyder, *An Age of Tyrants,* 8.

31. Smyth, *Warlords and Holy Men,* 19.

32. Oppenheimer, *The Origins of the British,* 326.

33. Ibid., 379.

34. Tolstoy, "Nennius Chapter 56," 118–62.

35. Rance, "Attacotti, Déisi and Magnus Maximus," 250.

36. Barber, *The Figure of Arthur,* 35.

37. Gidlow, *The Reign of Arthur,* 123.

38. Gildas, *De Excidio Britonum,* 28–36.

39. Gidlow, *The Reign of Arthur,* 113.

40. Barbieri, *History of Britain,* 407–597, appendix 10.

41. Gidlow, *The Reign of Arthur,* 95.

42. Ibid., 97.

43. Anderson, "The Dating Passages in Gildas's Excidium," 404.

44. Bromwich, *Trioedd Ynys Prydein,* 99.

45. Tolstoy, "Nennius Chapter 56," 131.

46. Bromwich, *Trioedd Ynys Prydein*, 42.
47. Koch, *The Gododdin of Aneirin*, xcvii–xcix.
48. Snyder, *An Age of Tyrants*, 14.
49. Koch, *The Gododdin of Aneirin*, 9.
50. Ibid., xlix.
51. Nennius, *Historia Brittonum*, 15.
52. Rowlands, "Warfare and Horses in the Gododdin and the Problems of Catraeth" 22; Koch, *The Gododdin of Aneirin*, 135.
53. Rowlands, "Warfare and Horses in the Gododdin and the Problems of Catraeth" 20.
54. Ibid., 27.
55. Ibid., 26.
56. Barbieri, *History of Britain*, 407–597, Book 8.
57. Collingwood and Myres, *Roman Britain and the English Settlements*, 323.
58. Barber, *The Figure of Arthur*, 52.
59. Rowlands, "Warfare and Horses in the Gododdin and the Problems of Catraeth," 29.
60. Ibid., 18.
61. Dent and Goodall, *The Foals of Epona*.
62. Bromwich, *Trioedd Ynys Prydein*, triad 17.
63. Rudgley, *Barbarians: Secrets of the Dark Ages*.
64. Snyder, *An Age of Tyrants*, 234.
65. Ibid.
66. Bachrach, "The Questions of King Arthur's Existence."
67. Padel, "The Nature of Arthur," 16.
68. Ibid.
69. Ibid.
70. Tolstoy, "Nennius Chapter 56," 121.
71. Ibid., 124.
72. Dark, *Britain and the End of the Roman Empire*, 93.
73. Tolstoy, "Nennius Chapter 56," 120.
74. Oppenheimer, *The Origins of the British*.
75. Tolstoy, "Nennius Chapter 56," 125
76. Ibid., 131–32.
77. Gidlow, *The Reign of Arthur*, 17.
78. Tolstoy, "Nennius Chapter 56," 118.
79. Ibid., 137–39.

80. Nennius, *Historia Brittonum,* 73.

81. Jackson, "Once Again Arthur's Battles," 50.

82. Tolstoy, "Nennius Chapter 56," 141.

83. Breeze, "Historia Brittonum and Arthur's Battle of Mont Agned."

84. Tolstoy, "Nennius Chapter 56," 143.

85. Nennius, *Historia Brittonum,* 46.

86. Marren, *Battles of the Dark Ages.*

87. Gidlow, *The Reign of Arthur,* 60.

88. Nennius, *Historia Brittonum,* 56

89. Dark, *Britain and the End of the Roman Empire,* 103.

90. Nennius, *Historia Brittonum,* 56.

91. Koch, *The Gododdin of Aneirin,* xvii.

92. Gidlow, *The Reign of Arthur,* 62.

93. Llywarch Hen, *Poetry,* 19.

94. Nennius, *Historia Brittonum,* 45.

95. Bromwich, *Trioedd Ynys Prydein,* triad 54.

96. Ibid., triad 53.

97. Gildas, *De Excidio Britonum,* 32.

98. Bromwich, *Trioedd Ynys Prydein,* triad 59.

99. Guest, *The Mabinogion,* 150.

100. Tolstoy, "Nennius Chapter 56," 126.

101. Bartrum, "Arthuriana from the Genealogical Manuscripts," 159.

CHAPTER 4. ARTHUR OF MYTH: GRANTER OF QUESTS

1. Haycock, "Some Talk of Alexander and Some of Hercules," 13.

2. Barber, *The Figure of Arthur,* chapter 8.

3. Gildas, *De Excidio Britonum,* 56.

4. Koch, *The Gododdin of Aneirin,* 45.

5. Matthews and Matthews, *Taliesin.*

6. Bromwich, *Trioedd Ynys Prydein.*

7. Nennius, *Historia Brittonum,* 73.

8. Bromwich and Evans, *Culhwch and Olwen.*

9. Gowans, *Cei and the Arthurian Legend.*

10. C. Matthews, *Mabon and the Guardians of Celtic Britain.*

11. Byrne, *Irish Kings and High Kings,* 186.

12. Cormac úa Cuilennáin, *Sanas Cormaic,* 1198, 1208.
13. Nennius, *Historia Brittonum,* 73.
14. Skene, *Four Ancient Books of Wales.*
15. C. Matthews, *Mabon and the Guardians of Celtic Britain,* 121–22.
16. Nennius, *Historia Brittonum,* 13.
17. C. Matthews, *Celtic Book of the Dead.*
18. Bromwich, *Trioedd Ynys Prydain,* 258.
19. C. Matthews, "Voices of the Wells," 14–15.
20. Skene, *Four Ancient Books of Wales.*
21. Matthews and Matthews, *Ladies of the Lake.*
22. C. Matthews, "The Spells of Women."
23. Ibid.
24. Chrétien de Troyes, *Arthurian Romances.*
25. Skene, *Four Ancient Books of Wales,* vol. 2, 368.
26. Koch, *The Gododdin of Aneirin,* 85.
27. Bromwich, *Trioedd Ynys Prydein,* triad 32.
28. Bryant, *The High Book of the Holy Grail.*
29. Bromwich, *Trioedd Ynys Prydein,* 411.
30. C. Matthews, *King Arthur and the Goddess of the Land,* 236ff.
31. Bullock-Davies, *Professional Interpreters and the Matter of Britain,* 16.
32. Reno, *The Historic King Arthur,* 317–18.
33. Bromwich, *Trioedd Ynys Prydein,* 169.
34. C. Matthews, *King Arthur and the Goddess of the Land,* 253ff.
35. Bromwich, *Trioedd Ynys Prydein,* 377.
36. Coe and Young, *The Celtic Sources for the Arthurian Legend.*
37. See also Williams, "An Early Ritual Poem in Welsh."
38. Ibid.
39. C. Matthews, *King Arthur and the Goddess of the Land,* 236ff.
40. Hill, *The Tristan Legend.*
41. Ibid.
42. Bromwich, *Trioedd Ynys Prydein,* triad 56.
43. Carey, "The Finding of Arthur's Grave," 3.
44. C. Matthews, *King Arthur and the Goddess of the Land,* 315.
45. Bromwich, *Trioedd Ynys Prydein,* triad 53.
46. See also C. Matthews, *Mabon and the Guardians of Celtic Britain,* 93–98 for parallel traditions concerning the "Long Arm."
47. See also Rowlands, *Early Welsh Saga Poetry.*

48. J. Matthews, *Merlin;* Tolstoy, *Quest for Merlin.*
49. Bromwich, *Trioedd Ynys Prydein,* triad 87.
50. Skeels, *The Romance of Perceval in Prose.*
51. C. Matthews, *Celtic Book of the Dead.*
52. C. Matthews, "The Spells of Women."
53. See also Chambers, *Arthur of Britain.*
54. C. Matthews, *Mabon and the Guardians of Celtic Britain,* 195.
55. Matthews and Matthews, *Encyclopaedia of Celtic Wisdom,* 115 ff.
56. Bromwich, *Trioedd Ynys Prydein,* triad 37.
57. Davies, *The Mabinogion.*
58. Bromwich, *Trioedd Ynys Prydein,* triad 37.
59. See also Padel, "The Nature of Arthur."
60. Chambers, *Arthur of Britain,* 221–27.
61. Skene, *Four Ancient Books of Wales,* vol. 2, 439.
62. Ibid.

CHAPTER 5. ARTHUR OF BRITAIN:
THE MAKING OF A KING

1. Coe and Young, *The Celtic Sources for the Arthurian Legend.*
2. Geoffrey of Monmouth, *Historia Regum Britanniae.*
3. Giles, *Old English Chronicles.*
4. Geoffrey of Monmouth, *Historia Regum Britanniae.*
5. Ibid.
6. Ibid.
7. Ashe, *Merlin.*
8. Geoffrey of Monmouth, *Historia Regum Britanniae.*
9. Bromwich, *Triodd Ynys Prydein.*
10. Giles, *Old English Chronicles.*
11. Ibid.
12. Kronk, *Cometography.*
13. Baillie, *Exodus to Arthur.*
14. Bromwich, *Triodd Ynys Prydein,* triad 28.
15. Ashley, *The Mammoth Book of King Arthur,* 257–58.
16. Bromwich, *Triodd Ynys Prydein.*
17. Gidlow, *The Reign of Arthur.*
18. Barbieri, *History of Britain,* 407–597.

19. Ashe, *Merlin.*

20. *Ceridwen's Cauldron: The Journal of the Oxford Arthurian Society.*

21. Matthews and Matthews, *Ladies of the Lake.*

22. Hunt, *Shadows in the Mist.*

23. Geoffrey of Monmouth, *Historia Regum Britanniae.*

24. Giles, *Old English Chronicles.*

25. Bromwich, *Trioedd Ynys Prydein,* triad 56.

26. *De Ortu Waluuanii.*

27. Gidlow, *The Reign of Arthur.*

28. Quoted in Loomis, *Arthurian Tradition and Chrétien de Troyes.*

29. Geoffrey of Monmouth, *Historia Regum Britanniae.*

30. Loomis, *Arthurian Tradition and Chrétien de Troyes.*

31. Hunt, *Shadows in the Mist.*

32. Ashe, *The Discovery of King Arthur.*

33. Ashley, *The Mammoth Book of King Arthur,* 274.

34. Geoffrey of Monmouth, *Historia Regum Britanniae.*

35. Gidlow, *The Reign of Arthur.*

36. Bede, *A History of the English Church and People.*

37. Gildas, *De Excidio Britonum.*

38. Geoffrey of Monmouth, *Historia Regum Britanniae.*

39. Quoted in Ashley, *The Mammoth Book of King Arthur.*

40. Chambers, *Arthur of Britain.*

41. Geoffrey of Monmouth, *Historia Regum Britanniae.*

42. Giles, *Old English Chronicles.*

43. Hammer, "Some Additional Manuscripts of Geoffrey of Monmouth's *Historia Regum Britanniae.*"

44. Geoffrey of Monmouth, *Vita Merlini.*

45. Ibid.

46. Ibid.

47. Mason, *Arthurian Chronicles.*

48. Ibid.

49. Ibid.

50. Ibid.

51. Loomis, *Celtic Myth and Arthurian Romance.*

52. Hunt, *Shadows in the Mist.*

53. Ashe, *The Discovery of King Arthur.*

54. Geoffrey of Monmouth, *Vita Merlini.*

55. *Annales Cambriae.*

56. Bede, *The Ecclesiastical History of the English People.*

57. Geoffrey of Monmouth, *Vita Merlini.*

58. Geoffrey of Monmouth, *Historia Regum Britanniae.*

59. Giraldus Cambrensis, *Itinerarium Cambriae.*

60. Ranulf of Higden, *Polychronicon.*

61. Geoffrey of Monmouth, *Historia Regum Britanniae.*

62. Geoffrey of Monmouth, *Vita Merlini.*

63. Ibid.

64. Ibid.

65. Wace and Layamon, *Arthurian Chronicles.*

66. Ibid.

67. Ibid.

68. Ibid.

69. Ibid.

CHAPTER 6. KING ARTHUR:
LORD OF CAMELOT

1. Chrétien de Troyes, *Arthurian Romances.*

2. Littleton and Malcor, *From Scythia to Camelot.*

3. Loomis, *Celtic Myth and Arthurian Romance.*

4. Bromwich, *Trioedd Ynys Prydein,* triad 80.

5. Chrétien de Troyes, *Arthurian Romances.*

6. C. Matthews, *King Arthur and the Goddess of the Land.*

7. J. Matthews, *The Quest for the Green Man.*

8. J. Matthews, *The Grail: The Truth behind the Legend.*

9. Jones, *The Mabinogion.*

10. Marie de France, *The Lays of Marie de France.*

11. Eisner, *The Tristan Legend.*

12. Thomas the Anglo-Morman, *Tristan in Brittany.*

13. Marie de France, *The Lays of Marie de France.*

14. Chestre, *Sir Launfal.*

15. Bullock-Davies, *Professional Interpreters and the Matter of Britain.*

16. Ibid.

17. Robert de Boron, *Merlin and the Grail.*

18. Jacobus de Voragine, *The Golden Legend.*

19. James, "Acts of Pilate."

20. Robert de Boron, *Merlin and the Grail.*

21. Hall, *The Knightly Tales of Sir Gawain.*

22. Jones, *Sir Gawain and the Green Knight.*

23. Hartmann von Aue, *Iwein;* Hartmann von Aue, *Erec.*

24. Ulrich von Zatzikhoven, *Lanzelet.*

25. Wolfram von Eschenbach, *Parzival.*

26. Wirnt von Grafenberg, *Wigalois: The Knight of Fortune's Wheel.*

27. Gottfried von Strassburg, *Tristan.*

28. Heinrich von dem Türlin, *The Crown.*

29. Der Stricker, *Daniel von dem Blühendental.*

30. Shave, *La Tavola Ritonda.*

31. Leviant, *King Artus.*

32. Kalinke, *Norse Romances.*

33. Bryant, *The High Book of the Holy Grail.*

34. Lacy, *The Lancelot-Grail.*

35. J. Matthews, *The Grail: The Truth behind the Legend.*

36. Malory (2000), *Le Morte d'Arthur.*

37. Malory (1963), *Le Morte d'Arthur,* introduction, xii.

38. Malory (2000), *Le Morte d'Arthur.*

39. Ibid.

40. Malory (1990), *Le Morte d'Arthur.*

41. Malory (2000), *Le Morte d'Arthur.*

42. Ibid.

43. Ibid.

44. Kittredge, "Who Was Sir Thomas Malory?" 85–106.

45. Hardyment, *Malory: The Life and Times of King Arthur's Chronicler.*

46. Ibid.

CHAPTER 7. ARTHUR OF FABLE:
A NATION'S HERO

1. See also Biddle, *King Arthur's Round Table.*

2. Rouse and Rushton, *The Medieval Quest for Arthur,* 54.

3. Ibid.

4. Ibid.

5. Giraldis Cambrensis, quoted in Barber, *The Figure of Arthur.*

6. Ibid.

7. Ibid.

8. Ibid., 128.

9. Geoffrey of Monmouth, *Vita Merlini.*

10. Barber, *The Figure of Arthur,* 127.

11. Ibid., 128.

12. Ibid.

13. Nicholson, *The Chronicle of the Third Crusade: The Itinerarium Peregrinorum et Gesta Regis Ricardi: A Translation of the "Itinerarium Peregrinorum Et Gesta Regis Ricardi."*

14. "King Arthur's Cross Rediscovered?" *Enfield Advertiser.*

15. See also Chambers, *Arthur of Britain.*

16. Barber, *The Figure of Arthur,* 115.

17. Prestwich, *Edward I,* 121.

18. See also Chambers, *Arthur of Britain.*

19. Fitch, "Edward III's Round Table At Windsor," 36–39.

20. Bolitho, *The Romance of Windsor Castle.*

21. Quoted in Hope, *Windsor Castle: An Architectural History.*

22. Ibid.

23. Biddle, *King Arthur's Round Table.*

24. Hughes, *Arthurian Myths and Alchemy,* 182–83.

25. Rouse and Rushton, *The Medieval Quest for Arthur,* 12.

26. Millican, *Spenser and the Round Table,* 14.

27. Hughes, *Arthurian Myths and Alchemy,* 307.

28. Biddle, *King Arthur's Round Table,* 459.

29. Millican, *Spenser and the Round Table,* 22.

30. Ibid., 26.

31. Ibid., 34.

32. Ibid., 44–45.

33. Ibid., 39.

34. Ibid., 38.

35. Ibid., 36.

36. Higham, *King Arthur: Myth-Making and History,* 138.

37. Ibid., 238.

38. Jonson, *The Complete Masques.*

39. Ibid.

40. Jonson, *For the Honour of Wales 11, in the Complete Masques,* 346–52.

41. Millican, *Spenser and the Round Table*, 71.

42. Milton, *Epitaphium Damonis*.

43. Percy, *Reliques of Ancient English Poetry*.

44. Ibid.

45. Scott, "The Bridal of Triermain."

46. Child, *The English and Scottish Popular Ballads*, ballad no. 30.

47. Blake, *Poetry and Prose of William Blake*, 609.

48. Ibid., 608–9.

49. Ibid., 609–10.

50. Nennius, *Historia Brittonum*, 73.

51. Gidlow, *The Reign of Arthur*, 182.

52. Padel, "The Nature of Arthur."

53. Alcock, *Arthur's Britain*.

54. Leyland's Itinerary, quoted in Barber, *The Figure of Arthur*, spelling modernized by us.

55. Plutarch, *Plutarch's Moralia XII*.

56. Plutarch, *On the Obsolescence of the Oracles Moralia V*.

57. Layamon quoted in Guest, *The Mabinogion*.

CHAPTER 8. ARTHUR EVERYWHERE: REX QUONDAM, REXQUE FUTURUS

1. Tennyson, *The Idylls of the King*.

2. Whitaker, *The Legends of King Arthur in Art*.

3. Higham, *King Arthur: Myth-Making and History*, 251.

4. Ibid.

5. Arnold, *Celtic Literature*.

6. J. Matthews, *The Barddas of Iolo Morganwg*.

7. Whitaker, *The Legends of King Arthur in Art*.

8. Ibid.

9. Lukitsh, "Julia Margaret Cameron's Photographic Illustrations."

10. Lacy, *The New Arthurian Encyclopaedia*.

11. White, *The Once and Future King*.

12. Attanasio, his 5-volume *Arthor* series.

13. Vansittart, *Lancelot;* Vansittart, *Parsifal*.

14. Frankland, *The Bear of Britain*.

15. Treece, *The Great Captains*.

16. Powys, *Porius*.

17. Sutcliff, *Sword at Sunset*.

18. Cornwell, *The Warlord Trilogy*.

19. Stewart, *Arthurian Saga*.

20. Holdstock, *The Merlin Codex*.

21. Masefield, *Midsummer Night and Other Tales in Verse*.

22. Eliot, *The Wasteland and Other Poems*.

23. Jones, *In Parenthesis*.

24. Jones, *Anathemata*.

25. Jones, *The Sleeping Lord and Other Fragments*, 85.

26. Lewis, "Launcelot," 95–103; Lewis, *That Hideous Strength*.

27. Williams, *Arthurian Poets: Charles Williams*.

28. Heath-Stubbs, *Artorius*.

29. Whitaker, *The Legends of King Arthur in Art*; Lacy, *The New Arthurian Encyclopaedia*.

30. Whitaker, *The Legends of King Arthur in Art*, 326–28.

31. Ibid., 331.

32. Jones, *Sir Gawain and the Green Knight*.

33. Barber, *King Arthur in Music*.

34. Lacy, *The New Arthurian Encyclopaedia*.

35. Barber, *King Arthur in Music*.

36. Ibid.

37. For these and others see Harty, *King Arthur on Film*.

38. J. Matthews, "A Knightly Endeavour."

39. Monaco, *Parsival*; Monaco, *The Grail War*; Monaco, *The Final Quest*.

40. Monaco, *Runes*.

41. Moorcock, *The War-Hound and the World's Pain*.

42. Skinner, *The Return of Arthur*.

43. Powers, *The Drawing of the Dark*; Anderson, *A Midsummer Tempest*.

44. Barr, *Camelot 3000*.

45. Zelazny, *The Last Defender of Camelot*.

46. Knight, "Lancer: Myth-Making and the Kennedy Camelot."

47. Bromwich, *Trioedd Ynys Prydein*, 268.

Bibliography/
Further Reading

Primary Sources: texts and translations
Secondary Sources: studies, commentaries, fiction, poetry, art, and film

PRIMARY SOURCES

"Acts of Pilate." in *The Apocryphal New Testament*. Edited by James, Montague
  Rhodes. London and Oxford: Oxford University Press, 1924.

Ammianus Marcellinus. Edited and translated by John C. Rolfe. Cambridge,
  Mass.: Harvard University Press, 1939.

The Anglo-Saxon Chronicle. Edited by George Norman Garmonsway. London:
  J. M. Dent & Sons, 1972.

Annales Cambriae: A Translation of Harleian 3859; PRO E.164/1; Cottonian
  Domitian, A 1; Exeter Cathedral Library MS. 3514 and MS Exchequer DB
  Neath, PRO E1 by Paul Martin Remfry. SCS Publishing, 2007.

Bede. *A History of the English Church and People*. Translated by Leo Shirley-
  Price. Harmondsworth, U.K.: Penguin Books, 1978.

———. *The Ecclesiastical History of the English People*. London: George Bell &
  Sons, 1907.

Brut Tysilio. *The Chronicle of the Kings of Britain*. Attributed to Tysilio.
  Translated by Peter Roberts. London: E. Williams, 1811. Facsimile reprint,
  Felinfach, Wales: Llanerch, 2002.

Culhwch and Olwen. Edited by Rachel Bromwich and E. Simon Evans. Cardiff: University of Wales Press, 1988.

Chestre, Thomas. *Sir Launfal*. Edited by Alan J. Bliss. London: Nelson, 1960.

Chrétien de Troyes. *Arthurian Romances*. Translated by William W. Kibler and Carleton W. Carroll. London: Penguin Books, 1991.

The Chronicle of the Third Crusade: The Itinerarium Peregrinorum et Gesta Regis Ricardi: A Translation of the "Itinerarium Peregrinorum Et Gesta Regis Ricardi." Edited by Helen J. Nicholson. London: Routledge, 2001.

Coe, John B., and Simon Young. *The Celtic Sources for the Arthurian Legend*. Felinfach, Wales: Llanerch, 1995.

Cormac úa Cuilennáin. *Sanas Cormaic*. Edited by Kuno Meyer. Halle, Germany: Max Niemeyer, 1912. Facsimile reprint, Felinfach, Wales: Llanerch, 1994.

De Ortu Waluuanii nepotis Arturi. Edited and translated by Mildred Leake. New York: Garland Publishing, 1984.

Der Stricker. *Daniel von dem Blühenden Tal*. Translated by Michael Resler. New York and London: Garland, 1990.

Dio Cassius. *Roman History*. Books 71–80. Translated by Earnest Cary. Cambridge, Mass.: Harvard University Press, 2001.

The Four Ancient Books of Wales. 4 vols. Translated by William F. Skene. Edinburgh: Edmonton and Douglas, 1868.

Geoffrey of Monmouth. *Historia Regum Britanniae*. Translated by Lewis Thorpe. London: Folio Society, 1966.

———. *Vita Merlini*. Edited and Translated by Basil Clarke. Cardiff: University of Wales Press, 1973.

Gildas. *De Excidio Britonum* [The Ruin of Britain]. Edited and translated by Michael Winterbottom. London and Chichester: Phillimore, 1978.

Giraldus Cambrensis. *Itinerarium Cambriae*. Edited by Betty Radice. Translated by L. Thorpe. Harmondsworth, Middlesex: Penguin Books 1978.

The Gododdin of Aneirin: Text and Context from Dark-Age North Britain. Edited by John Koch. Cardiff: University of Wales, 1997.

Gottfried von Strassburg. *Tristan*. Translated by Arthur T. Hatto. Harmondsworth, U.K.: Penguin Books, 1960.

Gregory of Tours. *The History of the Franks*. Translated by Lewis Thorpe. Harmondsworth, U.K.: Penguin Books, 1977.

The Knightly Tales of Sir Gawain. Edited and translated by Louis B. Hall. Chicago: Nelson and Hall, 1976.

The High Book of the Holy Grail: A Translation of the Thirteenth Century

Romance of Perlesvaus. Edited and translated by Nigel Bryant. Cambridge, U.K.: D. S. Brewer, 1978.

Historia Meriadoci. Edited by Mildred Leake Day. New York: Garland, 1988.

Hartmann von Aue. *Erec*. Translated by Thomas L. Keller. New York and London: Garland, 1986.

———. *Iwein*. Translated by Patrick M. McConeghy. New York and London: Garland, 1984.

Heinrich von dem Türlin. *The Crown: A Tale of Sir Gawein and King Arthur's Court*. Edited and translated by J. W. Thomas. Lincoln and London: University of Nebraska Press, 1989.

Herodian. *Works*. 2 vols. Translated by C. R. Whittaker. London: William Heinemann, 1969–70.

Herodotus. *The Histories*. Edited and translated byAubrey de Selincourt. Harmondsworth, U.K.: Penguin Books, 1954.

Jacobus de Voragine. *The Golden Legend*. Selected and translated by Christopher Stace. London: Penguin Books, 1998.

Jordanes. *The Origin and Deeds of the Goths*. Edited and translated by Charles C. Mierow. University of Calgary. 1914.

King Artus: A Hebrew Arthurian Romance of 1279. Edited and translated by Leviant, Curt. Syracuse, N.Y.: Syracuse University Press, 2003.

Koch, John T., and John Carey. *The Celtic Heroic Age: Literary Sources for Ancient Celtic Europe and Early Ireland and Wales*. Malden, Mass.: Celtic Studies Publications, 1995.

The Lancelot-Grail. Edited by Norris J. Lacy. New York: Garland, 1993–1996.

Lawman (Layamon). *Brut*. Translated by Rosamund Allen. London: J. M. Dent & Sons, 1992.

Llywarch Hen. *Poetry*. Translated by P. K. Ford. Berkeley: University of California Press, 1974.

Mabinogion. Edited and translated by Davies, Sioned. Oxford: Oxford University Press, 2007.

The Mabinogion. Edited and translated by Gantz, Jeffrey. Hamondsworth: Penguin Books, 1981.

The Mabinogion. Translated by Lady Charlotte Guest. Edinburgh: Ballantyne, Hanson, 1902.

Malory, Sir Thomas. *Le Morte d'Arthur*. Edited by John Matthews. London: Cassell, 2000.

———. *Le Morte d'Arthur*. Edited by John Rhys. Edinburgh: Everyman Library, J. M. Dent & Sons, 1906.

———. *Le Morte d'Arthur: King Arthur and the Legends of the Round Table*. Translated into the modern idiom by Keith Baines. London: Harrap, 1963.

———. *The Works of Sir Thomas Malory*. Edited by Eugene Vinaver. Oxford, U.K.: Clarendon Press, 1990.

Marie de France. *The Lays of Marie de France*. Translated by Glyn S. Burgess and Keith Busby. Harmondsworth, U.K.: Penguin Books, 1986.

Matthews, John, and Caitlín Matthews. *Celtic Myth and Legend*. London: Folio Society, 2006.

Nennius. *British History and The Welsh Annals*. Edited and translated by John Morris. London and Chichester: Phillimore, 1980.

———. *Historia Brittonum*. In British History and the Welsh Annals. Edited and translated by John Morris. London and Chichester: Phillimore, 1980.

Norse Romances. 3 vols. Edited and translated by Marianne E. Kalinke. Cambridge, U.K.: D. S. Brewer, 1999.

Perceforest: The Prehistory of Arthur's Britain. Edited by Nigel Bryant. Cambridge, U.K.: D. S. Brewer, 2011.

Plutarch. *On the Obsolescence of Oracles Moralia V*. Edited and translated by Frank Cole Babbitt. Cambridge, Mass.: Harvard University Press, 1957.

———. *Plutarch's Moralia XII*. Edited and translated by Harold Cherniss and William C. Helmbold. London: William Heinemann, 1957.

Ranulf of Higden. In Churchill Babington, ed. *Polychronicon Ranulphi Higden, monachi Cestrensis*. Cambridge, U.K.: Cambridge University Press, 2012.

Robert de Boron. "Merlin and the Grail: Joseph of Arimathea, Merlin, Perceval." In *Merlin and the Grail*. Translated by Nigel Bryant. Cambridge, U.K.: D. S. Brewer, 2001. *The Romance of Perceval in Prose: A Translation of the E Manuscript of the Didot Perceval*. Translated by Dell Skeels. Seattle and London: University of Washington Press, 1966.

Sidonius Apollinaris. *Letters*. Translated by O. M. Dalton. Oxford, U.K.: Clarendon Press, 1915.

Sir Gawain and the Green Knight. Translated by Simon Armitage. London: Faber & Faber, 2007.

Sir Gawain and the Green Knight: A Prose Translation. Edited and translated by Gwyn Jones. London: Golden Cockerel Press, 1952.

Tacitus. *The Agricola and the Germania*. Translated by Harold Mattingly. Harmondsworth, U.K.: Penguin Books, 2008.

Tales of the Elders of Ireland (Accalam na Sénorach). Translated by Ann Dooley and Harry Roe. Harmondsworth, U.K.: Penguin Books, 1977.

La Tavola Ritonda. Edited and translated by Anne Shave. Binghampton, N.Y.: Medieval and Romantic Texts and Studies, 1983.

Thomas. *Tristan in Brittany.* Translated by Dorothy L. Sayers. London: Ernest Benn, 1929.

Trioedd Ynys Prydein: The Triads of the Island of Britain. Edited by Rachel Bromwich. Cardiff: University of Wales Press, 2006.

Ulrich von Zatzikhoven. *Lanzelet.* Translated by Thomas Kerth. New York: Columbia University Press, 2004.

Wace, Robert, and Layamon. *Arthurian Chronicles.* Translated Eugene Mason. London: J. M. Dent & Sons, 1962.

William of Malmesbury. *The Deeds of the Bishops of England.* Translated by David Preest. Woodbridge, U.K.: Boydell Press, 2002.

———. *The Kings before the Norman Conquest (Gesta Regum Anglorum).* Edited and translated by Joseph Stevenson. Facsimile reprint. Felinfach, Wales: Llanerch, 1989.

Wirnt von Grafenberg. *Wigalois: The Knight of Fortune's Wheel.* Translated by J. W. Thomas. Lincoln: University of Nebraska Press, 1977.

Wolfram von Eschenbach. *Parzival.* Translated by A. T. Hatto. London: Penguin Books, 1980.

SECONDARY SOURCES

Alcock, Leslie. *Arthur's Britain.* London: Allen Lane, 1971.

Anderson, A. O. "The Dating Passage in Gildas's Excidium." Zeitschrift für Celtisch Philologie (1928): 403–6.

Anderson, Graham. *The Earliest Arthurian Texts: Greek and Latin Sources of the Medieval Tradition.* Lewiston, N.Y.: Edwin Mellen Press, 2007.

Anderson, Poul A. *Midsummer Tempest.* New York: Doubleday, 1974.

Arnold, Matthew. *Celtic Literature.* New York: Macmillan, 1983.

Ashe, Geoffrey. "A Certain Very Ancient Book." Speculum 56 (1981): 301–23.

———. *The Discovery of King Arthur.* Stroud, U.K.: Sutton Publishing, 2003.

———. *Merlin.* Stroud, U.K.: Tempus Publishing, 2007.

Ashley, Mike. *The Mammoth Book of King Arthur.* London: Constable & Robinson, 2005.

Attanasio, Alfred Angelo. *Arthor.* London: Hodder & Stoughton, 1995.

———. *The Dragon and the Unicorn*. London: Hodder & Stoughton, 1984.

———. *Kingdom of the Grail*. New York: HarperCollins, 1992.

———. *The Serpent and the Grail*. New York: HarperCollins, 1999.

———. *The Wolf and the Crown*. New York: HarperCollins, 1998.

Bachrach, Bernard S. "The Questions of King Arthur's Existence and of Romano-British Naval Operations." Haskins Society Journal (1990): 13–28.

Baigent, Michael, Richard Leigh, and Henry Lincoln. *The Holy Blood and the Holy Grail*. London: Jonathan Cape, 1982.

Baillie, Mike. *Exodus to Arthur*. London: Batsford, 1999.

Barber, Richard, ed. *The Figure of Arthur*. London: Longman, 1972.

———. *King Arthur in Music*. Cambridge, U.K.: D. S. Brewer, 2004.

Barbieri, Fabio P. *History of Britain, 407–597*. 2002. Faces of Arthur. Vortigern Studies, 1997–2007. www.geocities.ws/vortigernstudies/fabio/contents.html (accessed August 16, 2016).

Barr, Mike. *Camelot 3000*. (12 issues). Illustrated by Brian Bolland. New York: DC Comics, 1982–1985.

Bartrum, Peter C. "Arthuriana from the Genealogical Manuscripts." *National Library of Wales Journal* 14 (1965–66): 242–45.

———. *A Welsh Classical Dictionary*. Aberystwyth: National Library of Wales, 1993.

Bennett, Jack Arthur Walter. *Essays on Malory*. Oxford, U.K.: Clarendon Press, 1963.

Biddle, Martin. *King Arthur's Round Table*. Woodbridge, U.K.: Boydell Press, 2000.

Birley, Anthony. *Marcus Aurelius*. London: Batsford, 1987.

———. *The People of Roman Britain*. London: B.T. Batsford, 1979.

Blake, William. *Poetry and Prose of William Blake*. Edited by Geoffrey Keynes. London: Nonesuch Library, 1975.

Bolitho, Hector. *The Romance of Windsor Castle*. London: Evans Brothers, 1946.

Breeze, A. C. "Historia Brittonum and Arthur's Battle of Mont Agned." Northern History 40-1 (2003): 167–70.

Brown, Dan. *The Da Vinci Code*. London: Transworld Publishers, 2004.

Bruce, Christopher, ed. *The Arthurian Name Dictionary*. New York: Garland, 1999.

Bruce, James Douglas. *The Evolution of Arthurian Romance*. 2 vols. Gloucester, Mass.: Peter Smith, 1958.

Bryce, Derek. *Three Arthurs*. Lampeter, U.K.: Llanerch, 2006.

Brzezinski, Richard, and Mariusz Mielczarek. *The Sarmatians, 600 BC–AD 450.* Wellingborough, U.K.: Osprey Publishing, 2002.

Bullock-Davies, Constance. *Professional Interpreters and the Matter of Britain.* Cardiff: University of Wales Press, 1966.

Byrne, Francis John. *Irish Kings and High Kings.* London: B. T. Batsford, 1973.

Cambi, Nenad, and John Matthews, eds. *Lucius Artorius Castus and the King Arthur Legend.* Split, Croatia: Knjizevni Krug/Ogranak Matice Hrvatske, 2014.

Campbell, James. *The Anglo-Saxons.* Ithaca, N.Y.: Cornell University Press, 1982.

Carey, John. "The Finding of Arthur's Grave: A Story from Clonmacnoise." In Ildánach Ildírech, *A Festschrift for Proinsias Mac Cana.* Edited by John Carey et al., Andover, Mass.: Celtic Studies Publications, 1999.

Carley, James P., and Felictiy Riddy, eds. *Arthurian Literature XIII.* Woodbridge, U.K.: D. S. Brewer, 1995.

Carr, Gillian. "Woad, Tattooing and Identity in later Iron Age and Early Roman Britain." *Oxford Journal of Archaeology* 24 (2005): 273–92.

Castleden, Rodney. *King Arthur: The Truth behind the Legend.* London: Routledge, 2000.

Ceridwen's Cauldron: The Journal of the Oxford Arthurian Society, 1971. No other info available. This was a student infozine produced in house.

Chadwick, Nora. "Bretwalda-Gwledig-Vortigern." *Bulletin of the Board of Celtic Studies* 19 (1962): 225–30.

Chambers, Edmund Kerchever. *Arthur of Britain.* Cambridge, U.K.: Speculum Historiale, 1964.

Child, Francis J. *The English and Scottish Popular Ballads.* New York: Dover Books, 1965.

Colarusso, John, trans. and ed. *Nart Sagas from the Caucasus.* Princeton, N.J.: Princeton University Press, 2002.

Coleman, Kathleen M. "Launching into History: Aquatic Displays in the Early Empire." *The Journal of Roman Studies* 83 (1993): 48–74.

Collingwood, Robin George, and John Nowell Linton Myres. *Roman Britain and the English Settlements.* Oxford, U.K.: Clarendon Press, 1975.

Cornwell, Bernard. *The Warlord Trilogy.* 3 vols. The Winter King. Enemy of God. Excalibur. London: Michael Joseph, 1995–1997.

Dark, Ken. *Britain and the End of the Roman Empire.* Stroud, U.K.: Tempus, 2002.

Davies, John Reuban. *The Book of Llandaf and the Norman Churches of Wales.* Woodbridge, U.K.: Boydell Press, 2003.

Davies, Sioned, and Nerys Ann Jones, eds. *The Horse in Celtic Culture: Medieval Welsh Perspectives.* Cardiff: University of Wales Press, 1997.

Dent, Anthony A., and Daphne Machin Goodall. *The Foals of Epona: A History of British Ponies from the Bronze Age to Yesterday.* London: Gallery Press, 1962.

Dolukhanov, Pavel M. *The Early Slavs.* Harlow, U.K.: Addison Wesley Longman, 1996.

Dooley, Ann. "Arthur of the Irish: A Viable Concept?" In *Celtic Arthurian Literature.* Vol. 21 of *Arthurian Literature.* Edited by Ceridwen Lloyd-Morgan. Cambridge, U.K.: D. S. Brewer, 2004.

Dumézil, Georges. *Legends sur les Nartes.* Paris: Librarie Ancienne Honore Champion, 1930.

Eisner, Sigmund. *The Tristan Legend.* Evanston, Ill.: Northwestern University Press, 1969.

Eliot, T. S. *The Wasteland and other Poems.* London: Faber & Faber, 1940.

Evans, Stephen S. *Lords of Battle.* Woodbridge, U.K.: Boydell Press, 1987.

Fitch, Eric L. "Edward III's Round Table at Windsor." *Pendragon* 34, no. 1 (2006): 36–39.

Fleuriot, Leon. *Les Origines de la Bretagne.* Paris: Payot, 1980.

Foord, Edward. *The Last Age of Roman Britain.* London: George G. Harrap, 1925.

Frankland, Edward. *The Bear of Britain.* Oakland, Calif.: Green Knight Publishing, 1998.

Frere, Sheppard. *Britannia: A History of Roman Britain.* London: Routledge & Kegan Paul, 1974.

Gidlow, Christopher. *The Reign of Arthur: From History to Legend.* Thrupp, U.K.: Sutton Publishing, 2004.

Giles, John Allen. *Old English Chronicles.* London: G. Bell & Sons, 1910.

Gillies, William. "Arthur in Gaelic Tradition: Folktales and Ballads." *Cambrian Medieval Celtic Studies* 2 (Winter 1981): 47–72.

———. "Arthur in Gaelic Tradition: Romances and Learned Lore." *Cambrian Medieval Celtic Studies* 3 (Summer 1982): 41–75.

Gowans, Linda M. *Cei and the Arthurian Legend.* Cambridge, U.K.: D. S. Brewer, 1988.

Griffen, Toby D. *Names from the Dawn of British Legend.* Felinfach, Wales: Llanerch, 1994.

Hammer, Jacob, ed. "Some Additional Manuscripts of Geoffrey of Monmouth's Historia Regum Britanniae." *Modern Language Quarterly* 3, no. 2 (June 1942): 235–42.

Hammond, Mason. *The Antonine Monarchy*. Rome: American Academy in Rome, 1959.

Hardyment, Christina. *Malory: The Life and Times of King Arthur's Chronicler*. London: HarperCollins, 2005.

Harty, Kevin J., ed. *King Arthur on Film*. Jefferson, N.C.: McFarland, 1999.

Haycock, Marged. "Some Talk of Alexander and Some of Hercules: 3 Medieval Poems from the Book of Taliesin." *Cambridge Medieval Celtic Studies* 13 (Summer 1987): 7–38.

Heath-Stubbs, John. *Artorius: A Heroic Poem in Four Books and Eight Episodes*. London: Enitharmon Press, 1973.

Hicks, Edward. *Sir Thomas Malory, His Turbulent Career*. Cambridge, Mass.: Harvard University Press, 1928.

Higham, Nicholas J. *King Arthur: Myth-Making and History*. London: Routledge, 2002.

Hildinger, Erik. *Warriors of the Steppe*. Cambridge, Mass.: Da Capo Press, 2001.

Hill, Joyce. *The Tristan Legend*. Leeds, U.K.: University of Leeds Press, 1977.

Holder, Paul A. *The Roman Army in Britain*. London: B. T. Batsford, 1992.

Holdstock, Robert. *The Merlin Codex*. 3 vols. *Celtica. The Iron Grail. The Broken Kings*. London: Gollancz, 2001–2007.

Holmes, Michael. *King Arthur: A Military History*. London: Blandford Books, 1996.

Hope, William H. Saint John. *Windsor Castle: An Architectural History*. London: Country Life Office, 1913.

Hughes, Jonathan. *Arthurian Myths and Alchemy: The Kingship of Edward IV*. Stroud, U.K.: Sutton Publishing, 2002.

Hunt, August. *Shadows in the Mist: The Life and Death of King Arthur*. Kirkby Stephen, U.K.: Hayloft, 2006.

Jackson, K. H. "Once Again Arthur's Battles." *Modern Philology* 43 (1945–1946): 44–57.

James, John. *The Fourth Gwenevere*. Completed by John and Caitlín Matthews. London: Jo Fletcher Books, 2014.

Jarman, A. O. H. *Sieffre o Fynwy, Geoffrey of Monmouth*. Cardiff: University of Wales Press, 1966.

Jones, David. *Anathemata*. London: Faber & Faber, 1952.

————. *In Parenthesis*. London: Faber & Faber, 1937.

————. *The Roman Quarry*. London: Agenda Editions, 1981.

————. *The Sleeping Lord and Other Fragments*. London: Faber & Faber, 1974.

Jones, Terry, and Alan Ereira. *Terry Jones' Barbarians: An Alternative Roman History*. London: BBC Books, 2006.

Jonson, Ben. *The Complete Masques*. Edited by Stephen Orgel. New Haven, Conn.: Yale University Press, 1969.

Kennedy, Donald, ed. *King Arthur: A Casebook*. New York: Garland, 1996.

"King Arthur's Cross Rediscovered?" *Enfield Advertiser* 17.12. 1981.

Kittredge, George Lyman. "Who Was Sir Thomas Malory?" *Harvard Studies and Notes in Philology and Literature* 5 (1897): 85–106.

Knight, W. Nicholas. "Lancer: Myth-Making and the Kennedy Camelot." *Avalon to Camelot* 2, no. 1 (1988): 26–31.

Kronk, Gary W. *Cometography*. Cambridge, U.K.: Cambridge University Press, 1999.

Lacy, Norris J. *The New Arthurian Encyclopaedia*. Chicago: Saint James Press, 1991.

Lewis, C. S. "Launcelot." In *The Collected Poems of C. S. Lewis*. Edited by Walter Hooper. London: Geoffrey Bles, 1969.

————. *That Hideous Strength*. London: John Lane, 1945.

Littleton, C. Scott. "The Holy Grail, the Cauldron of Annwn, and the Nartyamonga: A Further Note on the Sarmatian Connection." *Journal of American Folklore* 92, no. 365 (1979): 32–33.

Littleton, C. Scott, and Linda A. Malcor. *From Scythia to Camelot*. New York: Garland, 2000.

Loomis, Roger Sherman. *Arthurian Tradition and Chrétien de Troyes*. New York: Columbia University Press, 1949.

————. *Celtic Myth and Arthurian Romance*. New York: Haskell House, 1967.

Lukitsh, Joanne. "Julia Margaret Cameron's Photographic Illustrations to Alfred Tennyson's 'The Idylls of the King.'" *Arthurian Literature* 7 (1987): 145–47.

Lumiansky, Robert Meyer, ed. *Malory's Originality*. Baltimore, Md.: Johns Hopkins Press, 1964.

Malcor, Linda A. "Lucius Artorius Castus 1: An Officer and an Equestrian." *The Heroic Age* 1 (Spring/Summer 1999). www.heroicage.org/issues/1/halac.htm (accessed August 16, 2016).

————. "Lucius Artorius Castus 2: The Battles in Britain." *The Heroic Age* 2 (Winter 1999). www.heroicage.org/issues/2/ha2lac.htm (accessed August 16, 2016).

———. "The Campanians of the Round Table: The Artorii, Flora and the Holy Grail." In *King Arthur: Tra storia e leggenda*. Edited by Mario de Matteis and Antonio Trinchese. Oberhausen, Germany: Athena, 2004.

Malory, Thomas. *Le Mort D'Arthur: The Birth, Life and Acts of King Arthur of His Noble Knights of the Round Table . . . with the Dolorous Death and Departing out of this world of them all.* Introduction by Sir John Rhys. Original designs by Aubrey Beardsley. Edinburgh: J. M. Dent & Sons, Aldine House, 1909. Facsimile reprint 1981.

Man, John. *Attila*. London: Bantam Press, 2005.

Marren, Peter. *Battles of the Dark Ages*. Barnsley, U.K.: Pen & Sword Books, 2006.

Masefield, John. *Midsummer Night and Other Tales in Verse*. London: Heinemann, 1928.

Matthews, Caitlín. *Celtic Book of the Dead*. London: Connections, 1992.

———. *King Arthur and the Goddess of the Land*. Rochester, Vt.: Inner Traditions, 2002.

———. *Mabon and the Guardians of Celtic Britain*. Rochester, Vt.: Inner Traditions, 2002.

———. "The Spells of Women." In *Verführer, Schurken, Magier*. Vol. 3 of *Mittelalter-Mythen*. Edited by Ulrich Müller and Werber Wunderlich. Saint Gallen, Switzerland: UVK Verlagsgesellschaft, 2001.

———. "Voices of the Wells." In *At the Table of the Grail*. Edited by John Matthews. London: Watkins, 2002.

Matthews, Caitlín, and John Matthews. *Encyclopaedia of Celtic Wisdom*. Shaftesbury, U.K.: Element, 1994.

———. *Ladies of the Lake*. London: Aquarian Press, 1992.

Matthews, John. *The Grail: The Truth behind the Legend*. London: Godsfield Press, 2005.

———. *King Arthur*. London: Carleton, 2004.

———. "A Knightly Endeavour." *Arthuriana* 14, no. 3 (2004): 112–14.

———. *Merlin: Shaman, Prophet, Magician*. London: Mitchell Beazley, 2004.

———. *The Quest for the Green Man*. Wheaton, Ill.: Quest Books, 2001.

———, ed. *At the Table of the Grail*. London: Watkins, 2002.

———, ed. *The Barddas of Iolo Morganwg*. York Beach, Maine: Weiser Books, 2004.

Matthews, John, and Caitlín Matthews. *Taliesin: The Last Celtic Shaman*. Rochester, Vt.: Inner Traditions, 2000.

Mattingly, David. *An Imperial Possession: Britain in the Roman Empire.* London: Penguin Books, 2006.

McKee, Ian. "Gildas, Lessons from History." *Cambrian Medieval Celtic Studies* 51 (Summer 2006): 1–36.

McKenzie, Peter. *Camelot's Frontier.* Morpeth, U.K.: Longhirst Press, 1999.

Millican, Charles Bowie. *Spenser and the Table Round.* London: Frank Cass, 1967.

Milton, John. *Lycidas and Epithaphium Damonis of Milton.* Hansebooks, 2016.

Moffat, Alistair. *Arthur and the Lost Kingdoms.* London: Weidenfeld & Nicolson, 1999.

Mommsen, Theodorus, ed. *Corpus Inscriptionum Latinarum.* Vol. 3 of *Inscriptiones Asiae, provinciarum Europae Graecarum, Illyrici Latinae.* Berlin: Reimer, 1873.

Monaco, Richard. *The Grail War.* New York: Pocket Books, 1979.

———. *The Final Quest.* New York: G. P. Putnam's Sons, 1980.

———. *Parsival, or A Knight's Tale.* New York: Macmillan, 1977.

———. *Runes.* New York: Ace, 1984.

Moorcock, Michael. *Elric at the End of Time.* London: New English Library, 1984.

———. *The War-Hound and the World's Pain.* London: New English Library, 1982.

Morris, John. *The Age of Arthur.* London: Weidenfeld & Nicolson, 1973.

Nash, Ernest. *Pictorial Dictionary of the Roman World.* London: Chatto and Windus, 1961–1962.

Nickel, Helmut. "The Last Days of Britain and the Origins of the Arthurian Legends." In *Lucius Artorius Castus and the King Arthur Legend.* Edited by N. Camby and John Matthews. Split, Croatia: Knjizevni Krug/Ogranak Matice Hrvatske, 2014.

———. "Wer waren Konig Artus Ritter? Über der geschichtliche Grundlage der Artussagen." *Zeitschrift der historischen Waffen- und Kostümkunde* 1 (1975): 1–18.

Nicolle, David, and Angus McBride. *Arthur and the Anglo-Saxon Wars.* Oxford, U.K.: Osprey Publishing, 1984.

Oppenheimer, Stephen. *The Origins of the British.* London: Constable, 2006.

O'Rahilly, Thomas F. *Early Irish History and Mythology.* Dublin: Dublin Institute for Advanced Studies, 1976.

Padel, O. J. "The Nature of Arthur." *Cambrian Medieval Celtic Studies* 49 (Summer 1994): 1–31.

Percy, Thomas. *Reliques of Ancient English Poetry Consisting of Old Heroic Ballads, Songs, and Other Pieces of Earlier Poets.* London: Dodsley, 1765.

Phillips, Graham, and Martin Keatman. *King Arthur: The True Story.* London: Arrow, 1992.

Poulson, Christine. *The Quest for the Grail: Arthurian Legend in British Art, 1840–1920.* Manchester, U.K.: Manchester University Press, 1999.

Powers, Tim. *The Drawing of the Dark.* New York: Ballantine, 1979.

Powys, J. C. *Porius.* Edited by W. T. Albrecht. Hamilton, N.Y.: Colgate University Press, 1995.

Prestwich, Michael. *Edward I.* New Haven, Conn.: Yale University Press, 1988.

Pryor, Francis. *Britain AD: A Quest for Arthur, England and the Anglo-Saxons.* London: HarperCollins, 2004.

Rance, Philip. "Attacotti, Déisi and Magnus Maximus: The Case for Irish Federates in Late Roman Britain." *Brittania* 32 (2001): 243–70.

Reid, Howard. *Arthur the Dragon King.* London: Headline, 2001.

Reno, Frank D. *The Historic King Arthur.* Jefferson, N.C.: McFarland & Co, 1996.

Richmond, I. A. "The Sarmatae, Bremetennacum Veteranorum and the Regio Bremetennacensis." *Journal of Roman Studies* 35 (1945): 15–29.

Rodway, Simon. "The Date and Authorship of Culhwch ac Olwen." *Cambrian Medieval Celtic Studies* 49 (Summer 2005): 21–44.

Rouse, Robert, and Cory Rushton. *The Medieval Quest for Arthur.* Stroud, U.K.: Tempus Publishing, 2005.

Rowlands, Jenny. *Early Welsh Saga Poetry.* Cambridge, U.K.: D. S. Brewer, 1990.

———. "Warfare and Horses in the Gododdin and the Problem of Catraeth." *Cambrian Medieval Celtic Studies* 30 (Summer 1995): 13–40.

Rudgley, Richard. *Barbarians: Secrets of the Dark Ages.* London: Channel 4 Books, 2002.

Scott, Sir Walter. "The Bridal of Triermain." 1813. Arthurian Miscellany. Internet Sacred Text Archive. Evinity Publishing, 2011. www.sacred-texts .com/neu/arthur/art155.htm.

Skinner, Martyn. *The Return of Arthur: A Poem of the Future.* London: Chapman & Hall, 1956.

Slavitt, David R. *Ovid's Poetry of Exile.* Baltimore, Md., and London: Johns Hopkins University Press, 1990.

Smyth, Alfred P. *Warlords and Holy Men: Scotland, AD 80–1000*. Edinburgh: Edinburgh University Press, 1984.

Snyder, Christopher. *An Age of Tyrants: Britain and the Britons, A.D. 400–600*. Stroud, U.K.: Tempus Publishing, 1998.

Steinbeck, John. *The Acts of King Arthur and His Noble Knights from the Winchester Manuscripts of Thomas Malory and Other Sources*. Edited by Chase Horton. London: Heinemann, 1976.

Stewart, Mary. *Arthurian Saga*. 4 vols. New York: Fawcett, 1985.

Sulimirski, Tadeusz. *The Sarmatians*. London: Thames & Hudson, 1970.

Sutcliff, Rosemary. *Sword at Sunset*. London: Hodder & Stoughton, 1963.

Takamiya, Toshiyuki, and Derek Brewer. *Aspects of Malory*. Cambridge, U.K.: D. S. Brewer/Rowman & Littlefield, 1981.

Tatlock, John S. P. *The Legendary History of Britain*. New York: Gordian Press, 1974.

Tennyson, Alfred. *The Idylls of the King*. London: Folio Society, 2006. First published by Edward Moxon, 1885.

Tolstoy, Nikolai. "Nennius Chapter 56." *Bulletin Board of Celtic Studies* 19 (1961): 118–62.

———. *The Mysteries of Stonehenge*. Stroud: Amberly, 2016

———. *The Quest for Merlin*. London: Hamish Hamilton, 1985.

Treece, Henry. *The Great Captains*. London: John Lane, 1956.

———. *The Green Man*. London: John Lane, 1956.

Vansittart, Peter. *Lancelot*. London: Peter Owen, 1978.

———. *Parsifal*. London: Peter Owen, 1988.

Wadge, Richard. "King Arthur: A British or Sarmatian Tradition." *Folklore* 98, no. 2 (1987): 204–15

Whitaker, Muriel. *Arthur's Kingdom of Adventure: The World of Malory's Morte d'Arthur*. Cambridge, U.K.: D. S. Brewer, 1984.

———. *The Legends of King Arthur in Art*. Cambridge, U.K.: D. S. Brewer, 1990.

White, Terence Hanbury. *The Once and Future King*. London: Collins, 1952.

Williams, Ann, and Alfred P. Smyth. *A Biographical Dictionary of Dark Age Britain*. London: Seaby, 1991.

Williams, Charles. *Arthurian Poets: Charles Williams*. Edited by David L. Dodds. Woodbridge, U.K.: Boydell Press, 1991.

Williams, Derek. *Romans and Barbarians*. New York: Saint Martin's Press, 1998.

Williams, Mary. "An Early Ritual Poem in Welsh." *Speculum* 13 (1938): 38–51.

Wood, Ian. "The Fall of the Western Empire and the End of Roman Britain." *Britannia* 18 (1987): 251–62.

Wordsworth, William. "The Egyptian Maid, or the Romance of the Water Lily." 1835. The Camelot Project. Robbins Library Digital Projects, University of Rochester. www.lib.rochester.edu/camelot/egypt.htm (accessed August 16, 2016).

Zelazny, Roger. *The Last Defender of Camelot*. New York: Pocket Books, 1980.

Zimmer, Heinrich. "Histoire littéraire de la France, tome XXX." *Göttingische Gelehrte Anzeigen* 20 (1890).

Arthurian Societies
and Resources

Arthuriana: The Journal of Arthurian Studies
Arthurian Society Quarterly, North American Branch
Scriptoriun Press
P.O. Box 750432
Dallas, Texas 75275-0432
www.arthuriana.org/arthurwel.htm

The Camelot Project
Arthurian texts online
Robbins Library Digital Projects
University of Rochester
www.lib.rochester.edu/Camelot/cphome.stm

International Arthurian Society
British Branch: Prof. Jane Taylor
Collingwood College, University of Durham
South Road, Durham DH1 3LT, U.K.
www.internationalarthuriansociety.com

Vortigern Studies: Dark Age resources
www.vortigernstudies.org.uk/vortigernhomepage.htm

Index